Lecture Notes in Computer Science 14716

The series Lecture Notes in Computer Science (LNCS), including its subseries Lecture Notes in Artificial Intelligence (LNAI) and Lecture Notes in Bioinformatics (LNBI), has established itself as a medium for the publication of new developments in computer science and information technology research, teaching, and education.

LNCS enjoys close cooperation with the computer science R & D community, the series counts many renowned academics among its volume editors and paper authors, and collaborates with prestigious societies. Its mission is to serve this international community by providing an invaluable service, mainly focused on the publication of conference and workshop proceedings and postproceedings. LNCS commenced publication in 1973.

Aaron Marcus · Elizabeth Rosenzweig ·
Marcelo M. Soares
Editors

Design, User Experience, and Usability

13th International Conference, DUXU 2024
Held as Part of the 26th HCI International Conference, HCII 2024
Washington, DC, USA, June 29 – July 4, 2024
Proceedings, Part V

 Springer

Editors
Aaron Marcus
Principal
Aaron Marcus and Associates
Berkeley, CA, USA

Elizabeth Rosenzweig
World Usability Day and Bubble Mountain
Newton Center, MA, USA

Marcelo M. Soares
Federal University of Pernambuco
Recife, Pernambuco, Brazil

ISSN 0302-9743   ISSN 1611-3349 (electronic)
Lecture Notes in Computer Science
ISBN 978-3-031-61361-6   ISBN 978-3-031-61362-3 (eBook)
https://doi.org/10.1007/978-3-031-61362-3

This Springer imprint is published by the registered company Springer Nature Switzerland AG
The registered company address is: Gewerbestrasse 11, 6330 Cham, Switzerland

If disposing of this product, please recycle the paper.

Foreword

This year we celebrate 40 years since the establishment of the HCI International (HCII) Conference, which has been a hub for presenting groundbreaking research and novel ideas and collaboration for people from all over the world.

The HCII conference was founded in 1984 by Prof. Gavriel Salvendy (Purdue University, USA, Tsinghua University, P.R. China, and University of Central Florida, USA) and the first event of the series, "1st USA-Japan Conference on Human-Computer Interaction", was held in Honolulu, Hawaii, USA, 18–20 August. Since then, HCI International is held jointly with several Thematic Areas and Affiliated Conferences, with each one under the auspices of a distinguished international Program Board and under one management and one registration. Twenty-six HCI International Conferences have been organized so far (every two years until 2013, and annually thereafter).

Over the years, this conference has served as a platform for scholars, researchers, industry experts and students to exchange ideas, connect, and address challenges in the ever-evolving HCI field. Throughout these 40 years, the conference has evolved itself, adapting to new technologies and emerging trends, while staying committed to its core mission of advancing knowledge and driving change.

As we celebrate this milestone anniversary, we reflect on the contributions of its founding members and appreciate the commitment of its current and past Affiliated Conference Program Board Chairs and members. We are also thankful to all past conference attendees who have shaped this community into what it is today.

The 26th International Conference on Human-Computer Interaction, HCI International 2024 (HCII 2024), was held as a 'hybrid' event at the Washington Hilton Hotel, Washington, DC, USA, during 29 June – 4 July 2024. It incorporated the 21 thematic areas and affiliated conferences listed below.

A total of 5108 individuals from academia, research institutes, industry, and government agencies from 85 countries submitted contributions, and 1271 papers and 309 posters were included in the volumes of the proceedings that were published just before the start of the conference, these are listed below. The contributions thoroughly cover the entire field of human-computer interaction, addressing major advances in knowledge and effective use of computers in a variety of application areas. These papers provide academics, researchers, engineers, scientists, practitioners and students with state-of-the-art information on the most recent advances in HCI.

The HCI International (HCII) conference also offers the option of presenting 'Late Breaking Work', and this applies both for papers and posters, with corresponding volumes of proceedings that will be published after the conference. Full papers will be included in the 'HCII 2024 - Late Breaking Papers' volumes of the proceedings to be published in the Springer LNCS series, while 'Poster Extended Abstracts' will be included as short research papers in the 'HCII 2024 - Late Breaking Posters' volumes to be published in the Springer CCIS series.

I would like to thank the Program Board Chairs and the members of the Program Boards of all thematic areas and affiliated conferences for their contribution towards the high scientific quality and overall success of the HCI International 2024 conference. Their manifold support in terms of paper reviewing (single-blind review process, with a minimum of two reviews per submission), session organization and their willingness to act as goodwill ambassadors for the conference is most highly appreciated.

This conference would not have been possible without the continuous and unwavering support and advice of Gavriel Salvendy, founder, General Chair Emeritus, and Scientific Advisor. For his outstanding efforts, I would like to express my sincere appreciation to Abbas Moallem, Communications Chair and Editor of HCI International News.

July 2024   Constantine Stephanidis

HCI International 2024 Thematic Areas
and Affiliated Conferences

- HCI: Human-Computer Interaction Thematic Area
- HIMI: Human Interface and the Management of Information Thematic Area
- EPCE: 21st International Conference on Engineering Psychology and Cognitive Ergonomics
- AC: 18th International Conference on Augmented Cognition
- UAHCI: 18th International Conference on Universal Access in Human-Computer Interaction
- CCD: 16th International Conference on Cross-Cultural Design
- SCSM: 16th International Conference on Social Computing and Social Media
- VAMR: 16th International Conference on Virtual, Augmented and Mixed Reality
- DHM: 15th International Conference on Digital Human Modeling & Applications in Health, Safety, Ergonomics & Risk Management
- DUXU: 13th International Conference on Design, User Experience and Usability
- C&C: 12th International Conference on Culture and Computing
- DAPI: 12th International Conference on Distributed, Ambient and Pervasive Interactions
- HCIBGO: 11th International Conference on HCI in Business, Government and Organizations
- LCT: 11th International Conference on Learning and Collaboration Technologies
- ITAP: 10th International Conference on Human Aspects of IT for the Aged Population
- AIS: 6th International Conference on Adaptive Instructional Systems
- HCI-CPT: 6th International Conference on HCI for Cybersecurity, Privacy and Trust
- HCI-Games: 6th International Conference on HCI in Games
- MobiTAS: 6th International Conference on HCI in Mobility, Transport and Automotive Systems
- AI-HCI: 5th International Conference on Artificial Intelligence in HCI
- MOBILE: 5th International Conference on Human-Centered Design, Operation and Evaluation of Mobile Communications

List of Conference Proceedings Volumes Appearing Before the Conference

1. LNCS 14684, Human-Computer Interaction: Part I, edited by Masaaki Kurosu and Ayako Hashizume
2. LNCS 14685, Human-Computer Interaction: Part II, edited by Masaaki Kurosu and Ayako Hashizume
3. LNCS 14686, Human-Computer Interaction: Part III, edited by Masaaki Kurosu and Ayako Hashizume
4. LNCS 14687, Human-Computer Interaction: Part IV, edited by Masaaki Kurosu and Ayako Hashizume
5. LNCS 14688, Human-Computer Interaction: Part V, edited by Masaaki Kurosu and Ayako Hashizume
6. LNCS 14689, Human Interface and the Management of Information: Part I, edited by Hirohiko Mori and Yumi Asahi
7. LNCS 14690, Human Interface and the Management of Information: Part II, edited by Hirohiko Mori and Yumi Asahi
8. LNCS 14691, Human Interface and the Management of Information: Part III, edited by Hirohiko Mori and Yumi Asahi
9. LNAI 14692, Engineering Psychology and Cognitive Ergonomics: Part I, edited by Don Harris and Wen-Chin Li
10. LNAI 14693, Engineering Psychology and Cognitive Ergonomics: Part II, edited by Don Harris and Wen-Chin Li
11. LNAI 14694, Augmented Cognition, Part I, edited by Dylan D. Schmorrow and Cali M. Fidopiastis
12. LNAI 14695, Augmented Cognition, Part II, edited by Dylan D. Schmorrow and Cali M. Fidopiastis
13. LNCS 14696, Universal Access in Human-Computer Interaction: Part I, edited by Margherita Antona and Constantine Stephanidis
14. LNCS 14697, Universal Access in Human-Computer Interaction: Part II, edited by Margherita Antona and Constantine Stephanidis
15. LNCS 14698, Universal Access in Human-Computer Interaction: Part III, edited by Margherita Antona and Constantine Stephanidis
16. LNCS 14699, Cross-Cultural Design: Part I, edited by Pei-Luen Patrick Rau
17. LNCS 14700, Cross-Cultural Design: Part II, edited by Pei-Luen Patrick Rau
18. LNCS 14701, Cross-Cultural Design: Part III, edited by Pei-Luen Patrick Rau
19. LNCS 14702, Cross-Cultural Design: Part IV, edited by Pei-Luen Patrick Rau
20. LNCS 14703, Social Computing and Social Media: Part I, edited by Adela Coman and Simona Vasilache
21. LNCS 14704, Social Computing and Social Media: Part II, edited by Adela Coman and Simona Vasilache
22. LNCS 14705, Social Computing and Social Media: Part III, edited by Adela Coman and Simona Vasilache

47. LNCS 14730, HCI in Games: Part I, edited by Xiaowen Fang
48. LNCS 14731, HCI in Games: Part II, edited by Xiaowen Fang
49. LNCS 14732, HCI in Mobility, Transport and Automotive Systems: Part I, edited by Heidi Krömker
50. LNCS 14733, HCI in Mobility, Transport and Automotive Systems: Part II, edited by Heidi Krömker
51. LNAI 14734, Artificial Intelligence in HCI: Part I, edited by Helmut Degen and Stavroula Ntoa
52. LNAI 14735, Artificial Intelligence in HCI: Part II, edited by Helmut Degen and Stavroula Ntoa
53. LNAI 14736, Artificial Intelligence in HCI: Part III, edited by Helmut Degen and Stavroula Ntoa
54. LNCS 14737, Design, Operation and Evaluation of Mobile Communications: Part I, edited by June Wei and George Margetis
55. LNCS 14738, Design, Operation and Evaluation of Mobile Communications: Part II, edited by June Wei and George Margetis
56. CCIS 2114, HCI International 2024 Posters - Part I, edited by Constantine Stephanidis, Margherita Antona, Stavroula Ntoa and Gavriel Salvendy
57. CCIS 2115, HCI International 2024 Posters - Part II, edited by Constantine Stephanidis, Margherita Antona, Stavroula Ntoa and Gavriel Salvendy
58. CCIS 2116, HCI International 2024 Posters - Part III, edited by Constantine Stephanidis, Margherita Antona, Stavroula Ntoa and Gavriel Salvendy
59. CCIS 2117, HCI International 2024 Posters - Part IV, edited by Constantine Stephanidis, Margherita Antona, Stavroula Ntoa and Gavriel Salvendy
60. CCIS 2118, HCI International 2024 Posters - Part V, edited by Constantine Stephanidis, Margherita Antona, Stavroula Ntoa and Gavriel Salvendy
61. CCIS 2119, HCI International 2024 Posters - Part VI, edited by Constantine Stephanidis, Margherita Antona, Stavroula Ntoa and Gavriel Salvendy
62. CCIS 2120, HCI International 2024 Posters - Part VII, edited by Constantine Stephanidis, Margherita Antona, Stavroula Ntoa and Gavriel Salvendy

https://2024.hci.international/proceedings

Preface

User experience (UX) refers to a person's thoughts, feelings, and behavior when using interactive systems. UX design becomes fundamentally important for new and emerging mobile, ubiquitous, and omnipresent computer-based contexts. The scope of design, user experience, and usability (DUXU) extends to all aspects of the user's interaction with a product or service, how it is perceived, learned, and used. DUXU also addresses design knowledge, methods, and practices, with a focus on deeply human-centered processes. Usability, usefulness, and appeal are fundamental requirements for effective user-experience design.

The 13th Design, User Experience, and Usability Conference (DUXU 2024), an affiliated conference of the HCI International conference, encouraged papers from professionals, academics, and researchers that report results and cover a broad range of research and development activities on a variety of related topics. Professionals include designers, software engineers, scientists, marketers, business leaders, and practitioners in fields such as AI, architecture, financial and wealth management, game design, graphic design, finance, healthcare, industrial design, mobile, psychology, travel, and vehicles.

This year's submissions covered a wide range of content across the spectrum of design, user-experience, and usability. The latest trends and technologies are represented, as well as contributions from professionals, academics, and researchers across the globe. The breadth of their work is indicated in the following topics covered in the proceedings, encompassing theoretical work, applied research across diverse application domains, UX studies, as well as discussions on contemporary technologies that reshape our interactions with computational products and services.

Five volumes of the HCII 2024 proceedings are dedicated to this year's edition of the DUXU Conference, covering topics related to:

- Information Visualization and Interaction Design, as well as Usability Testing and User Experience Evaluation;
- Designing Interactions for Intelligent Environments; Automotive Interactions and Smart Mobility Solutions; Speculative Design and Creativity;
- User Experience Design for Inclusion and Diversity; Human-Centered Design for Social Impact.
- Designing Immersive Experiences Across Contexts; Technology, Design, and Learner Engagement; User Experience in Tangible and Intangible Cultural Heritage;
- Innovative Design for Enhanced User Experience; Innovations in Product and Service Design.

The papers in these volumes were accepted for publication after a minimum of two single-blind reviews from the members of the DUXU Program Board or, in some cases, from Preface members of the Program Boards of other affiliated conferences. We would like to thank all of them for their invaluable contribution, support, and efforts.

July 2024   Aaron Marcus
                                                      Elizabeth Rosenzweig
                                                      Marcelo M. Soares

13th International Conference on Design, User Experience and Usability (DUXU 2024)

Program Board Chairs: **Aaron Marcus,** *Aaron Marcus and Associates, USA,* **Elizabeth Rosenzweig,** *World Usability Day and Bubble Mountain Consulting, USA* and **Marcelo M. Soares,** *Federal University of Pernambuco, Brazil*

- Sisira Adikari, *University of Canberra, Australia*
- Ahmad Alhuwwari, *Orange Jordan, Jordan*
- Claire Ancient, *University of Winchester, UK*
- Eric Brangier, *Université de Lorraine, France*
- Lorenzo Cantoni, *USI - Università della Svizzera italiana, Switzerland*
- Silvia De los Rios, *Indra, Spain*
- Romi Dey, *Solved by Design, India*
- Marc Fabri, *Leeds Beckett University, UK*
- Michael R. Gibson, *The University of North Texas, USA*
- Zaiyan Gong, *Tongji University, P.R. China*
- Hao He, *Central Academy of Fine Arts, P.R. China*
- Ao Jiang, *Nanjing University of Aeronautics and Astronautics, P.R. China*
- Hannu Karvonen, *VTT Technical Research Centre of Finland Ltd., Finland*
- Zhen Liu, *South China University of Technology, P.R. China*
- Wei Liu, *Beijing Normal University, P.R. China*
- Ricardo Gregorio Lugo, *Tallinn University of Technology, Estonia*
- Keith Owens, *University of North Texas, USA*
- Francisco Rebelo, *University of Lisbon, Portugal*
- Christine Riedmann-Streitz, *MarkenFactory GmbH, Germany*
- Patricia Search, *Rensselaer Polytechnic Institute, USA*
- Dorothy Shamonsky, *Brandeis University, USA*
- Qi Tan, *Central Academy of Fine Arts, P.R. China*
- Ana Velhinho, *University of Aveiro - Digimedia, Portugal*
- Elisangela Vilar, *University of Lisbon, Portugal*
- Wei Wang, *Hunan University, P.R. China*

The full list with the Program Board Chairs and the members of the Program Boards of all thematic areas and affiliated conferences of HCII 2024 is available online at:

http://www.hci.international/board-members-2024.php

HCI International 2025 Conference

The 27th International Conference on Human-Computer Interaction, HCI International 2025, will be held jointly with the affiliated conferences at the Swedish Exhibition & Congress Centre and Gothia Towers Hotel, Gothenburg, Sweden, June 22–27, 2025. It will cover a broad spectrum of themes related to Human-Computer Interaction, including theoretical issues, methods, tools, processes, and case studies in HCI design, as well as novel interaction techniques, interfaces, and applications. The proceedings will be published by Springer. More information will become available on the conference website: https://2025.hci.international/.

General Chair
Prof. Constantine Stephanidis
University of Crete and ICS-FORTH
Heraklion, Crete, Greece
Email: general_chair@2025.hci.international

https://2025.hci.international/

Contents – Part V

Innovations in Product and Service Design

Innovative Design for Enhanced User Experience

The Design of Humpback Correction Belt Under the Guidance of Healthy Behavior

Wa An[1(✉)], Yiwen Chen[1], Yuanhuai Liu[1], Zixun Lin[1], and Di Zhang[2]

[1] Guangzhou Academy of Fine Arts, Guangzhou 510006, China
anwa_design@163.com
[2] Zhongxuan Liquid Metal Technology Co., Ltd., Shenzhen 518063, China

Abstract. Through product research and user experienceanalysis of hunchback correction belts, we explore product design guidelines that meet user needs and provide a good experience. Qualitative research methods of user interviews and observation records were adopted, and the Fogg model was used as a method for product user experience needs mining and usability evaluation. The design principles of aesthetics, functionality, comfort, plasticity, ease of use, and concealment are proposed to effectively improve the use experience of correction belt products; combined with the application of new materials, the product's adaptability to the human body shape is improved, and the final design is both wearable products that are beautiful, easy to use, and can improve body posture.

Keywords: hunchback correction belt · behavioral research · user experience design · ergonomics

1 Introduction

As people's health awareness continues to increase, the problem of hunchback has also received much attention. Hunchback not only has a negative impact on a person's posture and temperament, but long-term hunchback can also cause muscle damage, limited movement, cervical spondylosis and other life and health problems. This article aims to help people improve the hunchback problem caused by bad posture. It uses design thinking, user research and product experience analysis to design a corrective belt with reasonable structure and comfortable wearing to help people cultivate health awareness and good posture.

2 Analysis of Hunchback Problem

2.1 Overview of the Hunchback Problem

The word "kyphosis" is often used to describe the excessive curvature of the upper back of the human body [1], which is medically called "kyphosis" or "kyphosis" [2], which can occur at any age [3]. The human spine is divided into three parts: cervical vertebrae,

A. Marcus et al. (Eds.): HCII 2024, LNCS 14716, pp. 3–15, 2024.
https://doi.org/10.1007/978-3-031-61362-3_1

thoracic vertebrae and lumbar vertebrae, each forming three natural curves on the side. This natural curvature is important for human balance and helps maintain normal posture. If any curve becomes too big or too small, the posture will be abnormal, which will lead to hunchback [4]. In general, the curvature of the spine measured using the Cobb angle in healthy humans is 20–45°, while the curvature in patients with kyphosis is above 50° [5]. Kyphosis can be caused by structural defects of the spine. The main types include Shulman's disease and congenital spinal deformities. It may be caused by osteoporosis, spinal fractures, or even congenital defects of the spine [6]. The causes are complex. And difficult to prevent. The hunchback problem faced by most people is postural hunchback [7].

Bad posture habits in life are an important reason for the formation of postural hunchback. With the popularity of electronic products such as smartphones, many people spend hours every day with their heads down. The normal human cervical spine is naturally lordotic. In addition to the flexion and extension movements of the neck, the elongation and retraction movements also play a role in the sagittal plane. Once the cervical spine remains in the extended position for a long time, abnormalities in the head posture will inevitably occur. Changes, leading to a bad posture called "forward head posture." [8] Laziness is also one of the bad postural habits that lead to hunchback. People's movements when they are slouched will increase the forward curvature of the spine, which in turn will stretch the extensor muscles of the back and the posterior ligaments of the spine, causing their function to increase with the Weakened with the passage of time [9]. Sitting for long periods of time can also induce hunching because it causes continued contraction of the head and neck muscles. According to statistics, China ranks 17th in the world in per capita use of mobile phones, with an average of 3.3 h of use per day; 58.6% of office workers sit for more than 1 h on average, of which 39.3% exceed 90 min; 43% sit in the office for at least 1 h every day, but seldom take the initiative to take a break; primary and secondary school students in China do homework for an average of 2.82 h a day, and 80% of children and adolescents spend more than 2 h sitting for a day; the average driving time in China is as high as 240 h every year, and they spend an average of 40 min in a car every day (see Fig. 2). In these scenes, static postures need to be maintained for a long time, which can easily lead to poor posture and hunchback problems.

As the habit of hunchback develops, frequent spinal and muscle injuries will continue to accumulate over time, bringing huge potential risks to our human health [10]. At the mental level, a hunchback makes people look listless, which can easily cause low self-esteem, depression and other psychological problems, affecting people's self-confidence and emotional state; at the pathological level, excessive pressure on the spine can cause pain, and if it causes additional pressure on the lungs, it can also cause pain. May cause difficulty breathing [11]. The longer the symptoms of postural kyphosis are ignored, the longer it will take to successfully correct the posture, and the possible consequences will be more serious. Early correction can effectively improve [12].

2.2   Treatment Methods for Postural Hunchback

Postural kyphosis usually does not damage the normal vertebral structure. Most people's hunchback occurs only in the muscles and can be corrected and controlled by themselves [13]. The course of postural kyphosis is usually benign [14], and prevention of deformation is better than treatment. Medical intervention is used to slow down deformation if lesions caused by posture are not corrected in time [15]. Effective methods to prevent hunchback include postural muscle training and the use of auxiliary products (see Fig. 1).

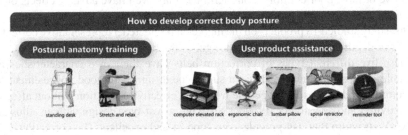

Fig. 1.   Effective methods to prevent and correct hunchback

1) Postural muscle training: Through stretching and relaxation training, stretch and relax tense muscles; through core strengthening exercises [16], activate and strengthen weak muscles, which can correct muscle imbalances.
2) Use auxiliary products: The effect of postural muscle training is limited by the patient's self-control, time and space requirements. Therefore, people often need to use external tools as assistance to maintain correct postures during study and work. The hunchback correction belt is one of the best-selling and most representative products on the market [17].

3   Humpback Correction Belt Product and User Experience Analysis

3.1   Product Function Analysis

The hunchback correction belt is a functional wearable product. The correction belts on the market can be roughly divided into two categories: (1) External force correction belts (2) Vibration reminders. External force correction belt products, represented by the back-to-back brand, usually use highly elastic and stretchable fabrics such as nylon and spandex to correct the user's shoulders, back, and waist through elastic stretching, thereby improving bad posture; in addition, there are reinforced correction belts that add rigid materials as keels to enhance support. The vibration reminder product has a built-in angle sensor, which uses vibration to remind the user to improve their posture in time based on the feedback of the body tilt.

By collecting reviews from Internet users such as Taobao and JD.com, we found that the correction belt products on the market provide users with obvious correction effects in the early stages of wearing them through external force correction and posture feedback. At the same time, they help users improve their control of back muscles and maintain Correct posture. However, forced external force correction under long-term use may cause muscle compensation in the user's body, aggravating the hunchback. The sensing data of the vibration reminder is inaccurate. What is actually obtained is cervical spine forward tilt data, which cannot accurately determine the current posture. It is prone to false alarms and will continue to interfere with the user, which has certain negative effects on the user's study or work process. Influence. All in all, it is difficult for existing products to combine comfort, invisibility, strong support, and high fit. They are either ineffective or have poor comfort. Long-term use may even have adverse effects on the body, and cannot meet the actual needs of users.

This study studied 18 products on the market and selected 5 representative correction belts for in-depth analysis from brand, design, evaluation, price, and sales volume.

These five different types of correction belts have their own characteristics and applicable groups. Product No. 1 has a strap-type design with good concealment and high comfort, and is suitable for people who want effective correction without affecting daily activities and appearance; Product No. 2 has a vest-type design with an adjustable double- Y structure that can provide even support and excellent The correction effect is suitable for people who want high-quality correction effects; Product No. 3 has an aluminum alloy keel that provides hard support and has obvious correction effects but is relatively bulky, so it is suitable for people who want better correction effects; Product No. 4 is a shoulder correction belt, focusing on It is suitable for mild shoulder correction, is friendly and comfortable, and is affordable. It is suitable for people who are new to correction belts or who have minor corrections. Product No. 5 has four small aluminum alloy keels arranged on the back, providing more even support and excellent results. It is also light and comfortable, suitable for people who want a moderate number of aluminum alloy keels and excellent effects.

In terms of shoulder tension, the double-Y structure correction belt's force-generating points are at the upper shoulder point and armpit, which enhances the backward pulling effect of the shoulder and has stronger tension than other structures; in terms of waist support, the small aluminum The horizontally arranged structure of the alloy keel will fit the human spine structure better than the bulky integrated metal keel, providing a good supporting effect; in terms of back support, the tension of the double Y structure correction belt converges on the back, which provides better support than other structures. More sufficient back support effect; in terms of concealment, a structure with a metal keel will be more obvious than a structure composed only of elastic bands, and a structure that fits the human body has a better hiding effect; in terms of flexibility, a pair of strong wrapping The Y structure and the oversized metal keel will limit the range of movement of the person. In contrast, the simple elastic band structure will be more flexible and agile. To sum up, each product has its own advantages and disadvantages based on comparisons in different aspects. Among them, product No. 5 has outstanding performance in lumbar support, while other products have excellent performance in shoulder tension, back support, concealment and flexibility.

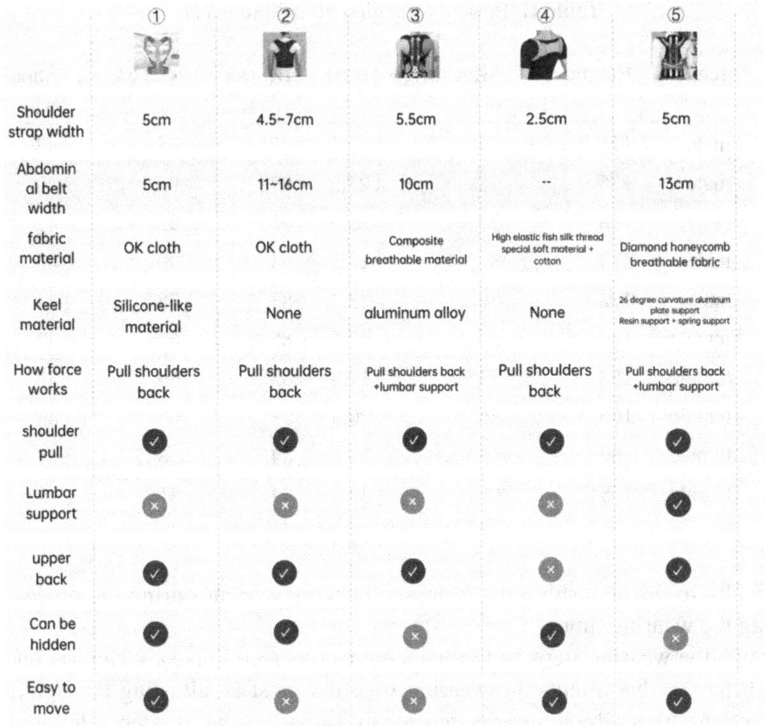

	①	②	③	④	⑤
Shoulder strap width	5cm	4.5~7cm	5.5cm	2.5cm	5cm
Abdominal belt width	5cm	11~16cm	10cm	--	13cm
fabric material	OK cloth	OK cloth	Composite breathable material	High elastic fish silk thread special soft material + cotton	Diamond honeycomb breathable fabric
Keel material	Silicone-like material	None	aluminum alloy	None	26 degree curvature aluminum plate support Resin support + spring support
How force works	Pull shoulders back	Pull shoulders back	Pull shoulders back +lumbar support	Pull shoulders back	Pull shoulders back +lumbar support
shoulder pull	✓	✓	✓	✓	✓
Lumbar support	✗	✗	✗	✗	✓
upper back	✓	✓	✓	✗	✓
Can be hidden	✓	✓	✗	✓	✗
Easy to move	✓	✗	✗	✓	✓

Fig. 2. Product information and function comparison chart

3.2 User Experience Analysis

This study recruited 10 young people with non-sports or dance professional backgrounds to voluntarily participate in the use experience test of 5 models of hunchback correction belts. To ensure accurate test results, subjects with significant spinal and shoulder disease were excluded. Subjects of different body types and genders were selected to observe the subjects' wearing reactions. The relevant body index of the subjects is shown in Table 1.

1. Experience analysis of the wearing process

Taking the subjects' wearing "time" and wearing "steps" as the main indicators, the subjects' wearing process of wearing 5 types of correction belts was recorded, and the "ease of use" of wearing the correction belts was analyzed. Product No. 3 took the longest to wear, taking 72 s. Because the shoulder strap structure is too cumbersome, it requires multiple adjustments to fit the human body size. The shortest one is product No. 4, which takes 22 s. Since the structure is the simplest, it only consists of shoulder straps, and there are very few steps to put it on. Among the wearing steps, the three longest steps are adjusting the correction strap, putting on the brace, and tightening the adjustment strap. The reason why it takes too long is that problems such as the adhesion of Velcro, adjustment of the pendant and cassette straps, backhand operation,

Table 1. Basic information of male subjects

Subject	gender	Height/cm	Weight/kg	BMI	Bust/cm	Waist/cm	Shoulder width/cm
1	male	175	54	17.6	77	75	43
2	male	175	78	25.5	97	95	48
3	male	168	73	25.9	95	92	42
4	male	184	81	23.9	94	90	46
5	male	172	70	23.7	83	78	44
6	female	160	50	19.5	85	69	37
7	female	163	53	19.9	85	69	38
8	female	166	56	20.3	88	66	40
9	female	160	55	21.5	84	68	38
10	female	168	66	23.4	94	81	39

and difficulty in distinguishing the front and back may occur during the process, thus increasing the wearing time.

Through the wearing steps and influencing factors (see Fig. 3), it can be concluded that the behavior that affects the wearing time the most is adjusting the tightness of the correction strap, which appears repeatedly in each wearing step. The adjustable structure of the correction belt will affect the user's wearing effort. Complex structure and cumbersome steps will make users spend more time and energy when using it. Therefore, when designing a correction belt, it is necessary to simplify the wearing steps as much as possible, reduce unnecessary adjustment structures, and optimize the wearing process on the shoulders, back, and waist while maintaining functionality, so as to make the wearing of the product simpler and smoother. The structural design of the posture correction belt should comply with ergonomics, facilitate single-person operation, and reduce the user's difficulty in wearing it.

2. Experience analysis of the correction process

After the subjects put on the products, the user experience during the correction period of the five correction belts was analyzed based on the four indicators of limb flexibility, body comfort, correction effect, and appearance acceptance (see Fig. 7).

In terms of limb flexibility: the width of the adjustment belt of 5 cm–15 cm can improve the comfort and stability of the correction belt, and has low restrictions on limb activities; the larger the coverage area of the correction belt, the better it can disperse the correction force and reduce the impact on local muscles. Restrictions; excessively large metal keels will increase the volume of the correction belt and cause greater discomfort to limb activities; too tight wrapping and low-elastic materials will reduce the space for muscle activity and increase pressure and discomfort on local limbs.

In terms of body comfort: the use of comfortable and soft fabrics reduces irritation and friction to the skin and increases wearing comfort; the keel that conforms to the

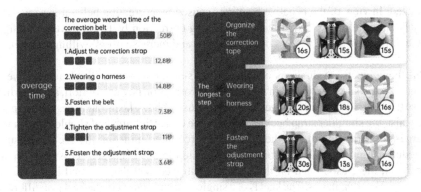

Fig. 3. Wearing Process Analysis Chart

curvature of the spine can ensure that it fits the curve of the human body, reducing the sense of oppression and foreign body sensation; the waist adjustment belt is suitable for The abdomen is squeezed, making it difficult to breathe during use; the shoulder and back adjustment straps are excessively compressed when passing under the armpits, causing discomfort and pain at the contact parts.

In terms of correction effect: the double Y-shaped structure can better support the back, make the correction force more uniform, and at the same time ensure the tension of the shoulder and improve the correction effect; the shoulder and back tension adjustment card label on the back can be adjusted according to individual conditions. Improve the pertinence and effectiveness of correction. The elasticity of the material is too large, causing the correction belt to be unable to provide sufficient correction force; the coverage area is too small, unable to cover key parts of the back, and a better correction effect is not achieved.

In terms of appearance acceptance: the use of three-dimensional tailoring design makes the correction belt fit the body curve more closely and the appearance is more natural; the use of high-quality fabrics, such as breathable, soft, comfortable cotton fabrics, etc., improves the comfort of wearing and the texture of the appearance. The oversized keel design makes the correction belt appear bulky and obvious, affecting the acceptance of the appearance; the color selection of the correction belt is too single and cannot be selected according to personal preference.

Through the test, it was found that the following problems were common among the subjects: the correction belt and the keel were misaligned and needed to be readjusted; the flexibility of squatting and reaching forward was limited due to the restraint of the upper body correction belt; the abdomen was bound by the belt., needing to take a big breath; because the shoulder straps cause tightness and pain in the armpits, the subjects will adjust the shoulder straps; because they are concerned about the eyes of others, they will put the correction straps on the outside and wear them inside.

In terms of emotions, the subjects will feel uncomfortable due to the constraints of the correction belt, and at the same time they will have feelings about the appearance of the product. Under the influence of negative emotions, subjects' willingness to use will gradually decrease as time goes by and eventually the wearing behavior will be terminated. In view of the negative emotions caused by correction belts, it is necessary to pay attention to users' experience when using correction belts, improve the design of the comfort and aesthetics of correction belts, and increase users' willingness to use them.

All the subjects' evaluations of the product's advantages and disadvantages were summarized and summarized from three aspects: correction power, comfort, and wearing process (see Fig. 4). The advantages include: the use of back keels enhances the support of the waist; the shoulder strap buckles enhance the correction force of shoulder opening; the large-area wrapping makes the correction force more uniform; the use of pressure pads reduces armpit pain; more contact The tensile force is dispersed across the face to reduce pain; the elastic band on the back is positioned with buckles and is not easily interrupted. Disadvantages: The keel is of a single size and cannot fit the backs of different subjects, leaving gaps; when leaning on, it is affected by external forces in the opposite direction, and the pulling force is weakened; the abdomen is tightened by the belt and breathing is difficult; the armpits are pressed for a long time and feel pain; The back belt is easily interrupted and inconvenient to wear; the belt gets stuck when adjusting the tightness; the back adjustment function requires backhand operation.

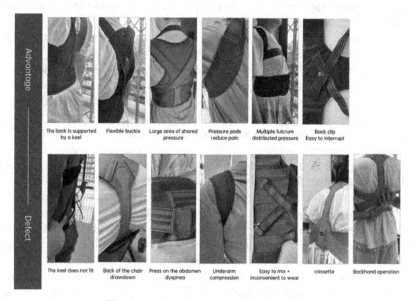

Fig. 4. List of advantages and disadvantages

4   Design Principles of Hunchback Correction Belt

This study uses the Fogg model as a guiding model for understanding the guidance of healthy behaviors for posture correction. This model analyzes and understands how human behavior is generated from the perspective of user behavior and psychology. This theory believes that the prerequisite for behavior to occur is that users must have sufficient behavioral motivation, behavioral capabilities and effective triggering mechanisms [18]. Based on the Fogg behavioral model, we can transform the design of "objects" into the design of "behaviors" by providing design guidance for correction belt products from three perspectives: motivation, ability, and trigger mechanism.

In the process of the user wearing the correction belt for humpback correction, the reasons that make users actively willing to wear them can be regarded as "user motivation"; the brainpower, time and body functions used by users can be regarded as "user capabilities"; the mechanism to encourage wearing can be seen As a "trigger mechanism". Therefore, if correction belts want to improve product usage, increase user stickiness and product competitiveness, they can further explore the design of correction belts from three directions: first, find motivation factors to increase the use of correction belts; second, improve user capabilities and lower the threshold for use; the third is to select appropriate trigger points to induce behavior.

Motives include issues such as painful correction process, concerns about the appearance of the correction belt, and doubts about the correction effect. The user needs gained from this can be summarized as creating a comfortable wearing experience for users, transforming and upgrading the correction belt, and improving the correction effect. In terms of capabilities, This includes issues such as repeated adjustments of the adjustment strap, complex wearing operations, and restricted behavior. The user needs can be attributed to providing smooth and easy operations and reducing restrictions on user behavior. In terms of mechanism, the main problem is the lack of wearing reminders. Insights from this The user demand is to add appropriate wearing reminders. Six design principles that are important in the design of hunchback correction belts are proposed: functionality, plasticity, comfort, ease of use, aesthetics, and concealment (see Table 2).

Functionality: Meet the correction needs of users. Provide users with effective support, help users improve their hunchback, and ultimately form correct posture habits.

Plasticity: Human bodies are all different and can be adapted to different types of users. Products need to have adjustment functions to improve form fit and meet the needs of users with different body types.

Comfort: Comfortable experience design needs to reduce user resistance. Through reasonable ergonomic design and skin-friendly materials, users are willing to wear and use it for a long time.

Ease of use: Complex operations are a hindrance for users. Reducing the difficulty of using correction belts and optimizing the wearing process of correction belts can increase users' willingness to use and help users form good usage habits.

Aesthetics: The aesthetics of a product is the prerequisite for users to like it. Through a more simplified design, the product can better match the user's clothing, while ensuring the functionality of the product itself and taking into account the overall wearing effect of the user.

Concealability: Users will have an uncomfortable sense of shame when wearing correction belts, which will hinder users from wearing them. Trying to weaken the visual presence of the correction belt can reduce the user's sense of shame to a certain extent.

Table 2. User needs and design principles of hunchback correction belt under Fogg Behavioral Elements

User issues	User needs	Behavior change	Design Principles
The correction process is painful and it is easy to give up wearing it The correction belt has a crude shape Don't mind other people's opinions, wear the correction belt inside Having difficulty breathing due to the tight belt on the abdomen Doubts about the effectiveness of correction	High-quality and comfortable correction experience Beautiful shape of correction belt Improve the concealment of correction belts Good correction effect	user motivation	aesthetic _ Feature comfort Hiddenness
The front and back of the incorrectly worn correction belt Adjustment straps tend to dangle and fall off Requires backhand operation to adjust the correction strap Adjust the adjustment strap repeatedly while wearing it The armpits are tightened and the shoulder straps are pulled Keel that adjusts displacement during use Corrective straps restrict movement	Fits human body structure Smooth wearing operation Reduce operational difficulty Reduce the number of adjustments Reduce restrictions on user behavior	User capabilities	plasticity Ease of use
lack of mention Easy to forget to wear	Appropriate wear reminder Interesting reminder mechanism	trigger mechanism	Feature Ease of use

5 Design of Hunchback Correction Belt

The design of kyphosis correction belt not only needs to consider its basic function, but also pay attention to the optimization of user experience and usage experience. The six design principles proposed above will guide design practices in aspects such as product structure, material use, appearance design, user psychology and behavioral processes, so as to achieve the best effect of product experience (see Fig. 5).

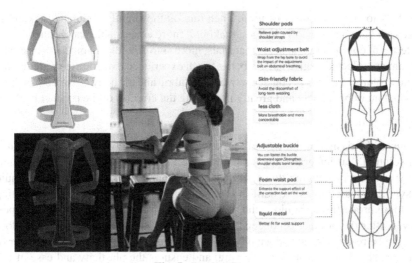

Fig. 5. Product Program

The design of the hunchback correction belt in this study uses liquid metal synthetic materials as materials. This material shows significant advantages such as low thermoforming temperature, good fit, light weight, and good shape temperature control memory [19]. Based on the low-temperature melting and plasticizing characteristics of liquid metal, after the liquid metal is heated to a certain temperature, it can be deformed, bent and shaped, and will gradually condense back to a solid state after being left at room temperature for tens of minutes. Its unique material properties provide a new design perspective for optimizing product functions and user behavior processes, helping users have a better product experience. This plan is designed based on the Fogg behavioral model from three aspects: motivation, ability, and trigger points:

1. Motivation design:

In terms of mechanical structure, we choose to add freely adjustable buckles on the back, so that users can still increase the pulling force a second time after wearing the product. And by adding a foam lumbar cushion for the thoracolumbar joint section of the back, the effect of supporting the thoracolumbar joint section can be achieved when the liquid metal condenses. While the shoulders and thoracolumbar joints are both supportive, it solves the problems of chest inclusion and hunchback, ensuring the functionality of the product. At the same time, the waist adjustment belt is optimized to wrap around the sternum and hip bones to disperse the force on the body and solve the problem of traditional correction belts pressing the abdomen and forcing users to breathe poorly. And by adding soft pads under the armpits, the force-bearing area is increased, allowing users to feel less pressure under the armpits (see Fig. 11), improving the comfort of the product.

In terms of appearance design, taking into account the hidden needs of users and the aesthetics of the product, we chose relatively low-key black and white, added a small amount of solid colors as embellishments, and minimized the size of the product to make it less likely to attract outside attention. Then rely on the slightly undulating texture to produce rich light and shadow changes, making it more concealable and aesthetic.

In terms of optimizing touchable materials, more skin-friendly nylon OK fabrics and EVA foam are selected to give users a better touch experience. And due to the reduction in product volume, the area of contact between the fabric and the body is reduced, making the product more breathable and greatly improving the comfort of the product itself.

2. Wearability design:

Terms of the design of the wearing process, we innovatively propose an integrated design solution that integrates the straps into the keel to solve the problems of corrective straps, straps hanging down and users' backhand operations. By using liquid metal synthetic materials as the built-in keel and utilizing the low-temperature melting and molding properties of liquid metal, it can better fit people of different body types. Moreover, after the product is condensed and set when used for the first time, it does not need to be re-condensed and adapted for a long time, which reduces the number of adjustments simplifies the steps of wearing, and ensures the plasticity and ease of use of the product.

3. Trigger mechanism design:

By setting timed reminders in WeChat mini-programs and pushing reminders through public accounts within a fixed period of time, using symbolic pictures and interesting copywriting, it can create visual and psychological stimulation for users. Pictures of hunchbacks will form negative positive motivation reinforcement and negative motivation reinforcement for users. Positive motivation reinforcement will make users aware of the changes in personal temperament caused by good posture, while negative motivation reinforcement will make users feel visual discomfort, so they can actively wear correction belts and develop correct sitting posture habits.

6 Conclusion

This study draws on professional medical kyphosis research literature, conducts user experience evaluation on related products that are best-selling on the market, and summarizes the usage problems and user experience needs of kyphosis correction belt products. Taking functionality, plasticity, comfort, ease of use, aesthetics and concealment as design guiding principles. Combined with the Fogg behavioral model, the correction belt product is designed from three perspectives: motivation, ability, and triggering mechanism. In terms of user motivation, the structure, appearance, comfort, and concealment are optimized to improve users' willingness to use; in terms of user ability, the plasticity of liquid metal and the integration of the keel are used to reduce the difficulty of wearing, reduce the number of adjustments, and allow users to More willing to use it for a long time; in terms of triggering mechanism, the purpose of wearing reminder is achieved through the content push of WeChat applet. This study takes healthy behavior guidance as the core concept, summarizes the design principles of the hunchback correction belt design, guides the design implementation, and serves as a reference for the design of healthy posture development products.

Fund Support. 2023 Guangdong Province Philosophy and Social Sciences Planning Project "Digital technology-driven Health Behavior Guidance and Habit Formation Design Research", no. GD23YYS19;2023 Guangzhou Philosophy and Social Science Planning Project "Research on the Design Mechanism of Digital Technology Involved in Healthy Lifestyle Cultivation", no.2023GZGJ316;2021 Guangzhou Academy of Fine Arts universal-level project "Research on the Design Method of Transformation and Upgrading of Traditional Manufacturing Industry Under AIoT Ecological Construction" no. 21XSB20.

References

1. Huang, P.: Analysis of poor posture and movement intervention in college students. Contemporary Sports Sci. Technol. **10**(05), 17–18 (2020)
2. Rohlmann, A., Klöckner, C., Bergmann, G.: The biomechanics of kyphosis. Orthopade, **30**(12), 915–8 (2001)
3. Dong, J.: Prevention and treatment of hunchback, different age methods are different, Family Med. Happy Health **8**, 26–27 (2020)
4. Jing, C.Y., Yao, X.J., Wu, H.R.: Child and adolescent health. Peking University Medical Press **7**, 20–29 (2012)
5. Lowe, T.G.: Scheuermann's kyphosis. Neurosurgery Clin. North America **18**(2), 305–315 (2007)
6. Zhang, Y.F., Sun, Y., Pang, H.L.: Research progress of kyphosis. Med. Rev. **22**(8), 1519–1522 (2016)
7. Li, P.: Investigation and intervention of poor body posture in ordinary college students. Xi'an Physical Education University (2016)
8. Thigpen, C.A., Padua, D.A., Michener, L.A.: Head and shoulder posture affect scapular mechanics and muscle activity in overhead tasks. J. Electromyogr. Kinesiol. **20**(4), 701–709 (2010)
9. Singla, D., Veqar, Z.: Association between forward head, rounded Shoulders, and increased thoracic kyphosis, A Review of The Literature. J. Chiropr. Med. **16**(3), 220–229 (2017)
10. He, H.C., Yang, L., Wang, Q.: https://www.icourse163.org/course/SCU1002203005?from=searchPage. Accessed 2021/5/3
11. Karen Gill, what is kyphosis? Medical News Today. Accessed 3 Jan 2022
12. "What is Kyphosis". Your Body Posture. 14 February 2018. Accessed 14 Feb 2018
13. Rudolfsson, T., Björklund, M., Djupsjöbacka, M.: Range of motion the upper and lower cervical spine in people with chronic neck pain. Man. Ther. **17**(1), 53–59 (2012)
14. Shum Hubert, P.H., Ho Edmond, S.L., Yang, J., et al.: Real-time posture reconstruction for Microsoft Kinect. IEEE Trans. Cybern. **43**(5) (2013)
15. Lifecare: "How to treat hunchback (and what causes it to begin with)". https://lifecarechiropracticandwellness.com/featured-articles/how-to-treat-hunchback/. Accessed 28 Jan 2020
16. Wang, J.Q.: LuJing, Study on physical rehabilitation methods of postural kyphosis, Shandong Sports. Sci. Technol. **01**, 68–70 (2008)
17. Wu, Y.H.: Intelligent research and design of posture correction belt, Guangdong University of Technology (2020)
18. Fogg, B.J.: A Behavior Model for Persuasive Design. France: Proceedings of the 4th International Conference on Persuasive Technology (2009)
19. Deng, Z.S.: A booming new liquid metal industry. Science **74**(02), 31–34+4 (2022)

A Framework for Applying Kansei Engineering Principles in the Design of Small Household Appliances

Shihao Cao, Fan Yang[✉], and Wenwen Yang

Guangzhou Academy of Fine Arts, No. 257, Changgang East Road, Haizhu District, Guangzhou, China
antony4d@hotmail.com

Abstract. The demand for added value in small household appliances gradually increased. However, existing theoretical design methods often struggled to achieve satisfactory results in the practical design of small household appliances. Sensitivity engineering (KE), by deeply understanding user perceptions, preferences, and emotions, incorporated these factors into design decisions, aiming to improve the quality and user satisfaction of products or services. Its core idea was to consider human emotions and intuitions in technical development and design. This study explored the effectiveness of integrating KE with iterativeprototype design in the context of small household appliance design methodologies. In the first phase, we explored user consumption trends and preferences for small household appliances and reviewed academic papers on the application of KE in product design. We proposed an innovative design theoretical model to meet user demands for in small household appliances. In the second phase, we employed case validation, applying the methodological model that integrated KE with iterative prototype design to the design of a humidifier, and received positive feedback. This research demonstrated the rationale of incorporating prototype design iteration methods into KE and provided valuable insights for the design and development of small household appliances.

Keywords: Product Design · Design Innovation · Sensitivity Engineering · Product Prototype Iteration · Small Household Appliances · Design Methods

1 Introduction

With the continuous technological advancement, the era of materialism is drawing to a close, and the era of sensibility has unfolded [1]. User demands for small household appliances have evolved beyond mere functionality, placing greater emphasis on visual experiences and emotional perception. In product design, consumers' expectations have shifted from functional aspects to emotional dimensions. When purchasing goods, consumers are not solely influenced by a single factor but conduct a comprehensive sensory evaluation of the product based on their own perceptions. The user base for small household appliances is gradually becoming younger. Younger consumers, when selecting products, consider not only the usability and practicality but also whether the product aligns with fashion trends and satisfies their personal spiritual needs [2]. Only when a product aligns with the emotional imagery within consumers' hearts, do they make purchase decisions.

Small household appliances are typically situated in home environments, necessitating designs that align with the overall decor style of homes and coordinate with furniture and spaces. They are relatively simple structures, and are updated frequently. Once new products were introduced to the market, they face a rapid influx of numerous competitors. In this fiercely competitive market, kitchen appliances (such as rice cookers and slow cookers) and environmental home appliances (such as air purifiers, humidifiers, vacuum cleaners, and robotic sweepers) emerged as popular products leading market trends. The sales volume of these products has shown a noticeable growth in recent years, making them a focal point of growth in the Chinese home appliance market over the past three years. This has also turned the small household appliances market into a highly scrutinized 'red ocean'. This new market trend not only underscored the intense competition within the small household appliances market but also revealed consumers' continuous desire for innovative products in the kitchen and environmental home appliance sectors. This demand has driven companies in the industry to accelerate the introduction of new products, continuously updating and iterating their product offerings. This dynamic market situation has made small household appliances a hotspot for research and attention [8].

Usability has long been recognized by design researchers and practitioners as a key to the success of product innovations [3]. More recently, greater emphasis was given to addressing users' emotional needs, within the product designing processes [1]. With the continuous development of technology, users have raised their expectations for product experience and convenience. Considerations for aesthetics and emotional appeal, including product appearance design, material selection, and human-computer interaction interfaces, need to address users' aesthetic and emotional demands [5]. It has been pointed out that effectively applying emotional into product designing, with a focus on capturing users' latent needs and requirements, assists in establishing a clearer resonance between the emotional features of interactive products and users [4]. The emergence of small household appliances signifies users' pursuit of higher living standards in terms of convenience, fashion, and efficiency after meeting basic life needs. Compared to large household appliances, small household appliances are more specialized, catering to specific usage needs, with more focused functionality and affordable prices. When purchasing small household appliances, users no longer solely consider factors such as quality, price, and brand but also place a greater emphasis on whether the product can evoke emotional resonance within the consumer. "Superiority" becomes one of the judgment criteria for consumers when choosing and purchasing large household appliances. Satisfaction and dissatisfaction are key standards by which users evaluate the purchase of small household appliance products.

The user experience is closely tied to users' emotional needs, and through human-centered design and simple, user-friendly interfaces, it is possible to enhance users' affinity for the product [6]. Research indicates that the development trend of small household appliances will increasingly focus on innovation and personalization. Products will pay more attention to personalized user needs, allowing different users to choose customized small household appliances based on their lifestyles and preferences [7]. Based on these characteristics, we believe that fully applying sensory engineering to the design and development of small household appliances helps designers gain a deeper understanding of users' subjective needs. Through in-depth research into users' perceptions and emotional feedback, it becomes possible to better meet users' expectations, achieve the fusion of user emotional experience and aesthetics in end products, and ultimately enhance the product's human-computer interaction experience and commercial success. The concept of "Kansei Engineering (KE)" was initially proposed by the former president of Mazda Corporation, Kenichi Yamamoto, during a speech at the University of Michigan. A more complete definition was given at the 10th International Symposium on Human-Computer Interaction, in 1988, that described KE as a translating technology of a consumer's feeling and image for a product into design elements, through qualitative and quantitative analysis. As pointed out by Luo et al. (2015), one distinctive characteristic of KE is the application of rational thinking is decoding handle sensory cognition, and then materializing the insight into design elements [5]. As a result, the application of KE allows designers to gain a deeper understanding of users' subjective needs, injecting richer humanistic content into product design.

KE methods have been employed by scholars to conduct a series of studies in the field of small household appliances. Shiyuan Ming introduced KE theory into the design of intelligent small household appliances, exploring from a narrative perspective how to utilize the Sensory Factor Analysis method in product design to better meet users' deep-seated psychological needs [10]. In a study using the example of the design of a wall-breaking cooking machine, Juan Du utilized KE theory as guidance. Through methods such as focus group discussions, cluster analysis, and morphological analysis, the relationship between consumers' sensory needs and product design was examined [11]. Yinqu Yang and Yanli Wei emphasized the importance of small household appliances in modern life and the issue of homogenization in their designs. They proposed a method of using prototype theory for small household appliances' design and conducted research based on the foundation of KE theory [6]. Yingying Miao highlighted the shift in societal values regarding products and applied the Sensory Catalog-based Value Creation System theory to small household appliances aimed at Chinese users [12]. However, these studies to focus on the application of KE to a single product or a specific aspect, lacking systematic studies on the overall scope of small household appliance products. Firstly, most existing studies tend to focus on the application of KE to a single product or a specific aspect, lacking a systematic exploration of the overall range of small household appliances and multiple sensory elements. Secondly, the methods used in research are relatively singular, and there is insufficient application of diverse research methods and technologies. Addressing the current shortcomings in research on the application of KE within the scope of small household appliances, we propose an innovative application framework for KE in the design of small household appliances.

2 Method

The study was divided into two stages: 1) market exploration and user studies, and 2) case validation. Market exploration and user studies were conducted to collect data on aesthetic trends and user preferences in product design. This data was then analyzed using the principles of sensory engineering to design product prototypes, which were subjected to a series of prototype testing and iterations. Case validation was done using the methodology. In the first stage, deeper understanding of user emotional needs and aesthetic expectations, and how they influenced product selection and usage, was achieved. The current aesthetic trends and user preferences in humidifier design were explored. Data was collected through market research and user studies, including questionnaire surveys targeting existing users and potential buyers of humidifiers. The survey covered aspects such as satisfaction with humidifier design, color and shape preferences, functional requirements, price sensitivity, etc. The questionnaire was distributed through email, social media, and home appliance stores. Representative individuals from the survey participants were selected for in-depth interviews. Additionally, social media analysis was conducted by collecting data from user comment sections on platforms such as Twitter, Facebook, and e-commerce sites using keywords such as "humidifier" and "design." Social media analysis tools were used for data collection and sentiment analysis. The collected data was analyzed using the principles and methods of sensory engineering to identify key design elements that impacted user emotions and preferences. The results led to the establishment of the new framework for applying KE in the design of small household appliances.

The framework was then evaluated and refined through a household humidifier design project. This type of household appliances was selected because their market performance was closely connected to the users' emotional experience. Besides, household humidifiers were more important to people's everyday life than ever, with the emerging consumer trends like 'home economy' and 'lazy economy', in the post-pandemic era [9]. However, in the design phase, smart humidifier products in the market often overlooked consumers' emotional needs, leading to an increasingly prominent issue of homogeneity in the appearance and design of similar products. Given the widespread use of humidifiers in home environments, they play a crucial role in providing a comfortable living environment. Furthermore, the usage of these humidifiers is closely related to users' lifestyle habits, health conditions, and other factors. Therefore, an in-depth study of their actual role in family life contributes to a better understanding and fulfillment of people's real needs at home, providing a more scientific basis for practical applications.

3 The Framework for Applying KE Principles in the Design of Household Appliances

The new framework incorporates the five key stages:

Stage One. In the initial stage, market research was conducted to clarify the target user group and the design positioning of the product. Subsequently, various humidifier samples with different styles in the market were focused on to ensure comprehensive sampling. Through methods such as on-site visits, online data analysis, literature reviews, etc., samples were systematically collected, constructing a rich library of humidifier product design samples. Following the typical product sample collection methods, after preliminary collection and organization, representative samples were ultimately summarized.

Stage Two. Relevant materials, product descriptions, advertisements, user reviews on e-commerce platforms or social media, design magazines and publications, browsing social media platforms, industry exhibitions, etc., were read. By comprehensively synthesizing information from these channels, a rich set of adjectives describing the sensibility of humidifiers could be obtained to better understand users' feelings and expectations for the product. During this process, special attention was given to adjectives suitable for describing design imagery. The collected adjectives were filtered, removing less common or similar-meaning words, and pairing adjectives with opposite meanings to construct an adjectival library of imagery. Subsequently, the database was categorized and preliminarily screened to exclude adjectives with high similarity and those unsuitable for evaluating humidifiers' sensibilities. An analysis and extraction of the collected sensibility adjectives were carried out using both online and offline methods, such as online reviews, face-to-face interviews, group brainstorming, etc. The adjectives for humidifier imagery were screened through these methods. Finally, through a questionnaire survey, the final sensibility adjectives were determined.

Stage Three. The hierarchical category analysis method was used to transform these sensibility adjectives into quantifiable features or design elements with physical properties. By artificially linking sensibility adjectives at various levels during the design phase, a more comprehensive understanding of the correlation between the characteristics of the humidifier product and the sensibility adjectives could be achieved.

Stage Four. Obtain the user's reaction intensity to product attributes. Design a questionnaire survey, and based on the sensibility adjectives determined in step three, score representative humidifier samples selected in step one. Choose the humidifier sample with the highest score as the initial prototype for product iteration.

Stage Five. Disassemble the representative samples selected in step one to summarize the key design elements affecting humidifier design. This step is crucial for subsequent design iterations.

Stage Six. Innovate the design of small household appliances, combining the key design elements identified in step five to iteratively innovate the product design.

4 Applying the Framework in the Design of a Household Humidifier

In the first stage, the innovative framework of KE in the design of small household appliances was practically applied through case studies. A total of 96 humidifier samples were collected through various channels, and after initial collection and organization, 27 representative samples were selected through screening. These 27 samples were categorized into 9 groups, from which 9 representative samples were further chosen, the representative samples were indicated by "N."This process aimed to gain in-depth insights into users' sensibility needs and preferences regarding humidifier styles. As shown in Table 1.

Table 1. Representative humidifier sample.

N1-N9

In the second stage, the collected sensory words were analyzed and extracted, resulting in 15 sets of corresponding sensory adjectives. Forty participants were selected, with no specific requirements for profession or age, comprising 20 men and 20 women randomly chosen. Subsequently, a survey questionnaire on sensory vocabulary was developed to identify six sets of words that best represented humidifier products (Table 2). A total of 40 questionnaires were distributed for this research project, 38 were collected, and 38 valid questionnaires were used for data analysis. The summarized statistical information is presented in Table 3.

From the survey information in Table 3, it is evident that six groups of vocabulary are most prominent. These words can most accurately represent the unique characteristics of humidifier products. The specific related vocabulary and descriptions are shown in Table 4.

In the third stage, the main task was to extract sensory design elements and, through the Analytic Hierarchy Process (AHP) [14], transform these sensory design elements one by one into quantifiable features or design elements with physical properties. Sensory design elements primarily focused on four key aspects: performance, material, appearance, and structure. The hierarchy diagram of the humidifier product is specifically (see Fig. 1).

In the fourth stage, a questionnaire survey using the sensory vocabulary and design elements identified in step three, was carried out to evaluate the representative samples of humidifiers from step one. A five-point scale of semantic differential method was

Table 2. Sensory vocabulary collection statistics.

Fifteen sets of sensory adjectives				
Modern/Traditional	Soft/Strong	Fresh/Dull	Eco-friendly/Energy consumption	Fashion/Plain
Humanized/Mechanized	Soothing/Stimulus	Fun/Boring	Novelty/Routine	Simplicity/Complexity
Streamline/Square	Large volume/Compact	Strong/Fragile	Smooth/ Rough	Safe/Dangerous

Table 3. The statistical information of the questionnaire data.

Perceptual vocabulary	Number of selections	Perceptual vocabulary	Number of selections
Modern/Traditional	32	Novelty/ Routine	30
Soft/Strong	6	Simplicity/Complexity	24
Fresh/Dull	23	Streamline/Square	19
Eco-friendly/Energy-consumption	27	Large volume/Compact	13
Fashion/Plain	22	Strong/Fragile	25
Humanized/Mechanized	10	Smooth/Rough	10
Soothing/Stimulus	29	Safe/Dangerous	6
Fun/ Boring	28		

Table 4. Finally sensory vocabulary

Six sets of sensory adjectives		
Modern/Traditional	Novelty/Routine	Soothing/Stimulus
Fun/ Boring	Humanized/Mechanized	Simplicity/Complexity

Table 5. Humidifier sample questionnaire

Product samples	Scores for sensory design elements
	Performance: □-2 □-1 □ 0 □1 □2
	Material: □-2 □-1 □ 0 □1 □2
N1	Appearance: □-2 □-1 □ 0 □1 □2
	Structure: □-2 □-1 □ 0 □1 □2

Table 6. Survey data for humidifier sample questionnaire

Product samples	Average scores of sensory design elements
N1	1.621
N2	1.379
N3	1.862
N4	1.586
N5	1.414
N6	2.517
N7	1.897
N8	1.655
N9	1.517

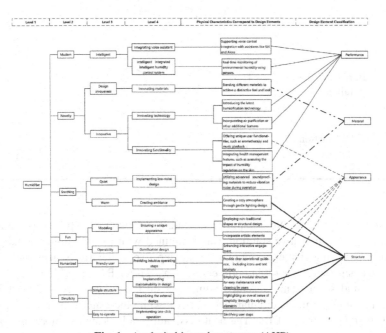

Fig. 1. Analytic hierarchy process (AHP)

utilized, ranging from "−2, −1, 0, 1, 2." Thirty target users, randomly selected without distinctions in occupation or age, with an equal distribution of 15 males and 15 females, were chosen. The questionnaire, as shown in Table 5, was developed and distributed for this round of testing, resulting in 30 distributed questionnaires, 29 of which were collected and considered useful. Statistical analysis was performed on the 29 questionnaires, and the total sum for each element of every sample was calculated. The average score for each sample's elements was obtained by adding up the total sum of each element and dividing it by 29. The humidifier sample with the highest average score in sensory design elements was selected as the initial prototype for product iteration. The objective of this step was to gauge the user's intensity of reaction to product attributes. The details are presented in Table 6.

Based on the survey data of the sample questionnaire, the average score of the Sensory design elements for the N6 humidifier sample was the highest. Therefore, the N6 humidifier sample was chosen as the initial prototype for the product.

In the fifth stage, The Key Styling Elements of the Humidifier Samples were produced, as illustrated in Table 7.

Table 7. Two-dimensional representation of humidifier styling elements.

In the sixth stage, the N6 humidifier sample, determined in step four as the initial prototype for the innovative solution, was combined with the two-dimensional graph of humidifier styling elements summarized in step five to iteratively generate various innovative design solutions for humidifiers, such as N1-A1-B1-C1, N1-A1-B2-C1, N1-A2-B5-C3, and so on. The presented humidifier design solution, N1-A3-B4-C3-C4, features a mist outlet in the circular shape of A3, while the water container adopts the irregular rectangle shape of B4. The heat dissipation hole design is more innovative, incorporating the concentric circles from C3 and the rectangular transformation from C4 onto the initial model. This completed the iterative and innovative design process of the product based on sensory elements (see Fig. 2 and Fig. 3).

Fig. 2. Final design solution (N1-A3-B4-C3-C4)

Fig. 3. Final design solution detail (Dissipation Hole)

5 Discussion and Conclusion

KE has long been proven as an effective method for product development and design. However, this theory has not been widely adopted in practical applications because it is challenging to quantify and can complicate the design process. This preliminary study suggests that the innovative design framework based on the integration of KE with product iteration is more suitable for product development in the small household appliance design field. As our results demonstrate, there are two critical processes in the innovation framework: (1) selecting a representative humidifier sample as the initial prototype through questionnaire scoring, understanding users' reaction intensities to sensory vocabulary design elements, and reducing the investment in design development and costs for small household appliances; (2) extracting and summarizing the key styling elements affecting the humidifier sample, enabling designers to quickly apply styling elements that meet users' sensory needs for design innovation.

The application of KE makes the design more focused on users' sensory and emotional needs, aligning products more closely with users' psychological expectations. By cleverly integrating KE with the product prototype iteration design method, not only can users' sensory and emotional needs be met, but also technical contradictions caused by design elements can be addressed. Continuously optimizing and adjusting during the design process helps to better balance the relationship between technical implementation and user experience, thereby enhancing the overall quality of the product. This innovation framework based on KE contributes to the creation of more innovative, practical, and user-expected products, driving the direction of small household appliance design towards greater humanization and user orientation.

After our case study on the innovative application framework of KE in small household appliance design, the research indicates that applying this innovation framework effectively promotes the iterative innovation of small household appliance products. Additionally, compared to traditional design processes, products designed using this framework can effectively capture users' sensory needs while, in the innovation process, clarifying users' reaction intensities to different initial sample prototypes through design surveys, better capturing users' sensory needs. Researchers can comprehensively consider various aspects of product design, ensuring that innovation is not limited to overall design but also focuses on precise shaping of individual details. This in-depth research will help improve the comprehensiveness and meticulousness of design, meeting users' more precise sensory needs and enhancing the market competitiveness of the product.

6   Limitations and the Next Step

There are also some limitations to the design strategy. Firstly, the paper does not mention market feedback, which is a potential limitation. The success of a product depends not only on the innovativeness of the design but also closely relates to market demand and feedback. Secondly, in the study, subjective evaluation was used for the investigation of imagery vocabulary for typical samples, and the selected sample size was relatively limited, which imposes certain constraints on the final results.

In the study, despite integrating many previous experiences, due to limited capabilities, certain theories still have some shortcomings. Additionally, users' sensory cognition plays a crucial role in this innovation framework, and in future research on small household appliances, it is necessary to consider introducing user evaluations and other sensory measurement methods, such as computer formula analysis or other experimental means, to deepen the research and form a more scientific and comprehensive innovation design framework. Existing design innovation frameworks will be improved over the long term.

Acknowledgments. This study was supported by Guangdong Planning Office of Philosophy and Social Science (Grant No. GD24CYS41); and the Department of Education of Guangdong Province (Grant No. 2023WTSCX052, and Grant No. 2023GXJK347).

References

1. Shi, Q.: The era of material happiness is over; how should we find new happiness. Life Companion (End of Month Edition), 000(005), 62–63 (2017). CNKI: SUN: RSBM.0.2017-05-032
2. Hou, J., Niu, S., Liu, J.: Research on emotional design of small household appliances under minimalism. Ind. Des. **2021**(10), 2. CNKI: SUN:KJYX.0.2020-10-020
3. Yang, F., Al Mahmud, A., Wang, T.: User knowledge factors that hinder the design of new home healthcare devices: investigating thirty-eight devices and their manufacturers. BMC Med. Inform. Decis. Mak. **21**(1), 166 (2021). https://doi.org/10.1186/s12911-021-01464-3
4. Lan, Y., Liu, P.: Emotional research of interactive products based on user experience. Packaging Eng. **012**, 040 (2019)
5. Luo, L., Hong, L.: Kansei Engineering Design. Tsinghua University Press (2015)
6. Yang, Y., Wei, Y.: Language consistency of small household electrical appliance design based on fuzzy cognitive experiment. J. Anyang Inst. Technol. **22**(2), 52–59 (2023)
7. Xu, Y., Zhao, K.: Research on emotional design strategy of generation Z small household appliances based on consumer characteristics. Design **36**(17), 85–87 (2023)
8. Qi, W.: Research on experiential design of small household electrical appliances. Art Quest **22**(1), 2 (2008). https://doi.org/10.3969/j.issn.1003-3653.2008.01.057
9. Sun, F., Kong, M.: Research on the status quo and development trend of small home appliances development in China. Home Appl. Sci. Technol. **2018**(6), 2. CNKI: SUN: JYDQ.0.2018-06-011
10. Shi, Y.: Research on intelligent small household appliances design based on perceptual narrative. Nanchang Hangkong Univ. (2022). https://doi.org/10.27233/d.cnki.gnchc.2022.000252
11. Du, J.: Research on assistant system of wall-breaking cooking machine modeling design based on perceptual image. Qilu University of Technology (2019)
12. Miao, Y.: Research on Chinese small household appliances design based on perceptual value creation. Nanjing University of Science and Technology, 2012 (2022)
13. Zhang, M.: Qingtong Capital Chen Huilin: The core technology is the moat of small household electrical appliance enterprises. Sci. Financ. **7**, 37–40 (2022)
14. Elisa, B., Fronzetti, C.A., Laura, S., et al.: Analytic hierarchy process for new product development. Int. J. Eng. Bus. Manage. **5**(1) (2013). https://doi.org/10.5772/56816

Comparative Analysis of the Presence and Decision Making in Romantic Visual Novels: Influence of Personalization and Sense of Presence

Vitaliy Davydovych[2,3]([✉]), Ernesto Filgueiras[1,2] [iD], and Anabela Marto[3] [iD]

[1] CIAUD, Research Centre for Architecture, Urbanism and Design, Lisbon School of Architecture, Universidade de Lisboa | UBI Polo, Lisbon, Portugal
evf@ubi.pt

[2] University of Beira Interior - UBI, Covilhã, Portugal
vitaliy.davydovych@ubi.pt

[3] CIIC, ESTG, Polytechnic of Leiria, Leiria, Portugal
anabela.marto@ipleiria.pt

Abstract. Video games have always had a significant impact on society, going beyond mere entertainment to become a cultural force that influences how we interact, learn, and perceive the world. This study explores how personalization and immersion affect decision-making in Visual Novels, a virtual environment that is often overlooked in research despite its importance. By incorporating moral aspects into decision-making and offering both personalized and non-personalized narrative options, the study aims to uncover potential connections between the types of choices players make, their sense of immersion, and the level of personalization. Two groups of participants played a decision-making game, one experiencing personalized narratives and the other pre-defined stories. The findings suggest that participants in personalized environments tend to make more conservative choices, indicating a possible relationship between personalization and decision-making. The study emphasizes the intricate nature of player experiences in romantic visual novels, highlighting how individual preferences and cultural backgrounds influence the subjective experience. Additionally, the results indicate that factors such as age, familiarity with the genre, and attraction to specific characters may also influence decision-making processes.

Keywords: Personalization · Decision-making · Interactive Romantic Visual Novels · Sense of presence and User engagement

1 Introduction

Videogames have long held a profound influence on society, transcending mere entertainment to become a cultural force that shapes how we interact, learn, and even perceive the world. From ancient pastimes to modern digital marvels, games have woven themselves into the fabric of human existence, impacting everything from social interactions and education to cognitive development and technological innovation.

A. Marcus et al. (Eds.): HCII 2024, LNCS 14716, pp. 28–46, 2024.
https://doi.org/10.1007/978-3-031-61362-3_3

Personalization and the feeling of presence have become increasingly important in modern media consumption, especially in the realm of interactive entertainment such as video games. As technology continues to advance, allowing for more immersive experiences, the importance of personalized engagement and feeling of presence will only continue to grow.

On the other hand, interactive Visual Novels (VN) are a unique medium for multi-linear storytelling. In contrast to traditional narratives, such as oral tales passed down through generations or books, they handle more intricately the human senses of hearing and vision, through their expressive character sprites, backgrounds, and elaborate sound design and music. Balancing between the fields of ludology and narratology, they offer a unique platform for exploring the interplay of personalization and the sense of presence.

This study addresses a critical gap in the current body of research, wherein the role of personalization and presence in interactive media, particularly within the context of VN's, remains understudied. By investigating the influence of personalized storytelling and its impact on the feeling of presence, this research aims to shed light on the intricate psychological and emotional dynamics that come into play during the consumption of interactive media. Moreover, it seeks to determine which variables within the realm of game design, encompassing elements such as narrative, graphics, and player behaviors, contribute to the development of more engaging and emotionally resonant VN's.

In an era where technology often dominates discussions of presence and immersion, this study intends to evaluate whether even within comparatively low-immersive environments, the design variables wield a significant influence on the sense of presence. Furthermore, it delves into the intriguing effect of real player data in Romantic Games on the tone of decision-making, highlighting that the inclusion or omission of players from the narrative can lead to divergent and contrasting outcomes.

Additionally, by introducing the element of moral decision-making, the study endeavors to establish that even in simple graphical settings, such as those found in Romantic Games, the degree of presence can significantly impact decision outcomes, guiding players toward choices that either mirror or deviate from their real-life inclinations.

The purpose of this pilot study is to test the conditions and methodologies for a larger experiment being conducted at the University of Beira Interior in Portugal, focus on the impact of personalization and sense of presence on decision-making in romantic visual novels, this preliminary investigation targets male participants in a predominantly sexual context. By exploring how customization and immersion influence player choices within romantic narratives, this study aims to lay the groundwork for a more comprehensive examination of user engagement and decision patterns in videogames and others interactive storytelling experiences.

2 State of the Art

It is important to explore the impact of personalization on presence and decision-making in video games. By allowing players to input personal information, the game can tailor the narrative to their preferences, potentially resulting in engaging, empathetic, and inclusive media experiences.

To test this hypothesis, a VN format was chosen due to its focus on narrative and minimum interactivity, making it ideal for focused and controlled testing. This choice was made after extensive research informed both by personal experience and direct observation of existing games in the genre.

2.1 Visual Novels

According to Kretzschmar & Raffel (2023) visual novels are "story-driven games that employ interactive elements, allowing the player to influence the story and characters". Cavallaro (2010), on the other hand, goes more technical and says that a visual novel is "a multi-branching and interactive ludic experience that enlists the player's creativity alongside the production studio's own artistry, and thus transcends the boundaries of other types of more controlling video gaming".

He also claims that a "visual novel typically articulates its narrative by means of extensive text conversations complemented by lovingly depicted (and mainly stationary) generic backgrounds (Fig. 1, A) and dialogue boxes (Fig. 1, B) with character sprites determining the speaker superimposed upon them (Fig. 1, C)."

Fig. 1. Interface from the VN "Clannad".

2.2 Player Experience

According to K.M. Lee (2004) presence can be defined as "a psychological state in which virtual (para-authentic or artificial) object are experienced as actual objects in either sensory or nonsensory ways."

Presence can only be felt through experience and "human experience can be categorized into three types—real experience, hallucination, and virtual experience" (K. M. Lee, 2004) so with the previous definition of presence, the author includes in the definition nonsensory experiences, such as hallucinations or daydreaming. As for para-authenticity, it is the property of virtual objects that have an equivalent in the physical world. It has long been believed that for video games, two factors invoke feelings of presence – vividness and interactiveness (Steuer, 1992) and this, as per K. M. Lee (2004), can be achieved through three specific dimensions:

- Social presence is defined as "a psychological state in which virtual social actors are experienced as actual social actors in either sensory or nonsensory ways." It "occurs when technology users do not notice the para-authenticity of mediated humans and/or the artificiality of simulated nonhuman social actors."
- Self presence is defined as "a psychological state in which virtual social actors are experienced as the actual self in either sensory or nonsensory ways." It "occurs when technology users do not notice the virtuality of either para-authentic representation of their own selves or artificially constructed alter-selves inside virtual environments."
- Physical presence is defined as "a psychological state in which virtual physical objects are experienced as actual physical objects in either sensory or nonsensory ways." It "occurs when technology users do not notice either the para-authentic nature of mediated objects (or environments) or the artificial nature of simulated objects (or environments)."

Numerous studies have demonstrated that various factors can influence the experience of presence in video games. These factors include the type of controller used (Skalski et al., 2011; Williams, 2013), audio quality (Skalski & Whitbred, n.d.), level of perceived violence, biological sex, and prior gaming experience (Nowak et al., 2008). However, the specific factors that contribute to presence in visual novels can be only translated and are not directly understood.

Examination of player experience often involves the exploration of presence and immersion, concepts that may still be used interchangeably in some studies. However, various authors have endeavored to delineate these constructs. According to Caroux (2023), immersion is predominantly linked to sensory perception, whereas presence, characterized by a sense of being 'in the game,' pertains more to a mental and psychological perception."

Cairns et al. (2014) refer to immersion as the "engagement or involvement a person feels as a result of playing a digital game", and a study they conducted has shown that "players were able to distinguish different levels of immersion in games and these corresponded to their sense of engagement and involvement in the game", defined sequentially, by their effect, as engagement, engrossment, and total immersion.

2.3 Game Design Elements

Personalization is a multifaceted term that can have various meanings depending on the context. When it comes to video games, Bakkes et al. (2012) uses the following definition: "A personalized game utilises player models for the purpose of tailoring the game experience to the individual player." He then further clarifies that the game is personalized when the adaptations made to it are informed by the player. Conversely, if the adaptations are autonomous, without any analysis of player's input, the game is "strictly adaptive". With this, it can be concluded that personalization can either occur by the game autonomously learning about the player and adapting the gameplay based on that newly acquired information or by the player providing it directly at the start which the game can later use to personalize the experience.

If we consider the latter scenario, it suggests that personalization will occur after the player is faced with a customization screen or menu at the start of the game. Although easily mistaken one by the other, there is an inherent difference between customization and personalization. Sundar and Marathe (2010) refers to customization as the "user deliberately tailors content by choosing options and/or creating content" while personalization entails "the degree to which the content is tailored by the system to individual tastes". In this definition, customization is used broadly and can include any customizable element, and in video games, it can be further subdivided on the type of desired customization; the one most relevant for this study is avatar customization.

In recent years, there has been an increasing number of games with customization (Cyberpunk 2077, Elden Ring, Baldur's Gate 3, Starfield), showing that it has become a crucial aspect of modern gaming. These games offer extensive avatar customization options, allowing players to not only choose their character's name but also tailor their appearance and traits to suit their preferences. Some effects of personalization in video games, as reported by existent research, are:

- Enhanced Player Engagement and Sense of Presence (Ng & Lindgren, 2013).
- Increase in Aggressiveness (Hollingdale & Greitemeyer, 2013).

On the other hand, decision making has been extensively researched across multiple fields. Per Shahsavarani and Abadi (2015), it is a mental process that is generally part of every human's life and is defined as a "problem-solving process which ends when a satisfying solution is reached". According to Damasio et al. (1996), decision-making "occurs at several levels within the central nervous system. At the highest level, the individual consciously uses both past experience and future predictions to choose an action. At the lowest level, decisions are made that do not reach consciousness until after actions are performed, and the individual is unaware of the process leading up to the particular choice."

Both of these decision-making levels can be translated into video games. They occur interchangeably and this can include selecting which weapons or abilities to use, deciding which quests or missions to pursue, and determining how to approach challenges or obstacles. This can lead to both instinctive and deliberate decision-making, depending on the context and player experience. Bracken and Skalski (2010) add that video games "provide models of decision-making processes that are not represented in television and other entertainment media where the user's role is passive. Thus, not only do video games have the capacity to provide more complete mental models than other media experiences, but the repeated enactment of these mental models during game play should strengthen the learning of decisional cues linked to associated behaviors".

In video games, decision making has been most extensively studied in regards to morality and ethics (Holl et al., 2020; Joeckel et al., 2012; Weaver & Lewis, 2012).

3 Methodology

Figure 2 presents a comprehensive methodology flowchart illustrating each sequential step in the development of this study. The process initiated with the selection of the research theme, followed by the identification of problems, an exploration of the current state of the art, formulation of the proposal and development methodology, execution of tests, analysis of results, and ultimately, the formulation of conclusions and future research.

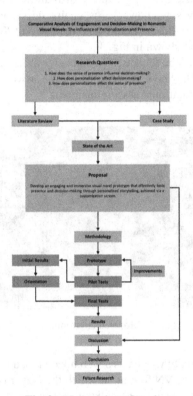

Fig. 2. Methodology flowchart.

3.1 Implementation

One of the most common settings in VN's is academic life. For this prototype, a small university campus library was chosen. It is a contained environment with objects that can be reused in 3D, saving time in the development process.

As for the plot, the general outline is as such: A student awakens well beyond closing hours on one of the library's tables and finds himself face to face with a mysterious woman. As they engage in conversation, he learns that she's the librarian, one who for some mysterious reason knows everything about him. Their dialogue unfolds, and when the situation reaches the peak of discomfort, she disappears. Following a process of trial and error, the narrative was successfully created, paving the way for the next step in the creative process – the construction of a storyboard. A great amount of time was invested in its development, particularly on the female character's expressions, poses and consistency throughout the frames.

The development of the prototype began with the creation of the library environment in 3D and then using an outline modifier and post-process effect to achieve a stylized 2D look. This greatly simplified the process and allowed switching camera perspectives without having to redraw each view by hand. It also allowed for the reuse of existing assets, including bookshelves, windows, vases, chairs, desks, and books. Through procedural techniques not only did the books automatically fit the bookshelves but also varied in size and texture, as shown in Fig. 3.

To make the drawings of the female main character fit in with the environment and stand out, an elaborate shading style was chosen for the artwork. Finally, followed by a series of iterative improvements and asset refinements.

Fig. 3. Modeled environment.

Since the story was initially written as a web novel, it had to be adapted to the first-person point of view to fit the VN format, in which the player is addressed as the main character, an important factor to aid personalization. The narrative was enhanced with a variety of visual and audio effects, implemented through a node-based narrative system to create a more immersive and engaging experience for the player. These included dynamic camera angles and close-ups on character's faces, accompanied by appropriate action sounds such as kissing, laughing, and falling, as well as carefully timed fade ins and outs to enhance the emotional impact of key moments in the story. Figure 4 how sprites underwent modifications to align with the narrative's bolder and ethically driven moral directions, aiming to provoke more powerful reactions from players.

Despite incorporating the storyboard's sequence of frames into the prototype, several frames failed to align both with the narrative and the choices. Adjustments had to be made, leading to the deviation from the original sequence in favor of a seamless player experience. Furthermore, choices in the game are presented in a randomized order to avoid any perceived pattern or bias in their tone.

Fig. 4. Evolution of Character Sprites (a) First bold version (b) Second version, bolder (c) Third version, even bolder, breaking the researchers' own ethical barriers.

As for the interface, the web browser was chosen as a more versatile and user-friendly alternative to an executable and it was implemented in such a way that players can only play once to prevent repeated results, assuring data accuracy. Figure 5 presents a shot of the final prototype.

Fig. 5. Final appearance of the playable prototype.

4   Tests and Feasibility

4.1   Sample

The sample consisted of 22 participants who voluntarily engaged in this study. The sample was carefully selected to represent a diversity of demographic profiles and gaming experiences, aiming to gain comprehensive insights into the influence of personalization in romantic games. The selection process adhered to one mandatory criterion, requiring participants to be male, as the scenario was tailored to this specific sexual orientation. The interaction within the scenario involves a male character engaging with a female character, and the narrative is presented from a male perspective.

For this study, only male volunteers who identified as predominantly heterosexual were considered, given that the scenario was tailored to attract a male audience and constructed with male-centric clichés. Homosexual women with preferences for the female gender were not included in this pilot study as it would require a deeper understanding of the attraction and sexualization dynamics specific to the female audience (Fig. 6).

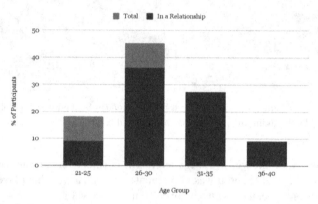

Fig. 6. Percentage of participants by age groups and relationship status.

Researchers at Northwestern University in the United States (Gerlach et al., 2018) examined data from over 1.5 million people and found that there are at least four distinct groups of social personalities:

– Average Type (People who tend to be more anxious and outgoing in public, but are not very open to trying new things).
– Reserved Type (Emotionally stable people who are not extroverted in public, but are pleasant and considerate of others).
– Role Model Type (People with low anxiety, trustworthy in public, and open to new ideas).

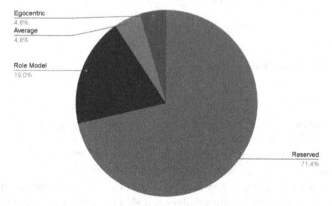

Fig. 7. Categorization of the participants' personalities.

– Self-centered Type (People who are introverted in public, have little openness to new experiences and show little empathy for others).

Figure 7 shows that the predominant personality type among the participants is Reserved, followed by Role Model and then Egocentric and Average the minority.

4.2 Sample Analysis

An analysis was made of the choices associated with each shot, categorized by the nature of the choice made—whether conservative, neutral, or bold. The examination incorporates a graphical representation illustrating the distribution of participant choices, accompanied by a comprehensive analysis for each respective shot.

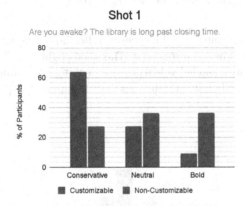

Fig. 8. Participant responses to Shot 1 categorized by customization type.

In the analysis of Fig. 8 (Shot 1), most choices made by participants fall within conservative and neutral, encompassing more than half of the selection spectrum. When scrutinizing the customizable versus non-customizable versions, a noteworthy pattern emerges. The customizable environment elicits a higher number of conservative choices, indicating a prevalent inclination towards risk-averse behavior among participants. This heightened conservatism in the customizable version is hypothesized to be attributed to personalization, suggesting that individuals might be more cautious and adherent to conventional choices when the narrative is tailored to their preferences. Conversely, the non-customizable version yields a higher number of bold choices, pointing towards a more adventurous decision-making approach when personalization is absent.

In the analysis of Fig. 9 (Shot 2), through an individual lens, it becomes evident that a substantial portion of the selection spectrum is dominated by conservative and neutral choices. This prevalence is further highlighted when comparing customizable and non-customizable options, revealing a striking similarity in the abundance of conservative and neutral choices across both versions. The observation emerges that this inclination towards more cautious decision-making may be attributed to the inherent simplicity and directness of the bold choice presented – "Stay longer? I'd love to!". The straightforward nature of this bold option may subconsciously encourage participants

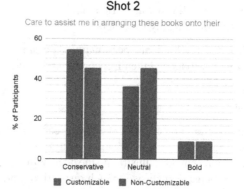

Fig. 9. Participant responses to Shot 2 categorized by customization type.

to opt for safer and less controversial responses, reflecting a broader societal tendency towards moderation and non-confrontation. This sheds light on the nuanced interplay between presentation style and individual decision-making, illustrating how the framing of choices can significantly influence the overall distribution of responses.

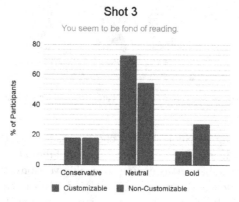

Fig. 10. Participant responses to Shot 3 categorized by customization type.

In the analysis of Fig. 10 (Shot 3), a notable trend emerges as participants make a higher number of neutral choices. This inclination towards neutrality becomes particularly pronounced when considering the participants' responses to the customizable versus non-customizable versions of the prototype. Interestingly, in the non-customizable version, there is a distinct increase in the number of bold choices made. This contrast suggests that the customization feature may impact decision-making, with individuals feeling more liberated to opt for bolder options when not constrained by their own persona. The observations further reveal a prevalent trend of risk aversion among participants, although in this instance, it manifests in a preference for neutral choices. This tendency is attributed to the participants' apparent reluctance to align themselves with the conservative option – "Itis indeed my passion." In essence, the higher frequency of bold choices in the non-customizable version reflects a sense of freedom from personal constraints, shedding light on the intricate dynamics of decision-making and risk perception within the context of customization features in the prototype.

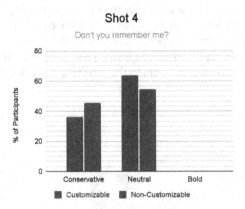

Fig. 11. Participant responses to Shot 4 categorized by customization type.

In the analysis of Fig. 11 (Shot 4), a notable absence of bold choices is observed, as the spectrum of decision-making predominantly leans towards conservative and neutral options. This lack of bold decisions is consistent across both customizable and non-customizable versions, while the Conservative and Neutral options reveal a balanced distribution, with neither version exhibiting a significant advantage over the other. The observations indicate a prevailing sense of risk aversion, with the bold choice, "'That's merely one of the things I'm fond of.' You wink at her" being perceived as overly provocative. It becomes evident that the avoidance of this bold option is likely driven by a desire to maintain a more restrained and less confrontational tone. The careful consideration of the customizable and non-customizable choices underscores a preference for subtlety and neutrality, emphasizing a deliberate avoidance of boldness in favor of a more conservative approach.

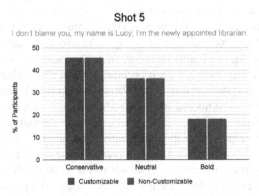

Fig. 12. Participant responses to Shot 5 categorized by customization type.

In the analysis of Fig. 12 (Shot 5), it becomes apparent that a significant portion of the decision-making spectrum is dominated by conservative and neutral choices. These choices collectively make up more than half of the decisions made, suggesting a preference for stability and moderation. Furthermore, when considering the duality between customizable and non-customizable options, a noteworthy observation emerges both versions offer an identical number of choices for each type. This parity raises questions about the significance of personalization in this scenario, and the similarity between the customizable and non-customizable versions implies that, in this instance, the decision-making moment is resistant to the recurring influence of personalization.

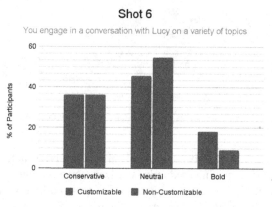

Fig. 13. Participant responses to Shot 6 categorized by customization type.

In the analysis of Fig. 13 (Shot 6), it becomes evident that most choices made by participants lean towards conservative and neutral, encompassing more than half of the decision-making spectrum. When observing the contrast between customizable and non-customizable choices, a notable pattern emerges – the customizable version features twice as many bold choices compared to its non-customizable counterpart. Delving deeper, it becomes apparent that the directness of certain options influences participants' decision-making. The participants may opt to avoid actions they perceive as morally or ethically questionable, and this aversion to perceived impropriety is particularly pronounced when confronted with bold choices. The inherent directness of the bold choice, "Lucy, I'm dying to know more about you!", may make it seem unsuitable for the specific scenario at hand, leading to a higher incidence of conservative and neutral choices.

In the analysis of Fig. 14 (Shot 7), it becomes evident that a significant portion of the selection spectrum is occupied by conservative and neutral choices. These choices, which lean towards the conventional and non-confrontational, make up more than half of the made choices. When comparing customizable and non-customizable environments, subtle fluctuations emerge within the conservative and neutral choices. The observations resulting from this analysis highlight a prevailing sense of risk aversion among individuals. Notably, the bold choice, "'I'm not trying to be too forward, but are you currently single?' You wink at her", stands out as too daring, with participants exhibiting

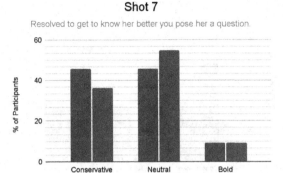

Fig. 14. Participant responses to Shot 7 categorized by customization type.

a tendency to avoid it, signaling a reluctance to take risks, possibly due to the perceived forwardness associated with it.

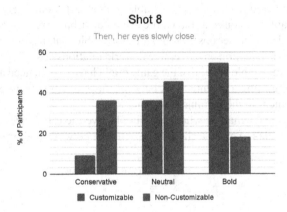

Fig. 15. Participant responses to Shot 8 categorized by customization type.

In the analysis of Fig. 15 (Shot 8), the Customizable version stands out for making the most daring decisions. A notable disparity emerges when comparing the Customizable and Non-Customizable versions, with a significantly higher frequency of bold choices evident in the former. This shot marks a pivotal juncture where participants must decide whether to reciprocate the female character's advances, and it becomes apparent that the majority of those engaging with the Customizable version opt for bold choices. This shift in behavior during this critical moment could be linked to the personalized narrative leading up to the decision point. Alternatively, it might be a culmination of a growing sense of intrigue, possibly spurred by the avoidance of bold choices in preceding instances. The connection between the customization feature and the willingness to take risks is underscored in this analysis, revealing how the tailored narrative experience influences participant responses in key decision moments.

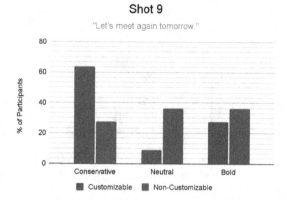

Fig. 16. Participant responses to Shot 9 categorized by customization type.

In the analysis of Fig. 16 (Shot 9), the overall results exhibit a noticeable dispersion. A noteworthy trend emerges when comparing the customizable and non-customizable versions. The customizable version reflects a significantly greater frequency of conservative choices compared to its non-customizable counterpart. Conversely, the results for the non-customizable versions exhibit a more evenly distributed pattern across all available option types. Upon closer observation, it is noticeable that this interaction moment may have triggered a reflection on players' real-world relationships. Consequently, those engaged in the customizable version of the game might have experienced an abrupt sense of detachment, suggesting a potential link between customization features and players' emotional engagement in the gaming experience.

Figure 17 presents a chart in which we can observe the differences in the average time it took participants to make a choice for each shot between both variants.

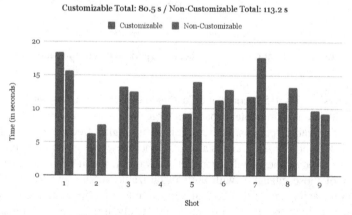

Fig. 17. Decision-Making: Average Time.

When comparing both versions, it is seen that participants in the customizable version displayed a significant lead in terms of quicker decision-making. This phenomenon was particularly pronounced in shots 5 and 7, where the customizable version exhibited the most significant disparity in decision-making time compared to its counterpart. On average, shots 1 and 7 emerged as instances where participants, irrespective of version, took a comparatively longer time to arrive at a decision. Interestingly, shot 2 stood out as an exception, with participants spending less time making decisions in both versions. The disparities in decision-making time during Shot 7 were particularly noteworthy, indicating that this specific shot played a crucial role in delineating the effectiveness of customization. These observations suggest that the customizable version facilitated quicker decision-making, possibly owing to the alignment of the narrative with participants' own personas, thereby underscoring the importance of personalization in enhancing cognitive processes and overall engagement (Fig. 18).

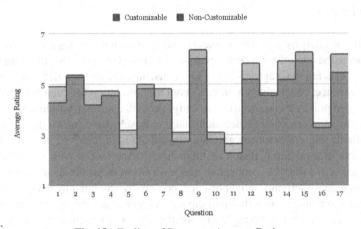

Fig. 18. Feeling of Presence: Average Rating.

Based on the Witmer & Singer (Singer, 2013) adapted questionnaire, the average presence values indicate a higher overall presence for the Non-Customizable version, with the Customizable version surpassing only in questions 2, 7, 9, 15, and 16. Participants in the customizable version who had a total of presence (sum of their presence rating for all questions) equal or higher than 60 opted for fewer bold choices than the participants within the same criteria in the non-customizable version. Number of bold choices: Customizable = 3/45 vs Non-Customizable = 12/54.

4.3 Research Limitations

Several limitations exist within the scope of this study, including:

– Limited interactions: A major limitation of the current prototype is that player choices are only limited to interactions with the female main character, which may severely restrict the sense of presence. To address this, the game could benefit from allowing players to switch positions or explore other areas between interactions with the character.

- While some basic information was collected about the user, this information may not be sufficient or personal enough to create a fully personalized experience.
- The sample size is small: Only 22 participants were used in the study. This makes it difficult to generalize the results to a larger population.
- Presence questionnaire: This questionnaire is only validated for the VR context, so it may not be appropriate to use in a visual novel setting. Additionally, some questions were removed as they didn't fit with the visual novel medium.
- Subjectivity: The experience of romantic visual novels can be highly subjective and influenced by individual tastes and preferences.
- Cultural differences: There may be cultural differences in how players perceive and engage with these types of games, which could affect the results.

5   Conclusion

The qualitative analysis has shown unexpected results, with average presence values being higher in the non-customizable environment. However, due to the limitations of this study (listed in detail in Chapter 5.3) that prevented an accurate statistical analysis of the feeling of presence, conclusive statements about the correlation between personalization and the sense of presence cannot be drawn, only speculated through an additional variable functioning as an intermediary – decision-making. Results have shown that participants in the customizable environment gravitate towards the conservative choices, this risk aversion hints at a potential fusion of their virtual experiences with their real-world personas, and thus a possible connection may exist between personalization and feeling of presence, namely self and social presence, potentially validated by decision-making.

Findings have also shown that participants subject to a personalized environment are prone to risk aversion, opting more for the conservative choices. These participants also exhibited faster overall decision-making times in comparison to their non-customizable counterparts. The discernible disparity in the decision-making type and time between both environments, observed through an individual analysis of each shot as well as an overall assessment, suggests a potential correlation between personalization and decision-making.

A potential cause for the participants in the customizable environment opting for the safer options, may be a result of specific dimensions of presence, such as self and social presence. Whether this inclination is a result of an increased feeling of presence remains uncertain, given the study's limitations in statistically analyzing the effects of the sense of presence due to the shortcomings listed previously.

Although direct correlation cannot be established due to limitations in the statistical analysis of the feeling of presence, it is noteworthy that participants in committed relationships predominantly favored conservative and neutral choices, more frequently than their counterparts in the same environment who are not in a relationship. Further research is required to ascertain whether this inclination goes hand in hand with an increased sense of presence.

Owing to the inherent limitations of this study, definitive conclusions remain elusive concerning the interplay between the sense of presence and decision-making type. Nonetheless, some provisional theories emerge, suggesting a symbiotic relationship between personalization and the sense of presence, as shown by participants in the customizable environment predominantly gravitating towards conservative choices, more often than their counterparts in the static confines of the non-customizable environment.

Results derived from the adapted presence questionnaire reveal consistently elevated ratings, despite the limited interaction character of the visual novel prototype. It's essential to note that the use of an adapted questionnaire is a limitation of this study, consequently, the previous statement should be regarded as speculative until a more comprehensive and precise analysis is conducted.

The results also suggest that there could be a discernible correlation between age, a player's familiarity with the genre, and their attraction for a particular character, all contributing factors that may influence decision-making.

5.1 Future Works

One promising direction for future research in the field of presence and decision making in videogames is the integration of emerging technologies such as VR and Augmented Reality (AR). These technologies have the potential to create even more immersive and realistic gaming experiences, which could enhance the sense of presence and further influence decision making. Another direction is how different types of graphics and visual rendering techniques affect the experience of presence and decision making in these immersive mediums.

Ongoing research will explore and advance studies focusing on the emotional potential inherent in video games. Within this overarching theme, research will specifically examine how various elements of video games, including narrative structures, artistic components, gameplay mechanics, and reward systems, intricately influence and shape human emotions. This research will not only seek to expand academic knowledge within the field but will also aim to shed light on the practical applications of such understanding, potentially informing the design and development of emotionally resonant and impactful interactive experiences.

Acknowledgements. This study was also partially supported by national funds through FCT - Fundação para a Ciência e a Tecnologia, I.P., under the Strategic Project with the references UIDB/04008/2020 and UIDP/04008/2020.

Disclosure of Interests.   The authors have no competing interests to declare that are relevant to the content of this article.

References

Kretzschmar, M., Raffel, S.: The history and allure of interactive visual novels. Bloomsbury Academic (2023)

Cavallaro, D.: Anime and the visual novel: Narrative structure, design and play at the crossroads of animation and computer games. McFarland & Co. (2010)

Lee, K.M.: Presence, explicated. Commun. Theory **14**(1), 27–50 (2004)

Steuer, J.: Defining virtual reality: dimensions determining telepresence. J. Commun. **42**(4), 73–93 (1992)

Skalski, P., Tamborini, R., Shelton, A., Buncher, M., Lindmark, P.: Mapping the road to fun: Natural video game controllers, presence, and game enjoyment. New Media Soc. **13**(2), 224–242 (2011)

Williams, K.D.: The effects of video game controls on hostility, identification, and presence. Mass Commun. Soc. **16**(1), 26–48 (2013)

Skalski, P., Whitbred, R. (n.d.): Image versus Sound: A Comparison of Formal Feature Effects on Presence and Video Game Enjoyment

Nowak, K.L., Krcmar, M., Farrar, K.M.: The causes and consequences of presence: considering the influence of violent video games on presence and aggression. Presence: Teleoperators Virtual Environ. **17**(3), 256–268 (2008)

Caroux, L.: Presence in video games: a systematic review and meta-analysis of the effects of game design choices. Appl. Ergon. **107**, 103936 (2023)

Cairns, P., Cox, A., Nordin, A.I.: Immersion in digital games: review of gaming experience research. In: Angelides, M.C., Agius, H. (eds.) Handbook of Digital Games, 1st ed., pp. 337–361. Wiley (2014)

Bakkes, S., Tan, C.T., Pisan, Y.: Personalised gaming: a motivation and overview of literature. Proceedings of the 8th Australasian Conference on Interactive Entertainment: Playing the System, 1–10 (2012)

Sundar, S.S., Marathe, S.S.: Personalization versus customization: the importance of agency, privacy, and power usage. Hum. Commun. Res. **36**(3), 298–322 (2010)

Ng, R., Lindgren, R.: Examining the effects of avatar customization and narrative on engagement and learning in video games. In: Proceedings of CGAMES'2013 USA, pp. 87–90 (2013)

Hollingdale, J., Greitemeyer, T.: The changing face of aggression: The effect of personalized avatars in a violent video game on levels of aggressive behavior. J. Appl. Soc. Psychol. **43**(9), 1862–1868 (2013)

Shahsavarani, A.M., Abadi, E.A.M.: The Bases, Principles, and Methods of Decision-Making: A Review of Literature 2(1) (2015)

Damasio, A.R., Damasio, H., Christen, Y. (eds.): Neurobiology of Decision-Making. Springer, Heidelberg (1996)

Bracken, C.C., Skalski, P.D. (eds.) Immersed in media: Telepresence in everyday life. Routledge (2010)

E., Bernard, S., Melzer, A.: Moral decision-making in video games: a focus group study on player perceptions. Hum. Behav. Emerging Technol. **2**(3), 278–287 (2020)

Joeckel, S., Bowman, N.D., Dogruel, L.: Gut or game? the influence of moral intuitions on decisions in video games. Media Psychol. **15**(4), 460–485 (2012)

Weaver, A.J., Lewis, N.: Mirrored morality: an exploration of moral choice in video games. Cyberpsychol. Behav. Soc. Netw. **15**(11), 610–614 (2012)

Gerlach, M., Farb, B., Revelle, W., Nunes Amaral, L.A.: A robust data-driven approach identifies four personality types across four large data sets. Nat. Hum. Behav. **2**(10), 735–742 (2018)

Witmer, B.G., Singer, M.J.: Measuring presence in virtual environments: a presence questionnaire. Presence Teleoperators Virtual Environ. **7**(3), 225–240 (1998). https://doi.org/10.1162/105474 698565686

Construction and Practice of Financial Management Professional Curriculum System Based on OBE Philosophy

Fang Fang, XiaoShi Chen[✉], and Qing Lan Li

Guangzhou City University of Technology, Guangzhou 510800, China
601668750@qq.com, 2942217488@qq.com

Abstract. This paper examines the construction strategy, implementation path and construction practice of the curriculum system in the reform of financial management professional talent training under the concept of OBE. Through literature review, case study, questionnaire survey method and other methods, this paper in-depth study of the application of the OBE concept in financial management education and puts forward a combination of social demand, student development and educational objectives of the curriculum reverse design construction framework system, including the development of student training from the talent training objectives of the expected results, to determine the course teaching content, teaching methods, sound and diversified assessment and evaluation system, continuous improvement of the whole process. Improvement of the whole process. The empirical analysis part will verify the implementation effect of the curriculum system through the data analysis of the practice process and the results of the questionnaire survey; summarize the results of the practice and discuss the direction of the future research and the problems that may be encountered. The findings of this paper are of great theoretical and practical significance for optimizing the curriculum design of financial management majors and improving students' professionalism and comprehensive ability.

Keywords: OBE (outcome-based) · financial management · curriculum system

1 Introduction

1.1 Background and Significance of the Study

In the process of deep development of the global economy, the society and so on put forward higher requirements for the ability quality of financial management professionals, and the applied undergraduate colleges and universities should pay attention to it. In order to meet the social demand for high-quality financial talents, more and more colleges and universities have carried out the reform of professional personnel training and curriculum system. The traditional financial management education often focuses on the transmission of knowledge, and ignores the cultivation of students' practical operation ability and problem solving ability, which is a certain disconnect with the actual demand for financial management talents in the current society. Therefore, in the construction of the financial management professional program system, how to innovate teaching methods, improve teaching quality, and cultivate financial management talents with high quality, innovation and practical ability has become an important issue facing higher education [1].

Outcome-Based Education (OBE) is a kind of education concept oriented to students' learning outcomes, which emphasizes that education should be designed and implemented around the competencies needed for students' future lives and careers [2]. The student-centered and output-oriented OBE concept is a fundamental way to realize the internal development of curriculum construction and teaching quality and the comprehensive development of students. W. G. Spady believes that OBE is an educational concept that clearly focuses and organizes teaching and learning activities around the key outcomes that can be obtained by all students at a certain stage of learning"1 [3]. Introducing the OBE concept into curriculum and teaching reform is a hot topic in educational research. The OBE concept has been widely noticed and applied in many disciplines, but there is relatively little research and practice in the field of financial management education. Therefore, the purpose of this paper is to discuss the construction strategy and implementation path of financial management professional curriculum system based on the OBE concept, so as to provide theoretical and practical reference for the reform of financial management education.

1.2   Research Issues and Objectives

The research questions in this paper include: Part 1, Construction strategy: how to apply the OBE concept to the curriculum design of financial management majors? Part 2, Implementation Path: How to construct the framework of financial management professional curriculum system based on OBE concept? Part 3, Result Evaluation: How to evaluate the implementation effect of the curriculum system of financial management major based on OBE concept?

In response to the above research questions, this paper deeply analyze the reform and implementation path of the application of OBE concept in financial management education; Construct a framework of financial management professional curriculum system that combines social demand, student development and educational goals; Verify the implementation effect of the financial management professional curriculum system based on the OBE concept through empirical research and questionnaire data analysis.

1.3   Research Methods and Data Sources

This paper adopts the methods of literature review, case analysis and questionnaire survey method to carry out the research. First of all, through the literature review to sort out the development history, basic connotation and application of OBE concept in the field of education; secondly, combined with the professional characteristics of financial management, social demand and practice exploration, to build the framework of financial management professional curriculum system based on OBE concept; finally, through the case practice data analysis to verify the implementation effect of the curriculum system framework. The data sources mainly include domestic and foreign related academic literature, practice process statistics and questionnaire research.

2 Strategies and Implementation Paths for the Construction of Financial Management Professional Curriculum System Based on the Concept of OBEBackground and Significance of the Study

2.1 Strategies for the Construction of Financial Management Professional Curriculum System Based on the Concept of OBE

The construction of financial management professional curriculum system based on OBE concept is a systematic project, which needs to be comprehensively considered and implemented in many aspects, such as cultivation objectives, curriculum structure, practical teaching, evaluation system, teacher quality and continuous improvement [4]. Through such a strategy, financial management professionals who are more in line with the needs of society can be cultivated.ted.

- Scientific determination of training objectives

Strengthen the concept of OBE, according to the national strategy, industry development and employer job demand, for stakeholders to carry out extensive demand research, take the form of issuing questionnaires, organizing symposiums, on-site interviews, third-party research, etc., to fully understand the needs of stakeholders and the formation of demand prediction, benchmarking demand prediction, combined with the positioning of the school and the characteristics of running the school. Scientifically determine the talent training objectives of the school, college and the specialty [5].

- Elaborate graduation requirements (learning outcomes)

Graduation requirements are the learning outcomes (ISLOs) that students are expected to achieve upon graduation. The graduation requirements are carefully formulated in accordance with the cultivation objectives and the standards for professional accreditation, focusing on the eight dimensions of business talent cultivation. The graduation requirements are itemized into achievable, measurable and logical indicators, which not only support the professional training objectives, but also reflect the characteristics of the program. At the same time, it provides a basis for the design of the organizational structure of the course system and the setting of the nature of the course elements.

- Reasonable construction of the curriculum system

According to the graduation requirements, set the course structure and credit ratio, rationalize the logic between courses, and all the courses included in the cultivation program should effectively support the talent cultivation objectives and graduation requirements, and each course can realize its role in the curriculum system [6]. Scientifically analyze and accurately prove the support matrix map of "graduation requirement, one training objective" and "curriculum system, one graduation requirement, one graduation requirement index point".

- Evaluation feedback for continuous improvement

The construction of the curriculum system should be continuously improved according to changes in demand [7]. In the process of implementation, it is necessary to carry out regular evaluation of the achievement of training objectives and graduation requirements and evaluation of the rationality of the curriculum system, optimize the elements and structure of the curriculum system according to the results of the evaluation and analysis, and ensure that the curriculum system can be adjusted with the changes in demand, so as to enhance its support and match with the training objectives and graduation requirements [8].

2.2 Implementation Path of Financial Management Professional Curriculum System Based on the Concept of OBE

To build the curriculum system of financial management based on the OBE concept, we should strengthen the awareness of demand and scientifically prove the talent cultivation objectives and graduation requirements [9]. Apply the method of reverse design curriculum system, make clear the effective support relationship between "cultivation goal, graduation requirement and curriculum system", decompose the talent cultivation goal to the curriculum goal layer by layer, and select the corresponding education content and teaching methods. Based on the graduation requirements, the course objectives and syllabus are formulated, and the teaching contents, teaching methods, assessment contents and methods support the achievement of the course objectives (Fig. 1).

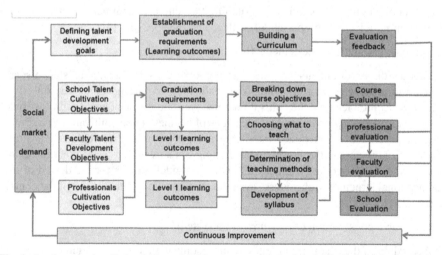

Fig. 1. Implementation Path of Financial Management Professional Curriculum System Based on the Concept of OBE

3   The Practice of Reverse Design Construction of Financial Management Professional Curriculum System Based on the Concept of OBE

School A is an application-oriented private university in Guangzhou, China, whose financial management major in the School of Management was accredited by the International Association for the Advancement of Business IACBE in 2019. Under the concept of results-oriented OBE, combined with the background of in-depth development of the global economy, the new environment and new tasks faced by the financial management major are also being changed by re-examining the new environment and new tasks, focusing on the new requirements of the global economic development on the professional talent cultivation, and carrying out the practice of the construction of the curriculum system of the financial management major based on the concept of OBE.

3.1   Determine the Training Objectives of Financial Management Professionals

First of all, clearly define the objectives of financial management professional training according to the talent objectives of the school and college, which are closely related to the expected results of the students and the demand of the employment market. This is the basis for building the professional curriculum system. The following is the talent cultivation objectives of the financial management major in school A (Table 1).

Table 1. Objectives for students in the financial management program in the School A

1.Objective 1: Students acquire subject matter knowledge and competencies related to the financial management program they are studying
2.*Objective2:* Students will be able to acquire knowledge of the various environments in which business operates
3.*Objective 3:* Students acquire professional skills in financial management
4.*Objective 4:* Students will be able to apply decision support tools and techniques to financial management decisions

3.2   Dentify Core Outcomes to Be Achieved by Financial Management Graduates

Develop graduation requirements based on the training objectives. These requirements should be clear, measurable and effective in measuring students' abilities and knowledge. Through in-depth cooperation with domestic and foreign industrial enterprises, we have gained a deep understanding of the industry's demand for talents, so as to determine the skills and qualities that graduates should have, and describe the core outcomes that applied undergraduates should achieve upon graduation from the university in eight dimensions. The core outcomes fully reflect the "student-centeredness" and use the form of "verb+" to emphasize the core competencies and qualities required of financial management graduates, such as financial statement analysis, financial decision-making, risk management and other aspects of competence (Table 2).

Table 2. Intended student learning Outcomes (ISLO) of Financial Management Program

	Dimension	ISLO (Level 1)	ISLO (Level 2)
1	critical Thinking	1.Demonstrate an ability to solve problems by using scientific and critical thinking skills	1.1 Students are able to access and process needed information
			1.2 Students will be able to use scientific and critical thinking skills to analyze problems and come up with solutions
2	Teamwork	2. Work effectively as a team member to contribute to high performance	2.1Students will be able to recognize the key elements of successful teams
			2.2 Students are able to work effectively in teams to promote high performance teams and collaborative environments
3	Communication	3. Communicate effectively and professionally within a wide range of audiences and context through oral and written skills	3.1 Students will be able to apply oral and written communication methods in a coherent and persuasive manner
			3.2 Students are able to communicate effectively and professionally across a wide range of audiences and environments
4	Business Core	Apply main concepts of the core areas to solve the practical problems	4.1 Students will be able to correctly understand the key concepts of the functional areas of business and the specialized areas of finance and economics
			4.2 Students are able to independently complete accounting, financial management, investment, financing and tax simulation labs
			4.3 Students are able to solve practical problems in accounting, investment and finance and taxation
5	Analytical Tools	5.Apply appropriate techniques and tools to make business decisions in the practice of Finance Management	5.1 Students are able to master important techniques and tools in the field of financial management administration

(*continued*)

Table 2. (*continued*)

Dimension	ISLO (Level 1)	ISLO (Level 2)
		5.2 Students will be able to apply techniques and tools related to accounting, financial management, tax planning and investment and finance studies to make business analysis decisions
6 Leaderships	6. Analyze the role of motivation and influence in achieving a coordinated goal	6.1 Students can master the skills of motivating and influencing people
		6.2 Students are able to effectively influence others to achieve coordination goals
7 Environment	7.Apply legal, ethical, and economic standards of business within a global environment	7.1 Students will be able to apply business law, business ethics and business economics standards in a global environment
		7.2 Students are able to demonstrate social skills and behaviors consistent with professional standards and ethical responsibilities, recognizing and accepting individual and cultural diversity
8 Scholarship	8.Utilize research skills to solve business problems	8.1 Students are able to utilize research skills in order to solve business problems
		8.2 Students have the ability to continue researching, exploring, and learning

3.3 Decomposition of Course Objectives

Decomposition of graduation requirements into course objectives. The course objectives of a major should directly support the graduation requirements and should be clear and measurable [10]. According to the skills and qualities that graduates should have, reverse design the curriculum system to ensure that the course content and teaching links are in line with the training objectives. In this process, attention should be paid to the logical relationship and sequence between courses to avoid content repetition and sequence confusion, and to prepare a map of course outcomes. The cumulative total of 68 courses (including graduation thesis, experimental and practical training courses, etc.) in the financial management program of School A, with a cumulative total of 271 supporting outcomes, support an average of about 4 learning outcomes per course, and each second-level learning outcome has been supported by more than 5 courses, and the repeated training and the proportion of outcomes reached is getting higher and higher (Table 3).

Table 3. ISLO and Course Objective Matching Map

Course Name	Nature of the course	credits	ISLO (Level 1) / ISLO (Level 2)	ISLO1		ISLO2		ISLO3		SLO4			SLO5	SLO6		SLO7		SLO8	
				1	2	1	2	1	2	1	2	3	1	2	1	2	1	1	2
Course 1	compulsory course	2	1.2\3.1\4.1\4.3\7.1																
Course 1	optional course	3	1.2\4.3\5.1\5.2\																
...	...	:	...																
Course 1 (8)	optional course	4	2.1\2.2\3.2\4.1\6.1\6.2\8.1																
Summary of Curriculum Support Outcomes			271	9	9	1		1		8	1	7	8	7		2		8	

3.4 Selection of Content and Teaching Methods and Development of Syllabus

Once the identification of the objectives of the curriculum is completed, the next step is to select the educational content and teaching methods that will support the objectives of the curriculum [11]. These content and methods are able to effectively impart knowledge and skills and, more importantly, aim to meet the needs of student outcome achievement. Based on the course objectives and educational content, a syllabus is developed. The syllabus of the professional courses in the syllabus is an important document to guide the teaching of financial management, mainly including the course introduction, teaching objectives, teaching content, teaching methods and tools, course evaluation and assessment methods. The most critical link here is: goal orientation, course objectives to support student learning outcomes (ISLO), course objectives and graduation requirements to maintain consistency, teaching content, teaching methods and evaluation feedback are to ensure that the course objectives are achieved.

Course Objectives and Support for Graduation Requirement Indicator Points. The course objectives correspond to the Indicator Points of Graduation Requirements (ISLOs). The course objectives take the form of "verbs+ " describing the level of knowledge and skills acquired by students (Table 4).

Table 4. Breakdown of course objectives corresponding to ISLOs

Num	Program Goals	Description of Objectives Course objectives based on learning outcomes	ISLO (Level 2)	ISLO (Level 1)
1	Program Goals1	Describe the concepts and fundamentals of ***** and explain the enterprise **** setup and management system	4.1	4
2	Program Goals 2	Apply ******* for processing and produce ***** reports	4.3	4
;;;	;;;	;;;	;;;	;;;

Reflecting the Relationship Between Instructional Content and Curriculum Objectives

Table 5. Teaching content and methods that correspond to the objectives of the course

Num	educational content	Expected Student Learning Outcomes	in-class school hours	method of teaching	Corresponding Course Objectives Program Objectives
1	General: ***Basic Concepts	(1) Explain ********** (2) Describe *********** (3) Appreciate the ********** relationship	2	Lecture method, exercise method	Program Goals 2
	*********	(1) *******; (2) Formation of ****** awareness	2	discussion	Program Goals 3

Table 6. Course Evaluation Assessment Form

Num	Program Goals	Assessment content	Proportion of assessment methods to total grade (%)					Course objectives as a percentage of total grade (%)
			process assessment				summative assessment	
			operation	Classroom Tests	deliberations	Lab Report	summative assessment	
1	Program Goals 2	***	5				10	16
2	Program Goals	***		5			20	40
.	...	...	...				...	...
合计			15	10	5	20	50	100

Course Evaluation and Assessment Methods. The evaluation and assessment of the course is mainly aimed at assessing the students' achievement of the course objectives and checking the students' mastery of each knowledge point [12]. The total evaluation grade includes the usual grade and the final examination grade. The grades of the usual and final exams are ultimately approved in the ratio of 5:5, with 60 points or more as a pass. Weekday grade is a process assessment, including homework, discussion and classroom presentations and other forms. The final examination is generally a summative assessment (Table 5).

4   Analysis of Empirical Evaluation of Financial Management Course Implementation

4.1   Constructing an Evaluation System for the Achievement of Professional Talents' Results

In order to better assess the achievement of the eight learning outcomes of financial management professional training and to make continuous improvement, School A has designed two types of assessment tools, direct assessment tools and indirect assessment tools. Direct assessment tools measure or count the objectives directly, such as scoring through comprehensive exams, dissertation evaluations, and inter professional internships, etc., to give specific data on the achievement of the outcomes, so as to accurately assess the achievement of the outcomes. Indirect assessment tools, on the other hand, extrapolate the status or evaluation of objectives through other variables or indicators. These methods require the use of other relevant data to be analyzed and extrapolated, for example, the level of outcome attainment can be assessed indirectly by analyzing student satisfaction surveys, etc. Below is a table of assessment tools corresponding to learning outcomes (Table 7).

At present, School A is vigorously carrying out the reform of the evaluation system of course achievement attainment, and every course of the major can well respond to the achievement of ISLOs, and the comprehensive examination, thesis and professional internship evaluation and assessment of the direct tools in the above table can be used

Table 7. ISLO Reach Assessment Tool Design

Type	Revised Evaluation Tools	ISLO							
		1	2	3	4	5	6	7	8
Direct	Comprehensive Examination	X			X	X	X	X	X
	Graduation Thesis Evaluation	X		X		X		X	X
	"Multi-disciplinary virtual simulation internship" Evaluation	X	X	X		X			X
Indirect	Senior Exit Survey	X	X	X	X	X	X	X	X

to obtain the direct evaluation data through the course achievement attainment. We can complete the direct assessment of ISLO achievement through course evaluation and assessment.

4.2 Reform of the Course Assessment System

Curriculum system is an important support for professional talent cultivation, and the achievement of course objectives is the direct evaluation data of learning outcomes. On the one hand, we determine the course objectives from ISLO; on the other hand, we need to choose diversified assessment methods to assess the achievement of the objectives. Traditional assessment methods are usually based on test paper examination, which is difficult to assess students' ability comprehensively. A diversified assessment and evaluation system that emphasizes both ability and knowledge assessment, including course tests, case studies, group discussions, laboratory reports, oral reports and other forms, can better assess the comprehensive quality of students; at the same time, we

Table 8. Sample Professional Program Assessment System

Assessment Methods	Time/number of times	proportion	Remarks
Classroom quizzes	Once in two classes	10%	Tests before or during class or after class, to be completed on the Learning Channel platform
Homework	Once a week	15%	Uploaded to the Learning Channel after the homework is changed in the workbook
Team Presentation	1 time	15%	Presentation at the end of the chapter
Laboratory report	One time for each experiment	10%	Complete the laboratory report after the experiment and submit it to the teacher according to the following schedule
Structural Modeling	Assessed Chapter	10%	Faculty required to make structural model and prepare proposal
Final Exam	End of semester	40%	Closed book exam

increase the proportion of process assessment results in the total results of the course, formulate a reasonable grading standard, and improve the monitoring, assessment and feedback mechanism of students' learning process. According to the actual situation and students' feedback, the assessment system will be adjusted and improved continuously.

Table 8 shows a sample assessment system for professional courses, and the proportion of each item are designed according to the objectives and teaching contents of different courses.

4.3 Analysis of the Effectiveness of the Reform of the Financial Management Program Based on the OBE Concept

The curriculum reform of financial management based on the concept of OBE has achieved various effects, including the improvement of students' learning effect, the enhancement of practical ability, the optimization of feedback mechanism, the improvement of teachers' teaching level and the improvement of course quality [10].

- Improvement of students' learning results: the OBE concept focuses on students' learning results, which better guides students to clarify their goals and improve their learning results during the learning process when reforming the curriculum system in School A. Since the implementation of the curriculum system reform in 2020, the achievement rate of the learning results in all eight dimensions has exceeded 80%, and students' learning results and abilities are improving (Fig. 2).

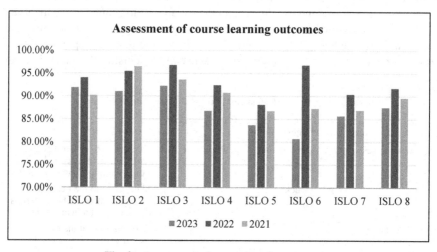

Fig. 2. Assessment of course learning outcomes

- Improvement of course quality: The reform of financial management program based on the concept of OBE has improved the teaching quality of the financial management program by constantly adjusting and improving the teaching content and teaching methods, and the satisfaction of the students is increasing. Figure 3 shows the statistical results of the questionnaire before the graduation of financial management students in 2021, 2022 and 2023, and the students' satisfaction with the teaching content and teaching methods of the specialized courses has been improved in the past three years.

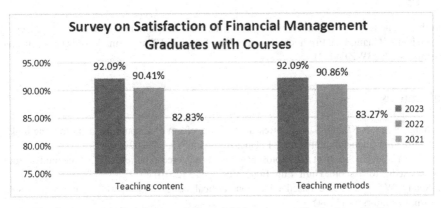

Fig. 3. Survey on Satisfaction of Financial Management Graduates with Courses

5 Conclusion and Outlook

Based on the OBE concept, this paper conducts an in-depth study on the construction and practice of the curriculum system of financial management majors, and finds that the application of the OBE concept provides a clear goal orientation for the financial management majors, which helps to improve the comprehensive quality and vocational competence of the students and enhance their employment competitiveness. The research.

- Systematically sorting out directly the application of OBE concept in the field of financial management education, and proposing a closed-loop implementation path of OBE concept in professional construction;
- A framework of financial management professional curriculum system based on OBE concept is constructed, which provides theoretical basis and practical reference for the reform of financial management education;
- Verified the implementation effect of the financial management professional curriculum system based on the OBE concept through empirical analysis, providing empirical support for the relevant educational reform.

However, the application of OBE concept in financial management majors still faces some challenges. For example, how to better combine the OBE concept with the characteristics of the financial management specialty, how to further improve the practical teaching system, and how to improve the practical teaching ability of teachers. Looking ahead, we will continue to deepen the application of the OBE concept in the financial management major, constantly improve the curriculum system, and improve the quality of teaching. We will actively explore new teaching methods and means, strengthen the practical teaching link, and improve students' practical ability and innovation ability. At the same time, we will also strengthen the cooperation with the industry to understand the needs of the society for financial management professionals in order to better serve the society.

Funding. The research is funded by Key Research Base of Humanities and Social Sciences in Universities of Guangdong Province: Research Base for Digital Transformation of Manufacturing Enterprises, (2023WZJD012).

References

1. Jiang, Y., Li, X., Jiang, S., et al.: Research on the reform of accounting talent training under the trend of financial intelligence. Financ. Acc. Mon. **13**, 95 (2022)
2. Xing, Y., Lu, B., Shi, J., et al.: Exploring a student-centered experiential teaching model: from knowledge to wisdom. High. Eng. Educ. Res. **5**, 123 (2016)
3. Spady, W.G.: Outcome based education: critical issues and answers. Am. Assoc. Sch. Administrators **17** (1994)
4. Ge, X., Yang, Y.: Exploration of practical teaching mode for accounting informatization course in higher vocational education based on OBE. Educ. Vocat. **9**, 101 (2022)
5. Zhao, H., Zhang, L., Wang, W.: Research on the training model of financial management professional talents based on OBE concept. Bus. Account. **17**, 105–108 (2019)
6. Cong, J., Wang, J.: Research on teaching reform of finance and economics majors in universities based on OBE concept. Heilongjiang Educ. (Theo. Pract.) **8**, 66–68 (2023)
7. Wang, Z., Zhang, J., Wang, J.: Construction and practice of financial management professional curriculum system based on OBE concept. In: Proceedings of the 2019 Academic Annual Meeting of the Higher Financial Education Branch of the Chinese Higher Education Association (2019)
8. Yang, Z., Liu, C., Wang, X.: Construction of an evaluation system for financial management professional courses based on OBE concept. Educ. Res. **07**, 88–91 (2020)
9. Liu, S., Wang, L., Zhang, L.: Research on teaching reform of financial management major based on OBE concept. China Manage. Informatization **23**(20), 25–28 (2020)
10. Wang, X., Zhang, L., Wang, L.: Research on the construction of financial management professional courses based on OBE concept. Friends Acc. **18**, 30–33 (2020)
11. Jing, C., Zheng, R.: Research on the reform of artificial intelligence curriculum system based on OBE concept. Sci. Educ. Guide **1**, 51–53 (2023)
12. Li, H., Zhang, Y., Wang, M.: Exploration of teaching reform in financial management professional courses based on OBE concept. Educ. Career **34**, 98–101 (2019)

Exploring Virtual Proximity in Sensory Food Experience

Ernesto Filgueiras[1,2(✉)] ⓘ, Eulerson Rodrigues[2,3] ⓘ, João Valente[1,4,5] ⓘ,
Flávio Almeida[2,3] ⓘ, Daniel Michalack[2], and Maria Nayara Albuquerque[2]

[1] Research Centre for Architecture, Urbanism and Design, CIAUD, Lisbon School of
Architecture, Universidade de Lisboa I UBI Polo, Lisbon, Portugal
`ernestovf@gmail.com`
[2] University of Beira Interior I Convento de Sto. António., 6201-001 Covilhã, Portugal
[3] Labcom-Communication and Arts, University of Beira Interior, Covilhã, Portugal
[4] Polytechnic Institute of Castelo Branco, Castelo Branco, Portugal
[5] BrainAnswer – Neuroscience in your hands, Castelo Branco, Portugal

Abstract. The aim of this paper is to explore the main sensory elements that
can increase the immersion of future digital tools and the feeling of distancing
between two people in different restaurants connected by videoconference. The
research is based on the growing relevance of videoconferencing as a means of
communication in a global context that seeks technological solutions for connectivity in times of social distancing. The proposal aims to integrate design elements
inspired by immersive online video game experiences into virtual restaurant environments, in order to offer a better understanding of the perception of distance in
interactions mediated by videoconferencing. By exploring how these immersive
tools can be applied in virtual restaurant environments, the study aims to provide a
socially enriching experience for participants, bringing the virtual sensation closer
to reality and enhancing interaction in virtual environments. The research aims
to identify and analyze visual and interactive elements that establish a specific
sensory consonance with specific types of food, contributing to the advancement
of knowledge about the interactions between technology, food and sensory experiences. It is hoped that the results of this study will provide valuable insights for
the creation of digital environments that promote proximity and social interaction
in contexts of physical distancing.

Keywords: Game Design experiences · Sensorial experiences · Virtual
environments

1 Introduction

The intersection between virtual environments and sensory experiences in the context
of digital games has garnered increasing interest in the scientific community. The relationship between open-world digital games and their ability to provide immersion and
engagement to players has been widely recognized. In this regard, the present research
aims to explore the potential connection between virtual scenarios and the empathy

experienced by players, investigating whether this empathy may be associated with certain types of food. Additionally, the study proposes to analyze the influence of virtual environments on the perception and preference for specific foods, seeking to understand the transformative potential of these environments on the sensory taste experience.

On the other hand, the growing relevance of video conferencing as a means of communication has driven the search for technological solutions that promote connectivity in times of social distancing. The perception of distance among participants in virtual environments still represents a significant challenge for the effectiveness of virtual communications. In this context, the broader project of which this research is part aims to integrate design elements inspired by immersive experiences of online video games into virtual restaurant environments, with the goal of offering a better understanding of distance perception in interactions mediated by video conferencing.

Given this scenario, this scientific article aims to investigate the relationship between virtual proximity and sensory experience in eating, exploring how visual and interactive elements in virtual environments can establish specific sensory consonance with certain types of food. Through meticulous analysis of taste perception in different environments using specific methodologies, the aim is to identify opportunities to create personalized sensory experiences that enhance the sensory appreciation of specific meals.

Thus, this study intends to fill a significant gap in understanding how open-world digital gaming technology can shape and expand the boundaries of sensory experiences, contributing to the advancement of knowledge about the interactions between technology and food. The proposed research aims not only to explore the relationship between virtual environments and food but also to provide insights for the creation of digital environments that enhance users' sensory experience, both in digital games and in interactions mediated by video conferencing.

This scientific article is structured around the investigation of virtual proximity in the sensory food experience, addressing the intersection between virtual environments, digital games, and the sensory perception of food.

1.1 Study Objectives

This study aims to investigate the impact of immersive virtual environments, inspired by open-world video games, on the perception of proximity and sensory experiences during remote dining interactions. It seeks to assess how immersive technologies, commonly utilized in video games, can be adapted and integrated into virtual restaurant settings to mitigate the sense of distance and enhance social connectedness during video conferencing. By exploring the correlation between visual and interactive elements within virtual restaurant environments and participants' sensory responses, particularly regarding food perception and preference, the study aims to examine the effectiveness of immersive virtual environments in bridging the gap between physical distance and social closeness during remote dining experiences. Moreover, it seeks to provide useful information into the design and implementation of immersive technologies in virtual restaurant environments, aiming to optimize sensory experiences and foster a sense of presence and community among participants engaged in remote dining interactions.

2   Literature Review

In this topic, we delve into an exploration of key elements shaping the modern gastronomic landscape. We begin by examining Sensory Food Experience, delving into the interplay between taste perception, environmental stimuli, and technological advancements. Next, we navigate through the dynamic realm of Virtual and Real Environments, exploring the evolution of dining spaces and the impact of immersive technologies on customer experiences. Finally, we explore the innovative strategy of Gamification in the restaurant industry, uncovering how game elements are reshaping customer engagement and enhancing culinary experiences. Through these discussions, we aim to illuminate the diverse dimensions of contemporary gastronomy and the pivotal role of sensory perception, technology, and interactive engagement in shaping the future of food experiences.

2.1 Sensory Food Experience

Renowned authors such as Charles Spence, author of "Gastrophysics," and Gibson, author of "Food Science and the Culinary Arts," have significantly contributed to understanding the complex interaction between the senses and elements beyond food, as well as the essential chemical processes in food product development. The relevance of environments in taste perception has been highlighted, emphasizing the importance of elements such as lighting, decor, background music, and spatial layout in shaping the gastronomic experience. Studies reveal that the surroundings exert a significant influence on how people interpret flavors and aromas, as discussed by Auvray & Spence (2008). Brain allocation for processing sensory information, such as smell and color, underscores the importance of anticipating flavor and nutritional properties of foods. Furthermore, the complexity of taste perception has been emphasized, considering the sensory contributions of taste buds, nasal olfaction, chewing-related proprioception, and swallowing, trigeminal sensation, as well as factors like touch, pain, temperature, visual expectations, and auditory stimuli. Manipulating food flavors while maintaining consistency has been cited as a relevant aspect of the gastronomic experience, as discussed color aspects by Chan & Kane-Martinelli (1997) and consistency by Horie, et al (2024). The incorporation of extended reality technologies, such as Augmented Reality and Virtual Reality, is recognized as an opportunity to provide a personalized and immersive customer experience, catering to both functional and emotional needs. Existing literature underscores the positive influence of these technologies on consumer perception, enhancing the gastronomic experience and food well-being, as evidenced by Batat (2021).

Considering this landscape, the scientific article "Exploring Virtual Proximity in Sensory Food Experience" seeks to deepen understanding of how virtual proximity can impact sensory experience in gastronomy, considering the interaction among technology, environment, and taste perception, based on the findings and contributions of the mentioned authors. The interaction between environment and taste perception, extensively explored across various disciplines, reveals the significant influence of environmental elements on flavor and aroma interpretation, highlighting the importance of sensory atmosphere in the gastronomic experience, as discussed by Turley and Milliman (2000).

Therefore, a comprehensive understanding of the interaction among sensory, environmental, and technological stimuli in food experience is essential for the evolution of gastronomy and the creation of more engaging and personalized gastronomic experiences. The critical analysis of these elements contributes to building a solid theoretical foundation underpinning research on the influence of virtual proximity on food sensory experience, opening new perspectives for innovation and continuous improvement in the gastronomic sector.

Moreover, the research addressed gamification and augmented reality in the restaurant industry, exploring how these smart technologies can transform the customer experience and promote global food well-being. Authors such as, Pamuru, Khern-am-nuai & Kannan, (2021); Sigala & Nilsson (2021); Alonso & O'Neill (2010) and Batat (2021) provided data about the impact of gamification and augmented reality in the restaurant sector, emphasizing the importance of personalization and immersion to meet consumer needs. Sensory atmosphere was also a highlight in the research, with authors like Auvray, M., & Spence, C. (2008) and Turley and Milliman (2000) providing insights into the influence of environmental elements such as textures, aromas, flavors, music, lighting, and layout on food perception and appreciation. Understanding these aspects significantly contributes to understanding consumer experience and developing effective strategies in the gastronomic sector.

2.2 Virtual and Real Environments

According to Kotler (1975), restaurants represent service entities characterized by direct interaction between providers and consumers within the physical confines of the establishment to ensure service delivery. These establishments offer physical products while providing a diverse array of services that significantly contribute to the customer experience. This direct interaction and coexistence of tangible and intangible elements position restaurants as unique spaces where product quality, atmosphere, service, and overall experience play pivotal roles in customer satisfaction. Hence, understanding the complexity of these organizations becomes imperative for devising effective management strategies and enhancing service quality.

Hanefors and Mossberg (2003) conducted research on the dimensions defining an extraordinary experience in gastronomic environments. They argue that extraordinary experiences are inherently atypical or unusual, presenting themselves as novel or scarce compared to everyday occurrences. Their research identifies five interconnected dimensions that delineate the unique journey of an exceptional dining experience: motivation and expectation, pre-experience phases; interaction and engagement, manifested during the event; and satisfaction, a dimension unfolding post-experience. These interrelated dimensions constitute a comprehensive framework, capturing the various stages composing an extraordinary restaurant experience.

In Kivela's study (1997) and Pierson, Reeve & Creed (2001), distinct responses regarding restaurant selection criteria were identified. While food quality emerged as a decisive criterion for choosing gourmet and themed restaurants, it was less determinative for popular or fast-food establishments. Conversely, atmosphere proved to be of utmost importance in the preference for themed and gourmet restaurants but did not exert the same significant influence on popular or fast-food venues.

2.3 Changing Dynamics of Dining Environments

Lia & Niemeyer (2019) discuss the transformations occurring in the bar and restaurant market, particularly in major urban centers, driven by changes in residents' lifestyles. The proliferation of food delivery apps like iFood, Uber Eats, and Rappi has enabled consumers to have meals from various establishments delivered to their homes or workplaces, including those that traditionally did not offer delivery services. Opting to order a meal through an app minimizes the influence of the restaurant's physical characteristics on the user experience during consumption, although these characteristics may still resonate in their memory and imagination, contributing subjectively to the construction of the experience. Consequently, the function of the dining environment undergoes a reconfiguration, necessitating it to compete to persuade consumers to forsake their original settings for dining, surpassing the convenience of enjoying restaurant cuisine without the need for physical displacement.

The theoretical model of Servicescape conceptualizes the physical environment as a composite entity comprising three interdependent dimensions: environmental conditions, which possess an inherently sensory nature; spatial layout and functionality, encompassing spatial configurations and the ability to facilitate task execution by individuals present in the environment; and signs, symbols, and artifacts, representing the communicative and distinctive elements of space aesthetics.

Thus, sensory design refers to strategies devised to stimulate and engage the five human senses: hearing, smell, touch, sight, and taste. In a 1998 article in the Harvard Business Review, "Welcome to the Experience Economy", the authors by Pine II and Gilmore (1998), the good aspects of an experience are directly related to the extent to which it can engage multiple senses. Understanding that the deliberate and harmonious incorporation of sensory stimuli enriches the user experience, resulting in a deeper and more enduring perception of interaction with a product, service, or environment. By expanding engagement beyond a single sense, sensory design aims to create more immersive and impactful experiences. Through careful consideration and application of sound elements, distinctive aromas, tactile textures, visual stimuli, and specific flavors, the experience becomes richer and capable of eliciting deeper emotional responses from the consumer.

2.4 Virtual Game Environments: A World of Complexity

Virtual game environments, found in open-world games, can vary significantly in complexity and size. The depth of these environments depends on various factors, including the level of interactivity allowed, the quality of graphics, the physics of the environment, the presence of simulation elements, and the artificial intelligence of characters, all of which are influenced and shaped by player actions.

Santos (2012) underscores that the fundamental characteristic of a digital game environment is the attempt to represent a context, whether derived from reality or constructed from fantastical elements. This representation is achieved through scripts that explore both audio and visual elements, incorporating physical principles. Scenarios are designed to provide players with a maximum immersive experience, aiming to make users feel truly integrated into the world they are exploring.

Expanding upon this notion of immersive virtual environments, another study (Elias *et al.*, 2021) delves into the concept of "world-building" as observed in select Rockstar Games' video games. These games intricately construct expansive digital landscapes, such as the replicated topography of California, utilizing advanced technical frameworks and "reality engines" to create immersive gaming experiences. The transition from "movie space" to "game space" is evident, with players navigating through intricately designed environments that mirror aspects of reality while offering unique gameplay elements. These open-world games, often referred to as "mirror-worlds," provide players with unprecedented freedom and unpredictability, blurring the lines between narrative-driven storytelling and player-driven exploration. The concept of "design fiction" emerges as these games not only tell stories but also shape entire worlds within a transmedia realm, connecting players to virtual portrayals of California's history and pop culture.

2.5 Gamification Improving Food Experiences

Gamification applied to the restaurant industry is an innovative strategy that utilizes game elements to engage and motivate customers, providing a more interactive and immersive experience in gastronomic establishments. This approach aims not only to entertain customers but also to create an emotional connection with food and make the gastronomic experience more memorable.

Gamification in restaurants can include elements such as challenges, rewards, competitions, scoring, progression levels, and engaging narratives. For example, a restaurant may implement a point-based loyalty system where customers accumulate points with each visit and can redeem them for prizes or special discounts. Another common approach is the creation of interactive games within the restaurant environment, such as quizzes about local cuisine, gastronomic treasure hunts, or even augmented reality to entertain customers while they wait for their orders.

Gamification in restaurants not only increases customer engagement but can also positively influence the perception of food quality, customer satisfaction, and loyalty. By making the gastronomic experience more fun and interactive, restaurants can differentiate themselves from the competition and create a unique atmosphere that encourages repeat visits and word-of-mouth recommendations.

Authors such as Harakal & Berger (2017), Lee & Lu (2023), Assimakopoulos (2023) and Batat (2021) have explored the impact of gamification in the restaurant industry, highlighting how this innovative approach can transform the customer experience and promote global food well-being. The integration of game elements into the gastronomic experience demonstrates the potential of gamification as an effective tool to captivate and retain customers, creating memorable and differentiated experiences in the restaurant sector.

3 Methodology

In this section, we provide an overview of the methodology employed in our study, encompassing the experimental protocol, applied procedures, selected environments, and the platform utilized for data collection. The methodology serves as the backbone of our research endeavor, as we aim to ensure the rigor, reliability, and reproducibility of our findings by the dynamics between technology, environment, and taste perception.

3.1 Selecting Environments

Before delving into the specifics of each type of environment selected for the study, it's crucial to outline the overarching methodology guiding their selection. The process involved an approach that aimed at capturing a diverse range of settings representative of real-world scenarios and virtual simulations.

Four distinct groups were created for analysis, each with its own characteristics and objectives: groups A (real environments), B (placebo environments), C (AI environments), and D (game environments). The Table 1 below outlines the groups with their names, descriptions, and objectives.

Table 1. Objectives and description of the group selection.

Group Name	Description	Objective
(A) Control: Real Environments	Real gastronomic environments	Provide a group with authentic gastronomic settings, where participants are exposed to traditional restaurant scenarios
(B) Treatment: Placebo Environments	Environments unrelated to gastronomy	Understand how participant expectations influence their sensory evaluation and experiences, even in environments without food stimuli
(C) Experimental 1: AI Environments	Environments generated by artificial intelligence	Aim to stimulate the gastronomic experience of real environments, allowing the analysis of participants' responses between real and artificially generated environments
(D) Experimental 2: Game Environments	Environments selected from digital games	Enable analysis of participant reactions to environments presented in digital games, through an interactive and lucid approach, exposing participants to simulated gastronomic environments in digital games

The selection criteria for group A involved analyzing five different restaurant (Fig. 1) categories: meat, fast food, pasta, fish, and salads, based on the prevalence of modern cuisine. Factors such as colors, lighting, materials used for tables, chairs, decorations, and walls were considered. Visits to restaurants provided direct analysis of decorative elements. Online research sought references for similar restaurants to enhance selection criteria. Realistic environments with high-quality images were chosen to immerse participants during testing.

Fig. 1. Group (A) Control - Real Environments: (1) steakhouse, (2) fast food restaurant, (3) pasta restaurant, (4) fish restaurant, and (5) salad restaurant.

Criteria for selecting images for group B (Fig. 2) included comfortable settings suitable for meals, each with distinct lighting, textures, and decorations. Placebo images were online lobby photos of hotels, maintaining consistency among them. These neutral settings provide a reference point for comparing experimental groups, isolating visual influences on food perception.

AI-generated environments (Fig. 3) were created using specific prompts tailored to replicate visual cues of steakhouse, pasta, fast food, and salad establishments. Utilizing Leonard.ai, these prompts aimed to simulate realistic virtual environments consistent with research findings. By generating digital representations based on identified characteristics, participants were exposed to visually immersive scenarios, allowing for an exploration of the relationship between visual stimuli and food perception.

Criteria for game environments (Fig. 4) included the presence of accessible restaurant settings, open-world exploration, and realistic graphics for participant immersion. Five

Fig. 2. Group (B) Treatment: Example of Placebo Environments, the room above is a hotel lobby, not a restaurant.

Fig. 3. Group (C) Experimental 1: AI Environments

distinct game environments were chosen based on realism and varied themes, allowing participants to associate foods with different contexts. Looping videos of game environments enriched understanding of how digital contexts impact food perception, enhancing comprehension of gastronomic experiences and visual stimuli.

Fig. 4. Group (D) Experimental 2: Game environments on research protocols.

3.2 Brain Answer Platform

The BrainAnswer platform is an online tool dedicated to collecting neurosensory data to provide detailed analysis of the impact of products, brands and advertising on consumers. Through multisensory measurements, the platform identifies points of attractiveness, memorization and emotional impact, providing valuable information for improving brand communication and developing products that meet the needs of participants. The platform records participants' biosignals in real time, such as ECG, RESP, PPG and EDA, integrated into the implementation of each study, allowing the creation of personalized and comprehensive protocols that combine different media (sound, video, games, etc.) and controlled stimuli during the experiment (Fig. 5).

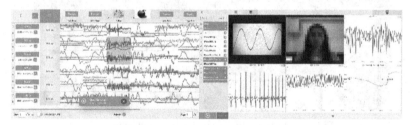

Fig. 5. The BrainAnswer platform controls the stimuli and records the participants' reactions during the interaction.

This study used the BrainAnswer platform to implement the protocols that guided the participants' experience, including restaurant scenarios and food consumption, along with questionnaires and signal collection by biosensors. The platform allowed for dynamic interaction between the participants and the stimuli presented, making it easier to understand the individuals' behaviors and reactions. In addition, centralizing the data on the platform simplified the analysis and interpretation of the results, contributing significantly to the development and conclusion of the Design research. The BrainAnswer platform played a central role in conducting the studies, providing a flexible and comprehensive framework for collecting neurosensory data. Through protocols designed on the platform, participants were guided through experiments involving restaurant scenarios and food consumption, while simultaneously answering questionnaires and providing signals through biosensors.

3.3 Testing and Data Collection

The pilot study's setup for data collection involved creating a protocol using the BrainAnswer platform, outlining participant data collection procedures and methods. The protocol included video capture via webcam, voice capture via microphone, and the use of biosensors to gather participant data. Additionally, specific foods corresponding to real-world scenarios chosen for the study were selected. The food type selection includes fish, pasta, and fast food.

Due to the extended duration of the tests, as identified during the pilot testing, it became necessary to reduce the number of food options from five (each representing a single restaurant) to three. This adjustment was made to streamline the testing process and ensure participant engagement and compliance throughout the study. By limiting the food choices to three options, the duration of each test session was effectively shortened, allowing for more manageable and focused data collection while maintaining the study's integrity and objectives (Fig. 6).

Fig. 6. Images taken during the pilot study: From left to right, disposable cups with portions of food prepared on the day of the test, images of the pre-test with volunteers.

For the video call simulation between participants and the mediator, chroma key technology was employed in both study stations, allowing for different looping backgrounds (looping from group, A, B, C or D) during the call. A high-definition webcam was used to enhance immersion during the test, while the laptop webcam recorded the participant's reactions. The chosen test scenarios were edited to create background consistency for the mediator, ensuring participants could view each selected environment and become familiar with them. This familiarity facilitated responses to questionnaires in a manner that closely resembled the taste experienced during meals.

3.4   Post-testing Questionnaire

In the post-study questionnaire, participants were asked a series of questions to gather detailed feedback on their experience and perceptions during the interaction. Each question is assigned a code and has a specific objective. The questions are presented in the following table (Table 2). Questions 1 and 2 are demography related and will be discussed on part 4 (Results and Discussion).

Table 2. Post-Testing questions and objectives

Code	Question	Objective
Q1	According to the data presented during your participation, what is the purpose of this interaction?	Verify participants' understanding of the study objective
Q2	Based on your experience, is there any relationship between the foods and the presented scenarios? If yes, please describe it	Verify if participants associated the offered foods and the scenarios in any way
Q3	Did any of the presented scenarios catch your attention? If yes, please describe it	Identify which environments stood out during the study from the participant's perception
Q4	Did any of the presented scenarios seem familiar? If yes, please describe them	Identify which environments brought back memories for the participant

After reformulating the protocol with all the necessary changes, the new studies began, starting with real environments, then placebo environments, AI environments and finally gaming environments.

Participant data is collected using the biosensors mentioned above (Fig. 7), as well as video capture for analysis and, at the end of the test, the completion of a specific form for the study of each group. As the aim of this study does not involve analyzing environments generated by artificial intelligence, the results obtained from the studies of this group will not be studied.

After reformulating the protocol, the test consists of four foods, one of which is only for the explanatory part of the protocol for the person carrying it out, thus leaving only three foods to make the relationship between taste and environment, even with five environments and only three foods, it was not necessary to cut any of the scenarios to carry out the tests, after tasting the participant has the option of choosing one of the five environments for each of the two questions that are asked and at the end of the test the participant answers a form designed to check their understanding of the test and explain their choices in more detail.

Fig. 7. Volunteer during a test with real environments, where we can see the glasses with portions of food, the interlocutor with the virtual environment and the biosensors collecting data simultaneously.

4   Results and Discussion

The study sample included 20 volunteers (n = 20). Male participants represent most part of volunteers, being 14 male and 6 female participants. Most participants were aged between 19 and 36 years old (18 in total). The greater presence of young adults as participants is important because of the relevance of this demographic group for consumption and for building market trends. However, we are aware of the importance of extending this study to a more heterogeneous sample.

4.1   Food Environment Association

In Table 3, representing the Control group's responses to real environments, we observed distinct patterns in the most common and preferred eating places for each food type.

For instance, while the local codfish dish is commonly associated with pasta and fish restaurants, participants show varied preferences, with some favoring steakhouses settings. Similarly, preferences for pasta and burgers differ, with pasta restaurants and steakhouses emerging as preferred choices.

Table 4 depicts responses from the Treatment group, exposed to placebo environments.

Here, we notice shifts in preferences, with participants showing preferences for specific ambient settings over traditional eating places. Interestingly, the local codfish dish sees a notable preference for Ambient 3, while pasta preferences are more evenly distributed across various environments.

Table 3. (A) Control: Real Environments.

Food Type	Most Common Eating Place	Preferred Eating Place
Local Codfish Dish	Steakhouse (20%)	Steakhouse (20%)
	Fast food restaurant (0%)	Fast food restaurant (0%)
	Pasta Restaurant (40%)	Pasta Restaurant (40%)
	Fish Restaurant (40%)	Fish Restaurant (20%)
	Salad Restaurant (0%)	Salad Restaurant (20%)
Pasta	Steakhouse (0%)	Steakhouse (20%)
	Fast food restaurant (0%)	Fast food restaurant (0%)
	Pasta Restaurant (40%)	Pasta Restaurant (0%)
	Fish Restaurant (20%)	Fish Restaurant (40%)
	Salad Restaurant (40%)	Salad Restaurant (40%)
Burger	Steakhouse (20%)	Steakhouse (60%)
	Fast food restaurant (60%)	Fast food restaurant (0%)
	Pasta Restaurant (20%)	Pasta Restaurant (0%)
	Fish Restaurant (0%)	Fish Restaurant (20%)
	Salad Restaurant (0%)	Salad Restaurant (20%)

Table 4. (B) Treatment: Placebo Environments.

Food Type	Most Common Eating Place	Preferred Eating Place
Local Codfish Dish	Ambient 1 (0%)	Ambient 1 (0%)
	Ambient 2 (20%)	Ambient 2 (40%)
	Ambient 3 (40%)	Ambient 3 (40%)
	Ambient 4 (0%)	Ambient 4 (0%)
	Ambient 5 (40%)	Ambient 5 (20%)
Pasta	Ambient 1 (20%)	Ambient 1 (40%)
	Ambient 2 (40%)	Ambient 2 (20%)
	Ambient 3 (20%)	Ambient 3 (20%)
	Ambient 4 (20%)	Ambient 4 (20%)
	Ambient 5 (0%)	Ambient 5 (0%)
Burger	Ambient 1 (0%)	Ambient 1 (0%)
	Ambient 2 (20%)	Ambient 2 (0%)
	Ambient 3 (40%)	Ambient 3 (20%)
	Ambient 4 (0%)	Ambient 4 (0%)
	Ambient 5 (40%)	Ambient 5 (80%)

Moving to Table 5, representing the Experimental 1 group exposed to AI environments, we observe a blend of traditional eating places and AI-generated environments.

Table 5. (C) Experimental 1: AI Environments

Food Type	Most Common Eating Place	Preferred Eating Place
Local Codfish Dish	Steakhouse (20%)	Steakhouse (40%)
	Fast food restaurant (0%)	Fast food restaurant (0%)
	Pasta Restaurant (40%)	Pasta Restaurant (20%)
	Fish Restaurant (20%)	Fish Restaurant (20%)
	Salad Restaurant (20%)	Salad Restaurant (20%)
Pasta	Steakhouse (0%)	Steakhouse (0%)
	Fast food restaurant (20%)	Fast food restaurant (0%)
	Pasta Restaurant (20%)	Pasta Restaurant (40%)
	Fish Restaurant (0%)	Fish Restaurant (20%)
	Salad Restaurant (60%)	Salad Restaurant (40%)
Burger	Steakhouse (40%)	Steakhouse (0%)
	Fast food restaurant (60%)	Fast food restaurant (20%)
	Pasta Restaurant (0%)	Pasta Restaurant (20%)
	Fish Restaurant (0%)	Fish Restaurant (60%)
	Salad Restaurant (0%)	Salad Restaurant (0%)

Table 6. (D) Experimental 2: Game Environments

Food Type	Most Common Eating Place	Preferred Eating Place
Local Codfish Dish	Ambient 1 (0%)	Ambient 1 (20%)
	Ambient 2 (40%)	Ambient 2 (0%)
	Ambient 3 (0%)	Ambient 3 (20%)
	Ambient 4 (40%)	Ambient 4 (20%)
	Ambient 5 (20%)	Ambient 5 (40%)
Pasta	Ambient 1 (0%)	Ambient 1 (0%)
	Ambient 2 (40%)	Ambient 2 (60%)
	Ambient 3 (0%)	Ambient 3 (0%)
	Ambient 4 (20%)	Ambient 4 (0%)
	Ambient 5 (40%)	Ambient 5 (40%)
Burger	Ambient 1 (80%)	Ambient 1 (80%)
	Ambient 2 (20%)	Ambient 2 (20%)
	Ambient 3 (0%)	Ambient 3 (0%)
	Ambient 4 (0%)	Ambient 4 (0%)
	Ambient 5 (0%)	Ambient 5 (0%)

While steakhouse remains a preferred choice for the local codfish dish, pasta preferences shift towards AI-generated pasta restaurants, indicating a willingness to explore novel dining experiences facilitated by AI.

Finally, in Table 6, depicting responses from Experimental 2 participants exposed to game environments, we see a divergence in preferences, with participants favoring game environments over traditional eating places.

Notably, Ambient 1 emerges as the preferred choice across all food types, highlighting the allure of immersive gaming experiences in shaping dining preferences.

4.2 Post Testing Answers

In the following section, we discuss the post-testing questionnaire administered to participants. This questionnaire served to our understanding about the relationship between food and environment, and their reactions to specific scenarios presented during the test.

Most of the participants answered indicating their understanding of the study's objective (Q1). However, one participant suggested an alternative goal, relating the study to the creation of food-related businesses, like another participant's understanding in the real-world environments group. Both interpretations associated the test with entrepreneurship in the restaurant industry.

Another question asked if the participant was able to find any relationship between the foods and the presented scenarios. Participants generally perceived a positive relationship between the foods offered and the presented scenarios (Q2). One participant associated flavors with specific spices commonly used in certain locations, reflecting personal experiences. Another participant emphasized the role of individual experience and memory in associating foods with different environments, highlighting how past experiences influence perceptions.

All responses were positive about scenarios being attractive (Q3), with the medieval environment being the most frequently mentioned. Participants highlighted elements of the medieval setting that stood out to them, such as its uniqueness compared to the present-day world. They commented on how these elements influenced their perception of the scenario, making it stand out among the presented environments.

About the familiarity of the scenarios (Q4), one participant mentioned an environment resembling an Arabian bazaar, while others cited familiarity with diner and bar settings, likely due to frequent visits to such establishments.

5   Conclusions

Although this is a pilot study for a more comprehensive investigation, the data obtained offers a substantial analysis that enriches the understanding of the association between virtual and real environments and the perception of food. This data is extremely important for crucial areas of game design, providing a solid basis for future developments in this constantly evolving field.

Despite the small sample size of this study (n = 20), the study was able to delve deeper into the individual perceptions and experiences of the participants, allowing for a detailed analysis of the associations between specific foods and the chosen environments. This more intimate approach made it possible to identify interesting trends and individual preferences.

The findings of this pilot project lay a solid foundation for future research on a larger scale. Even with a small sample, the data obtained has the potential to guide subsequent research, especially regarding the combination of sensory elements in gastronomic environments and the influence of immersive experiences, whether in real or virtual environments. The limited participation of 5 people per group in this specific study emerges as a strategic choice, providing a valuable platform to explore concepts and methodologies, assisting in the creation of more suitable protocols for larger research, marking a crucial starting point for more comprehensive investigations in the future.

The research has made a significant contribution to understanding the association between virtual or real environments and food. The methodology used, when extended to a larger sample, could provide important data for the creation of more functionally integrated environments. In this context, the role of game design areas is crucial in creating or adapting environments to meet their function, whether in real or virtual spaces. The development of experimental protocols that validate the environment/food association is fundamental for an increasingly demanding market in terms of user experience, contributing to the success of products or services.

5.1 Future Studies

One point to be improved in future studies is the selection of foods with more distinct and perceptible flavours. As the analyses showed, not all participants were able to identify the foods offered in the experiment. Choosing foods with more refined flavours could be crucial for further research for studies involving digital gaming environments, a potential improvement is the selection of scenarios with a greater variety of different visual elements. This could provide a more accurate analysis of the associations between food and environments, allowing for a deeper understanding of the influence of these elements on participants' perceptions.

The use of biosensors to capture participants' physiological signals presented challenges during the study, including possible data saturation or capture failures. For future research, it is recommended to investigate alternatives to keep the biosensors calibrated and ensure accurate data collection.

The results obtained in this pilot study provide a solid basis for future research. Despite the limitations, the data obtained can inform improvements to the experimental protocol and guide more comprehensive investigations in the future. The preliminary findings of this study can contribute significantly to the advancement of knowledge in the areas of human-computer interaction and user experience design.

Acknowledgments. This study was also partially supported by national funds through FCT - Fundação para a Ciência e a Tecnologia, I.P., under the Strategic Project with the references UIDB/04008/2020 and UIDP/04008/2020.

Disclosure of Interests. The authors have no competing interests to declare that are relevant to the content of this article.

References

Alonso, A.D., O'Neill, M.A.: Consumers' ideal eating out experience as it refers to restaurant style: a case study. J. Retail. Leis. Prop. **9**, 263–276 (2010)

Assimakopoulos, A.: Gamification for mid-sized restaurants in Helsinki: Challenges and Opportunities (2023)

Auvray, M., Spence, C.: The multisensory perception of flavor. Conscious. Cogn. **17**(3), 1016–1031 (2008)

Batat, W.: How augmented reality (AR) is transforming the restaurant sector: Investigating the impact of "Le Petit Chef" on customers' dining experiences. Technol. Forecast. Soc. Chang. **172**, 121013 (2021)

Chan, M.M., Kane-Martinelli, C.: The effect of color on perceived flavor intensity and acceptance of foods by young adults and elderly adults. J. Acad. Nutr. Diet. **97**(6), 657 (1997)

Elias, H., Almeida, F., Filgueiras, E., Rodrigues, E.P.F., Alexandre, S.C.: No-places and immersion in open world games: a rock star case study. In: Advances in Design and Digital Communication, 166–179. Springer (2020). https://doi.org/10.1007/978-3-030-61671-7_16

Gibson, M.: Food science and the culinary arts. Academic Press (2018)

Hanefors, M., Mossberg, L.: Searching for the extraordinary meal experience. J. Bus. Manag. **9**(3), 249–270 (2003)

Harakal, K.L., Berger, P.D.: The effects of gamification on restaurant consumer-retention. Bus. Econ. Res. **7**(1), 58–67 (2017)

Horie, F., et al.: Flavor intensity is reduced in pureed food: A study using instrumental and sensory analyses. Food Quality and Preference, 105121 (2024)

dos Santos, L.V.V.: A Nacionalidade em Jogo: Representações do Brasil em Jogos Digitais. 2012. 141 f. Dissertation (Master's Degree) - Multidisciplinary Postgraduate Programme in Culture and Society, Institute of Humanities, Arts and Sciences, Federal University of Bahia, Salvador (2012). <https://repositorio.ufba.br/ri/bitstream/ri/16633/1/Dissertação de Leandro Viana Villa dos Santos.pdf>. Access in: 28/11/2023

Kivela, J.: Restaurant marketing: selection and segmentation in Hong Kong. Int. J. Contemp. Hosp. Manag. **9**(3), 116–123 (1997)

Kotler, P., Murray, M.: Third sector management-The role of marketing. Public Adm. Rev. **35**(5), 467–472 (1975)

Lee, W., Lu, L.: Designing gamified interactions with self-service technology at restaurants. Int. J. Hosp. Manag. **113**, 103503 (2023)

Lia, N., Niemeyer, L.: O papel do ambiente físico na experiência de comer em restaurantes. SIMPÓSIO DE PÓS-GRADUAÇÃO EM DESIGN DA ESDI, 5 (2019)

Pierson, B.J., Reeve, W.G., Creed, P.G.: The Relative Importance of Criteria Used by Consumers When Selecting a Restaurant (2001)

Pine II & Gilmore: Bem-vindos à economia das experiências. Harvard Business Review (1998)

Sigala, M., Nilsson, E.: Innovating the restaurant industry: the gamification of business models and customer experiences. Gamification Tourism **92**, 100 (2021)

Pamuru, V., Khern-am-nuai, W., Kannan, K.: The impact of an augmented-reality game on local businesses: a study of Pokémon go on restaurants. Inf. Syst. Res. **32**(3), 950–966 (2021)

Turley, L.W., Milliman, R.E.: Atmospheric effects on shopping behavior: a review of the experimental evidence. J. Bus. Res. **49**(2), 193–221 (2000)

Influences of ICT Tools on the Empathizing Phase of the Design Thinking Process of Design Students

Upeksha Hettithanthri[1,2](✉) [ID], Preben Hansen[1] [ID], and Harsha Munasinghe[3] [ID]

[1] Department of Computer and Systems Sciences, Stockholm University, PB 7003,
SE-164 07 Kista, Sweden
upeksha@nsbm.ac.lk, {dilini,preben}@dsv.su.se
[2] Department of Design Studies, NSBM Green University, Pitipana, Homagama, Sri Lanka
[3] School of Architectural Studies, George Brown College, Toronto, Canada
hmunasinghe@georgebrown.ca

Abstract. The notion of design thinking initiates discussions regarding its process and practices in many fields, including education. However, the design thinking process within the architectural domain and among architectural design students has not been sufficiently addressed in education and scientific research. This study explores the design thinking process of the design students while working in a conventional design studio context, further, expanding towards exploring the influences which could be made by ICT tools to the design process adopted by students. For this study, twenty-five interior design undergraduates were selected through convenient sampling technique. The students were divided into five random groups and were assigned with a design task to engage. Conventional design studio at NSBM Green University, Sri Lanka was utilized as the study context. Each study was conducted through three studio days with six hours allocated per day. Data was collected using naturalistic observation, focus group interviews, narrative samplings, and photographs to ensure the credibility of the data by adopting multiple data collection techniques. Six phased thematic analysis was utilized for data analysis. Results have shown that ICT tools have facilitated students to start their design thinking process from Ideation. Empathizing phase was critically neglected by students as a result, and we identified it as a major problem which needs further research.

Keywords: ICT tools · Design thinking process · Conventional design studio

1 Introduction

Design pedagogy has given a greater priority to the design studio education. Design studio is a place where the design courses and projects are conducted, which is a specific environment designed to engage in collaborative, pedagogical activities related to designing [12, 19]. The design thinking process emerging within the conventional design studio context has varied features which are exclusive to architectural design domain

A. Marcus et al. (Eds.): HCII 2024, LNCS 14716, pp. 79–92, 2024.
https://doi.org/10.1007/978-3-031-61362-3_6

[34]. Design thinking is not only applied in the field of HCI and design, it has contributed immensely towards various fields such as innovation [9], business [25], IT, education [31]. However, the design thinking process of novice designers who are learning to design by engaging in many design projects in conventional design studio context have not been addressed in many discussions in scientific world.

In current pedagogical context, design students have their own ways of starting design thinking [23]. Even though there are established design thinking models such as IDEO DT model [21], and Double Diamond Design thinking model [14], the design thinking process undergone by architectural design students is not clearly established. Design students receive pedagogical training to think and work as designers and are provided with design tasks which are associated with ill-defined problems which needs to be solve through a design [12].

The established design thinking models are providing a systematic guideline in solving a given problems [5, 6]. However, the application of design thinking guidelines/models in architectural design domain is not clear and need further investigation. Students who work in conventional design studio environments are not specifically supported with contextual and real-life experiences [10]. They engage in given design tasks while being in a studio setup located in an institutional environment [15]. However, the design tasks which are given to the students contain complex problems which are associated with socio, cultural and contextual situations. The exposure to the outside real world problem scenarios is limited and students are more inclined to explore the world outside through ICT tools, than situating themselves in real problem scenarios and contexts. Therefore, how design thinking and design thinking processes have been molded in a conventional design studio context is necessary to explore and understand in order to identify how architectural design students engage and solve design problems.

This study will explore the design thinking process of design students within the Conventional Design Studio (CDS) context. Furthermore, it seeks to examine the influences of Information and Communication Technology (ICT) tools on the design thinking processes employed by the architectural design students.

1.1 Application of ICT Tools in Design Studio

Information and Communication Technology (ICT) is playing a vital role in education. ICT tools are contributing towards collaboration, networking, visualization of design imagery, design exploration, to integrate multidisciplinary knowledge to a particular field [16]. ICT tools are designed to increase the interaction between human and the tool [39]. The interaction with ICT tools got increased due to multiple functions provided in a user friendly manner [27]. Due to the excessive facilities and apps created, it became easier for students to engage via digital devices they have in hand [26]. Mobile phones, tabs, laptops contain many user centered design features which increased the dependency and trust on those devices [2, 3]. Students who are designing in CDS context are utilizing mobile phones, tabs and laptops for multiple purposes [18]. The most common ICT tool in hand is the mobile phone, which is mainly being used to connect with people and to be connected to other digital platforms which brings quick and fast information related to any field.

When it comes to the process of designing, ICT tools play a vital role. Students feel easier to browse the internet than moving outside into real world design situations. The ICT tools available such as apps, social media, online design platforms made them attractive and bonded to the device and increasing the onscreen time [28]. Using computers, digital devices bring instant visual graphics which could be worth than reading thousand words in searching information through other medias [38]. Visual presentations and visual Information which are related to design domain are heavily available in online platforms and mobile phones and other ICT tools make students easily accessible to those design repositories. It is evident that visual information is a more retainable stimulant than abstract information presented in written format [40]. This fact make students more connected to ICT devices at hand.

Design thinking could get influenced by those tools, because they connect students to rich domains which are having several architectural solutions. Design students are able to find multiple design solutions from digital platforms and this could limit the design thinking ability of students. With the usage of ICT tools, design students are facing a risk of losing their own creativity, intrinsic knowledge and usage of human senses in the decision-making process which is related to the task of designing. Students need to have a rational and logical thinking mindset to identify and develop most suitable and human friendly design solutions [24]. The over utilization of ICT tools might be able to influence the natural design thinking process of students which could be dangerous. Devices could increase mindlessness of students due to over exposure [27]. Designers need to be capable of giving creative solutions to complex problems [29, 30]. However, currently, students are capable of finding millions of similar solutions on online platforms which were given by other designers. This could potentially hamper and limit the creativity, imagination processes and abilities of the students. Therefore, the importance of exploring the influences of ICT tools on the design thinking process of students is rising.

2 Problem Statement

Students who work in the CDS context use ICT tools to search for information, inspirations, novel ideas, and to develop prototypes [22]. This may lead the students to be more information centric and to neglect knowledge from real life scenarios [37, 40]. The conventional design studio context is the typical academic setup where students engage in design activities. In previous research, we have observed the design thinking process which occurs within the conventional design studio has many limitations [17, 18]. This study aims on exploring the influences of ICT tools on design thinking process of students while working in conventional design studio context.

2.1 Research Questions

1. How do ICT tools influence students' architectural design thinking process in Conventional Design Studio Context?
2. How do ICT tools influence the Empathizing phase of the architectural design thinking?

3 Research Methodology

For this study we applied Constructivist Grounded Theory (CGT). Constructivist epistemology is grounded on the statement that the practice of doing scientific research depends on social factors [41]. The data gathered through naturalistic observation, focus group interviews and participant narrative samples shows the patterns, phases, activities and usage and influences of the ICT tools on the design process of the students. Naturalistic observation is a qualitative research methodology which is heavily applied on collecting data of a sample without disturbing to the natural behavior of the observed party [33].

3.1 Data Collection

We employed a comprehensive approach to data collection, including multiple data collection methodologies, such as naturalistic observation, focus group interviews, photographic study, participant narrative sampling, and video recordings.

Naturalistic observation was recorded in the time sampling sheet, describing all the activities, tools and methods utilized for the design thinking process of the students. Notes were created by the researcher in time sampling sheet in every hour, summarizing the activities and tools utilized. Recording the natural design thinking process of students was the primary focus of naturalistic observation [13]. The other data collection technique utilized is the field diaries. Field diaries contain detailed descriptions of situations and incidents. It is a real time documentation which contains rich descriptions [7]. The reason of utilizing field diary along with the time sampling sheets to increase the richness of data with descriptive explanations.

Another method utilized in data collecting is the focus group interviews. Focus group interviews are a qualitative data collection methodology which is specifically focused on getting in-depth insights and reflections of the participants [8]. The focus group interviews were conducted by the researcher using open ended questions. The interviews were fully audio recorded and transcribed for the purpose of data analysis.

Consent-obtained video recordings of all groups were taken and cross-checked with time sampling sheets and field diaries during data analysis. To ensure unbiased information, participants were asked to produce narrative samplings, offering their perspectives on the design process, activities and tools used. Photographs were taken throughout the study, capturing significant incidents and labelled for easy reference according to group number and hour of engagement. The inclusion of a second-year studio class, comprising 12 male and 13 female students, through a convenience sampling technique, aimed to reflect the natural distribution of skills in a typical architectural studio without manipulation by the researcher [1, 13].

3.2 Data Analysis

The data was analyzed through six phased Thematic analysis, which mainly searches the patterns or themes in relation to various epistemological and ontological positions [4, 20]. We applied inductive Thematic analysis. This is a bottom-up approach where the themes were generated by the data itself rather than applying prevailing theories and frameworks to construct themes.

The data collected from multiple sources have been individually prepared for the analysis. As the initial step, we separated text data and non-text data for initial screening. The data collected from Naturalistic observation, focus group interviews and participants' narrative sampling were counted as text data and video recordings, photographs come under the category of non-text data. The six phased thematic analysis consists the following stages: (a) familiarizing with data, (b) generation of initial codes, (c) searching for themes, (d) review and refining themes, (e) definition and naming themes. As the initial step, we started coding text data. The interviews were audio recorded and transcribed for analysis. We have done a careful scanning of all the text data in hand including transcriptions, observation records, data on field diary and participant's narrative sampling. All the text data was scrutinized, and important areas were flagged. Identifying potential codes was the next step.

Initial codes generated through the words, phrases transferred the idea of the entire text. These initial codes which were identified in textual data generated through observation notes, narrative samples and transcribed audio text. At the initial stage, this was done on desk, by highlighting meaningful insights through labelling. Highlighting the text and sticky notes were utilized to identify initial codes through data. Non-textual data such as photographs were coded aligning with the meanings or reflections identified in textual data. Further, non-textual data was coded independently with meaningful expressions narrated by the researcher along with the photographs. Same technique was applied for the video poses.

4   Results

Upon creating a thematic map based on the results, we discerned a total of 17 codes, 11 categories, 10 themes, and 6 dimensions. This comprehensive mapping sheds light on the influences of ICT tools on the architectural design process, along with the positioning of the empathizing phase in architectural design thinking (refer to Fig. 1: Thematic map).

The initial phase of data analysis involved in the systematic examination of data collected through various methods, including observational records, time sampling, narrative sampling, field diaries, and focus group interviews. Through a meticulous process, the textual and graphical data obtained from these sources underwent open coding. This approach involved closely scrutinizing the content to generate initial codes that captured the essence of the information.

The open codes were then interconnected by discerning patterns and relationships among them. This process facilitated the identification of commonalities, distinctions, and supported on emergent of categories within the dataset. The objective was to organize the diverse array of information into meaningful themes that could later contribute to a comprehensive understanding of the research context. By employing open coding and categories developed, themes were identified. Through the themes developed, six dimensions were identified which could provide answers to the research questions created. This analytical process laid the groundwork for understanding the influences of ICT tools and the placement of empathizing phase in architectural design thinking.

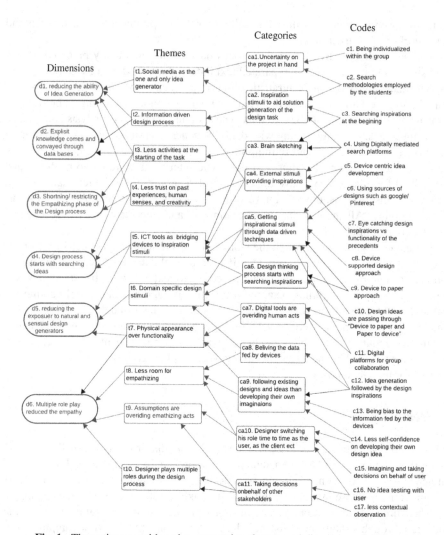

Fig. 1. Thematic map with codes, categories, themes and dimensions developed

5 Discussion

5.1 ICT Tools and Its Influences in Architectural Design Thinking

Research question one aims on identifying influences of ICT tools on architectural design thinking. We identified five dimensions which could provide answers to the RQ1. The results depict that ICT tools have had the following influences on students' design thinking process: (refer d1- d5 in Fig. 1).

- d1) Reducing the ability of idea generation,
- d2) Explicit knowledge comes and conveyed through databases
- d3) Shortening and restricting the empathizing phase of the design process

- d4) Design process starts with searching ideas
- d5) Reducing the exposure to natural and sensual design generators

The dimension 1 (d1) explains the influence on the students' idea generation due to usage of ICT tools. The dimension 1 was developed through the themes generated from t1 – t4. The first theme (t1) "social media and digital repositories are the key design generators" is explaining how the ideation process of students got influenced through the usage of ICT tools. Students were using individual mobile phones at the beginning of the design process. They used their individual mobile phones to browse design inspirations to start the design process. This was mainly done individually and less collaboration was visible during this phase.

The second theme (t2) "information driven design process" explains another major influence caused by ICT tools. The students use mobile phone, which is the most common ICT tool available with students throughout the design process. Once the task assigned, they started searching design inspirations through previously done precedents which are available in very popular web-based design domains. They spent significant amount of time (nearly 4 h of the first day) with the device searching inspirations. Being overexposed to the ICT tools during the early stages of the design thinking process has compressed their design thinking ability and reduced the ability of novel idea generation through their intrinsic creativity. The web-based design domains brought millions of design solutions to their fingertip. However, this has made the design thinking and imagination spectrum of students narrow. The third and fourth themes further explains the influences of ICT tools on the design process.

The third theme (t3), elucidating "less activities at the initiation of the design process," highlights a significant influence resulted from excessive exposure to ICT tools. Students tend to search design ideations individually through their mobile phones and this has made them individual centric and less collaborative among the group members. Brain storming sessions, collaborative developments and idea testing sessions were not much visible as a result of the utilization of ICT tools during the design process.

The second dimension (d2) we developed "explicit knowledge comes and conveyed through data bases" explains how the students receive design knowledge during the design process. In the development of dimension 2 (d2), contributions were made through the incorporation of information found in themes 2 and 3 (t2 & t3). The students were heavily biased on the design ideations which came through digitally mediated platforms. The complex consolidation of previous experience, human senses, anthropometric and ergonomic facts, and socio contextual demands were heavily neglected. This trend is leading the design industry towards a hazardous end where many aesthetically pleasing, eye catching design solutions could be visible with lack of functionality, which could not cater complex human needs including socio cultural demands of the context.

Another major influence we identified is (d3) "restricting the empathizing phase of the design process". In developing dimension 3, theme 3(t3) and theme 4 (t4) were heavily contributed. In typical design thinking models empathizing phase was placed at the beginning. Empathizing consisting of several empathizing acts. However, students in conventional design studio context have shown very less activities at the beginning of the design process (t3) and they have kept on searching inspirational stimuli than empathizing. Moreover, students exhibit diminished reliance on their own experiences, senses, and creativity, as evidenced by theme 4 (t4). We recognized this as a substantial effect stemming from the heightened human-computer interaction experienced by students while working within the conventional design studio context. The fourth dimension (d4): "Design process starts with searching ideas" was developed through the themes labeled as t3, t4 & t5. Theme 5 (t5), which elucidates the role of ICT tools as a connecting mechanism to inspirational stimuli, delineates another significant influence attributed to ICT tools. In the realm of architectural design education, ICT tools have revolutionized the traditional design process of students. They are always seeking novel ideas through a device and those devices have given them lenses to investigate the world.

The fifth dimension (d5) "reducing the exposure to natural and sensual design generators" is showing us more dangerous influence caused by ICT tools. The dimension 5 (d5) was developed based on the contributions made through t5, t6 & t7. The ICT tools were the connecting bridge to the inspirational stimuli found in web-based domains (t5). Through these ICT tools, individuals gained access to a diverse array of motivational content and creative influences. The web-based platforms, rich with multimedia and interactive features, offered a dynamic space for students to explore and draw inspiration from. The results depict that ICT tools have played a crucial role in bridging students to the wealth of inspirational resources available on the internet.

The sixth theme (t6) "domain specific design stimuli" explains the fact that design students are getting them connected to the inspirational stimuli through the ICT tools they have in hand and they are not inspired through natural inspirations or past memories, incidents or other ways of getting inspired. The inspirations they received was exactly downloaded from specific design domains available in internet (t6). This has reduced the natural imagination ability of the students. Being sensible and sensitive about the problem at hand is an important quality to become a good designer. Designers must possess the sensitivity to comprehend user demands and the capacity to empathize, understanding how others will utilize their design solutions once completed. Human sensitivity is diminishing as individuals tend to avoid engaging in thoughtful processes, choosing to alleviate cognitive burdens. Now they can see multiple solutions generated by former designers without much hesitation, which leads them being less sensitive to the problem at hand. The theme 7 (t7)" Physical appearance over functionality" explains the choice of students when they are selecting design stimuli. The students have picked eye catching design solutions generated in other contexts. They got inspired through the features and ideas communicated through those designs and tried hard to replicate those ideas in the contexts which they have to provide design solutions. They did not consider contextual demands and user demands when giving solutions and were based on the inspirations they found on the internet. This is showcasing a major influence caused by ICT tools on design thinking process. To generate realistic, human friendly design solutions, the designer must feel the problem in a correct way. The empathizing phase is placed at the beginning in most of design process models developed, because the designer needs to understand the periphery of the scope in hand first. But unfortunately, the exposure to ICT tools has shrunk the ability to see the real world through their naked eye.

5.2 ICT Tools and It's Influences on Empathizing Phase in Architectural Design Thinking

D4 & d6 along with t3, t4, t5, t7, t8, t9 and t10 contributed towards answering RQ2. The empirical study revealed a notable observation regarding architectural design students, indicating that they initiate the design process without engaging in the empathizing phase of design thinking. Rather than starting with an empathetic understanding of the users or context, the students demonstrated a tendency to immediately embark on the search for novel ideas (d4). This departure from the traditional design thinking sequence suggests a potential gap in their approach, as empathy is a foundational step in understanding the users' needs and experiences. The study's findings imply a deviation from the established design thinking models, highlighting the importance of revisiting the initial stages of empathizing before delving into the generation of novel ideas.

The 8th theme (t8) "less room for empathizing" explains the amount of priority or attention given by the students in understanding the problem domain. Empathizing acts were not visible during the initial stages of the design thinking process. During the study we identified that students are assuming user needs, and they think on behalf of the user instead of deep interviewing, observing, or exploring user and their behavior (t8) & (t9). Therefore, empathy kept in a distance in architectural design process adopted by the students. We have marked this as an assumption based empathizing phase in the model, we developed to explain the influences of ICT tools on empathizing phase (refer Fig. 2).

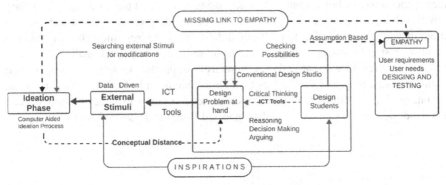

Fig. 2. Influences caused by ICT tools on architectural design thinking process of the students (developed by authors)

As identified by theme 10 (t10): "designer plays multiple roles during the design process". Design students are switching their role from the designer to the user and the client and to many other stakeholders. They take decisions on behalf of the users without any prior checking. This has made them less sensitive and less empathetic.

The sixth dimension (d6), which addresses the reduction of empathy due to the multiple roles played by students, delineates the consequences of diminished empathetic engagement. In Fig. 2, we have highlighted this as an additional factor contributing to the identification of a missing link to empathy.

In IDEO design thinking model empathizing has been placed at the beginning [11, 21]. Empathizing phase has been identified as the initial step which is followed by many designers to make themselves familiarized to the problem they got to solve. Typical empathizing phase comprises with empathizing acts which make the designer more grounded to the problem at hand. However, the results led us to identify architectural design thinking process of students, which they have started their design thinking from the ideation phase (refer Fig. 3). In IDEO [11] and double diamond design thinking models [14] Ideation phase comes as the third phase which is followed by empathizing and defining phases. Empathizing phase is creating a sufficient background for the designer to understand socio, economical and human context of the problem given, and the defining phase supports the designer to explore, research, observe, understand and to develop point of views. The ideation phase is typically followed by the above two steps in established design thinking models. However, we identified, architectural design students are starting the design thinking process from Ideation phase (d4), by searching potential design ideas and inspirational stimuli to develop new design ideas (refer Fig. 3). They are critically ignoring the empathizing acts and understanding the problem at hand, instead, they make themselves so busy on searching potential external stimuli to develop solutions to the problem at hand (t6). The results depicted that, they are spending a significant amount of time, searching external stimuli to start the design process by searching in popular digital design repositories by using their mobile phones (t5). Mobile phone has been acting as a bridging device to connect the student to the external stimuli (t5).

Empathy is a critical component of any type of design and for architectural design, since it encompasses human interacting and using spaces and places designed for their activities. It allows designers to get a better understanding of the context and the user whom they are designing for, to understand their needs, desires, and behavior. Without empathy, design becomes a sterile exercise in aesthetics and functionality, devoid of the emotional resonance that makes designs truly impactful. Design students, in their newfound roles, may find themselves making decisions on behalf of users and clients without conducting thorough research or empathetic inquiry (d6). Lack of empathy can lead the design solutions which are disconnected from the actual needs of the user.

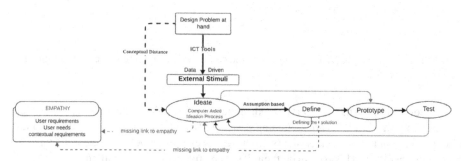

Fig. 3. Design thinking process adopted by students (Extended design thinking model developed by authors based on IDEO design thinking Model [11])

Based on the results, we have developed a conceptual design thinking model (see Fig. 3) which could specifically be applied for architectural design students. The design thinking started from Ideation phase and define phase were followed by the Ideation phase. But in typical design process models such as IDEO DT model and double diamond DT model defining phase comes secondly and thirdly Ideation happens. The major difference is, architectural design students in a CDS context, are starting from Ideation and then they moved in to define phase to define the possible solutions that they could generate (d3 & d4). In typical design thinking model, during the defining phase designers are defining the problem at hand. But in architectural design thinking, students are defining the solutions that they could generate. We identified a missing link to the empathizing phase (refer Fig. 3). There were no major empathizing acts obtained by the students. They have simply neglected exploring socio, cultural, human context of the problem at hand. They did it very lightly and, instead of empathizing, they tend to assume situations which are favorable to the solutions they identified during internet searching at Ideation phase.

We identified, that there is a conceptual distance between ideation phase and problem identification which is related to empathizing at the beginning. T5, t6 & t7 contributed to identify the conceptual distance. Due to the inspirations, they followed (t6) made them away from real world scenarios, and the solutions they identified are mostly away from the real human needs. Most of the ideas they developed contain aesthetically pleasing features, but those are heavily missing addressing to deep socio physical needs of the user (t7). This occurred due to inspirations they received from the internet which were done by several designers in other contexts (t1, t2, t3 & t4 in table 1). Direct applications of those ideas made them neglect user and contextual demands. Empirical study we conducted, resulted in identifying a placement variation of design thinking phases of students (refer Fig. 3). Being so centric to digital devices and digital platforms, have made students away from real life situations. The danger is, over exposure to ICT tools have made them less sensitive. We identified this as a very dangerous situation, because designers should jump in to the shoe of the user. The user needs cannot be hypothetically assumed, all this design solution should be acceptable by the user. The user acceptance comes with a good, functional design solution. Aesthetically pleasing design solutions which are commonly available in digital platforms are not fulfilling the real life needs of the user. Therefore, starting the architectural design process form Ideation has created several problems which made the architectural students less sensitive and less confident on own creativity and abilities, plus it kept them away from empathy which is very important to become a good designer.

In addressing Research Question 2, we have recognized that the architectural design thinking process employed by students differs from the established models of design thinking worldwide. While many established design thinking models commence with the empathizing phase, the outcomes of our study (refer Fig. 3) illustrates that the architectural design thinking process initiates from the Ideation phase. This happened due to searching external stimuli through ICT tools at the beginning. Considering the integral incorporation of ICT tools in the routines of design students, we emphasize the necessity for additional research endeavors focused on discovering effective approaches to mitigate the negative influences of ICT tools on the architectural design thinking process.

6   Conclusion

The goal of this study was to identify the influences caused by ICT tools on architectural design thinking process of students. We also examined the placement of the empathizing phase in architectural design thinking. For this study we have observed 25 interior designing undergraduates throughout 18 studio hours. We utilized naturalistic observation, focus group interviews and participant narrative sampling techniques along with photographs and video recordings to collect data. Six phased thematic analysis has been utilized to analyze the data.

The empirical study conducted has resulted in identifying significant influences of utilization of ICT tools during the design thinking process of students (refer Fig. 2). Reduction of ability of idea generation through own imagination and creativity was identified as a result of using ICT tools. Due to usage of ICT tools, students have given less effort to develop novel ideas, instead they borrow it from the Internet. This fact could create many repercussions in design thinking domain and need more research to mitigate negative influences of it. Due to usage of ICT tools at the beginning of the design thinking process, the empathizing phase got restricted and shortened.

The conceptual design thinking model we have developed, as depicted in Fig. 3, reveals a notable absence of empathy in the initial stages. This absence is attributed to a detachment stemming from the use of ICT tools for Ideation before engaging in empathetic understanding of the problem at hand. Consequently, the prioritization of idea generation takes precedence in the design thinking process of architectural design students. The model we developed (Fig. 3) underscores a departure from the conventional design thinking sequence, where empathy typically precedes defining and idea generation. In the architectural design thinking process, Ideation takes the lead, followed by the defining phase. However, our analysis, as illustrated in Fig. 3, has identified a notable absence of empathy preceding the ideation or defining stages. This observation emphasizes the influences of ICT tools on the design thinking process of students, suggesting that the use of technology may influence the sequencing and emphasis of crucial stages in the architectural design thinking.

This study highlights the necessity for further research endeavors aimed at enhancing the empathy of architectural design students. As the architectural design thinking process underscores the importance of empathy, future studies can contribute valuable insights to cultivate a more empathetic approach among design students. These efforts are crucial for refining design education and ensuring that students are equipped with a comprehensive skill set that encompasses both technological proficiency and a deep understanding of user needs.

References

1. Bansal, P. (Tima) et al.: New ways of seeing through qualitative research. Acad. Manage. J. **61**(4), 1189–1195 (2018)
2. Benyon, D.: A data centred framework for user-centred design. In: Nordby, K., et al. (eds.) Human—Computer Interaction: Interact '95, pp. 197–202 Springer, Boston (1995). https://doi.org/10.1007/978-1-5041-2896-4_33
3. Benyon, D.: Spaces of interaction, places for experience. Springer Nature (2022)

4. Braun, V., Clarke, V.: Using thematic analysis in psychology. Qual. Res. Psychol. **3**(2), 77–101 (2006). https://doi.org/10.1191/1478088706qp063oa
5. Brown, T., Katz, B.: Change by design. J. Prod. Innov. Manag. **28**(3), 381–383 (2011)
6. Brown, T., Wyatt, J.: Design thinking for social innovation. Dev. Outreach. **12**(1), 29–43 (2010)
7. Creswell, J.W.: Mixed-method research: Introduction and application. In: Handbook of Educational Policy, pp. 455–472 Elsevier (1999)
8. Creswell, J.W., Poth, C.N.: Qualitative inquiry and research design: choosing among five approaches. Sage publications (2016)
9. Cross, N.: Design thinking: understanding how designers think and work. Berg, Oxford (2011)
10. Cuff, D.: Architecture: The story of practice. Mit Press (1992)
11. Dam, R. F, I.D.F.: The 5 Stages in the Design Thinking Process, Interaction Design Foundation. https://www.interaction-design.org/literature/article/5-stages-in-the-design-thinking-process
12. Demirbaş, O.O., Demirkan, H.: Focus on architectural design process through learning styles. Des. Stud. **24**(5), 437–456 (2003). https://doi.org/10.1016/S0142-694X(03)00013-9
13. Denscombe, M.: The Good Research Guide : For Small-scale Research Projects. McGraw-Hill Education, Maidenhead, Berkshire (2014)
14. Design Council, Technology Stratergy board: Design Council 2011, Technology Stratergy Board (2011)
15. Boling, E., Smith, K.M.: Critical Issues in Studio Pedagogy: Beyond the Mystique and Down to Business. Design in Educational Technology : Design Thinking, Design Process, and the Design Studio. 37 (2013). https://doi.org/10.1007/978-3-319-00927-8_3
16. Gaver, W.W., et al.: Ambiguity as a resource for design. Presented at the Proceedings of the SIGCHI conference on Human factors in computing systems (2003)
17. Hettithanthri, U., et al.: Exploring the architectural design process assisted in conventional design studio: a systematic literature review. Int. J. Technol. Des. Educ. (2022). https://doi.org/10.1007/s10798-022-09792-9
18. Hettithanthri, U., et al.: Exploring the Collaborative Design Process at Conventional Design Studio. Springer, Cham (2022). https://doi.org/10.1007/978-3-031-15273-3_25
19. Hettithanthri, U., Hansen, P.: Design studio practice in the context of architectural education: a narrative literature review. Int. J. Technol. Des. Educ., 1–22 (2021). https://doi.org/10.1007/s10798-021-09694-2
20. Hoskyns, S.: Thematic analysis. In: Collected Work: Music therapy research. 3rd ed. rev. Published by: Dallas: Barcelona, 2016. (AN: 2016–21423). Barcelona, Dallas (2016)
21. Kelley, T.: The art of innovation: Lessons in creativity from IDEO, America's leading design firm. Currency (2001)
22. Kim, J., Ryu, H.: A design thinking rationality framework: framing and solving design problems in early concept generation. Hum.-Comput. Inter. **29**(5–6), 516–553 (2014). https://doi.org/10.1080/07370024.2014.896706
23. Kvan, T., Jia, Y.: Students' learning styles and their correlation with performance in architectural design studio. Des. Stud. **26**(1), 19–34 (2005). https://doi.org/10.1016/j.destud.2004.06.004
24. Mamdouh, A., et al.: Analysis of the gap in architects' skills of lifelong learning. Ain Shams Eng. J. **13**, 6 (2022)
25. Martin, R.L.: The design of business: Why design thinking is the next competitive advantage. Harvard Business Press (2009)
26. Meyer, M.W., Norman, D.: Changing design education for the 21st century. She Ji: The Journal of Design, Economics, and Innovation. **6**(1), 13–49 (2020)
27. Nass, C., Moon, Y.: Machines and mindlessness: Social responses to computers. J. Soc. Issues **56**(1), 81–103 (2000)

28. Norman, D.: Emotion & design: attractive things work better. Interactions **9**(4), 36–42 (2002)
29. Norman, D.: The design of future things. Basic books (2009)
30. Norman, D.A.: Affordance, conventions, and design. Interactions **6**(3), 38–43 (1999)
31. Plattner, H., et al.: Design thinking. Springer (2009)
32. Rahbarianyazd, R., Nia, H.A.: Aesthetic cognition in architectural education: a methodological approach to develop learning process in design studios. Int. J. Cognitive Res. Sci. Eng. Educ. (IJCRSEE), 61–69 (2019)
33. Ryan, T.G.: Naturalistic observation of engagement and disengagement within professional development in education. Int. Online J. Educ. Teach. **6**(1), 37–54 (2019)
34. Salama, A.: New Trends in Architectural Education: Designing the Design Studio (1995)
35. Schon, D.A.: Educating the Reflective Practitioner. Toward a New Design for Teaching and Learning in the Professions. The Jossey-Bass Higher Education Series (1987)
36. Schön, D.A.: The Reflective Practitioner : How Professionals Think in Action. Routledge, London (2016)
37. Shneiderman, B.: Leonardo's laptop: human needs and the new computing technologies. Mit Press (2003)
38. Shneiderman, B.: The eyes have it: A task by data type taxonomy for information visualizations. Presented at the Proceedings 1996 IEEE symposium on visual languages (1996)
39. Shneiderman, B., Plaisant, C.: Designing the user interface: Strategies for effective human-computer interaction. Pearson Education India (2010)
40. Turkle, S.: Life on the Screen. Simon and Schuster (2011)
41. Ward, K., et al.: Analysis in Grounded Theory—How Is It Done? Examples From a Study That Explored Living With Treatment for Sleep Apnea. London (2021). https://doi.org/10.4135/9781473989245

Observation and Reflection: The Behavioral Fields of UX Industry and Its Dilemma

Jingpeng Jia$^{(\boxtimes)}$ and Xueyan Dong

Beijing Union University, Beijing 100101, China
tjtjingpeng@buu.edu.cn

Abstract. The pursuit of a common theoretical framework of User Experience (UX) is challenging but important, as Experience Design, being an emerging and rapidly evolving discipline, encompasses diverse backgrounds, hindering the establishment of universally accepted principles. Our study aims to identify potential strategies to navigate this dilemma. We conduct a qualitative examination of the UX industry over the past decade, revealing that the conventional industry and academic perspectives often overlook behavioral fields indirectly related to UX practice. These fields, however, unveil crucial underlying factors that impede the development of a unified UX theory. Our findings highlight the need for directed efforts to overcome the obstacles in theory-building and provide a comprehensive overview of the eight behavioral fields relevant to UX. This serves to contextualize hidden causal factors and offers a panoramic view of the UX industry, laying a foundation for the development of a unified UX theory.

Keywords: User experience · Behavior field · Industry dilemma · Common theoretical framework

1 Introduction

In 1995, cognitive psychologist Donald Norman introduced the term 'user experience' at the HCI conference, leading to its widespread adoption in the design field [1]. Concurrently, UX design practice and related academic research flourished. UX, as an inherently interdisciplinary field [2], draws theoretical resources from diverse areas such as design psychology, human factors, business, marketing, and economics. Experts across these disciplines have contributed to defining 'user experience' and developing innovative experience design practices [3]. This has enhanced understanding of the 'user experience' phenomenon, but the loose and sometimes conflicting relationships between various theoretical models have hindered the formation of a unified discussion platform [4]. Wolfgang contends that piecing together concepts from different theorists, even if they are from the same discipline, disrupts the coherence of theoretical constructs [5]. Over the past two decades, scholars have emphasized the need to develop a unified theoretical framework for 'user experience' to facilitate coherent understanding among practitioners and expedite systematic UX theory building [6]. However, this goal remains elusive. Peter Benz attributes this to the fact that experience design is still too young,

A. Marcus et al. (Eds.): HCII 2024, LNCS 14716, pp. 93–103, 2024.
https://doi.org/10.1007/978-3-031-61362-3_7

varied, and contextually diverse to form a coherent theoretical framework or an accepted canon of texts [7]. The same phenomenon has been interpreted and utilized differently across various disciplinary frameworks, complicating the integration of these theoretical models and concepts [6].

Is this challenge truly insurmountable? Recent developments in artificial intelligence suggest that a significant barrier to complete AI implementation may stem from the paradox of using human brain to study itself [8, 9]. This perspective sheds light on a similar situation in the theoretical study of UX: the construction of a unified UX has predominantly focused on the explicit behavioral aspects of UX practice. One must consider whether a broader field of relevance exists beyond this focus. Could exploring a wider field provide valuable insights and directions for the development of a unified UX theory. Informed by the above review, we embraced the concept of Epoche from phenomenology [10] to focus more closely on the diverse local aspects of UX. This approach extended beyond deep immersion in UX scholarship to encompass an exploratory tour of the UX industry. Our aim was to identify all behavioral fields associated with UX, considering both direct and indirect connections, while maintaining an objective, broad perspective. Our focus centered on examining the core behaviors and intrinsic features within each field, as well as uncovering the interactive relationships among these fields. Simultaneously, we anticipated that this exploration might lead to unexpected yet insightful discoveries. We are pleased to report two significant findings from this approach.

Firstly, our examination revealed that, in addition to the causes identified by scholars like Benz and Pieter, there are more subtle causes within behavioral fields that often elude conventional industry and academic perspectives. While the connection between these hidden causes and the construction of UX theory is more indirect compared to explicit causes, their implications are potentially more profound. Therefore, these subtle causes might offer deeper and more valuable insights into the dilemma of building a unified UX theory.

Secondly, uncovering additional relevant behavioral fields, which are often overlooked in traditional academic and industry contexts, can lay a crucial foundation for developing a comprehensive theory of UX. This approach enables the creation of a more detailed panoramic view of UX, highlighting the behavioral structures, features, and challenges prevalent in the UX industry. The map allows for a richer interpretation of certain aspects of UX, while also revealing content that is only identifiable through this broader overview. Therefore, utilizing this comprehensive illustration as a starting point, or at least as an essential element, is a logical step in constructing a unified UX theory. This approach offers a 'view from the mountaintop,' fostering a foundational understanding of UX.

2 Materials and Methods

Strictly speaking, our research is not an independent study but rather a sub-topic within a broader research problem. This problem originated from our curiosity about why experience innovation is so challenging and what possibilities exist for addressing these challenges. To find answers, we embarked on a comprehensive exploration of the UX industry from 2013 to 2017. In early 2014, we identified a key issue: the absence of a systematic methodology for experience innovation, which directly contributed to the challenges in its practice. This led to a new question: why is there a lack of a systematic methodology for experience innovation, and how can it be established? The emergence of this question guided the direction of our subsequent research and serves as the starting point for the work presented in this paper. By the beginning of 2017, we had not only understood the UX industry's fundamental view of the theory-building dilemma but had also developed a more comprehensive understanding of the entire behavioral field related to UX and the challenges it faces. Ultimately, we discovered deeper, implicit reasons that hinder the construction of a unified UX theory. Based on this insight, we gained a clearer understanding of both the starting point and the direction for developing this theory. Since then, building on the aforementioned research foundation and supported by interdisciplinary theories, we have begun to develop and refine a methodology for systematic experience innovation. This framework was completed in early 2019. Over the past three years, we have tested the validity of our research findings primarily through practical application and teaching, making refinements based on the feedback received.

This raises a question: Have the reported results lost their validity since our research commenced at the beginning of 2017? In fact, the progress achieved prior to 2017 has enabled us to carry out subsequent work effectively. However, since then, we have continuously monitored developments and changes in the behavioral field of UX, enriching our research with new findings and deeper insights. This article presents a comprehensive overview of these elements.

The research presented in this paper was conducted primarily using qualitative research methods. A fundamental principle of qualitative research is to approach the field with an 'empty glass' mentality, meaning without preconceptions [13]. Initially, we were fortunate to have a relatively straightforward sampling range. However, to obtain comprehensive answers to our questions, the scale and complexity of the sampling in this study exceeded standard norms. It appeared nearly impossible to uncover all phenomena that might offer answers and clues. In this case the best design for collecting data is no design [11]. Our strategy involved conducting recursive research [12], where answers to the initial question lead to further inquiry. These answers were then used to refine and clarify the question. Subsequently, we sought new answers repeatedly until an explicit, consistent answer emerged. Our aim was to gain insights from multiple disciplines, as clear definition of the research problem is essential to anticipate all possible answers. This approach was utilized throughout the study, though it does not imply that we disregarded the importance of research methods. In fact, we adhered to standard methodological guidelines for qualitative research [13–15] to examine and reflect on each stage of our research methods. Specifically, the output at each stage was compared with typical research problems, employing methods such as grounded theory [16], descriptive phenomenological analysis [17], interpretive phenomenological analysis [18], action research [19], and critical incident technique [20]. Additionally, we incorporated the advantages of these methods into our research.

As Zahavi pointed out, when facing with the specific needs of a new problem, it is important to exceed the advice and paradigms given in the existing literature for applying and exploring methods [21]. The research in this paper falls roughly into a similar situation. When readers are faced with similar research questions that require flexibility in organizing their research methods, it is hoped that the content of this paper will provide some possible inspiration and lessons. In the following section, we present the critical issues involved in the methodology of the study.

2.1 The First Author's Education Background

In 2001, the first author commenced undergraduate studies in new media design, a curriculum akin to an interaction design program, at the Beijing Institute of Graphic Communication. This college was chosen because its program was the first in China to win the first prize in the Morpheus International Multimedia CD-ROM Design Competition. Nearing graduation, he made a fascinating discovery: effective interactive design often necessitates robust dynamic design. Consequently, he forsook a lucrative position as an interactive designer at an internet company to pursue studies in animation design for two years. His supervisor was Professor Ma Kexuan, a renowned animation director in China known for successful productions like 'Twelve Mosquitoes,' 'Five Men the Greatest Showman,' and 'Little Tadpole Finds His Mother.' As he approached his master's graduation, he had acquired substantial theoretical and practical skills in the hypothetical characteristics of animation art, animation performance, and the principles of animation movement. However, he was not immediately inclined to apply this knowledge to create better interactive dynamic designs. Instead, he pondered questions such as 'Why does knowledge of the laws of animation movement exist? Where does this knowledge originate, and why is it valid? To seek answers, he consulted Professor Ma. After a moment of silence and lighting a cigarette, Professor Ma said, 'I share the theory with you, yet you ask why this knowledge exists – a question I cannot answer. Come with me. Professor Ma then gave him a book titled 'A Walk in Aesthetics' by Mr. Zong Baihua, the first philosophical book he had ever encountered. Professor Ma added, 'To find answers, you must turn to philosophy.' He heeded this advice. In September 2012, he began his doctoral studies in aesthetics at the School of Philosophy of Renmin University of China, under the supervision of Professor Wang Xuxiao, an expert in applied aesthetics.

It is noteworthy that, since 2005, the author's attunement to cutting-edge issues in interaction design diminished, likely due to his focus on animation studies. In 2009, the author observed the innovative performance of the iPhone and subsequently recognized the challenge of experience innovation in 2011. However, none of these observations prompted the author to delve deeper into or reflect further on these issues. It wasn't until early 2013 that his curiosity, fueled by the study of aesthetic theory and the commencement of his PhD thesis, led him to ponder, 'Why is making experience innovation like the iPhone so difficult? This nearly neglected issue suddenly regained the author's attention, and he became intrigued to discover the answer. To meet the demands of his research, over the next three years, he engaged in courses covering philosophy of science, cultural theory, and psychology, along with philosophical aesthetics, while staying abreast of the latest issues and literature in these fields.

2.2 Sampling

The research employed several sampling methods, the first of which was snowball sampling. Given our research problem, it was necessary to explore all behavioral fields related to UX. Initially, we were unaware of the specific behavioral fields associated with UX. It was also unclear which fields were relevant to the impediments in constructing UX theory. We questioned whether there were complex, intertwined relationships between these fields, but initially, we had no clear idea. As our research deepened, we began identifying the explicit behavioral fields. For instance, the annual UX industry conference organized by the Interaction Design Committee in China served as our initial study object to uncover clues about potential behavioral fields. Subsequently, we followed these leads to discover additional relevant fields. The second method was purposive sampling, aimed at identifying people, behaviors, and events that could offer key information and possible answers. The third method employed was typical case sampling. In this approach, for instance, we conducted interviews for academic research on UX with figures like Donald Norman, Honorary Life President of the International Chinese Association of Computer Human Interaction (ICACHI), Ren Xiangshi, and UX experts from Fortune 500 companies. Regarding experience innovation, we investigated practical projects from renowned companies like BMW, Land Rover, and Xiaomi. The fourth method was stratified sampling. In this method, we frequently invited academic experts, industry professionals, and general practitioners to share their perspectives on specific issues. The fifth method was convenience sampling. In this approach, we leveraged our capabilities, economic, and social status to access research subjects in fields that were convenient and accessible to us.

2.3 Data Collection and Analysis

To address the questions posed at the outset, we have been exploring and examining the entirety of UX-related industries since mid-2013. Throughout this process, our approach varied: at times, we stood on the sidelines to observe; at other times, we actively participated in practices, discussed with experts from various fields, or retreated to a quiet location to review and analyze all that we had seen, heard, thought about, and to consult relevant literature. In other words, we maintained a state of active engagement without becoming overly immersed, continually seeking to understand the various behavioral fields related to UX and uncovering deeper reasons that hinder the theoretical construction of uniformity in UX. Generally, data collection and analysis were not distinct phases in our research. Furthermore, the entire research process was distinctly unstructured. Throughout the process, we continuously gained new experiences, updating our answers based on these insights, which in turn led to the discovery of new research tasks. This means that new fields often emerged gradually as the research progressed, rather than being preconceived. Chance inspiration and fortuitous occurrences aided in the discovery of these new fields. Many of these discoveries were unexpected. For instance, we did not maintain a rigorous record of every detail, but rather focused on the overall atmosphere and understanding of each field. Our aim was to gain maximum experience and awareness of the entirety of the UX behavioral field and to uncover the implicit connections, patterns, and logic within events. Additionally, our interviews were often informal in nature. Furthermore, to ensure a sufficiently in-depth and comprehensive study, we did not adhere to a strict timetable for data collection and analysis.

Compared to conventional studies, the research approach described above is somewhat unorthodox. However, this approach was necessary and proved to be effective for our research. This relaxed, strolling approach afforded us ample time to comprehensively understand the various aspects of the UX behavioral fields, to fully reflect on their key and puzzling elements, and to uncover many issues and scenarios that often go unnoticed in conventional industry and academic perspectives. Regarding our findings, focusing on such contents and reflecting on them played a crucial role in answering our initial questions.

2.4 Determination of Research Saturation

Two main criteria were used to determine the research saturation. Firstly, we assessed whether additional materials collected duplicated the content of information gathered earlier, with duplication primarily referring to patterns of behavior and relationships. In this study, no new information was available to further answer the research questions [14]. Secondly, over the past three years, we have shared our findings with over 20 UX practitioners, 15 relevant academics, and over 180 UX-oriented master's students. Many, particularly those who have encountered difficulties in experience innovation, resonated with our results, thereby empathically validating our findings [22]. Some expressed that we had provided a systematic explanation for aspects they found confusing yet difficult to articulate, while others felt we helped them view their problems from a broader perspective. Some even experienced a moment of enlightenment, followed by silence, due to a lack of resources to effectively achieve their desired goals. Therefore, reassessing their experience innovation strategy, or even their business strategy, became necessary. Encouraged by this feedback, we became increasingly eager to share our findings with more colleagues and fellow researchers.

3   Results

Our analysis reveals that the UX behavioral field comprises at least eight interconnected sub-fields. Five sub-fields are directly related to UX: practice of experience innovation, experience consumption, development of UX theory, corporate perceptions of UX, and UX education. The remaining three - academic, business, and cultural atmospheres - have an indirect yet significant influence on UX. Surface-level observations suggest a thriving UX industry; however, deeper analysis uncovers complex challenges, both overt and covert. This creates an apparent contradiction within the vibrant UX sector. The issues in the direct sub-fields form the explicit part of this dilemma, while the challenges in the indirect sub-fields, deeply embedded in societal inertia and cultural norms, present even more formidable obstacles, intensifying the overall dilemma.

3.1   Behavioral Fields Directly Related to UX

Experience Innovative Practice. To explore this topic, two conceptual issues must be clarified. Firstly, our investigation into business practices, design work, and consumer behavior indicates that the core value of UX is the practice of experience innovation, specifically product experience innovation. This means enhancing product design to provide customers with new and better experiences. Secondly, in actual business practice, product innovation essentially equates to product experience innovation. However, this concept is not yet universally acknowledged among all product innovation practitioners, leading to variations in its application. We have collected and analyzed information on experience innovation under various terminologies, such as experience innovation, product experience innovation, and product innovation. It has been observed that the key indicator of successful experience innovation is the economic return a company receives, which reflects consumer perceptions of the value of the innovation. Examples of successful experience innovations include the Hoover vacuum cleaner and desk telephone by Henry Dreyfuss, Walt Disney's Disneyland, Apple's iPod and iPhone, Airbnb, and Tesla Motors, with the iPhone being particularly notable for its commercial profitability and market response. However, such success stories are rare. As per Stephen Wunker's statistics as of 2017 [23], more than 50% of new product launches fail to meet company expectations, only one in a hundred can recoup development costs, and merely one in three hundred significantly impacts customer buying behavior and company growth. Our observations suggest no significant change in this trend before the submission of this paper. Post-iPhone, most product experience innovations have been minor, focusing on aesthetic and usability refinements rather than significant user improvements. Others have promoted experience innovation concepts without substantial innovation.

Experience Consumption. The concept of UX has been integral to business since the 1970s, but it was not until 2007, with the launch of the first iPhone, that the concept of experience truly penetrated the mass consumer market. This revolutionary product awakened a new consumer demand for quality and innovative experiences, a trend that soon extended beyond smartphones. Consumers began to expect continuous innovation akin to what Apple had delivered. However, around 2011, there was a growing realization that even for Apple, maintaining the pace of quality experience innovation was challenging. This acknowledgment did not diminish consumer awareness of the need for innovative product experiences, highlighting a gap in market supply.

The Construction of UX Theory. The concept of the 'Experience Economy' was first introduced by American futurist Alvin Toffler in his 1970 book 'The Impact of the Future.' In 1995, cognitive scientist Donald Norman introduced the concept of UX at the Human-Computer Interaction Conference in the USA, defining it as encompassing both functional and emotional experiences [24]. Since then, UX has gained rapid acceptance, especially in interaction design [25]. In 1998, economists Joseph Pine II and James Gilmore provided a more systematic explanation of experience consumption and the workings of the experience economy in their book 'The Experience Economy' [26]. Alvin Toffler, Donald Norman, and Joseph Pine laid a solid foundation for UX theory. However, despite these contributions, the emergence of a unified UX theory has been hindered by various factors.

Corporate Perceptions of UX. Following the iPhone's success, many companies established UX departments from 2008 onwards. However, the roles and strategic integration of these departments within organizations were unclear, resulting in diverse definitions of UX department functions based on the department heads' knowledge or the companies' main business focus. Initially, companies were willing to explore and financially support the UX departments' development, leading to UX becoming a popular and well-compensated position. However, it soon became evident that achieving effective product experience innovation was challenging, and UX departments struggled without sufficient theoretical guidance. By the end of 2017, with economic downturns and shifts in the tech industry, many companies began reassessing and reducing their investment in UX, although the complete elimination of UX departments was not common. This was partly because most companies recognized the market need for experience innovation but lacked effective methods to implement it, leaving room for further experimentation.

UX Learning. When UX first became a popular career, learners were in three distinct states. Some practitioners with a strong foundation in interaction design or multimedia visual design equated UX with higher quality design in their respective fields and did not feel the need to explore UX philosophical underpinnings. Others, from non-design backgrounds, eagerly learned about design thinking, interaction design, interface design, and other UX skills, facing pressure but not significant anxiety due to the manageable learning curve. However, sensitive practitioners recognized the challenges in systematically learning about UX due to the lack of rigorous organization among various UX knowledge types. This situation, as reported by Idyawati in 2014 [27], reflects the ongoing challenges in UX education and learning. By the end of 2017, as companies began scrutinizing the value of UX roles and reducing resources, many practitioners realized the complexity and fragmentation of UX knowledge, leading to anxiety about systematically learning UX. This anxiety was shared by both practitioners and students, as the academic community had not yet fully accepted UX as a distinct discipline. Consequently, universities offering UX programs often based course content on existing disciplines, leading to distinctive program focuses, such as a bias towards interaction design, psychological approaches, or big data research.

Combining the above five fields, we can see that the UX industry is currently in the following situation: on the one hand, in the field of mass consumption, the awareness of experience consumption has been generally awakened, which has established a solid fulcrum for the existing value of the UX industry. On the other hand, the lag in the construction of UX theories has, firstly, led to a lack of methodological guidance for the practice of experience innovation, such as, people are not able to carry out the practice of experience innovation in a structured way, thus making the practice of experience innovation an inefficient practice. One reason is that it is difficult for UX learners to obtain an effective knowledge map and carry out systematic learning based on it. Another reason is it makes UX practitioners unable to learn systematically. In short, the lag in developing UX theory is the root cause of the current dilemma in the UX industry. In this regard, promoting a unified UX theory is imperative to help the UX industry out of its current impasse. In fact, in addition to the reasons outlined in 3.1.3, there are two indirectly related fields that are implicitly impeding the start of UX theory building, which constitute the more significant dilemma behind the UX dilemma.

3.2   Behavioral Fields Indirectly Related to UX

Academic Atmosphere. The modern academic system, focusing on specialization and the ability to make singular, groundbreaking discoveries, contrasts with the broader inquiries of scholars like Plato, Newton, and Darwin. This environment shapes current academic behaviors. For instance, in the summer of 2018, Professor Ren Xiangshi, Honorary Life President of the International Chinese Association of Computer Human Interaction (ICACHI), visited China for a lecture exchange. Upon discussing research with the first author, Professor Ren inquired about the pressures of publication, highlighting the challenges faced by scholars who seek to explore new research methods and questions despite these pressures. This academic climate often labels unconventional research approaches as unorthodox, yet these are necessary for progress in fields such as UX [28].

Business Atmosphere. The drive for efficiency, fueled by competition, profit motives, and capital logic, has led businesses to prioritize speed and precision. While these goals are understandable in a business context, they often result in a rushed and superficial pursuit of objectives. This business climate, focusing on immediate results, imposes constraints on the development of a unified UX theory, as it often overlooks the depth and complexity required for substantial theoretical advancements.

Cultural Atmosphere. Interpretive phenomenology teaches that no analysis can completely detach from established knowledge and experience. These existing theoretical models provide essential support for researchers to develop valid observational perspectives and thinking frameworks [21]. Although we lack the historical and cultural theoretical background to conduct an in-depth analysis of contemporary cultural forms, our study has identified several elements of the current cultural climate that influence the behavioral characteristics across the aforementioned fields.

4   Discussion

Our investigation has led to three significant insights regarding the development of a unified UX theory.

4.1   Direction and Challenges in Building a Unified UX Theory

The current review literature provides a basis but is insufficient for a comprehensive theoretical framework. We propose returning to fundamental questions about the scope, tasks, and methods of UX practice. Addressing these questions requires an interdisciplinary approach, incorporating diverse disciplines to fully interpret the range of experiential phenomena. Brenda Laurel's assertion that a lack of knowledge in relevant disciplines limits the scope of work underlines the importance of a multi-perspective approach [22]. The challenge lies in integrating diverse models and concepts across disciplines, which requires going against established academic, commercial, and cultural habits.

4.2　Interdisciplinary Perspective in Academic Evaluation

We advocate for an academic evaluation mechanism that supports and encourages an open approach to research, not requiring exhaustive exploration in each discipline but rather sketching key contours and points. This approach, based on theoretical intuition and an interdisciplinary perspective, may initially seem vague but can yield valuable insights and guide future research. Collaborative research with experts in relevant disciplines can refine and enrich preliminary theories. Ron Wakkery's work exemplifies the effectiveness of this approach [29]. Additionally, we call for incorporating corporate research and design practice findings into academic discourse, as these frontline experiments can provide critical insights.

4.3　Constructing a Unified UX Theory

This paper presents a broader view of the UX landscape, uncovering fields and behavioral structures not easily accessible from conventional academic and industry perspectives. This comprehensive view enriches our understanding of known issues and reveals new, critical ones. However, we acknowledge that our study has limitations in terms of researcher capacity, sample size, and the evolving nature of the UX industry. Our ongoing work will further detail the history and evolution of the UX industry and monitor significant changes in related fields.

References

1. Hassenzahl, M., Tractinsky, N.: User experience - A research agenda. Behav. Inf. Technol. **25**, 91–97 (2006)
2. VelsenThea, L.V., GeestThea, V., Klaassen, R., et al.: User-centered evaluation of adaptive and adaptable systems: a literature review. Knowl. Eng. Rev. **23**(03), 261–281 (2008)
3. Law, L.C., Roto, V., Hassenzahl, M., et al.: Understanding, scoping and defining user experience: a survey approach. In: Proceedings of the 27th International Conference on Human Factors in Computing Systems, Boston, USA, 4–9 April 2009
4. Desmet, P., Hekkert, P.: Framework of product experience. National Sci. Council Taipei **1**(1), 57–66 (2007)
5. Wolfgang, I.: How to Do Theory, 1st edn., pp. 154–196. Nanjing University Press, Nanjing, China (2008)
6. Thoring, K., Mueller, R.M., Desmet, P., et al.: Toward a unified model of design knowledge. Des. Issues **2**, 38 (2022)
7. Benz, P.: Experience Design Concepts and Case Studies, 1st ed. Bloomsbury: London, British; p. 171 (2015)
8. Zhang, C.: Critique of artificial reason intelligence: phenomenological reflection on Dreyfus'philosophy of artificial intelligence. J. Chongqing Univ. Technol. (Social Science) **12**, 9–20 (2018)
9. Pirozelli, P., João, F.N.: The beauty everywhere: how aesthetic criteria contribute to the development of AI. In: Proceedings on "I (Still) Can't Believe It's Not Better!" at NeurIPS 2021 Workshops, 12 Dec (2021)
10. Husserl, E.: Ideas: General Introduction to Pure Phenomenology, pp. 120–126. Routledge, New York (2012)

11. Englander, M., Morley, J.: Phenomenological psychology and qualitative research. Phenomenol. Cogn. Sci. **22**, 25–53 (2021)
12. Xiang, B.: Global "Body Shopping": An Indian Labor System in the Information Technology Industry, pp.15–16. Princeton University Press, Princeton (2007)
13. Ravitch, S.M., Mittenfelner Carl, N.: Qualitative Research: Bridging the Conceptual, Theoretical, and Methodological, 2nd edn. SAGE Publications Ltd, Vilnius, Lithuania, 2019; pp. 34–39 (2020)
14. Aurini J.; Heath M.; Howells S. *The How To of Qualitative Research,* 2nd ed; SAGE Publications Ltd:Vilnius, Lithuania, 2022; pp. 75–79
15. Denzin, N.K.: The SAGE handbook of qualitative research. Asian J. Soc. Psychol. **10**(4), 277–279 (2007)
16. Frederick W., et al.: Five ways of doing qualitative analysis: phenomenological psychology, grounded Theory, discourse, pp. 130–135. Guilford Press, New York (2013)
17. Rangarajan, V., Onkar, P.S., Barron, K.D.: A descriptive phenomenological approach to perception of affective quality in design inspiration. Design Stud. **78**, 101072 (2022)
18. Smith, J.A.: Interpretative phenomenological analysis: getting at lived experience. J. Positive Psychol. **12**(3), 1–2 (2017)
19. Costello, P.J.: Action Research. Bloomsbury, London, British, pp. 203–206 (2003)
20. Flanagan, J.C.: The critical incident technique. Psychol. Bull. **51**(4), 327–358 (1954)
21. Dan, Z.: Phenomenology: The Basics, 1st edn., pp. 154–196. Routledge, New York (2019)
22. Xue, H., Desmet, P.: Researcher introspection for experience-driven design research. Des. Stud. **63**, 3 (2019)
23. Wunker, S.M., Wattman, J., David, F.: Jobs to Be Done: A Roadmap for Customer-Centered Innovation, AMACOM, New York, USA, pp. 38–46 (2016)
24. Buccini, M., Padovani, S.: Typology of the experiences. In: Proceedings of the 2007 International Conference on Designing Pleasurable Products & Interfaces. Helsinki, Finland, 22–25 August 2007
25. Hendrik, N.J.: Product Experience, 1st edn., pp. 136–142. Elsevier Science, Amsterdam, Netherlands (2007)
26. II B., Gilmore J.H.: The Experience Economy, With a New Preface by the Authors: Competing for Customer Time, Attention, and Money, 1st edn., pp. 78–85. Harvard Business Press, Boston, USA (2019)
27. Hussein, I., Mahmud1, M., Tap, A.: A survey of user experience practice: A point of meet between academic and industry. In: Proceedings of the 3rd International Conference on User Science and Engineering (i-USEr), Shah Alam, Malaysia, 2–5 Sep (2014)
28. Explore, C.I.: Understand. Share and Show How: Four ways to use hermeneutic phenomenology to inspire human-centred creativity in engineering design, Akademisk kvarter/Academic Quarter **09**, 291–307 (2014)
29. Wakkary, R.: Two years or more of co-speculation. ACM Trans. Comput.-Hum. Interact. **29**(5), 1–44 (2022)

Design and Research on the Integration of Gamification Design and Agricultural Harvesting

Zhenze Ju, ZiYang Li, XianDong Cheng$^{(\boxtimes)}$, and WenXi Wang

Art and Design Academy, Beijing City University, Beijing, China
`xiandongC@126.com`

Abstract. In recent years, helping farmers has been the focus of attention of the whole society. With the rapid development of digital technology and the rise of the digital economy, the agricultural sector has also been exploring innovative strategies combined with gamification thinking, and how to precisely help farmers in the digital era is an important topic. Digitalisation has become a new trend in agriculture and rural development. In order to promote the optimisation of rural industry more effectively, a new model combining game participatory interaction with agricultural products picking using digital technology has emerged. Taking rural industry optimisation as the goal and gamification theory as the framework, this topic promotes the development of the agricultural product picking industry through gamification, targeting the degree of user participation, interaction and market development. It aims to build a complete picking participation platform to meet the production activity management needs of farmer users and make the picking of agricultural products more reasonable, scientific and interesting. In this paper, we studied the interactive way of the game, specifically combed the flow of the picking activity, and improved its structure to design the interactive application. The design aspect emphasises interactivity and fun, while meeting the development needs and current situation of rural areas. It is hoped that this research attempt can effectively promote the development of rural industry, achieve the purpose of accurate support for agriculture, and provide more digital solutions for this purpose.

Keyword: Gamification · agricultural harvesting · user experience · helping farmers

1 Introduction

Agricultural development has always been a hotspot of social concern, and innovative methods and strategies need to be found in order to improve the efficiency of agricultural production and promote the sustainable development of communities. In recent years, gamification has gradually attracted widespread attention as an emerging way to attract users.

Gamification is the incorporation of game design principles into non-game environments in order to stimulate participants' interest, increase productivity and promote goal achievement. In the field of agriculture, especially in activities centred on harvesting, the concept sof gamification opens up entirely new possibilities for agricultural production. By embedding game elements into the agricultural production process, it is possible to increase user engagement, optimise the production process and promote community synergy.

This paper will focus on the integration of gamification and agricultural production, using picking and farm assistance as entry points to explore how gamification strategies can be used to enhance the effectiveness of agricultural production and promote community participation. By examining the fundamentals of gamification, the current situation of picking activities, and the mechanism of helping farmers and community interaction, it aims to provide an innovative and sustainable development path for the agricultural sector.

The fundamentals and applications of gamification will first be introduced, followed by an in-depth analysis of the potential impact of picking gamification in agriculture. Next, the concepts of helping farmers and community engagement will be explored and how gamification can play an active role in this process will be explored. Finally, by reflecting on the relationship between gamification and the sustainable development of agriculture, possible future trends and challenges will be looked at, with a view to providing new concepts and methods for sustainable innovation in the agricultural sector.

In this era of digitisation and intelligence, the combination of gamification and agriculture injects a new vitality into agricultural production and promotes the sustainable development of agriculture. Through in-depth research on this topic, it is expected to inject new vigour into the field of agriculture and provide more innovative and sustainable solutions for the future mode of agricultural production.

2   Background of the Study

2.1   Research on the Integration of Gamification and Agriculture

Gamification has shown great potential as an emerging way to engage people in different fields. Its fundamentals include the integration of game elements into non-game environments in order to stimulate participants' interest, increase productivity and facilitate goal achievement. In the field of agriculture, especially in activities related to harvesting and helping farmers, the concept of gamification is gaining attention and is seen as a new way to increase the efficiency of agricultural production and promote mass. The fundamentals of gamification and its applications in different fields are explored in more detail below.

In recent years, the concept of gamification has been gradually introduced in the field of agriculture to enhance the efficiency, sustainability and attractiveness of the agricultural sector. Pavlenko T, Paraforos DS, Fenrich D, et al. proposed the use of simulation-based agricultural games to promote the adoption of precision agriculture technologies. This study focused on the development of precision agriculture to increase farmers' acceptance of new technologies through agricultural simulators. Through the gamification approach, it succeeded in capturing the interest of farmers and increasing their awareness of precision agriculture technology, thus improving the efficiency of agricultural production. Tingting Zhang, Zi Yang, Miaoshen Gong suggested that combining games with agriculture in the context of the experience economy can lead to the comprehensive development of agriculture. This study analyses autonomy, competence and social needs as dimensions in the dynamics of gamification, which leads to the manifestation of gamification in agricultural experiences. More importantly, the study distills design strategies to enhance the sense of mastery, interaction and achievement in agricultural experiences, providing an important reference for future agricultural development. Yichen Li, Mingxia Wu, Yinsen Pu, Zhenjia Fan focused on a digital agricultural game marketing model to alleviate poverty in specialised industries. Through fieldwork in Yunnan, the researchers found that gamification, as an emerging agricultural poverty alleviation model, applies information and communication technology (ICT) to the marketing of agricultural products, and attracts users to participate in farming activities by means of gamification, which improves user engagement and quality of experience. This study highlights the potential of gamification in promoting agricultural development and poverty alleviation. Dandan Liu, Tingting Wen explored the design of agricultural gamification services based on urban community spaces. The study approaches the service design from a service design perspective and through the innovative application of gamification strategies, it aims to increase the motivation of urban community residents to participate in community agriculture, promote interactions within the community, and optimise the user experience in community agriculture. This study enriches the agricultural service system in urban community spaces and provides new ideas for the development of urban community agriculture. Junxiang Wang focuses on the design of gamified urban agriculture services for commercial spaces, arguing that gamification can improve service engagement, user community interaction and collaboration, and user experience. By introducing gamification tools, this study attempts to optimise the shortcomings of existing urban agriculture models and provide new ideas for the sustainable development of urban agriculture. Martin J, Torres D, Fernandez A, et al. explored the application of citizen science gamification in the field of agriculture. The study highlights the importance of public participation in scientific research and introduces the public to the process of co-production of agricultural knowledge through a gamification approach. This approach facilitates the dissemination and sharing of agricultural knowledge and is expected to provide new ideas for solving challenges in agriculture. Tjernstrm E, Lybbert TJ focused on virtual practices and belief renewal in smallholder agricultural production. The study focused on the heterogeneity of soil quality faced by farmers in parts of Africa and updated their beliefs and behaviours through an interactive application that allowed farmers to try different agricultural inputs on a virtual farm. The results showed that farmers adjusted their allocation of agricultural inputs and increased their acceptance of new technologies through the virtual learning application.

Overall, the studies show that the application of gamified thinking in agriculture has become an important trend that can increase user engagement, improve user experience, and promote agricultural development and poverty alleviation. These studies provide theoretical and practical basis for the combination of agriculture and gamified thinking, and provide new ideas for the sustainable development of Chinese agriculture.

2.2 Fundamentals of Gamification

At its core, gamification is about motivating participants by setting clear goals, creating attractive reward systems, creating interactivity, and fostering competition and co-operation. **Specifically:**

- **Goal setting:** Gamification sets clear goals, gives participants a clear idea of what they need to accomplish, and provides clear paths and feedback mechanisms for achieving those goals.
- **Reward system:** Gamification will enhance participant motivation through a reward system. These rewards can be virtual, such as points, badges or level-ups, or they can be tangible, such as gifts, coupons or other physical rewards.
- **Interactivity:** Gamification focuses on the interaction between participants and the system so that participants feel they have an impact on the outcome and are encouraged to actively participate in the activity.
- **Competitive and cooperative:** gamification can both motivate participants through competition and enhance team cohesion through cooperation. This competitiveness and co-operation can be realised at the individual, team or community level.

2.3 Applications of Gamification in Different Domains

Gamification has been successfully applied in a number of fields, including education, health management, and corporate training. In these fields, gamification not only increases participants' interest and engagement, but also effectively promotes the achievement of goals. **Specifically:**

- **Education:** Gamification is widely used in education, e.g. through online learning platforms that allow students to improve their learning efficiency and motivation by completing tasks and earning achievements.
- **Health Management:** Health apps use gamification to encourage users to exercise and maintain healthy eating habits to improve their lifestyles.

Enterprise management: Within enterprises, gamification is used for employee training, performance management, etc., to motivate employees' motivation and creativity by setting up goals and reward systems.

By understanding the fundamentals of gamification and examples of its use in other fields, the potential role of gamification in agriculture can be better understood and provides a basis for subsequent discussion. Next, the focus will be on the application of gamification in harvesting and farming assistance activities, exploring its specific role in improving agricultural production efficiency and promoting community engagement.

2.4 Current Status of Harvesting Activities

Picking is a crucial link in the agricultural production chain, directly related to the quality and yield of agricultural products. The application of gamification in picking activities can effectively stimulate the participation of farmers and volunteers, optimise the picking process, and improve the yield and quality of agricultural products. This section will delve into the application of picking gamification in agriculture and demonstrate its potential benefits and impacts through case studies.

How gamification can enhance engagement in picking activities?

Setting up challenges and rewards: Setting up various challenges and targets, such as picking a certain amount of produce within a specified period of time, completing a picking task in a specific area, etc., and setting up corresponding rewards, such as in-kind rewards, gift cards or honours, to motivate farmers and volunteers to actively participate.

Gamification brings optimization effects to the agricultural production process Introducing gamification elements can not only enhance the participation of picking activities, but also optimize the agricultural production process, improve production efficiency and product quality; gamification can stimulate the participants' motivation and enthusiasm, make them more focused on the task, and thus improve the efficiency of the picking and the output; through the optimization of the picking process and the improvement of the work efficiency, the human costs and time costs, reducing the waste of resources, thus reducing the production costs of agricultural products; participants are more engaged in the gamified environment, paying more attention to the quality of work, reducing omissions and errors, thus improving the quality and reputation of agricultural products.

3 Research Design

In order to further explore the use of picking gamification in agriculture, a mobile application called "Fruit Delight" will be designed and integrated with Augmented Reality (AR) technology. The application will aim to improve the efficiency, quality and user engagement of produce picking. This section describes the research design of the application in detail.

3.1 Preliminary Research

Preliminary research was an important prerequisite for the design and development of the "Fruit Joy" application, aiming to gain an in-depth understanding of the actual situation of orchard picking activities and user needs. Firstly, several local orchards were selected as research targets, and contact was made with the orchard managers and their intention to co-operate. Then, a detailed research plan and research tools were formulated to ensure that the research was comprehensive and systematic.

In terms of orchard interviews, a specialised research team was arranged to visit the orchards to conduct field interviews. During the interviews, in-depth exchanges were made with the orchard managers to understand the basic situation of the orchard, planting varieties, picking process, staffing, equipment use, as well as existing problems and challenges. Through the communication with the orchard managers, we obtained first-hand information about the orchard picking activities, which provided important references for the subsequent application design and development.

At the same time, research on the orchard site was conducted. In the practice of orchard picking activities, the layout and conditions of the site environment have an important impact on the smooth running of the picking activities. Therefore, a detailed investigation and record of the orchard site was carried out, including the distribution of fruit trees, orchard roads, rest area facilities, and picking tool storage. By investigating the site, the actual conditions of the orchard can be better understood, providing practical support for the design and functional development of the application.

During the research process, the focus was also on the participants of the orchard picking activities, including farmers, volunteers and tourists. Through exchanges and interviews with them, we learned about their views, experiences and needs for the picking activities, and collected their suggestions and opinions. This information is important for understanding user needs, optimising application features and enhancing user experience.

In summary, through the preliminary research, we have gained an in-depth understanding of the actual situation of orchard picking activities and user needs, which provides an important foundation and guidance for the subsequent application design and development. At the same time, the first-hand information and user feedback obtained during the research process also provide valuable reference and inspiration.

3.2   User Analysis

People for whom the Fruit Delight App is suitable.

As an application focusing on enhancing the experience of orchard picking activities, Fruitjoy App is suitable for a user group covering people of different ages, occupations and interests. Through in-depth analyses, we have come up with a list of people who are suitable for using Fruitful App, as well as their needs and expectations for the app (see Fig. 1).

Fig. 1. Research process

Fruit Joy App has a positive effect on garden owners, tourists and other people. Fruit Joy App provides convenient orchard management functions, wmeishi hich can help them keep track of the ripening of fruit trees in real time, record the amount of picking, and manage sales channels. They can easily manage the daily work of the orchard through the app and improve production efficiency. The abundant agricultural technology information and practical tips are very attractive to fruit farmers and agricultural practitioners. They can access real-time information about orchard management and agricultural technology through the app to support healthy orchard growth. For community residents and student volunteers, the Fruit Joy App provides detailed information on picking activities and task schedules, which can help them better participate. They want to access clear task guidelines and opportunities for social interaction through the app to increase the enjoyment of participating in the activity. Family tourists usually want to get a close-to-nature experience by participating in picking activities, and enjoy the fun of rural life with their families. The Fruit Delight App can provide a variety of picking activity experiences to bring family tourists an enjoyable outdoor experience. For city dwellers and tourists, Fruitful App provides the opportunity to learn about orchard culture and participate in picking activities, allowing them to feel the beauty and fun of nature. They would like to get detailed information and guided routes of the activities through the app to increase their interest and experience in participating in the activities (see Fig. 2).

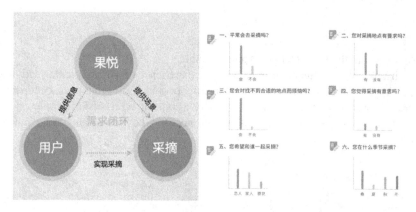

Fig. 2. Research data statistics

3.3 Combining Picking with Gamification

With the development of technology, the enhancement of user experience has become a key aspect of application design. In the interface design of Fruit Picking Assistant, gamification elements can provide users with a more interesting and interactive experience, while stimulating their interest and increasing their stickiness. In the interface of Fruitjoy Picking Assistant, some gamification elements can be introduced, such as the small game of sweeping fruits and fruit collection tasks. Users can get rewards, such as coupons, points or special props, by participating in these mini-games in the process of using the application. This not only enhances the user's sense of participation, but also motivates the user. Combined with the picking AR technology, users can capture fruits in real time through their mobile phone cameras, integrating the virtual image of fruits with the actual scene, making users feel like they are really picking fruits in the orchard. This interactive experience can increase user immersion and make the picking process more interesting. Incorporating the fruit introduction into the gamified interface, users can click on the fruit icon to get detailed information about the fruit, including origin, characteristics, nutritional value, etc., during the process of sweeping the fruit. This not only increases the user's knowledge of the fruit, but also allows them to learn more through a fun way. Design a reward system where users can get rewards for completing fruit picking tasks, participating in games and other activities. These rewards can be virtual, such as coupons and points, or real, such as free tickets and special gifts. The reward system can stimulate users' participation and increase their interaction. In order to make users understand the orchard more deeply, a tour guide IP can be designed to introduce an interesting tour guide character to provide users with an interesting introduction to the orchard through voice and text. The guide IP can be personalised to increase the sense of interaction between the user and the app. Design a coupon system where users can get coupons after completing game tasks or participating in activities, and these coupons can be used when shopping in the orchard or purchasing tickets. This will not only attract users to participate, but also increase their spending in the orchard. By combining picking with gamification, the interface design of Fruitjoy Picking Assistant can better meet users' needs for fun and interactivity, enhance user experience, and at the same time bring more user participation and retention to the Fruitjoy platform. This design concept will not only be limited to providing picking services, but also bring users an interesting entertainment experience, while achieving the goal of helping farmers (see Fig. 3).

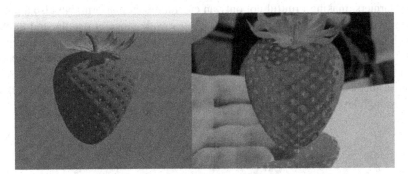

Fig. 3. Rendering

4 Design Strategies

4.1 Interface Design

Fruitjoy's interface design follows a number of important principles, which include simplicity of operation, personalisation and customisation, and visualisation rules. These principles aim to improve users' ease of use and comfort. In the interface design, the user's reading habits are taken into account, and visual rules are used to guide the user's attention and reduce the user's memory burden. The UI structure design adopts the mode of personalised customisation, which is arranged in logical relationships and sequences to form orderly units, and is visually graded to facilitate the user's rapid discovery of the required information. In the design of interface elements, the appearance of text, the choice of fonts, and the use of colours are all carefully considered to maintain the aesthetics and legibility of the overall interface. The interface as a whole is green in colour, reflecting the characteristics of Fruitful Joy, while focusing on the use of fonts of their respective specifications on different systems. The overall page layout design includes page displays at all levels, such as real-life views of the fruit garden, introductory information, user reviews, etc., aiming to provide users with a clear and organised browsing experience. The choice of interface size takes into account the monitor size and screen resolution to ensure that users can get a good interface display on different devices. Common shapes such as rectangles and circles are used in the graphic design, focusing on the shape and modelling of the pattern to match the overall design style. The layout and editorial design of the text focuses on clearly displaying the content, adopting different typesetting methods such as skeleton type, top and bottom type, etc., in order to achieve good aesthetics and information communication. The placement and design of pictures emphasises on illustrations and text, ensuring that text and pictures complement each other and enliven the design interface. The design of the mall and the communication interface gives full consideration to the needs of users, enabling them to browse and communicate conveniently, while cartoon fruit elements are added to the mall to increase the fun. The change in design concept is reflected in the choice of colours and the addition of functions, from red to green, while more functions are added to help farmers, making Fruitful not only an entertainment platform, but also a part of helping farmers. Lastly, Fruitjoy's market targets a wide range of people, and through research data, it is found that users of different age groups have different preferences, which provides more references for Fruitjoy's positioning. Overall, Fruitful's interface design focuses on user experience, based on the design principles of simplicity, clarity and aesthetics, and through continuous adjustments and improvements, Fruitful can achieve a high level of user interaction and functionality (See Fig. 4).

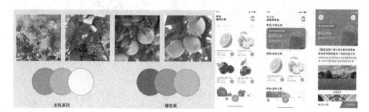

Fig. 4. Interface design and color matching

4.2 Interaction Design

The core principle of Fruitjoy's interface design is simplicity and ease of use, guiding the user's attention and reducing the burden of memory through an interface design that conforms to visualisation rules. In the UI structure design, a personalised model is used to classify information through ordered units and visual hierarchies so that users can quickly find the required logo. The design of interface elements pays attention to the wholeness and unity of the text, avoiding the use of excessive styles and sizes, as well as the use of respective specifications on iOS and Android systems. The overall page layout design should focus on the mastery of the main tone, the use of a layout that meets the principles of aesthetics, to maintain the density of the elements, to achieve the effect of the overall layout. In the choice of interface size, consider the monitor size and resolution to avoid exceeding the screen range and the need to increase the scroll bar. In the graphic design, common shapes are used to make the pattern shape round, soft and symbolic. Text layout and editorial design should focus on the collocation of text, fonts, colours and words to achieve the best effect of aesthetics and transmission of information. The design of pictures should consider the visual impact, so that the illustrations and text, text and pictures complement each other, enriching the artistic design expression. The mall interface adds cartoon fruit elements, provides shopping cart and shop functions, and users and sellers can make comments and replies. The communication interface adopts a minimalist approach, which is convenient for users to view fruit pictures and promotes detailed communication between users. The design concept was to provide entertainment experience at the beginning, and later changed to bring user experience while achieving the goal of helping farmers and promoting the sales of agricultural products. For the market demographic, research shows that more people are willing to share the picking time with their lovers, so the interface and functions are designed accordingly for users of different age groups. The design of the map includes a route interface, which makes it easy for users to locate nearby orchards through positioning. In the colour design, green was chosen as the dominant colour to convey a vibrant atmosphere, while colourful colours were used to create a variety of effects (see Fig. 5).

Fig. 5. Usage mode

4.3 Gamification Design

Gamification design is a design strategy that can improve user engagement and experience. In the interface design of Fruitjoy, the addition of gamification elements can make users feel more enjoyable and interactive in the process of using it. Firstly, an interesting gamified interactive session is designed by combining the characteristics of picking AR. While sweeping the fruits, users can get information such as the introduction and ripeness of the fruits, and at the same time, they can also participate in small games, such as finding the treasure hidden in the orchard or unlocking special achievements. Completing game tasks can earn points or coupons, stimulating users' motivation and desire to explore. Secondly, a unique and interesting virtual tour guide character is designed by introducing tour guide IP elements. Tour guides can accompany users to browse the orchard and provide interesting stories, history and plant knowledge, while rewarding users with virtual gifts or tour guide-exclusive coupons when they complete specific tasks or reach a certain level, increasing user stickiness and loyalty. In addition, combined with user research data, different gamification designs can be customised according to the needs of users of different age groups. For example, for young users, more creative and challenging games can be designed; while for family users, games suitable for parent-child interaction can be designed to allow family members to participate together. In gamification design, focus on balancing the difficulty of the game, avoiding too complex or too simple, and ensuring that users can easily get started and enjoy the game process. At the same time, timely collection of user feedback, continuous optimisation of the game experience, to maintain the freshness and interest of the game. Finally, the gamification elements are organically combined with the functions of Fruitful Joy mall and communication interface, so that users can obtain asctual benefits or welfare in the process of the game, and enhance users' willingness to use Fruitful Joy and satisfaction. Through the above gamification design strategy, Fruitjoy can better attract users' attention, improve user experience, achieve closer interaction between users and the platform, and at the same time realise the goal of helping farmers, and build a more interesting and beneficial bridge between orchards and users. (see Fig. 6).

Fig. 6. Storyboard

5   Concluding Remarks

In this article, we aim to design and develop a mobile application called "Fruit Joy", which uses gamification and augmented reality technology to improve the efficiency and quality of picking agricultural products, and at the same time enhance user participation. Through the preliminary research, we gained an in-depth understanding of the actual situation of orchard picking activities and user needs, which provided an important foundation and guidance for the design and development of the application. In the user analysis, it is clear that "Fruit Joy" is suitable for a wide range of people, including gardeners, farmers, volunteers, family tourists, as well as urban residents and tourists.A detailed user needs analysis ensures that Fruit Joy can provide personalised services to different user groups, from orchard management to detailed information on picking activities, as well as a gamified experience. Combining picking with gamification is a key strategy in the design, and several gamification design elements are proposed, such as fruit sweeping game, tour guide IP, reward system, etc., aiming to improve user participation and interaction, and make the picking process more interesting. This design concept not only provides users with picking services, but also brings them an interesting entertainment experience, while achieving the goal of helping farmers.In the design strategy, the principles and techniques of interface design, interaction design and gamification design are emphasised. Through the reasonable use of colour, layout design, text layout, etc., we are committed to improving the user's ease of use and comfort. The change of design concepts, from the initial entertainment experience to the later combination of entertainment experience and helping farmers, has enabled "Fruitjoy" to achieve a high level of user interaction and functionality.

In the gamification design, we focus on balancing the difficulty of the game, and customise different gamification elements according to the age group of the users to ensure that the users can enjoy a pleasant experience during the game. Through the organic combination with the Fruitful Joy mall and the communication interface, it is hoped that users can obtain actual benefits and welfare in the game, and enhance their willingness to use "Fruitful Joy" and their loyalty. Through the design scheme of this paper, we are committed to creating an application that is both entertaining and achieving the goal of helping farmers. It is believed that "Fruit Joy" will bring users a new picking experience, and at the same time, establish a more interesting and useful connection between orchards and users, promote the sale of agricultural products, and realise the organic fusion of agriculture and science and technology. We look forward to "Fruitjoy" becoming a partner in users' life and injecting new vigour into the agricultural industry.

References

1. Zhang, T., Yang, Z., Gong, M.: Agricultural experience design strategy under gamification thinking. Pop. Liter. Art: Acad. Vers. (3), 2 (2019)
2. Li, Y., Wu, M., Pu, Y., et al.: The construction of digital agricultural game marketing model for poverty alleviation in characteristic industries-Taking Yunnan field investigation as an example. Agric. Libr. Inf. Sci. (2021)
3. Liu, D., Wen, T.: Research on agricultural gamification service design based on urban community space. Ind. Des. (4): 2 (2020)

4. Wang, J.: Research on Urban Agricultural Gamification Service Design for Commercial Space. Jiangnan University (2023)
5. Jia, X., Li, K.: Will farming in the future be as addictive as playing games? artificial intelligence will take the lead in the rise of agriculture. China Econ. Weekly (006), 74–75 (2021)
6. Li, Y., Wu, M., Pu, Y., Fan, Z.: The construction of digital agricultural game marketing model for poverty alleviation in characteristic industries-taking Yunnan field investigation as an example. Agric. Libr. Inf. Sci. **033**(004), 22–34 (2021)
7. Jie, C.: Pinduoduo joined hands with Chucheng to help the new consumption experience of agricultural products through gamification operation. China Sci. Technol. Wealth (2019)
8. Si, Z., Yu, D.: Research on the interactive design of rural news games in the communication scene of interactive ritual chain. Ind. Eng. Des. **4**(5), 15–22 (2022)
9. Pan, L.: The development and utilization of local resources in parent-child activities from the perspective of curriculum gamification. Exam. Weekly (45), 1–5 (2023)
10. Shang, J.: What is gamification?. China Inf. Technol. Educ. (08) 2015
11. Xi, Y.: Research on Gamification Service Design for Agricultural Tourism. Xihua University (2022)
12. Gong, M.: Research on service design strategy based on ecological agriculture. Public Art (06) (2018)
13. Zhang, B., Wan, J., Wen, X.: Comparison and experience reference of foreign agricultural tourism model. Agric. Econ. Issues **32**(05) (2011)
14. Pavlenko, T., Paraforos, D.S., Fenrich, D., et al.: Increasing adoption of precision agriculture via gamification: the farming simulator case. In: 13th European Conference on Precision Agriculture (2021)
15. Martin, J., Torres, D., Fernandez, A., et al.: Using citizen science gamification in agriculture collaborative knowledge production. In: International Conference on Human-Computer Interaction. ACM (2018)
16. Kovács, T., Szilágyi, R., Várallyai, L.: The role of gamification in sustainable agricultural higher education. Bio-Econ. Agri-prod. (2021). https://doi.org/10.1016/B978-0-12-819774-5.00017-5
17. Tjernstrm, E., Lybbert, T.J., Hernández, R.F., et al.: Learning by (virtually) doing: experimentation and belief updating in smallholder agriculture. J. Econ. Behav. Organ. **189**, 28–50 (2021)

Smart Digital Technology Driven Experience Design of Job Seeking Social Skills Training for University Students in Campus Scenarios via Business Model Innovation

Yixin Liu[✉] and Zhen Liu

School of Design, South China University of Technology, Guangzhou 510006, People's Republic of China
`yixinliu1004@126.com`

Abstract. The development and application of digital technology have led to changes in the employment structure and working style of the labor market, and the lower the density of interpersonal skills in the occupation, the easier it is to be replaced by artificial intelligence. However, emerging technological competitiveness drives innovation in user-centered business models creating more jobs. As such, smart digital technology-driven social skills training for university students in campus scenarios via business model innovation is conducive to mitigating the employment impact by the development of artificial intelligence, striking a balance between the objectives of technological development and stable employment. However, the current research lacks the exploration of the influence mechanism of smart digital technology and business model innovation on user experience at the theoretical level, which is necessary to investigate the structural relationship among experience design, business model innovation, and smart digital technology. In addition, at the application level, there is a lack of evaluation and feedback on user experience in the field of social skills training, as well as product and platform assistance in the social skills training experience process. Therefore, this paper aims to investigate the mode mechanism of social skills training experience driven by smart digital technology and business model innovation and design a new experience of job-hunting social skills training in campus scenarios.

Keywords: Smart digital technology · Campus scene · Social skills training · Social skill model · Experience design · User experience · Business model

1 Introduction

In the current era, great changes are being experienced in which interconnected societies are demanding new ways to reformulate society, human interactions, and education [1]. 77% of jobs in developing countries, including China, will be at risk of automation because of the development of smart city technology, resulting in huge volatility in the current labor market, such as millions of workers needing to change careers and work locations [2]. Researches express that the employment growth rate of occupation is positively correlated with the interpersonal skills required [3]. The social skills model suggests that enhancing social skills promotes good interpersonal relationships, which improves personal reception, processing, and expression skills by developing the perception of social stimuli and situations, cognitive processing of information, and appropriate responses in social situations [4]. Furthermore, the integration of smart city technology and business model innovation is considered to offer new perspectives to address problems of employment in the ever-evolving digital job market [5].

At present, attentions have been paid to the cultivation of middle school students' digital skills [6] and basic education [7]. Hence, how to improve university students' social skills in campus scenarios, combined with the smart city technology and business model factors, should be paid attention to by researchers. Therefore, this paper aims to explore the structural relationship between smart digital technology, experience design, and business model innovation; investigate the mode mechanism of social skills training experience driven by smart digital technology and business model innovation; design a new experience of job-hunting social skills training in campus scenarios, for which the following three questions (RQ) are addressed in this paper as research rationale (Fig. 1):

1. What is the structural relationship between smart digital technology, experience design, and business model innovation?
2. How can smart digital technology and business model innovation drive the social skills training experience?
3. How to transform theoretical mechanisms into practical application scenarios through design practice in campus scenarios?

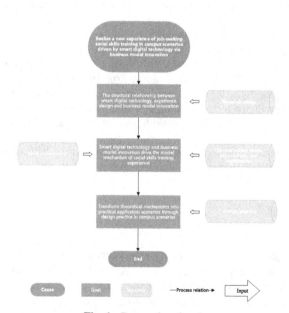

Fig. 1. Research rationale.

2 Method

Firstly, theoretical research through the methods of literature review and qualitative analysis has been carried out to determine the structural relationship between smart digital technology, experience design, and business model innovation. Secondly, a user interview, scene investigation, and statistical analysis have been conducted using affinity map and user portrait to explore the user's deep needs, expectations, and experiences, which suggest a mode mechanism of social skills training experience driven by smart digital technology and business model innovation. Finally, in design practice, a structured design method of the double diamond model is adopted to implement the user experience in the form of interaction between applications and actual products (Fig. 2).

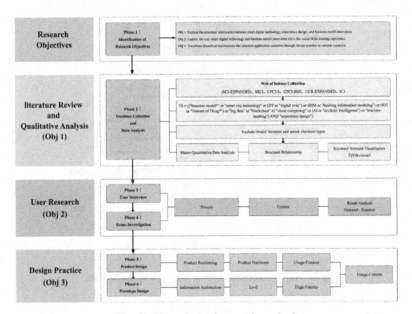

Fig. 2. Flow chart of research method.

3 Result

3.1 Literature Review and Qualitative Analysis

The data has been obtained from the Web of Science Core Collection that was imported into VOSviewer (1.6.20) software for co-analyzing the keywords to generate the corresponding cluster map by using the VOS clustering algorithm. In the network visualization generated by VOSviewer (1.6.20) as shown in Fig. 3, circles and labels make up a unit, units of various colors from different clusters, and various colors represent different research directions, respectively. The size of the node indicates how often the keyword appears, the larger the node, the more often the same keyword appears in different articles. The relationship between keywords is indicated by the distance between two nodes and the association is stronger the closer the distance. The width of line reveals how strongly the terms are related to one another.

The keyword co-occurrence network visualization of research connected to smart digital technology, experience design, and business model innovation is shown in Fig. 3, which has four clusters in different colors (yellow, blue, red, and green). Big data, artificial intelligence, machine learning, and the Internet of Things as a bridge between technology and experience design have received the most attention. Human-computer interaction has become a hot spot in this field, while service design and user research are the most focused parts of experience design.

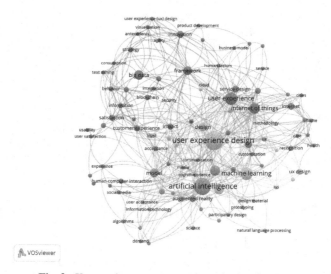

Fig. 3. Keyword co-occurrence network visualization.

3.2 User Research

This study provides insight into user needs through user interview and scene investigation. A total of 12 volunteers were interviewed and 4 representative users were selected for detailed content insight. Furthermore, user needs are deepened through the scene investigation with the participation of 15 volunteers.

User Interview. According to Fig. 4, the data was collected from primary user, the university students, who need to improve their social skills during job hunting or pre-job hunting, and the secondary users are personnel specialists responsible for recruitment and university staff in charge of graduate employment dispatch, which is used to obtain the competitiveness of college students in job search and employment scenarios based on social skills modeling by exploring their need for social skills in the job search stage. And the interview results are analyzed in the form of affinity map (Fig. 5). The results show that students with different personalities all show social intention and expect to participate in non-purposeful social activities, and enhance social ability and workplace competitiveness through activities. HR expresses concern about the lack of social skills among contemporary university students and says there is a lack of proper assessment mechanisms. The Employment Guidance Office of the university emphasizes the disconnection between the university and the market economy in the aspects of personnel training mode, training structure, and service strategy.

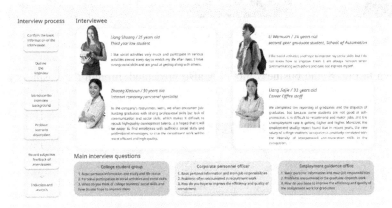

Fig. 4. Interview content.

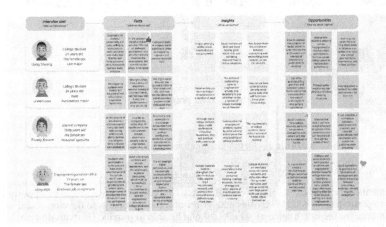

Fig. 5. Analysis of interview results.

Scene Investigation. This research further carries out scene investigation to explore the deep needs, expectations, and experiences of users and get more scientific and effective information feedback (Fig. 6).

Result Analysis. The results of user interview and scene investigation are later analyzed to create user portrait (Fig. 7) and transform them into design function points (Table 1).

Fig. 6. Scene investigation.

As shown in Fig. 8, the business model is also presented through the business model canvas.

Fig. 7. User portrait.

Table 1. Demand-function transformation

Demand	Function
How to enhance the motivation of university students to participate in social activities and make them realize the importance of social skills in the workplace?	Activity salon is considered to be opportunities for university students to develop social skills and be able to provide HR with diverse recruitment scenarios
How can university students develop their social skills by participating in various social activities?	Creating stories and role play enable university students to step back from their environment and think about their actions when necessary

(continued)

Table 1. (*continued*)

Demand	Function
How to enhance the interest of social activities and arouse the interest of university students to participate in more social activities?	AIGC, combined with game mechanics, is an important tool to increase fun and expand new social experiences for university students
How to feedback the status and performance of university students in social activities?	A realistic but safe environment based on the combination of verbal and non-verbal behaviors enables university students to train specific behaviors to adapt to socially challenging situations
How to promote enterprises, students and schools to form an organic connection between employment and entrepreneurship?	Appropriate incentive systems appeal to university student. At the same time, a rating system was implemented to reward participants with virtual currency to improve their performance

Fig. 8. Business model canvas.

3.3 Design Practice

The use environment, target user, product positioning, and product carrier are determined according to the results of qualitative analysis and user research. Results show that social skills of university students can be improved by the intelligent communication bracelet and holographic projection audio linkage. This design not only cultivates the social skills of social terror groups, but also meets the self-realization of social cattle groups, and finally enhances the employment competitiveness of university students.

Product Design. Figure 9 and Fig. 10 show intelligent communication bracelet and holographic projection audio respectively. Figure 11 and Fig. 12 show the product interactive display and product gesture display respectively.

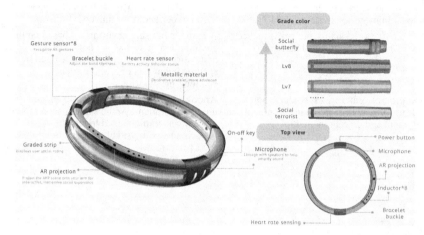

Fig. 9. Product hardware display.

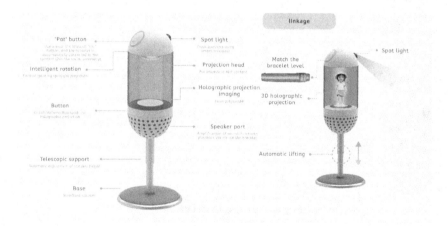

Fig. 10. Product hardware display.

Prototype Design. According to Fig. 13 and Fig. 14, APP consists of five sections: Home page, Scale detection, Bracelet status, Advanced intensive and Mine. "Home page" displays real-time playground activity status, and supports creating activities and viewing activity scenes. The "Scale detection" section can measure the level of personal social skills through the SSI scale. The "Bracelet status" board can monitor the user's heart rate in real-time, record the user's verbal and non-verbal information, and generate behavioral performance reports. The "Advanced intensive" section provides books and periodicals of different scenarios, different groups and different topics for users to learn.

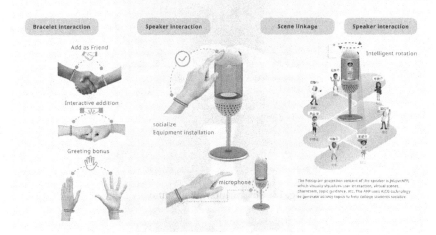

Fig. 11. Product interactive display.

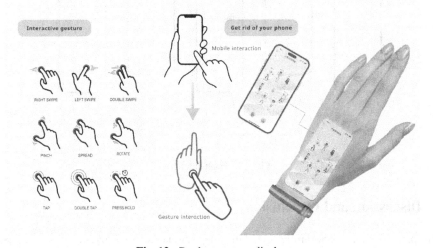

Fig. 12. Product gesture display.

"Mine" section displays personal information and allows you to view your level and task route.

Fig. 13. Information architecture.

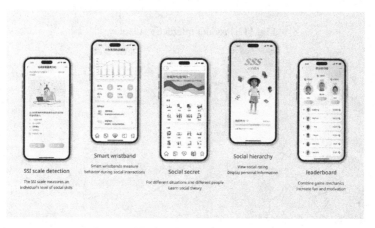

Fig. 14. High-fidelity.

4 Discussion and Conclusion

This paper reveals a panoramic view of the integration of smart digital technology, experience design, and business model innovation, which explores the structural relationship between smart digital technology, experience design, and business model innovation, as well as concludes the solutions that promote social skills training experience based on smart digital technology and business model innovation. Finally, the intelligent communication bracelet and holographic projection audio are put into practical application in campus scenarios.

The results show that smart digital technology and business model innovation can drive social skills training experience in four ways: behavioral rehearsal, corrective feedback, positive reinforcement, and weekly assignments. Meanwhile, business model innovation and smart digital technology can be used to enhance the user experience and describe the process, such as the activity scene of the campus activity salon, the activity content of creating stories and role-playing, the activity form of combining AIGC and game mechanism, the process of combining verbal and non-verbal activity diversity, and the grade assessment system in the campus social skills training. The campus activity salons provide university students a chance to practice their social skills and give businesses a variety of recruiting settings. Creating stories and role-playing activities enables university students to remain relatively independent in social situations and to consider their actions when appropriate. The integration of AIGC and game mechanics increases the fun and motivation of participants and creates new social experiences for the students. Verbal and nonverbal cues work together to provide a realistic and safe setting, in which college students can practice certain behaviors to deal with socially problematic situations. At the same time, appropriate incentive mechanisms should be included to maintain the participation of the students. In addition, to raise participant performance, a grade assessment system could be implemented using a virtual money reward system.

The research has some limitations. Firstly, there may be a sample bias as the study is based on a specific school or regional context, making it challenging to generalize the findings to other environments. Besides, the choice of research methods and data collection approaches can influence the study's conclusions, necessitating further validation and comparative research. Lastly, due to the sensitivity of business model innovation, the research could be influenced by commercial partners or stakeholders, introducing potential biases.

References

1. Carrasco-Sáez, J.L., Careaga Butter, M., Badilla-Quintana, M.G.: The new pyramid of needs for the digital citizen: a transition towards smart human cities. Sustainability **9**(12), 2258 (2017)
2. Brantner, C., Saurwein, F.: Covering technology risks and responsibility: automation, artificial intelligence, robotics, and algorithms in the media. Int. J. Commun. **15**, 5074–5098 (2021)
3. Evans, D., Mason, C., Chen, H., et al.: Accelerated demand for interpersonal skills in the Australian post-pandemic labour market. Nat. Hum. Behav. **8**, 32–42 (2024)
4. Beauchamp, M.H., Anderson, V.: SOCIAL: an integrative framework for the development of social skills. Psychol. Bull. **136**(1), 39 (2010)
5. Viriyasitavat, W., Anuphaptrirong, T., Hoonsopon, D.: When blockchain meets Internet of Things: characteristics, challenges, and business opportunities. J. Ind. Inf. Integr. **15**, 21–28 (2019)
6. Segredo, E., Miranda, G., León, C., Santos, A.: Developing computational thinking abilities instead of digital literacy in primary and secondary school students. In: Uskov, V.L., Howlett, R.J., Jain, L.C. (eds.) Smart Education and e-Learning 2016, pp. 235–245. Springer, Cham (2016). https://doi.org/10.1007/978-3-319-39690-3_21
7. Santos, T., Alves, P., Sá, S.: Learning in the context of digital technologies: what lessons can we learn from Covid-19 in basic education? In: Mesquita, A., Abreu, A., Carvalho, J.V., Pinto de Mello, C.H. (eds.) Perspectives and Trends in Education and Technology: Selected Papers from ICITED 2022, pp. 775–784. Springer, Singapore (2023). https://doi.org/10.1007/978-981-19-6585-2_69

Let Go of the Non-digital Past: Embracing the 4Rs for a New Life - Recallable, Relaxing, Repayable, and Reconnected Experiences

You Lyu[1], Jiayi Hu[1], Ziyi Wang[1], Jiaqing Xiong[1], Mingjun Liu[1], Hao Lyu[1], Xindi He[1], Jiayi Lu[1], Cheng Yong[1], Zhen Wang[1], Lijun Xu[1], Mengzhen Xiao[2(✉)], Taiyu Huang[2], and Ruonan Huang[1]

[1] Beijing Key Laboratory of Applied Experimental Psychology, National Demonstration Center for Experimental Psychology Education (Beijing Normal University), Faculty of Psychology, Beijing Normal University, Beijing 100875, China
[2] Department of China Digital Technology, The LEGO Group, Shanghai 200031, China
202328061029@mail.bnu.edu.cn

Abstract. With the arrival of the digital era, the traditional toy industry is encountering both new opportunities and challenges. While innovative digital play experiences strongly attract the Generation Z user group, the tactile and emotional connection offered by traditional physical toys cannot be completely abandoned. The toy industry has dived into digital transformation, seeking to merge traditional physical toys with digital elements, utilizing interactive methods like virtual reality (VR), augmented reality (AR), etc., to elevate the user experience of toy products. Building upon this groundwork, this study, employing the Human-Centered Design (HCD) process, has delineated four distinct user personas and Jobs-to-be-done (JTBD). The primary focus revolves around the essential 4Rs - Recallable, Relaxing, Replayable, and Reconnected, leading to inventive product design. The outcomes of this study showcase how, through Project-Based Learning (PBL) practices, user-driven design can be propelled, offering innovative insights for the future of the digital play experience in the toy industry.

Keywords: User eXperience · Human-Centered Design · Digital Play · The LEGO Toys · Generation Z · Interaction Design

1 Introduction

With the rapid evolution of media technology and artificial intelligence, our lifestyles and ways of interacting with the world have undergone a revolutionary transformation [1, 2]. People's needs, work methods, learning approaches, and even modes of creation are rapidly changing. We can now communicate with others, access information, learn, and even work anytime, anywhere through digital platforms. The widespread adoption of artificial intelligence has automated many repetitive tasks, freeing up more time for individuals to focus on creative endeavors. We have entered an era that redefines human interaction, learning, and creation through technological innovation. This shift continues to shape our lives, opening broader possibilities for the future.

A. Marcus et al. (Eds.): HCII 2024, LNCS 14716, pp. 128–140, 2024.
https://doi.org/10.1007/978-3-031-61362-3_10

In this context, the toy industry is also undergoing an unprecedented transformation. The emergence of entertainment forms such as electronic toys and virtual reality games poses both challenges and opportunities to the traditional toy industry [3, 4]. On one hand, these emerging forms of entertainment attract a large consumer base with their innovative technology and interactive experiences, gradually altering people's entertainment habits and purchasing behaviors. On the other hand, the traditional toy industry possesses the tactile and emotional connection of physical toys, something electronic toys and virtual reality games cannot replace. In this digital age, if traditional toy manufacturers wish to achieve further development and identify new growth points, "digital transformation" is undoubtedly worth exploring. The traditional toy industry needs to keep pace with the trends of the times, continually innovating and improving its products. By introducing technological elements and combining traditional toys with digitization, it can offer a more enriching, enjoyable, and interactive experience to meet consumer demands. The future form of toys is likely to be a fusion of traditional and digital toys.

In the process of digital transformation, the LEGO Group has explored various methods with its unique approach to play, including utilizing AR and VR technologies to enhance user experience. For example, "LEGO Hidden Side" employs AR technology, allowing users to scan physical LEGO models and overlay virtual elements to simultaneously perceive two different types of information, thereby activating hidden story elements. Leveraging technological innovation to increase product interactivity, comfort, fun, and sociability meets the emotional needs of Generation Z users [5, 6]. This helps them relax, alleviate stress, address social isolation, enhance a sense of belonging, and explore the endless value of play. The ideal future of digital transformation lies in finding a balance between traditional and modern, virtual and real, and continually benefiting from progress.

The purpose of this study is to explore how, amid the rapid development of digitization and technology, designing appropriate solutions that cater to the potential needs of Generation Z can impact the toy industry. In the fall semester of 2023, 20 transdisciplinary graduate students formed four teams to collaboratively complete a design task: designing games for Generation Z, with a focus on the interaction between people and products. We explored the social and connective aspects of interacting with the LEGO toys and contemplated the value of "play" through digital solutions. Simultaneously, through this research, we aim to provide crucial design and development opportunities for the Department of China Digital Technology (CDT). This study seeks to address the following questions:

- What are the characteristics of the target user groups?
- What are the typical user scenarios and journeys?
- What are the new design concepts to enable the playful experience?

2 Methodology

2.1 User Needs

In practical user research projects, desktop research often marks the initial step, providing insights into the future trends and user demographics of the research project [7–9]. Desktop research can be broadly divided into three steps—finding and collecting data, analyzing and organizing information, and summarizing key points in an output report. Our research aims to dive deep into the user characteristics and pain points of Generation Z LEGO toy players, along with the digital transformation achievements of the LEGO Group and other companies. To achieve this objective, we consulted various academic journals such as China National Knowledge Infrastructure (CNKI) and Google Scholar in online academic repositories. These resources offered an abundance of academic papers and research reports, facilitating a comprehensive understanding of the academic background and current research status related to the topic. However, relying solely on academic journals might not provide a holistic understanding of actual user phenomena and market dynamics.

We also referred to some mainstream industry reports from companies like iResearch and Aurora Mobile to gain further insights into industry research and real-time data. Additionally, we paid attention to some self-media and social platforms, such as Xiaohongshu (The Little Red Book) and others, where LEGO toy players share experiences and discussions, offering us more authentic and intuitive user feedback and market dynamics. Through these platforms, we gained insights into Generation Z users' profound memories during the LEGO building process, players' preferences in game themes and technological elements, as well as their engagement in community activities, individual building preferences, specific design elements such as music, stories, challenges, and more. The entire process of finding and collecting data, analyzing and organizing information, and summarizing key points in an output report in the user research phase has significantly aided us in understanding user needs and behaviors, along with market development trends.

2.2 Collection of User Needs

In this project, we conducted in-depth analysis and research on the Generation Z target group, observing the potential challenges and pain points they might encounter in daily life. We also conducted on-site investigations into the experiences that the LEGO toys provide for users in physical stores [10–14]. To assist observers in integrating information, we employed an observation framework due to the possibility of incomplete or omitted data during the observation process. Through brainstorming, we derived usage scenarios from refined requirements, forming the preliminary PEOMS framework to document the research results of user interaction behaviors.

Subsequently, we collected and analyzed user labels such as social attributes, lifestyle habits, and consumption behaviors to depict a virtual user persona. This user persona is derived from real users but represents different types based on variations in behavioral concepts, organized together to form user personas of that type. This allows us to understand and track changes in the demands of each user type, analyze the reasons behind these changes, and make precise positioning.

By accurately defining users, we can update products more purposefully, achieve more emotionally driven designs, and uncover unmet user pain points. Through multi-dimensional user segmentation, we aim to provide corresponding product services, discard pseudo-needs and impractical scenarios, and truly discover the users' points of need when using the product. Based on this, we design the LEGO toys that align with the demands of being "Recallable, Relaxing, Replayable, and Reconnected." Recallable—simultaneously addressing practicality and emotional value, bringing more touchable moments of reminiscence to Generation Z; Relaxing—alleviating stress in the work and life of Generation Z; Replayable—enhancing the playability of the LEGO toys, increasing loyalty and repurchase rates for Generation Z; Reconnected—strengthening connections with friends through the LEGO toys, mitigating the loneliness that Generation Z may face during the transition from school to the workplace.

2.3 Analysis of User Needs

Following the interviews, we organized the gathered information by refining user needs through steps such as integrating synonyms, eliminating duplicate requirements, and standardizing concise language. Using the Affinity Diagram method, we classified user needs based on certain connections, forming secondary functional requirements. Subsequently, we categorized them into primary functional requirements based on each classification and assigned names to these requirements. We then employed the JTBD method to explore critical tasks (Jobs) in specific scenarios [15]. After summarizing by each team, we established the final 4R model: Recallable, Relaxing, Replayable, Reconnected. We listed the desired effects under each Job. Simultaneously, using the Flower Map, we contemplated potential solutions to address problems and the services that could fulfill user needs, generating numerous innovative ideas. Through the C-Box matrix, we categorized a multitude of design concepts and assessed their innovativeness and feasibility. Eventually, we selected ideas located in the first quadrant of the axis, indicating high feasibility and innovativeness, as the direction for future product design.

Subsequently, we created the current journey map of the product, analyzing pain points and touchpoints in the emotional curve during the current user's process of assembling the LEGO toys. Issues such as easily lost assembly instructions and difficulty in finding assembly components and lack of replay value after completion were identified. Based on this, we derived a vision journey map of the user's entire process and emotional states when using our designed the LEGO toys, integrating the expected functionalities and keywords derived from the C-Box. With this foundation, we conducted conceptual design, creating an approximate prototype for future products and outlining the process flow when using the product through functional analysis.

2.4 Iteration of User Needs

After completing the prototype design, we proceeded to create a low-fidelity user interface and utilized the UEQ, an economical and efficient questionnaire tool, for product usability testing [16–18]. The assessment covered pragmatic quality, reflecting the basic usability and user-friendliness of the LEGO prototype design, and hedonic quality, reflecting the enjoyment and perceived additional value provided by the LEGO prototype design. Each project team recruited 12 visitors matching the user personas for testing. After collecting user responses, descriptive statistical analysis was conducted using the UEQ data analysis tool to identify strengths and issues in the designed digital LEGO toys.

Combining user feedback from usability testing and the results of data analysis, targeted optimizations were applied to the low-fidelity interface, continually iterating to form a high-fidelity user interface more aligned with real usage scenarios. For instance, the team focusing on "Replayable" as the design core achieved scores above average in attractiveness, transparency, and satisfaction but below average in efficiency, reliability, and stimulation. This indicates that the low-fidelity user interface design by the project team is straightforward and user-friendly but lacks fun and efficiency. In subsequent iterative improvements, emphasis are placed on enhancing visual interface interactions and diversifying functionalities.

3   Results

After completing the entire workflow, each of the four teams identified their respective JTBDs and confirmed their key JTBDs: 4Rs—Recallable, Relaxing, Replayable, and Reconnected. Table 1 presents the personas and JTBDs selected by each team. The following sections showcase each team's user personas, usage scenarios, specific JTBDs, and their respective solutions.

Table 1. Mapping of the teams, personas, and JTBDs of the results.

Team	Persona	Key JTBDs
1	Office Workers, 26–28	Making the LEGO toys a means of relaxation for themselves
2	Young Professionals, 22–25	Addressing loneliness, providing companionship, and offering emotional value
3	College Students, 18–22	Replayable value: Using new technology to keep the LEGO toys constantly fresh
4	Young Female Professionals, 22–26	Simplifying the setup of my rented space, providing a sense of home convenience

3.1   Gap Day

The team selected the research target as Generation Z office workers aged 26–28. This demographic, after a week of hard work, eagerly seeks relaxation during the weekends. According to the research findings, they prefer lightweight and immersive relaxation methods that offer a brief escape from reality, such as watching short videos, playing games, watching movies, and TV series. Office workers generally believe that assembling the LEGO toys requires a significant amount of time and effort, typically engaging in such activities only during long holidays like the Spring Festival or National Day, rather than incorporating it into their daily relaxation routines. Therefore, the team's primary research focus is on making LEGO toy assembly more effortless and increasing its immersive experience.

After conducting interviews with users, the team performed affinity analysis and identified 5 JTBDs: (1) Assembling the LEGO toys at home should be easy to understand at a glance; (2) Assembling the LEGO toys at home should also become a form of relaxation; (3) Experiencing richer product content while assembling the LEGO toys; (4) Enjoying the LEGO toys should come with comprehensive services; (5) Assembling the LEGO toys should also showcase my ideas.

In response to these 5 JTBDs, the team brainstormed and focused on generating the final product concept: using AR glasses and motion-sensing devices to help users alleviate assembly fatigue and enhance the immersive experience. Users can see virtual assembly instructions through AR glasses, enter storyline experiences related to the product after completing a stage, and engage in corresponding motion-sensing activities within the plot. After completing the assembly, a personalized assembly poster and corresponding digital collectibles are generated (see Fig. 1).

The team's value innovation lies in: (1) Focusing on hidden user pain points: While the LEGO toys are a form of entertainment, the actual user experience reveals that assembling the LEGO toys does not provide a relaxing effect; (2) Making the LEGO toys a genuine relaxation method for Generation Z office workers: Adding motion-sensing interaction during assembly, allowing users to relax both physically and mentally without compromising the assembly experience; (3) Enriching the LEGO toy assembly experience: Adding storyline elements during assembly to immerse users in the experience.

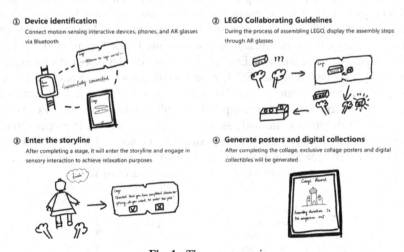

Fig. 1. The user scenario.

3.2 Rhapsody Pack

The team's research focuses on young professionals from Generation Z, aged 22–25, who enjoy playing with the LEGO toys during their leisure time. Through research, it was found that their most significant challenge is the shift in interpersonal relationships. College friends are scattered across the country, and there are few close friends in their current city. Interactions with colleagues are generally limited. Therefore, the team's primary research direction is to address the "loneliness" of this group, improve their interpersonal relationships, and provide an entertaining way to alleviate stress through the LEGO toys.

After conducting interviews with real users, the team used affinity analysis to extract information from the interviews, refine user needs, and transform them into product requirements. They ultimately identified 5 JTBDs: (1) Provide reusable components and replaceable parts; (2) Offer various gameplay options for both self-entertainment and social play with friends; (3) Provide personified emotional support, companionship, and the ability to communicate with friends; (4) While adding online features, the core remains the offline assembly experience; (5) Provide a community sharing platform, enabling users to find friends with similar interests.

In brainstorming sessions to fulfill these 5 JTBDs, the team envisioned functional features that meet product requirements (see Fig. 2): standardized format for functional plugins, customizable installation for a more enjoyable experience; two gameplay modes – solo and connected with friends – to meet different needs; mood detection and proactive real-time interaction for a more humane companionship, addressing loneliness; retaining the basic assembly mode while adding functional plugins for free combination, along with appearance upgrade packs and more iterative features; an auxiliary online app to help players find more friends in the "fantasy world."

The team's value innovation lies in: (1) Emphasizing physical interaction, where users can experience companionship by interacting with smart physical toys, making the LEGO toys feel like friends, providing companionship to solve loneliness after a tiring day at work; (2) Extending the joy of LEGO toy assembly: In contrast to current LEGO toy assembly, the team's designed assembly marks the beginning of a second interactive experience. The finished LEGO toy is not just a display piece but an interactive companion toy; (3) Combining the LEGO toy design with an online app, allowing users to explore more features, entertainment modes, and make new friends with similar interests, improving their interpersonal relationships; (4) A multi-modal interactive LEGO toy to enhance the user experience. In mode selection, users can engage in games through motion interaction, voice interaction, and physical LEGO pieces. The smart companion LEGO toy can also monitor user emotions in real-time and provide proactive care, making it more like a user's partner compared to other smart assistants.

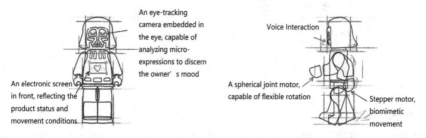

Fig. 2. The user scenario.

3.3 Play House

For college students aged 18–22, the challenge arises when they lose interest in the LEGO toys after completing a set. Most of the play value of the LEGO toys is confined to the initial assembly process, and once it is completed, the interest wanes. Users attempt to address this dilemma by using the completed the LEGO toys as decorations or by disassembling and reassembling them to experience it again. However, these approaches have drawbacks like fragility and a decrease in enjoyment, and they do not fundamentally solve the problem. Therefore, when these students play with the LEGO toys in their personal space during free time, they need a lower economic burden and higher immersion to keep the LEGO toys fresh.

After conducting user interviews, the team identified 5 JTBDs: (1) Replayable value: Use new technology to always keep the LEGO toys fresh; (2) Controllable investment: Play with the LEGO toys in leisure time without worrying about economic burden; (3) Exclusive process, shared results: Share my achievements after completing the LEGO toys without disturbance; (4) Diverse and enjoyable gaming experience: Have fun playing games during leisure time; (5) Desire to repurchase: Always make me want to buy another toy.

The team designed a set of AR-based interactive storytelling games to enhance the user experience. In the team's designed app, users can scan specific LEGO toy sets to unlock stories and receive prompts to reshape the scene before advancing the storyline (see Fig. 3).

The team's value innovation lies in: (1) Increasing replayability: By combining storytelling games and reshaping the LEGO toys, they address the issue of the LEGO toys losing interest once assembled, promoting environmental themes and increasing reuse; (2) Enhancing play experience: Utilizing VR and storytelling games to enhance the

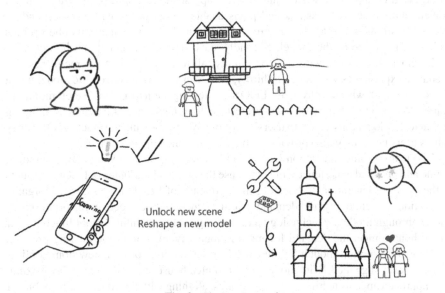

Unlock new scene
Reshape a new model

Fig. 3. The user scenario.

overall play experience of the LEGO toys after assembly; (3) Edu-tainment: The design can easily integrate with educational content, aiding students in learning through play.

3.4 Recallable Toys

This team turned its focus to young female professionals from Generation Z, aged 22–26, who have recently entered the workforce. Having left their campuses and hometowns to work in different cities, these individuals face the challenge of frequent relocation due to unpredictable circumstances. They often find themselves in shared living spaces, with an average area of around 15 square meters. Limited physical space, coupled with a lack of proper planning, leads them to frequently purchase storage boxes of inappropriate sizes, resulting in the inconvenience of frequent returns. Additionally, being away from home, these young professionals experience intense feelings of loneliness. Through research, the team identified that this target user group desires effective guidance for organizing and storing belongings, enabling them to quickly create a comfortable living environment, fostering a sense of warmth and belonging. Consequently, "recallable" became the emotional theme for this team.

After a series of design tools and deductions, the team derived five JTBD points: (1) Practical value: I can always find a reasonable arrangement for space within a short time when moving; I can always make my new home look better and more interesting; I can find and compare home supplies that meet my psychological price within a few minutes; (2) Preserving memories: I can often communicate with like-minded people after moving and preserve memories of the old house; (3) Personalized customization: I can always find decoration solutions that suit my personal style and can be linked to preferred IPs.

The solution proposed by this team is an app with three main functions. Firstly, based on AI ranging and modeling technology, the app scans real spaces, generates virtual models, automatically measures and plans usable areas, and provides corresponding storage solutions integrated into the model (see Fig. 4). Users can arrange their rooms under the guidance of the model. Secondly, each new home model can be uploaded to the cloud and shared with the community, allowing users to leave memories and exchange experiences with others. Thirdly, users can choose to convert the model into a proportionally downsized physical LEGO toy, allowing them to assemble their miniature homes. Recognizing that "a person's greatest wealth is memories," this team, by applying digital technology, fully caters to users' emotions. While meeting the practical efficiency values users need, they also provide high emotional and enjoyable value.

The team's value innovation lies in: (1) Enhancing practical value: By combining online and physical experiences, they increase the practical attributes of LEGO products in the eyes of Generation Z, boosting the frequency of LEGO toy usage; (2) Organic integration of technology and demand: From a functional perspective, restoring rented houses through modeling technology and creating exclusive online layout functions for rented houses meet the demand for more rational layouts during the moving process; (3) New consumption model: While experiencing the creation of a new home online, users can exchange the LEGO model of their rented house in proportionate downsizing. This approach appeals to high-spending groups, aligning with the consumption habits of contemporary young people, potentially boosting sales, intensifying brand effects, and generating profits for the enterprise's long-term development.

Fig. 4. The user scenario.

4   Discussion and Conclusions

Through the analysis above, we have identified various scenarios and personas facing Generation Z, including university students and young professionals entering the workforce. The primary pain points for Generation Z, such as university students and young professionals, revolve around feelings of loneliness and exhaustion. The opportunity lies in their high acceptance of digital products and their willingness to experience innovative solutions. Analyzing their journey map in using the LEGO toys reveals that the major pain points are weak replayability, a lack of ease, and limited interactivity, which are crucial aspects for us to address in our design. Based on this information, we aim to enhance the LEGO Group's user experience by introducing new design concepts that address these issues, incorporating AR technology, sensor-based interaction, fusion and reshaping, and miniature models.

4.1   Feedback from the LEGO Group

All four teams presented their projects at the LEGO Group report meeting. During the presentation, the LEGO Group experts fully recognized the achievements of the project teams, acknowledging their creativity and implementation capabilities in addressing product issues and improvements. They commended the research and design approach focused on the pain points of the target users, considering it highly effective in ensuring product design that meets the specific needs of users. Understanding user expectations and needs through an in-depth analysis of their pain points allows for effective positioning of product features and characteristics.

Each team designed products that can contribute to solving user pain points, signifying that the products are not only innovative but also practical, providing valuable solutions in users' daily lives. This is expected to enhance the market acceptance and competitiveness of the products. The experts emphasized the potential of the projects, believing that these innovative methods and iterative adjustments would contribute to improving product competitiveness and user satisfaction.

The LEGO Group shared their perspectives and recommendations. Regarding the four theme reports, they expressed that our product designs well encompass the 4Rs: addressing the pain point of moving for modern young people, transforming previous furniture arrangements into LEGO miniature models effectively makes it "Recallable"; focusing on weekend entertainment for working individuals, combining the LEGO toys with AR not only enhances immersion but also achieves true "Relax" through sensor-based interaction; the inherent disposability of LEGO toy assembly is addressed by the potential for "Replay" through fusion and reshaping; given that most of Generation Z has just entered the workforce and has not found a sense of belonging, the way friends become the LEGO toys for interaction makes "Reconnected" more heartwarming. They provided suggestions for refining each project, such as changing the concept of the Recallable Toys mini-program to an app for better data support in modeling; integrating our ideas with the LEGO toys' existing Builder application for Gap Day to more easily and diversely meet user needs; enhancing virtual reality technology for a better immersive experience in the Rhapsody Pack; and finding suitable ways to shorten the user wait time for reshaping in Play House to ensure real improvements in sustainability for the product.

4.2 What if We Start All Over

Based on the feedback from the LEGO Group and the experience gained during the practice of PBL, we are reconsidering our project with the question: what if we start all over?

Our success in uncovering user pain points and conducting research and design based on this orientation, along with the positive feedback from the LEGO Group, suggests that we should continue to adhere to this research method. Further exploration of user groups and needs is crucial. For instance, considering the diverse span of LEGO toy users from children to Generation Z, prioritizing target users is essential to accurately focus on user pain points. In terms of user needs, we have learned from interviews that user demands can sometimes be ambiguous. Thus, diving deeper into understanding user pain points, aligning various pain points expressed by users, and making their needs clear is vital. This ensures that the solutions obtained are human-centered, meeting actual user needs.

Considering the improvement suggestions from the LEGO Group, we should strive to minimize additional costs for users during the product design process. Leveraging existing products for design improvements or feature integration can make new products more accessible and user-friendly. Additionally, reducing the time users spend waiting would lower their time costs. Throughout the process, the strategic use of various tools is crucial. Utilizing tools such as videos and visual presentations in product concept design and progress reports can effectively convey our design ideas to users. Given another opportunity, we aim to complete the project more efficiently and with higher quality.

4.3 Prospects

As the era progresses, there are various future trends in the digital transformation of the LEGO toys. The LEGO Group experts emphasize the importance of continuous attention to user needs and market trends to ensure product alignment with the market. They continuously explore methods to reduce resource waste and environmental impact, integrating these considerations into future product design to maintain sustainability while meeting market demands. In terms of sustainability, future considerations involve making all packaging sustainable and introducing new bio-based materials made from bio-polyethylene components. This initiative aims to reduce plastic pollution, aligning with the environmental keywords in the United Nations Sustainable Development Goals.

In the future digital transformation plan for the LEGO toys, greater consideration can be given to integrating technology with sustainability goals. Increased investment in sustainability can accelerate development, aligning with social responsibility initiatives.

Regarding advancing quality education, the LEGO Group provides hands-on STEM and STEAM courses, using the building process of LEGO bricks to inspire children's learning interests and creativity. Future considerations include incorporating technology into classrooms to provide students with a richer and more engaging learning experience. Integration of VR, AR, and holographic projection can expand course content from traditional two-dimensional spaces to more three-dimensional, immersive learning environments. By blending LEGO bricks with virtual graphics, students can experience real-world scenarios in various STEM and STEAM fields, interact with virtual elements in real classrooms, enhancing their understanding of subject concepts, stimulating creativity, and imagination.

The LEGO Group's digital transformation not only focuses on meeting market demands but also actively addresses environmental protection, sustainable social responsibility, and development aligned with the United Nations Sustainable Development Goals. This strategic approach not only propels the company's sustainable development but also makes a positive contribution to future developments in society, the environment, and education.

References

1. Skilton, M., Hovsepian, F.: The 4th Industrial Revolution. Springer, Heidelberg (2018). https://doi.org/10.1007/978-3-319-62479-2
2. Ai, M., et al.: How can BOLE identify, cultivate, and judge user experience (UX) talents? inspiring and designing the playful experience of tomorrow. In: Marcus, A., Rosenzweig, E., Soares, M.M. (eds.) Design, User Experience, and Usability: 12th International Conference, DUXU 2023, Held as Part of the 25th HCI International Conference, HCII 2023, Copenhagen, Denmark, July 23–28, 2023, Proceedings, Part I, pp. 16–26. Springer, Cham (2023). https://doi.org/10.1007/978-3-031-35699-5_2
3. Miller, C.H.: Digital Storytelling 4e: A Creator's Guide to Interactive Entertainment. CRC Press, Boca Raton (2019)
4. Yuen, S.C.Y., Yaoyuneyong, G., Johnson, E.: Augmented reality: an overview and five directions for AR in education. J. Educ. Technol. Dev. Exchange **4**(1), 11 (2011)
5. Fan, A., Shin, H.W., Shi, J., Wu, L.: Young people share, but do So differently: an empirical comparison of peer-to-peer accommodation consumption between millennials and generation Z. Cornell Hosp. Q. **64**(3), 322–337 (2023)

6. Xin, X., et al.: X thinking in the experience economy era: 23 personas that identify generation z interaction qualities. Creat. Innov. Entrepre. **74**, 86–94 (2023)

7. Visser, F.S., Stappers, P.J., Van der Lugt, R., Sanders, E.B.: Contextmapping: experiences from practice. CoDesign **1**(2), 119–149 (2005)

8. Norman, D.A.: Design for a Better World: Meaningful, Sustainable, Humanity Centered. MIT Press, Cambridge (2023)

9. Liu, W., Lee, K.P., Gray, C.M., Toombs, A.L., Chen, K.H., Leifer, L.: Transdisciplinary teaching and learning in UX design: a program review and AR case studies. Appl. Sci. **11**(22), 10648 (2021)

10. Kokotsaki, D., Menzies, V., Wiggins, A.: Project-based learning: a review of the literature. Improv. Sch. **19**(3), 267–277 (2016)

11. Desmet, P.M., Xue, H., Xin, X., Liu, W.: Demystifying emotion for designers: a five-day course based on seven fundamental principles. Adv. Des. Res. **1**(1), 50–62 (2023)

12. Wu, X., Liu, W., Jia, J., Zhang, X., Leifer, L., Hu, S.: Prototyping an online virtual simulation course platform for college students to learn creative thinking. Systems **11**(2), 89 (2023)

13. Bullock, B., Learmonth, C., Davis, H., Al Mahmud, A.: Mobile phone sleep self-management applications for early start shift workers: a scoping review of the literature. Front. Public Health **10**, 936736 (2022)

14. Desmet, P., Hekkert, P.: Framework of product experience. Int. J. Des. **1**(1), 57–66 (2007)

15. Liu, W., et al.: Designing interactive glazing through an engineering psychology approach: Six augmented reality scenarios that envision future car human-machine interface. Virt. Real. Intell. Hardw. **5**(2), 157–170 (2023)

16. Schrepp, M., Hinderks, A., Thomaschewski, J.: Design and evaluation of a short version of the user experience questionnaire (UEQ-S). Int. J. Interact. Multimedia Artif. Intell. **4**(6), 103–108 (2017)

17. Zhu, D., Wang, D., Huang, R., Jing, Y., Qiao, L., Liu, W.: User interface (UI) design and user experience questionnaire (UEQ) evaluation of a to-do list mobile application to support day-to-day life of older adults. Healthcare **10**(10), 2068 (2022)

18. Zhu, Y., Tang, G., Liu, W., Qi, R.: How post 90's gesture interact with automobile skylight. Int. J. Hum.-Comput. Interact. **38**(5), 395–405 (2022)

Models for the Assessment of Stimulus Conditions Favoring Harm and Excessive Loads in *Home Office* Environments

Manuela Mello Fernandes[1]([✉]) [iD], Elisângela Vilar[2,3] [iD], and Lourival Costa Filho[1] [iD]

[1] Centro de Artes e Comunicação, Universidade Federal de Pernambuco,
Av. Prof. Moraes Rego, Cidade Universitária, 50670-901 Recife, PE, Brasil
{manuela.fernandes,lourival.costa}@ufpe.br
[2] CIAUD, Research Centre for Architecture, Urbanism and Design, Lisbon School of
Architecture, Universidade de Lisboa, Rua Sá Nogueira, Polo Universitário do Alto da Ajuda,
1349-063 Lisboa, Portugal
ebpvilar@edu.ulisboa.pt
[3] ITI- LARSyS, Universidade de Lisboa, Rua Sá Nogueira, 1349-063 Lisboa, Portugal

Abstract. Seeking to connect the knowledge of Environmental Psychology and Ergonomics of the Built Environment to provide guidelines to assist home office projects, this article presents the preliminary results of the first stage of the doctoral research conducted at UFPE in Brazil, in collaboration with FAUlisboa in Portugal. This research aimed to formulate an assessment model for the environmental conditions that promote discomfort and excessive loads in home office environments. To achieve this, the study considered the aspects of privacy control, biophilia, office clutter, and coherence (achieved through reduced contrast). The empirical investigation in this initial stage, structured through Facet Theory, employed the Multiple Sorting Procedure to collect data from 58 Brazilians and 45 Portuguese participants. The data were analyzed using the multidimensional scaling technique of Similarity Structure Analysis with the aid of the computer program HUDAP (Hebrew University Data Analysis Package) computational program. The empirical results revealed that the home office environment with a dedicated workspace, privacy control, the presence of biophilia, the absence of office clutter, and minimal to moderate contrast, is associated with conditions that promote the reduction of excessive loads and perceived state anxiety in the investigated environments. Furthermore, there was partial consensus in the majority of results between the two groups under study.

Keywords: home office · ergonomics of built environment · facet theory · environmental harm

1 Introduction

During the COVID-19 pandemic, both companies and schools had to halt their in-person operations, adapting to remote work. Activities started being carried out from the homes of employees and students, adopting the home office system. Although this type of work

© The Author(s), under exclusive license to Springer Nature Switzerland AG 2024
A. Marcus et al. (Eds.): HCII 2024, LNCS 14716, pp. 141–157, 2024.
https://doi.org/10.1007/978-3-031-61362-3_11

offers more flexibility, allowing daily tasks to be carried out and providing more time with family, if the home office environment is poorly designed, it can affect working conditions and, in turn, its users.

According to Xiao et al. [1] highlights that working in poorly structured environments and for long hours can cause discomfort and dissatisfaction regarding the quality of the work environment, due to the lack of aesthetic and environmental comfort. With the home office, the line between work and personal life becomes blurred, and having a clear separation between these two dimensions (i.e., work and personal life) is crucial to creating the perception of a defined work environment and the activities carried out. in it, as highlighted by Moser [2]. This can lead to overwork by employees, without defined time limits, resulting in unpaid overtime, as observed by Xiao et al. [1]. Additionally, factors such as a lack of technological skills and familiarity with the virtual world can also pose challenges for adapting to remote work, as pointed out by Elliot & Bibi [3].

Therefore, it is assumed that home office environments require greater attention due to environmental stimuli that can harm users, such as multitasking, distractions, and other factors that may affect privacy control, as well as emotional instability, stress, and anxiety, thereby damaging human performance and behavior.

Although home offices have always existed, the COVID-19 pandemic has heightened conflicts related to working and living in the same space, so that scrutiny of the home office environment has gained prominence. Therefore, this is an opportune moment to study these issues.

Thus, the goal of this article is to present preliminary data from a larger research project currently being developed in the Graduate Program in Design at the Federal University of Pernambuco, in collaboration with the Faculty of Architecture at the University of Lisbon, as part of a doctoral thesis. The overarching goal is to propose a conceptual procedure for evaluating excessive and potentially harmful burdens in home office environments. The specific objectives include: identifying facets related to environmental stimulus conditions that contribute to harmfulness and excessive burdens in home office environments (DEFINE VARIABLES); examining the relationship between these facets; testing the effects of these facets on harmfulness and excessive burdens, as well as on anxiety levels of home office users (VALIDATE MODEL); conducting a comparative study between two population groups in Brazil and Portugal (TRANSCULTURAL TEST).

2 Methodology

Aiming to propose a model for evaluating the conditions of environmental stimuli, which favor harmfulness and excessive loads in home offices, this phase of research adopted as a basis the Facet Theory, created and developed by Louis Guttman in the mid-1950s ([4–6]), also relying on the "objectified evaluation of the place", addressed by Canter [7].

According to Shey (1978, p. 6) [8] Louis Guttman defined Facet Theory (TF) as "The general hypothesis that, in the long run, an optimal strategy for developing laws is the specification of certain formal roles for facets in a mapping sentence […]".

To Canter [9], the facet approach, when combined with appropriate procedures (Multidimensional Scaling – MDS), provides the basis for finding hidden structures in qualitative data. Among the multidimensional techniques most associated with facet analysis, Similarity Structure Analysis (SSA) stands out.

TF can also be characterized as a metatheoretical procedure, as it is a hybrid method between methodology and theory itself, which means that it offers principles to outline research for the systematic collection of data, as well as a formal reference framework that facilitates the development of theories [6].

Its use initially involves the identification of the different concepts or dimensions that outline the research, coming from literature or on-site explorations [10, 11]. This step consists of establishing hypotheses, finding the facets, which are elements that correspond to the classifications of variables regarding the thematic aspect of the empirical research, and defining the elements that creates them, meaning, identifying the variables that will be researched. Subsequently, it presents a variety of data analysis methods and, finally, allows hypotheses to be expressed, which can be tested empirically and thus validate them or not [6].

Regarding facets, Bilsky [6] states that they can be summarized into three main types. The first type of facet refers to the sample population (population facet). The second type covers the content of the researched variables (content facet) and, together with the facet of the population addressed, defines the domain of this research. The third type describes the possible responses in this field of research (range facet). Each facet represents a conceptual category, made up of subcategories of elements to be researched. Every phenomenon studied can have as many categories or facets as the researcher desires [10], therefore, the Facet Theory (TF) can be seen as the hypothesis of the empirical structure [12].

Thus, different aspects of people's experience with a certain content can be summarized through a mapping sentence, which describes the components of the research and the way they are experienced by the participants. The mapping sentence, therefore, defines the specific research [6, 13].

Typically, there are three content facets for environmental evaluation, each one representing a component of the place investigated: referent, focus, level. The first facet defines what refers to the experience and exposes the different aspects on which people base their assessments; the focus facet considers that there are essential and peripheral elements, and that people respond to general or specific questions differently, but it is the general questions that represent the synthesis of the experience.

The focus modulates the referent of the experience, therefore, it depends on the referent of the experience and the type of place being evaluated; the level facet considers the existence of the environmental scale, which interferes in the evaluation of spaces, for example, a residence has bedrooms, living rooms, kitchens and so on, each of these rooms represents a different level [10, 13, 14]. The content facet combined with the population facet (people being investigated) forms the research domain.

Regarding the variables to be analyzed, the dependent variables are the participants' preferences in relation to scenes from home office environments, as well as the participants' emotional responses in relation to these spaces.

As for the independent variables, there are scenes considered positive in the sense of reducing excessive stimulus loads and perceived anxiety and negative ones being those that favor excessive stimulus loads influencing perceived anxiety.

In this way, 4 phases were established for this stage. Starting with the Systematic Literature Review, followed by the definition of the mapping sentence, definition of stimulus elements and Results.

2.1 Sample

The conducted research is characterized as a field investigation of exploratory nature, employing non-probabilistic sampling. In this type of sampling, there was no predetermined determination of the number of participants or the percentage of reliability attributed to the collected data [15]. However, the population proposed to be evaluated in this research consists of two different types of individuals with an interest in the same home office environments. In the first group, Brazilians, and in the second group, Portuguese individuals, who work or have worked in home office settings, in order to identify if there is consensus in the results among the participants.

These groups were selected for this research due to the likelihood of having different perspectives on the same investigated environment. Therefore, it will be possible to assess different views on the same environmental characteristics, facilitating a cross-cultural test.

In total, 58 Brazilians and 45 Portuguese participants responded to this survey. The Brazilian group was predominantly composed of females (74.13%) and males (24.49%), with the majority having completed postgraduate education (41.37%) and undergraduate degrees (32.75%). The participants were aged between 28 and 37 years (41.37%), with a mean age of 31 (SD = 5.86).

As for the interviewed Portuguese participants, the majority were males (57.77%), followed by females (42.22%), with the majority having completed undergraduate education (46.66%), followed by completed postgraduate education (24.44%), and with an age range between 28 and 37 years (M = 30 SD = 5.75).

2.2 Systematic Literature Review

For such an approach, this research relied on studies in Environmental Ergonomics (EE), along with Environmental Psychology (EP), stemming from the interest of these two research areas in how people perceive and make decisions in the environments they inhabit (human-environment interaction). Drawing on a definition aligned with the focus of this study, Bessa and Moraes [16] assert that environmental ergonomics can be defined as the application of knowledge drawn from environmental psychology in the planning of the environment at any of its stages – before, during, or after occupation – with the aim of establishing parameters to be implemented in the space or evaluated after implementation. This assessment aims to understand its functionality, whether the project was conceived with ergonomic considerations or not.

It can also be said that EE is concerned with the development of psychosocial aspects, requiring attention to human perception and cognition, as well as people's judgments regarding built environments.

To better understand this subject of study (home office), we turned to conducting a systematic literature review as a strategy to analyze what has been addressed in research—both nationally and internationally—over the last two years regarding detrimental/harmful stimuli in home office environments.

Through this review, the following variables were identified: privacy control, which refers to the ability to isolate yourself or become accessible to others; biophilia, representing the presence of natural elements or scenes that resembles nature in the space; contrast, achieved through reduced coherence, allowing for better spatial readability at lower levels; office clutter, defined as the abundance of work-related objects making the environment disorderly; and emotional variables, such as anxiety, specifically in this study, state anxiety, which manifests in specific moments like interviews or task submissions. Therefore, these variables were selected as the foundation for this research due to their likely influence on the perception of conflicts in home office environments.

2.3 Mapping Sentence

Following the Facet Theory Metatheory, which proposes the definition of a structuring sentence, this phase aims to present the sentence established for the proposed research.

In this research, the facets were established as follows:

a) Population facet: represented by individuals who currently work or have worked in a remote work setting in Brazil and Portugal.
b) Level facet A| environmental scale: represented by environments dedicated to remote work, such as home offices, and non-dedicated environments, like living rooms and bedrooms. These locations were selected because they are commonly used for work-related tasks. The choice of the home office also serves to assess whether a space exclusively dedicated/designed for this type of activity influences the perceived ease of task execution.
c) Referent facet B| privacy control: represented by the presence of barriers/opaqueness that allow for privacy control or permeability/transparency that reduces privacy levels. Privacy levels were specified as minimal to moderate, as environmental scales (living room and bedroom) do not always allow for a 100% private environment; otherwise, the space would be characterized as an office environment.
d) Referent facet C| office clutter: represented by the presence or absence of the accumulation of office-related consumables.
e) Referent facet D| biophilia: represented by the presence or absence of elements that evoke nature, whether real (woods, plants, aquariums, nature views, among others) or artificial elements (photographs, textures resembling those found in nature).
f) Referent facet E| contrast: represented through colors that can have minimum or maximum contrast, as these characteristics are indicated by theories, as mentioned in the theoretical framework, to have the most influence on human perception.
g) Range facet: systematized by a five-point Likert scale (nothing, little, somewhat, much, too much).

The focus was not considered in the sentence as content facets, as the focus was related to the internal elements of the referent facets (Fig. 1).

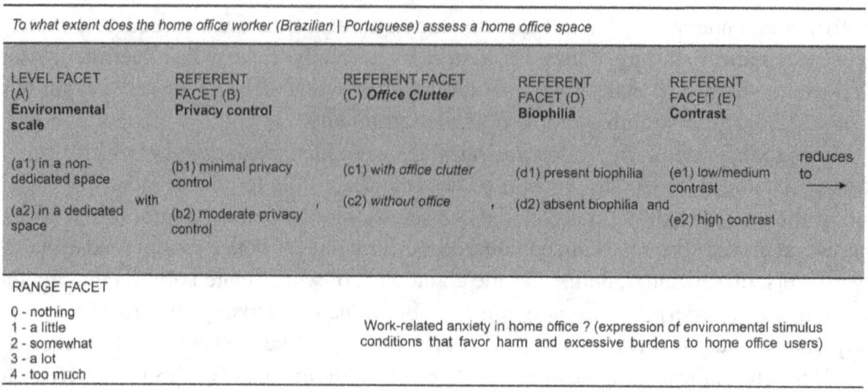

To what extent does the home office worker (Brazilian | Portuguese) assess a home office space

LEVEL FACET (A) Environmental scale	REFERENT FACET (B) Privacy control	REFERENT FACET (C) *Office Clutter*	REFERENT FACET (D) Biophilia	REFERENT FACET (E) Contrast	
					reduces to →
(a1) in a non-dedicated space	(b1) minimal privacy control	(c1) *with office clutter*	(d1) present biophilia	(e1) low/medium contrast	
(a2) in a dedicated space	(b2) moderate privacy control	(c2) *without office*	(d2) absent biophilia and	(e2) high contrast	

with ... , ... ,

RANGE FACET

0 - nothing
1 - a little
2 - somewhat
3 - a lot
4 - too much

Work-related anxiety in home office ? (expression of environmental stimulus conditions that favor harm and excessive burdens to home office users)

Fig. 1. Mapping Sentence for home office evaluation.

All facets were selected considering that these physical-environmental characteristics can directly influence the assessment of home office spaces. The internal elements of the five adopted content facets (environmental scale, privacy control, office clutter, biophilia, and contrast), related in a mapping sentence for the evaluation of harm and excessive loads in a home office environment (Fig. 2), organized as in a combinatorial analysis ($A2 \times B2 \times C2 \times D2 = 32$), produce 32 different sets of images used as stimulus elements for data collection, conveying a specific relationship or situation to be evaluated through a common rationale within this domain.

This structuring sentence serves as a conceptual model for evaluating the conditions of environmental stimuli that favor harm and excessive loads in home offices. It is analyzed in relation to empirical results that should either support or refute the hypotheses raised. Thus, after data analysis, there is sufficient information to construct a new sentence or not, to be structured as a direct consequence of the empirical results obtained.

2.4 Data Collection Method (MSP)

The method defined for data collection in the investigation was the Multiple Sorting procedure (MSP) for the first stage, which proposes the use of stimulus elements to be presented to participants. Below, the reasons and definitions of the data collection method used for the classifications will be explained.

The Multiple Sorting Procedure technique involves requesting information from participants to classify the same elements multiple times, which will be grouped based on their similarities. Elements within the same group are likely to share something important and distinctive from others. The purpose of the Multiple Sorting Procedure is to understand participants' ideas about the study object. Its choice was primarily motivated by the minimal influence of the researcher on the individuals involved, allowing for more reliable responses regarding their understanding of the questions [11].

Multiple Sorts can be divided into two different types: free sorts and directed sorts. In the first type, participants can perform as many sorts as they deem necessary, meaning they can divide the elements into as many categories as they imagine. Free sorts are accompanied by the criteria that guided them. The second type is carried out according to criteria pre-established by the researcher, based on the research's interests [10, 17]. In this study, directed sorting will be used, and it will take place through the response scales presented by the rationale.

Due to the qualities presented above, the Multiple Sorting Procedure becomes a method for collecting reliable empirical data.

Participants approached in the research were asked to assess to what extent each of the scenes favored the reduction of the anxiety in the home office environments. Participants´ opinions were indicated on 5 different points, ranging from "nothing" (minimum preference) to "too much" (maximum preference) in favor of being or remaining in the presented environments.

2.5 Data Analysis Method (SSA)

The obtained data were analyzed using the multidimensional scaling technique called Similarity Structure Analysis (SSA), with the assistance of the software HUDAP (Hebrew University Data Analysis Package), developed by Amar and Toledano [18]. SSA is a technique for similarity-based data analysis that provides a metric representation of non-metric information based on relative distances within a set of points [19]. The proximity of variables in the multidimensional space of SSA is proportional to the degree of correlation they exhibit. These similarity relationships can form contiguity regions, allowing for the verification of whether the initial hypotheses are transformed into regional hypotheses. It is expected that distinct regions will be highlighted, encompassing the internal elements of each facet. Analyses of the diagrams plotted by SSA can reveal patterns and implicit data in the results, which may be imperceptible in usual quantitative analyses [20].

According to Costa Filho and colleagues [21], facets play a specific role in structuring SSA diagrams. Each region is specified for a given subset of variables in the SSA space, identifying them through a common internal element of each facet of the mapping sentence. These regions take very specific separation forms (patterns), such as parallel strips (axial), circular configurations (modular), or angular patterns (polar).

The form of separation found in a multidimensional analysis, according to Bilsky [6], depends on whether it results from ordered facets, meaning each internal element denotes a higher degree of the attribute compared to the preceding one. An ordered facet can play an axial or modular role in dividing the SSA diagram, depending on its relationship with the other facets of the mapping sentence. If it has no relation with the other facets, it will appear as axial; whereas when it is related to one or more facets, its elements will manifest in a modular way. In addition to ordered facets, there is another type where elements differ qualitatively but without any obvious order. Such facets have a polar role.

If the regional hypotheses are validated, they reveal relatively stable aspects of the investigated concept, providing it with legitimacy, and confirming the internal structure of concepts and attributes, enabling the perception of empirically verifiable components and how they interrelate [5]. The SSA also allows testing and confirming whether a particular group operates in the same way as another in the focused evaluation. To achieve this, it is possible to register participant groups as external variables that do not interfere with the result of the SSA's original component diagram or map. This type of external variable, according to Monteiro and Roazzi [19], is considered a significant advancement in SSA, as it allows the integration of subpopulations into the map of original components, reducing the number of evaluations.

2.6 Definition of Stimulus Elements

The Multiple Sorting Procedure (MSP) allows the use of various types of elements as stimuli, including the use of colored images. As determined by Stamps [22, 23], when assessing the visual quality of the environment, highly reliable results can be obtained

Fig. 2. Scenes of home office environments representing the relationships between the facets of environmental scale, privacy control, office clutter, biophilia, and contrast. You may access this figure in a bigger picture by entering the link below https://shorturl.at/sAGJL

by using colored photographs, videos, slides, pictures, photomontages, and simulations as stimulus elements. For this reason, the stimulus elements in this study consisted of different images of home office environments.

The images formulated through the mapping sentence were generated using the 3D modeling software, Sketchup Pro 2022 (SKP), and the image rendering program, Lumion version 11. The generation of this set, however, needs to be directly associated with the variables of this research. All variables are listed in the mapping sentence for this type of evaluation, precisely establishing the relationship between all involved parts, namely, the sample group, the aspects intended to be evaluated concerning the experience, as well as the range. The modeling program allows the manipulation of the environment following all proposed variables for empirical investigation.

At total, 32 scenes were created with different environmental stimulus conditions. All scenes were colored and of the same size, related to the environment under investigation. The directed sorts were recorded on a specially designed form. Since all participants underwent the same procedures, the varying data is limited to the specific information of each group (Brazilian and Portuguese), restricted to the first page of the proposed model (Fig. 2).

2.7 The Test (Research Procedures)

The participant research was conducted online through a multiple sorting software, Optimal Workshop. The participation link was distributed through WhatsApp groups, emails and also a survey distribution website, aiming to reach a larger number of participants.

The participants were asked to complete an anxiety questionnaire, DASS 21, in order to screen them. The DASS 21 test consists of 7 questions that assess the anxiety levels of the participants. This screening is important as it allowed identifying whether the participants had trait or state anxiety, considering that one of the exclusion criteria defined for the research was individuals with trait anxiety.

Subsequently, the participants ranked all scenes used as stimulus elements, evaluating their perceptions of anxiety in performing activities in a home office. The images were ranked considering the environmental stimulus conditions that favor harm and excessive loads on home office users, influencing perceived anxiety. Responses could vary based on the rationale established in the structuring sentence: nothing, little, somewhat, much, or too much.

The images were presented to participants from both groups (Brazilian and Portuguese), with labels indicating the rationale assigned in the structuring sentence. After the classifications were completed, participants were asked to answer some questions in an online questionnaire to form a profile.

Participants from both groups went through the same classification processes, and at the end of each directed sort, they were asked about the reasons that led them to rank the images in a certain way, aiming for a better understanding of their evaluation. Subsequently, the responses were transferred to a form developed by the researcher.

3 Results

To test the facets in the original SSA diagram, each of the 32 scenes graphically represented by points in this Euclidean space received colors indicating their membership in a specific internal element of the facets. Subsequently, the existence or absence of known patterns in the division of the SSA map into contiguity regions was analyzed.

The SSA also provides the disattenuation coefficient, which indicates the reliability of the graph results; an increase in dimensionality reduces the disattenuation coefficient. In Facet Theory, a disattenuation coefficient up to 0.15 is considered satisfactory. For this solution, the disattenuation coefficient in three-dimensionality was 0.09.

It was found that both Facet C (Fig. 3) and Facets D (Fig. 4) and E (Fig. 5) formed contiguity regions, meaning they are adherent or determinant to the conditions of stimuli that favor harm and excessive loads in home office environments. In contrast, Facets A and B failed to exhibit well-formed regions, indicating that they were not adherent to this assessment.

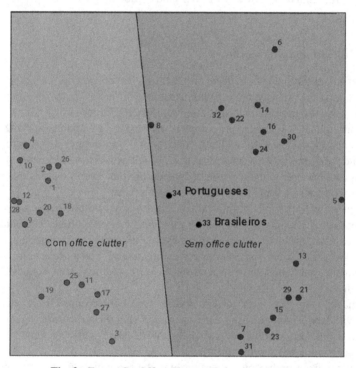

Fig. 3. Faceta C - Office Clutter. (Color figure online)

In Fig. 3, the diagram of Facet C, office clutter, shows an inclined line that divides the SSA space into two contiguity regions in a hierarchical order—defined through scores obtained in the data collection of scenes in classifications. It starts from the right blue region (without office clutter) and moves towards the left (with office clutter). This is because scenes on the blue side, represented by points on the diagram, scored higher than scenes on the red side.

This ordered facet clearly plays an axial role on the diagram, and participants were able to perceive office clutter as an adherent feature for the focused assessment, along with its two different levels. This supports one of the research hypotheses initially defined in the mapping sentence, indicating that participants prefer home office environments without office clutter in the evaluation of conditions that favor harm and excessive loads in these spaces.

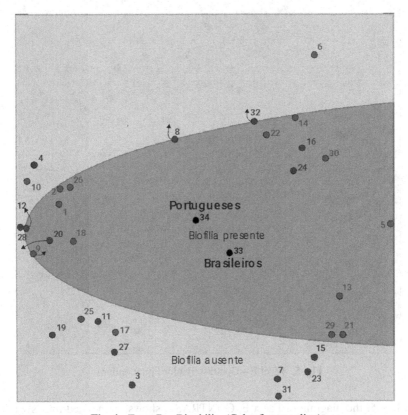

Fig. 4. Facet D – Biophilia. (Color figure online)

As explained by Bilsky [6], images in the center of the ellipse develop a central pattern in evaluations. For this study, it means that scenes in the central region played a more general than specific role in this type of assessment. It is important to note that questions of a general nature represent the synthesis of the experience. This indicates that scenes with present biophilia played a guiding role in reducing harm and excessive loads in home office environments, without a characteristic specific to these environments that was more pronounced for the respondents (Fig. 4).

While it cannot be asserted that these are the preferred home office scenes, it can be said that environments with present biophilia play a regulatory role in the assessments according to the respondents. It is also noticeable in Fig. 4 that there are some exceptions, scenes number 16 and 24, which, despite having absent biophilia (blue), were perceived as scenes with present biophilia. Meanwhile, scenes number 6, 10, 17, and 25 with present biophilia (red) were perceived as scenes with absent biophilia (blue). However, these exceptions do not invalidate the results.

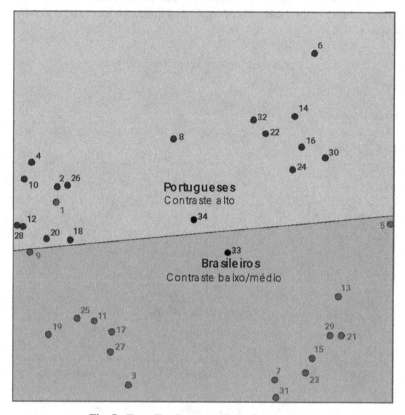

Fig. 5. Facet E – Contrast. (Color figure online)

In Fig. 5, the diagram of Facet E, CONTRAST, shows an inclined line, similar to Facet C, dividing the SSA space into two contiguity regions in a hierarchical order that, based on scene scores, begins in the blue region (high contrast) and moves towards the red region of the diagram (low/medium contrast).

Facet E, also ordered, plays an axial role in the SSA diagram, revealing that participants perceived the contrast of scenes as an adherent feature for the evaluation of these spaces, along with its two different levels. This supports another hypothesis of the research initially defined in the structuring sentence, indicating that the participants prefer low to moderate contrasts in home office environments, in this case, as suggested by the theory.

The SSA diagram for contrast shows only one regional exception, scene number 1, with low/medium contrast perceived as high. When observing the similarity matrix, scene number 1 has a high correlation with scene number 2, both having identical characteristics except for the contrast, suggesting that chromatic contrast guided this perception.

When analyzing the scores obtained for each scene in the directed sorts, it is noticeable that the scene with the highest score was number 29, featuring a dedicated home office environment, moderate privacy control, no office clutter, present biophilia, and low/medium contrast. On the contrary, according to the respondents, the scene with the lowest score was number 20, whose characteristics are exactly opposite (Fig. 6).

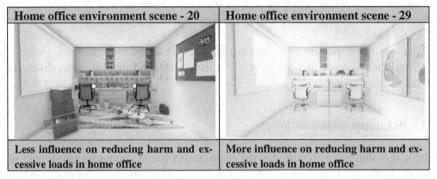

Fig. 6. Scenes that most and least influence the reduction of harm and excessive loads in home offices according to the participants.

The results reveal that out of the 5 tested facets, 3—OFFICE CLUTTER, BIO-PHILIA, and CONTRAST—proved to be adherent to the proposed assessment. Additionally, the home office work environment with a dedicated workspace, moderate privacy control, no office clutter, present biophilia, and low/medium contrast has more stimulus conditions favoring the reduction of harm and excessive loads in home office environments. Therefore, the findings of this research align with existing theories. This implies that, in support of design guidelines to assist in planning stimulus conditions, a home office environment with a dedicated workspace, moderate privacy control, no office clutter, present biophilia, and low to medium contrast facilitates the reduction of harm and, consequently, perceived anxiety in these spaces.

The assessments undertaken in this research also sought to analyze whether there was consensus in the results between the two selected groups. Additionally, based on the SSA diagrams, each group was incorporated into the SSA projections for the facets of ENVIRONMENTAL SCALE, CONTROL OF PRIVACY, OFFICE CLUTTER, BIOPHILIA, and CONTRAST as external variables.

Thus, the diagrams shown depict both the regional structure and the different groups as external variables, defined by numbers 33 (Brazilians) and 34 (Portuguese), as shown in Figs. 3, 4, and 5.

Based on Figs. 3, 4, and 5, both the Brazilian and Portuguese groups in this research are located in the region without office clutter (in blue) and with present biophilia (in red). As for the contrast facet, it is observed that the Brazilian group, located at the bottom of the diagram in Fig. 5, represented in red, is in areas that bring together home office work environments with high contrast (low coherence), while the Portuguese are located in the same diagram in the low/medium contrast region (medium/high coherence), represented in blue.

From the above, and specifically, it is demonstrated that the Brazilians surveyed prefer a home office environment with a dedicated space, privacy control, no office clutter, present biophilia, and low contrast (high coherence). On the other hand, the Portuguese share the same preferences, differing only in terms of contrast – they prefer home office environments with high contrast (low/medium coherence).

As observed in the correlation matrix and scores, the scene with the highest correlation for the Brazilian group is scene number 29, while for the Portuguese, it was scene number 14. Additionally, for both groups, the scene with the lowest correlation was scene number 20.

This result is important as it demonstrates consensus between the two groups for the environmental scale, privacy control, office clutter, and biophilia, but divergence regarding contrast.

4 Conclusion

Initially, it is important to note that the main results found cannot be considered in a simplistic manner, as they are specific to the type of stimulus element presented to the participants, the time, and the location in which the collected data were obtained.

Seeking to identify whether the characteristics of ENVIRONMENTAL SCALE, PRIVACY, OFFICE CLUTTER, BIOPHILIA, and CONTRAST in home office environments adhered to the proposed evaluation, it was found that the last three proved to be determining, as they formed contiguity regions among their internal elements.

However, the first two failed to form regions in the diagrams, indicating that they were not adherent to this research. It is believed that, being home office environments, their location within the home does not make a difference to their users. Although the scenes chosen by participants as having the most influence on stimulus conditions that favor the reduction of excessive and harmful loads in this type of space, especially in terms of perceived anxiety, were scenes in office environments, i.e., a dedicated workspace at home. The same occurred for privacy control, contradicting theoretical findings. For this research, the privacy facet had difficulty dividing the multidimensional space, in which participants did not identify whether or not such type of control existed in the scenes used as stimulus elements.

As levels of privacy control were minimal (little privacy, without screens or partitions) or moderate (featuring some partition/screen), and analyzing the observations provided by participants, it was identified that by leaving some part of the environment open to other rooms or accessible to other people, all environments did not present (for these participants) any type of privacy, although the scene that most positively influenced the participants was one with moderate privacy.

In this perspective, the mapping sentence for the evaluation of stimulus conditions that favor harmfulness and excessive loads in home office environments, assisting in reducing perceived anxiety, proved to be partially consistent for the assessment. However, such a result does not invalidate the research and mostly corroborates with one of the hypotheses of this study.

It is recommended, however, that for future research, the proposed sentence be rewritten, removing the environmental scale and privacy control. If privacy is to be maintained, it is suggested that control levels be more evident in the scenes and at more detailed levels, such as minimum, moderate, and maximum. However, for home office research, this type of detailing becomes unfeasible since having maximum privacy control loses the sense of a home office, becoming an isolated office environment in the house.

Examining the effects of the 5 characteristics of home office environments taken for study, it is concluded that an environment with a dedicated workspace, moderate privacy, without office clutter, with biophilia present, and low/medium contrast has a higher potential to reduce excessive and stress-inducing factors in home office settings. On the other hand, another environment with a dedicated workspace, minimal privacy, office clutter, biophilia absent, and high-contrast (low coherence), as suggested by the theory presented in the theoretical considerations, represents the opposite.

In this perspective, for design guidelines that assist in reducing the environmental stimuli conducive to excessive loads in home office settings, a home office environment with a dedicated workspace, coupled with moderate privacy control, devoid of office clutter such as excess papers, boxes, and books, featuring biophilic elements such as wood, earth tones, and greenery, and low to medium contrast, i.e., neutral colors, promotes the reduction of perceived state anxiety in a home office.

Based on the above, the overall objective of this research— to propose a conceptual procedure for evaluating excessive and potentially harmful loads in home office environments—has been fully achieved. It is hoped that these guidelines can assist in design decisions for such spaces, as they integrate empirical analyses, in line with Environmental Psychology and Built Environment Ergonomics principles.

Acknowledgement. This study was financed in part by the Coordenação de Aperfeiçoamento de Pessoal de Nível Superior - Brasil (CAPES) - Finance Code 001. This study was also partially supported by CIAUD Project UID/EAT/4008/2020, ITI -LARSyS-FCT Pluriannual funding 2020–2023 (https://doi.org/10.54499/UIDB/50009/2020) and the Fundação para a Ciência e Tecnologia - FCT (https://doi.org/10.54499/DL57/2016/CP1365/CT0003).

References

1. Xiao, Y., Becerik-Gerber, B., Lucas, G., Roll, S.C.: Impacts of working from home during COVID-19 pandemic on physical and mental well-being of office workstation users. J. Occup. Environ. Med. **63**(3), 181–190 (2021). https://doi.org/10.1097/JOM.0000000000002097

2. Moser, G.: A Psicologia Ambiental: competência e contornos de uma disciplina. Comentários a partir das contribuições. In: Psicologia USP (2005). https://doi.org/10.1590/s0103-656420 05000100030

3. Elliot, M.A.A., Bibi, D.: The office at home: information technology and work-life balance among women in developing countries. In: AISWN International Research Workshop on Women, IS and Grand Challenges 2020 (2020)

4. Guttman, R., Greenbaum, C.: Facet theory: its development and current status. Eur. Psychol. **3**(1), 13–36 (1998). https://doi.org/10.1027//1016-9040.3.1.13

5. Shye, S., Elizur, D., Hoffman, M.: Introduction to Facet Theory: Content Design and Intrinsic Data Analysis in Behavioral Research. Sage, London (1994)
6. Bilsky, W.: A Teoria das Facetas: noções básicas. Estudos de Psicologia (Natal) 8(3), 357–365 (2003)
7. Canter, D.: The purposive evaluation of places: a facet approach. Environ. Behave. 15(6), 659–698 (1983). https://doi.org/10.1177/0013916583156001
8. Shye, S. (ed.): Theory Construction and Data Analysis in the Behavioral Sciences. Jossey-Bass, San Francisco (1978)
9. Canter, D.: Qualitative structural theory: practical possibilities of partial order projections. In: Shye, C.S., Solomon, E., Borg, I. (eds.)15th Internacional Face TV Theory V Conference. Anais, New York (2015)
10. Costa Filho, L.L.: Midiápolis: comunicação, persuasão e sedução da paisagem urbana midiática. 272f. Tese (Doutorado em Desenvolvimento Urbano), Universidade Federal de Pernambuco, Recife (2012)
11. Costa Filho, L.L.: O enfoque da Teoria das Facetas na avaliação de lugares. In: V ENEAC – Encontro Nacional de Ergonomia do Ambiente Construído e VI Seminário Nacional de Acessibilidade Integral, Rio de Janeiro, Anais. Rio de Janeiro, PUC-Rio, LEUI/PUC – Rio (2014)
12. Levy, S., Guttman, L.: On the multivariate structure of wellbeing. In: Michalos, A.C. (ed.) Citation Classics from Social Indicators Research: The Most Cited Articles Edited and Introduced by Alex C. Michalos, pp. 145–172. Springer Netherlands, Dordrecht (2005). https://doi.org/10.1007/1-4020-3742-2_7
13. Shey, S.: The essence of Facet Theory: a unified view of faceted multivariate research methods. In: 17th Facet Theory Conference Proceedings, pp. 5–17 (2020)
14. Cerqueira, V.D.F.D., Monteiro, C.: Environment indicators for river restoration: a facet approach to reveal the interplay of environmental, spatial and social dimensions. In: 17th Facet Theory Conference Proceedings, pp. 130–140 (2020)
15. Marconi, M.A., Lakatos, E.M.: Técnicas de pesquisa: Planejamento e execução de pesquisas, amostragens e técnicas de pesquisas, elaboração, análise e interpretação de dados, 5nd edn. Atlas, São Paulo (2002)
16. Bessa, O.F.M., Moraes, A.: A Ergonomia do Ambiente Construído. In: Moraes, A. (ed.). Ergodesign do Ambiente Construído e Habitado: ambiente urbano, ambiente público, ambiente laboral. iUsEr, Rio de Janeiro (2004)
17. Figueiredo, D.M.F.: O monumento habitado: a preservação do patrimônio de sítios históricos na visão dos habitantes e dos arquitetos especialistas em patrimônio. O caso de Parnaíba. 159f. Dissertação (Mestrado em Desenvolvimento Urbano), Universidade Federal de Pernambuco, Recife (2001)
18. Amar, R., Toledano, S.: HUDAP Manual. Hebrew University of Jerusalem, Jerusalem (2005)
19. Roazzi, A., Monteiro, C.M.G., Rullo, G.: Residential satisfaction and place attachment: a cross-cultural investigation. In: Cohen, A. (ed.) Facet Theory and Scaling: In Search of Structure in Behavioral and Social Sciences, pp. 81–97. Facet Theory Association Press, Tel Aviv (2009)
20. Borg, I., Lingoes, J.: Multidimensional Similarity Structure Analysis, p. 390. Springer, New York (1987)
21. Costa Filho, L.L., Oliveira, I.F., Yokoyama, S.A.A.: qualidade percebida em cenas do comércio varejista do centro de Caruaru. In: VI ENEAC – Encontro Nacional de Ergonomia do Ambiente Construído e VII Seminário Nacional de Acessibilidade Integral, Recife, pp. 541–552. UFPE, Anais, Recife (2016)

22. Stamps, A.E.: Perceptual and preferential effects of photo montages simulations of environments. In: Perceptual and Motor Skills, no. 74 (1992)
23. Stamps, A.E.: Use of static and dynamic media to simulate environments: a meta-analysis. Percept. Motor Skills **111**, 355–362 (2010)

Connecting the Dots for Positive Change: Designing an Enabling Digital Platform for Social Innovation for a Depopulated Territory in Portugal

Ana Melo[✉] and Marco Neves

CIAUD, Research Centre for Architecture, Urbanism and Design, Lisbon School of Architecture, Universidade de Lisboa, Lisbon, Portugal
anapintomelo@gmail.com

Abstract. The article describes the development of a prototype for an enabling digital platform through a research through design process. The platform serves as an idea bank, triggering social innovation projects in an inland Portuguese territory facing population decline. Employing a design for social innovation approach, by recombining existing resources, it aims to act as a hub to connect locals, stakeholders, and other interested communities in locally implemented projects, generating sustainable and innovative solutions for mutual benefits. The platform aims to foster dialogue around shared interests, catalyzing place-making, community activation, and triggering communities of action to implement transformative social innovation projects for the territory. Various interaction design methods, such as wireframing, user-journey mapping, and formative testing, were used during this research. As part of a broader ecosystem to drive design-led social innovation initiatives, the platform was evaluated by experts and achieved positive results in articulating various crucial dimensions for the territory. The Topia Digital Platform asserts itself as an artefact of interaction design and a vehicle for design for social innovation.

Keywords: Interaction design · Enabling platform · Design for social innovation · Design for territories · Population decline

1 Introduction

Digital platforms are relevant instruments for infrastructuring (Hillgren et al. 2011) social innovation, understood as a process of recombining existing resources to conceive sustainable responses for local communities' needs (Mulgan 2019; Murray et al. 2010). The creation of enabling digital hubs can promote and facilitate the participation of hybrid communities of interest and action (Manzini 2015; 2019). They allow social innovation initiatives to expand their reach to wider audiences, bring together scattered human resources, and provide diverse and accessible channels and modes of collaboration.

Interaction design asserts itself in this framework as an area capable of meeting specific needs of social innovation initiatives, namely by developing digital artefacts

© The Author(s), under exclusive license to Springer Nature Switzerland AG 2024
A. Marcus et al. (Eds.): HCII 2024, LNCS 14716, pp. 158–173, 2024.
https://doi.org/10.1007/978-3-031-61362-3_12

for communication and participation that enable the circulation of new meanings and place-making approaches that are relevant for territories (Krucken 2012; Parente and Sedini 2018). Furthermore, they can support strategies for sociability, facilitating the creation of new social relationships and new ways of collaborating between various actors. Acting as a digital meeting point between local and external communities, they address critical mass gaps and generate or strengthen communities of action (Emilson and Hillgren 2014; Emilson et al. 2014).

The article describes the development of an enabling digital platform (Manzini 2005; Manzini and Menichinelli 2021) for promoting digital and hybrid interactions between various stakeholders in a sparsely populated Portuguese territory, Aldeias de Montanha, a network of 41 small rural mountain villages in Serra da Estrela. The platform collects proposals from local communities, thus functioning as a repository of ideas with transformative potential for the territory. The project also aims to draw the participation of designers, researchers and design students in local activities that creatively recombine available resources and enhance the territory sustainability, recognizing the role of design as a holder of ways of thinking and doing potentially relevant to territories (Parente and Sedini 2017).

Low population density is a systemic problem that affects multiple rural interior regions of many European countries (Čipin et al. 2020; Vinãs 2019) and has left many villages in Portugal, Spain or Italy depopulated (Sechi et al. 2020 Viñas 2019). Population decline highlights the existence of a negative European cycle that is both cause and consequence of several factors such as population ageing, lack of capacity to maintain residents and attract new inhabitants, absence of investment, and insufficient employment and services (Čipin et al. 2020; European Commission 2020; UMVI 2016). The European Union stresses how this issue threatens territorial cohesion and originates social inequalities (Camarero and Oliva 2019; European Commission 2020). The loss of inhabitants also has as a direct consequence the deterioration of material and intangible cultural heritage and, in the case of Aldeias de Montanha territories, of natural ecosystems. Population decline makes them more vulnerable to forest fires and causes the degradation of protected forest areas (Fernandes et al. 2016). Neo-endogenous social innovation approaches, characterized by local, multi-sector, bottom-up and experimental initiatives, are recognized as having the potential to contribute positively to revitalizing territories and reactivating local communities (Neumeier 2012). Thus, design for social innovation practices can have a relevant contribution for mitigating depopulation, triggering and supporting local communities to reinvent what inland rural territories can mean and offer to new residents in the near future.

Based on a series of previous exploratory methods, including a multiple case study of social innovation initiatives focused on the activation of territories (Melo and Neves 2022), we applied a research through design (RtD) process that included several interaction design methods and tools. Generative activities included wireframing, user-journey mapping, and formative testing with users. The process originated a medium/high fidelity prototype of Topia Digital Ptalaform (TDP), a web-based platform for promoting social innovation initiatives at Aldeias de Montanha (AM).

TDP acts as a hub to articulate various strategic actors, such as local communities, communities of interest, local stakeholders and designers, providing streamlined channels for idea submission and collaboration on projects. Additionally, it serves as a repository for ideas, promotes visibility for implemented projects, and expands and strengthens the design network. The design-led approach underlying the platform aims to harness the specific value of design by applying methods and tools to transform ideas into tangible projects that generate impact for AM.

Beyond serving as a digital meeting point, TDP encourages on-site presence and collaboration, facilitates contact between participants, and provides tools for learning, communication, and project management. It acts as an instrument for knowledge circulation and capacitation (Hillgren et al. 2011; Manzini and Rizzo 2011). Also, the website allows different levels of involvement, ranging from light contributions to deeper engagement in various projects, considering the need of resilience of social innovation initiatives (Manzini 2015; 2019).

The platform is part of a broader system, framed by a strategic design process, that proposes a living lab model to trigger and support design-led social innovation in Aldeias de Montanha. Although it is not the focus of this article, this system is mentioned since it provides a context in which the platform is instrumental. This multi-touchpoint and hybrid system aims to aggregate resources and actors, ignite and sustain more lasting and effective social innovation processes in the territory, as well as to gather design knowledge that can be transferred to other similar contexts. The development of the system also highlighted how, within the scope of design for social innovation, interaction design works closely with strategic design, system design, service design and communication design.

A functional prototype of the platform, as well as the living lab model, was evaluated by a group of experts from the most relevant fields to the project (territorial innovation, social innovation and design). The project collected positive feedback regarding innovation, applicability and relevance for the territory.

1.1 Research Question and Objectives

The RtD process aims to respond to the following research question: how can interaction design generate a digital artefact, embedded in a broader hybrid system, to trigger and strengthen potentially transformative social innovation dynamics for the territory of Aldeias de Montanha, with a focus on mitigating population desertification?

Thus, the process described in the article had the following main objectives:

i. Design a tool for igniting, promoting, facilitating, and supporting social innovation initiatives in AM.
ii. Prototype a website to establish a channel for participation and collaboration for local communities and to attract and expand communities of interest (possibly physically distant from the villages), thereby triggering communities of action.
iii. Strategically structure a website with three main functionalities: an idea bank for social innovation in AM; an enabling ecosystem to facilitate the implementation of co-creative projects; a repository of results and cases implemented in other contexts.
iv. Develop a model for a digital platform with the potential to be replicated in other European low-density population territories.

1.2 Digital Platforms as Facilitating Devices for Social Innovation

Interaction design emerges as a relevant player in a context where the physical and digital realms are increasingly seamlessly integrated (European Commission 2023; Schwab 2015): objects and users interact in hybrid systems through computational capability, sensors, and networks (Schoder 2018); data, information, and knowledge as central assets (Deguchi et al. 2020; Fukuyama 2018); multimodality, including visual, haptic, voice, and bodily interfaces (Rafael 2020); and a permanent and exponential expansion of new possibilities for human-computer interaction led by artificial intelligence and machine learning.

In this scenario, interaction design asserts itself as an interdisciplinary practice permeable to technological issues and grounded in dialogues with other areas of design and fields related to human-computer interaction. Acting as a mediator in interactions among people, the natural environment, and the artificial environment, interaction design plays a central role in producing socio-technological contexts (Höök and Löwgren 2021). In this perspective, a reflection on social, ethical, and political dimensions is crucial, along with the development of critical and speculative capabilities.

Particularly in the field of social innovation, considered as a possible path to address the challenges of our time (Emilson 2015; European Commission 2015; Manzini 2015), interaction design plays an increasingly relevant role, given the capacity of digital artefacts to support community initiatives aiming for transformative and sustainable actions (Manzini and Menichinelli 2021). Information and communication technologies (ICT) play a fundamental role in promoting open and participatory processes, enabling real-time collaboration in common projects without the need for users to share a physical infrastructure. They provide essential tools to facilitate hybrid collaboration processes for social innovation. This became particularly visible during the Covid-19 pandemic, during which numerous hybrid communities of place (Manzini 2020; Manzini and Menichinelli 2021) thrived at physical-digital spaces, supported by digital platforms. The concept of what is local has thus been expanding, going beyond the circumscription to a physical territory, incorporating the idea of cosmopolitan localism: communities interact with the world, although rooted in a specific geographical place (Manzini 2008). The strategic convergence of local and global elements; the sustainable development of local resources, both physical and socio-cultural; ICT enabling access to global networks and resources; all give rise to new opportunities for fostering synergy between these two dimensions, as suggested by Manzini (2008).

Interaction design can thus facilitate distributed activities of networked social innovation by fostering the creation of hybrid communities, connecting local communities to broader communities enabled by digital platforms. They become instrumental tools for communicating initiatives globally, disseminating knowledge and promoting participation. Moreover, a specific contribution is the setting of online infrastructures that strengthen and empower these hybrid communities, turning them into communities of action. Digital means also facilitate the creation of open content and the production of low-cost replication tools, such as digital toolkits, thus contributing to the amplification and replication of initiatives and other roles that design plays in social innovation (Melo and Neves 2020; 2022).

Some cases highlight the essential role of digital and hybrid platforms, driving collaboration, collective learning, and sociability in the context of community activation. The Frena la Curva project (Criado et al. 2020; Ruiz-Muzquiz 2020), originated during the Covid-19 pandemic, promoted collaborative responses to the emergency, using an open and collaborative online map and involving more than a thousand activists in online projects. Amplifying Creative Communities (Manzini and Rizzo 2011; Penin et al. 2009), from the Parsons DESIS Lab, mapped and communicated social innovation initiatives in New York, using interactive exhibitions that became a conversational tool to support creative communities. In Malmö, Sweden, projects like Blue Promo and Urblove (Linde and Book 2014) used bluetooth technology to distribute music on buses and created mobile games, fostering place-making and collaborative participation of younger communities. These three cases highlight how it is crucial for interaction design to address experiences, users, and contexts holistically (Bagnara and Smith 2006), expanding the concept of user experience to include co-experience (Battarbee and Koskinen 2005), highlighting the collective nature of the production of meaning, places and communities.

2 Methods

A set of preliminary activities contributed to defining the problem space, providing the context for developing the digital platform, outlining its scope of action, and the design principles that guided it. These activities consisted of a literature review, a multiple-case study addressing three social innovation initiatives focused on revitalizing communities of action and practice in Portuguese territories, participant observation activities, and a co-creation session with experts from the AM territory. The activities began with participant observation of various ongoing projects in the AM, deployed by ADIRAM, a local development association that, among other tasks, triggers and coordinates initiatives to mitigate depopulation. These activities allowed direct contact with the territory, identifying relevant stakeholders, as well as existing opportunities and challenges in implementing design for social innovation projects in the region.

After these initial stages, a research through design process was deployed, consisting of designing and prototyping a medium/high-fidelity enabling digital platform. The research developed through a practical and reflective approach, characterized by direct intervention in the object of study (Hult and Lennung 1980) and allowing for the design project to be the vehicle for research (Frayling 1994). The research unfolded in cycles of action and research similar to those described by Zuber-Skerritt (2003) and consisted of planning (defining study focus, procedures and objectives), action, observation, and reflection - obtaining a critical synthesis that often resulted in a new cycle of action and research. The process was documented, allowing peer reviewing and self-evaluating (Swann 2002), as well as tracing of information, events, and decisions, facilitating subsequent analysis and discussion of results (Neves 2012).

The various development phases included benchmarking, establishing design principles, defining user profiles, user-journey mapping, information architecture and wireframing, medium-fidelity prototyping, iterative testing, development of the visual interface identity, and high-fidelity prototyping.

The user testing phase included five iteration cycles, using formative tests (online and in-person) to improve the prototype's usability (Nielsen 1993; Barnum 2020). The number of participants was defined based on Nielsen and Landauer (1993), suggesting three to five participants as the ideal number, in terms of effort/benefit, for conducting small studies. Before conducting the tests, a user profile was defined within the typology of a community of interest, i.e., users who do not reside in the villages but express interest in participating in projects to be implemented in the AM. The users were given specific scenarios and three tasks to complete, and a think-aloud protocol (Baxter et al. 2015) gathered participant feedback on the user experience, as well as insights regarding various dimensions of the experience (Barnum 2020).

The high-fidelity prototype was evaluated by eight experts in individual online sessions that adapted the concept walkthrough method (Barnum 2020; Salazar 2022). The aim was to ascertain their understanding and acceptance of the platform in terms of adequacy and relevance to the proposed objectives, and the experts provided their feedback through a questionnaire consisting of closed and open-ended questions.

3   Prototyping an Enabling Platform: A Social Innovation Design Process in the Territory

The research through design process was informed by a multiple case study of the social innovation initiatives Loulé Design Lab (LDL n.d.), Laboratório Cívico Santiago (LCS n.d.), and Loulé Sou Eu! (LSE n.d.). The results revealed how digital platforms, such as websites and social networks for the projects, were crucial for communicating activities, expanding visibility, and attracting diverse audiences. Furthermore, they functioned as infrastructure, capable of sustaining the impact of initiatives over time and played a crucial role in constructing meaning and place-making.

In the participant observation of ongoing projects in the AM territory, the crucial role of various digital artefacts, such as websites, was also noted (Projeto Queijeiras n.d.; Coworks Cooperativa @ Aldeias de Montanha n.d.; Plataforma Lugar n.d.). These were instrumental in attracting partners, increasing project visibility and influence, as well as engaging the community. Moreover, their ability to enable direct and close involvement of participants, create a sense of ownership within communities, and enhance relational dimensions between local and external audiences was highly relevant for gathering and building critical mass.

In continuing to explore the problem space, a co-creation session with AM experts was conducted (Fig. 1), allowing for gathering insights about the importance of actively involving residents; the relevance of creating open and inclusive structures for mutual learning; and building a positive perception of villages as innovative, creative, and dynamic territories. These insights were incorporated into the platform requirements, determining content, information architecture, and functional specifications.

Benchmarking. The research through design process began by benchmarking various case studies of social innovation and enabling digital platforms identified during the literature review (Cipolla et al. 2007; Criado et al. 2020; Linde and Book 2014; Manzini and Rizzo 2011; Ólivan and Horrillo 2020). Open innovation platforms (Chesbrough and Di Minin 2014; Fayard and Levina 2017) were analyzed, focusing on their operational models, participation mechanics, idea implementation, user journey for collaboration,

Fig. 1. Co-creation session with AM experts.

information architecture, and issues related to authorship and transparency. The analysis informed the definition of design principles, guiding the strategic and conceptual development of the platform.

Design Principles. The identified design principles became the foundation for all subsequent decisions in the development of the platform and the prototype. They encompass ease and simplicity of use, accessibility (navigation and language), transparency (of ongoing processes and project results), empowerment (providing tools and encouraging knowledge sharing), inclusion, aggregation (making everyone welcome and bridging between participants and stakeholders), proximity (relational and friendly), inspiration, and fostering dialogue between the user and the platform. Navigation was designed to be simple and direct, and the graphical interface uses diagrams and images to facilitate comprehension for various audiences.

User Profiles. In determining the target audience for TDP, a segmentation strategy (Goyat 2011; Martin 2011) was employed to create user profiles that guide design principles, communication strategy, and design decisions, following a user-centered approach. Four main target audiences were identified for the TDP: local communities, interest communities, stakeholders (such as municipalities and businesses) and designers (as potential project activators). The "Community of Interest" profile defines a user with interest in AM derived from geographical connections, family or emotional ties, motivation to participate in social innovation actions, or links to partners in the stakeholder network.

User-Journey Mapping. To clarify the user experience, we mapped the key moments of interaction with the hybrid system, which comprises both the platform and touchpoints in the villages, as well as interactions with project implementation teams. Visual representations such as sketches, diagrams, and user-journey maps (Fig. 2) were employed to illustrate the diverse dimensions of the user experience. These helped to identify touchpoints, pain points, and opportunities for enhancing the overall user experience (Marquez et al. 2015; Stickdorn et al. 2018). To further refine the definition of the system and its components, we established the main user stories of the website, outlining the actions available to the user.

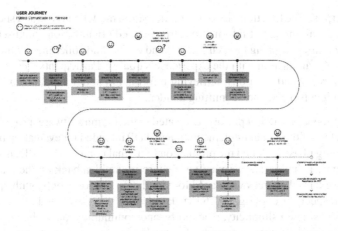

Fig. 2. User-journey map for Community of Interest user profile.

Wireframes. The development continued with the creation of wireframes, initially in low fidelity sketched on paper, allowing testing of various hypotheses of structural organization and navigation flow through multiple iterations. After iterative cycles, the creation of a functional prototype based on medium-fidelity wireframe navigation using Figma software began for user testing (Fig. 3).

Priority was given to evaluating the understanding of the platform's purpose and the ability to navigate to perform key tasks. Distinctive graphic elements were not included to avoid diverting users' attention from these objectives. However, an explanatory diagram of the platform's operation was presented, visually providing an understanding of the idea and project generation system and the flow between phases and involved actors. This visual synthesis complemented explanatory texts, reinforcing the articulation between the system's operation and the platform's purposes.

Fig. 3. Wireframes and medium-fidelity prototype used in user testing.

User Testing. Tests were structured with specific objectives, guided by dimensions such as efficiency, effectiveness, experience quality, error tolerance, and ease of learning (Barnum 2020). These objectives encompassed evaluating the comprehension of the website's purpose, the functionality of the participation model, the ease and speed of task completion, the alignment of information structure and organization with users' mental models, observation of navigation challenges and errors, and soliciting qualitative feedback on overall satisfaction with the experience's quality. Participants were tasked with completing three specific actions: retrieving information about the platform's purpose, participating in a project, and submitting an idea.

Prototype. The high-fidelity prototype, created in the Figma software, provided a more accurate artefact of the actual implementation of TDP intended for evaluation by experts. The prototyping phase included the production of textual content and collection of cases (identified during the literature review) to feature in the idea bank on the platform (all images from external sources were used for simulation purposes only, with appropriate credits and respect for copyright). The visual identity was developed based on design principles, focusing on simplicity, readability, and communication of the attractiveness of the territories, using images provided by ADIRAM.

The main page (Fig. 4) succinctly presents the TDP concept, with call-to-action buttons for key features (participate and submit ideas) and includes a diagram synthesizing the objectives and how the platform operates. The visual interface uses images, simple geometric shapes, typography, and a colour palette centred on pastel tones, highlighting main areas with vibrant colours. The inclusion of black and white images, along with geometric shapes, creates a visually uncluttered backdrop for important information.

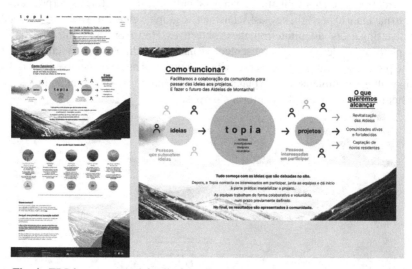

Fig. 4. TDP homepage and detail of the diagram depicting how the platform works.

The main menu provides direct links to main pages (Fig. 5) and a login area for project participants. The What You Can Do on This Site and How It Works sections describe the platform's features in an accessible manner, with diagrams and step-by-step information about the process underlying the participation in projects. An Idea Bank section allows navigation between ideas, projects, and results of already implemented projects. The

Ideas page presents previously submitted ideas, each with a brief description and image, along with the call-to-action to submit ideas, supported by a submission form. The Projects page features a catalogue of ongoing projects, with information about the village, participants, and the option to join the project. The reserved area allows participants to access detailed information about projects they participate in and resources, including learning materials, relevant documents and information about the project's team. A Call for Designers page is aimed at professionals, students, researchers, and design educators, seeking their participation in ongoing projects.

Fig. 5. TDP Prototype, Idea Bank and Project pages.

4   Results and Discussion

The TDP prototype was evaluated by eight experts, and all participants agreed that TDP can bring benefits to AM and enhance social innovation initiatives, thus fostering a positive perception of inland territories as promising and full of opportunities.

In general, the experts agreed on TDP's ability to serve as a critical mass aggregator and considered it a relevant tool to involve design students in social innovation projects in AM and foster productive partnerships between the territory and academic research in design. Questions directed to social innovation experts further underscored a positive outlook on TDP's effectiveness in gathering contributions from communities, promoting participation, and supporting the success of social innovation initiatives in AM.

Territorial innovation experts positively assessed TDP's ability to foster productive partnerships and synergies among local stakeholders, and attract social innovation projects and innovators, indicating its potential to revitalize the territory. The evaluation was also very positive regarding the platform's ability to encourage the participation of local communities and facilitate the actions of social innovators in the field.

Some less favourable evaluation feedback involves experts noting the potential exclusion of local communities with an ageing population due to higher rates of digital illiteracy. Additionally, concerns were raised about the possibility of the digital nature of the platform undermining the essence of social innovation, which revolves around local actions, activating communities, and fostering personal relationships.

In this regard, it will be important to accommodate the suggestions made by the experts to find ways to further integrate the platform with the geographical places. One suggestion is to promote more human interactions in the digital environment, facilitating quick direct contacts between project participants and local communities, such as phone calls, field visits, or online meetings. Indeed, strengthening affective dimensions and sociability, as pointed out by the literature and the multiple case study, is crucial for the long-term sustainability of initiatives.

Another relevant suggestion was to promote a hybrid system of on-site interactions. This concern was already addressed by the strategic program that includes TDP as a digital component supporting a broader enabling system, shaping a proposal for a living lab model that allows for infrastructuring social innovation initiatives that can be transformative for AM territories (Fig. 6). Nonetheless, taking note of the feedback from the experts, the designing of modes of synergy between the digital platform and the physical interactions in the villages can be further explored.

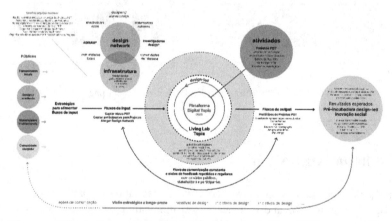

Fig. 6. Diagram of the strategic program/living lab model that includes TDP as an enabling digital platform.

The funding of the platform and the system was also identified by experts as a potentially problematic aspect, as it constitutes a critical factor in ensuring long-term effectiveness. Several experts also emphasized the need to carefully consider power relations between external participants, including designers, and local communities. The evaluation also highlighted the platform's capacity as an instrument to map resources and social innovators in the territory, thus triggering synergies.

4.1 Limitations

The user testing conducted during the platform development encountered some limitations. It was not possible to carry out tests with users from local communities, whose feedback could have provided valuable insights into the perceived usefulness and relevance of the platform. This limitation also hindered addressing issues related to accessibility, especially considering the higher age demographic of the population in AM.

Another limitation was the absence of post-test questionnaires for participants. However, this was mitigated by the data collected through the think-aloud protocol, which involved requesting verbal opinions on utility, ease of use, and navigation at the end of each test, along with suggestions for improvement.

A third limitation regards the fact that all participants were tolerant, meaning individuals close to the researcher who fit the defined profile; however, they had no prior knowledge of the platform, the study objectives, or the tasks to be performed during the tests.

5 Conclusions

The research through design described in the article resulted in a digital enabling platform dedicated to promoting networks of social innovation in the Aldeias de Montanha territory, triggering and facilitating collaborative processes, co-learning, and knowledge circulation. It becomes a community activator around local projects and, therefore, around the territory. It is enabling in the sense that it creates a digital channel that allows sharing, interaction, learning, and collaboration among the various actors relevant to the territory.

The PDT prototype received a positive evaluation in terms of its innovation, relevance, and suitability from eight experts in social innovation, depopulated territories, territorial innovation, and design education (with experts emphasizing the need for complementing on-site activities to avoid the risk of excluding local communities where digital illiteracy is an issue and to support the situated and relational nature of social innovation).

Regarding future research, it is suggested to implement a pilot of the TDP (pending funding), which will serve as a test capable of producing new iterative cycles. It is also recommended that the potential implementation be assessed for impact using frameworks such as Social Return on Investment (SROI) and tools like Civimetro. Although the entire RtD development has always considered the issue of replicability to other territories with a similar low-density population context to AM, further research is needed to assess the applicability of the platform in other territories.

In the scope of interaction design practice for social innovation, the research contributes to explore ways for design to be involved in mitigating the challenges of inland depopulated territories. Furthermore, to act as an engine to set in motion design-led social innovation. Providing a digital channel to drive the generation and development of social innovation in inland territories, it can strengthen local communities, congregate communities of interest, activate creative communities, and promote the sense of agency along various actors. The strategic use of digital means, combined with on-site actions, enables hybrid approaches and expands the platform's reach. The main objective is to facilitate practices and projects that contribute to breaking negative cycles of population loss, generating transformative and regenerative dynamics for the AM territory.

To bring the value of design to depopulated territories, it is necessary to establish infrastructural devices that act as enabling co-creation mechanisms for sustainable social innovation. Guided by design principles and utilizing its methods, tools, and practices, these devices can generate interventions at the local level through situated design initiatives, intending to impact macro-level systems. These devices can function as listening laboratories, allowing local communities to forge alternative projects for experiencing the territory. Guided by design, they become platforms for experimentation, encouraging risk taking, learning, and co-creation. These activities, geared towards environmental, social, and economic sustainability, must adhere to principles of collaborative co-creation, democratic participation, emancipation, empowerment, mutual learning, knowledge transfer, power circulation, and autonomy training for participants, partners, and teams.

Interaction design can contribute by providing digital and hybrid tools that enable transformative projects deployed through the action of local and virtual communities and supported by design. Digital enabling platforms, such as TDP, can act as sustaining devices that trigger, empower, capacitate, mediate, and sustain processes of recombining existing resources through the agency of hybrid communities of place and practice.

Acknowledgments. This work is financed by national funds through FCT - Fundação para a Ciência e a Tecnologia, I.P., under the Strategic Project with the references UIDB/04008/2020.

Disclosure of Interests. The authors have no competing interests to declare that are relevant to the content of this article.

References

Bagnara, S., Smith, G.C. (eds.): Theories and Practice in Interaction Design. CRC Press, Boca Raton (2006)

Barnum, C.M.: Usability Testing Essentials: Ready, Set... Test! Morgan Kaufmann, Burlington (2020)

Battarbee, K., Koskinen, I.: Co-experience: user experience as interaction. CoDesign 1(1), 5–18 (2005)

Camarero, L., Oliva, J.: Thinking in rural gap: mobility and social inequalities. Palgrave Commun. 5(1) (2019)

Chesbrough, H., Minin, A.: Open social innovation. In: Chesbrough, H., Vanhaverbeke, W., West, J. (eds.) New Frontiers in Open Innovation, pp. 169–187. Oxford Academic (2014)

Čipin, I., Klüsener, S., Recaño, J., Ulceluse, M.: A long-term vision for the development of rural areas in Europe: insights from demography. Pop. Europe (2020)

Cipolla, C., Franqueira, T., Conditi, R.: Enabling solutions in creative cities: the cohousing.it case. In: Conference Emergence 2007: Exploring the Boundaries of Service Design, Pittsburgh (2007)

Criado, J.I., Guevara-Gómez, A., Villodre, J.: Using collaborative technologies and social media to engage citizens and governments during the COVID-19 Crisis: the case of Spain. Digital Gov. Res. Pract. 1(4), 1–7 (2020)

Cooperativa Coworks @ Aldeias de Montanha (n.d.). https://coworkaldeiasdemontanha.pt/

Deguchi, A., et al.: What is society 5.0. Society **5**, 1–24 (2020)

Emilson, A.: Design in the space between stories. design for social innovation and sustainability— from responding to societal challenges to preparing for societal collapse. [Doctoral thesis, Malmö University]. DiVA (2015)

Emilson, A., Hillgren, P.A.: Connecting with the powerful strangers: from governance to agonistic design things. In: Ehn, P., Nilsson, E.M., Topgaard, R. (eds.) Making Futures: Marginal Notes on Innovation, design, and Democracy, pp. 63–84. The MIT Press, Cambridge (2014)

Emilson, A., Hillgren, P.A., Seravalli, A.: Designing in the neighbourhood: beyond (and in the shadow of) creative communities. In: Ehn, P., Nilsson, E.M., Topgaard, R. (eds.) Making Futures: Marginal Notes on Innovation, Design, and Democracy, pp. 35–61. The MIT Press, Cambridge (2014)

European Commission. Industry 5.0 (2023). https://research-and-innovation.ec.europa.eu/res earch-area/industrial-research-and-innovation/industry-50

European Commission. Social policy innovation: Meeting the social needs of citizens (2015). https://doi.org/10.2767/59875

European Commission. Report on the impact of demographic change (2020). https://ec.europa. eu/info/sites/info/files/demography_report_2020_n.pdf

Fayard, A.L., Levina, N.: An interstitial space for social innovation. In: Academy of Management Proceedings, vol. 2017, no. 1, p. 12167. Academy of Management (2017)

Fernandes, J.A.R., Chamusca, P., Bragança, P., Formigo, N., Marques, H., Silva, Â.: Aldeias de Montanha: os problemas, as perspetivas e as propostas, vistos desde as serras da Aboboreira, Marão e Montemuro, no Noroeste de Portugal. Revista de Geografia e Ordenamento do Território **1**(9), 113–137 (2016)

Frayling, C.: Research in art and design. In: Royal College of Art Research Papers, vol. 1, no. 1 (1993/4) (1994)

Fukuyama, M.: Society 5.0: aiming for a new human-centered society. Japan Spotlight **27**(5), 47–50 (2018)

Goyat, S.: The basis of market segmentation: a critical review of literature. Eur. J. Bus. Manag. **3**(9), 45–54 (2011)

Hillgren, P.-A., Seravalli, A., & Emilson, A. (2011). Prototyping and infrastructuring in design for social innovation

Höök, K., Löwgren, J.: Characterizing interaction design by its ideals: a discipline in transition. She Ji: J.0 Des. Econ. Innov. **7**(1), 24–40 (2021)

Hult, M., Lennung, S.-Å.: Towards a definition of action research: a note and bibliography. J. Manage. Stud. **17**(2), 241–250 (1980). https://doi.org/10.1111/j.1467-6486.1980.tb00087.x

Krucken, L.: A re-descoberta do lugar e do artesanato. In: Albino, C. (ed.) Design, Artesanato & Indústria, pp. 22–30 (2012). ISBN 978-989-98473-9-2

LCS (n.d.). https://labcivicosantiago.wordpress.com/

LDL (n.d.). https://louledesignlab.pt/

LSE (n.d.). https://www.facebook.com/loulesoueu/

Linde, P., Book, K.: Performing the city: exploring the bandwidth of urban place-making through new media tactics. In: Ehn, P., Nilsson, E.M., Topgaard, R. (eds.) Making Futures: Marginal Notes on Innovation, Design, and Democracy, pp. 87–97. The MIT Press, Cambridge (2014)

Manzini, E.: Creative communities and enabling platforms: An introduction to a promising line of research and actions on sustainable production and consumption. In: Tangen, D., Thoresen, V.W. (eds.) Taking Responsibility: Conference of The Consumer Citizenship Network Proceedings, Bratislava 2005, pp. 33–41 (2005)

Manzini, E.: A cosmopolitan localism: prospects for a sustainable local development and the possible role of design. In: Clark, H., Brody, D. (eds.) Design Studies: A Reader, pp. 448–453. Berg, Oxford (2008)

Manzini, E.: Design, When Everybody Designs: An Introduction to Design for Social Innovation. MIT Press, Cambridge (2015)

Manzini, E.: Politics of the Everyday. Bloomsbury Visual Arts (2019)

Manzini, E., & Menichinelli, M. (2021). Platforms for re-localization. Communities and places in the post-pandemic hybrid spaces. Strategic Design Research Journal, 14(1), 351–360

Manzini, E., Rizzo, F.: Small projects/large changes: participatory design as an open participated process. CoDesign 7(3–4), 199–215 (2011)

Marquez, J.J., Downey, A., Clement, R.: Walking a mile in the user's shoes: Customer journey mapping as a method to understanding the user experience. Internet Ref. Serv. Q. 20(3–4), 135–150 (2015)

Martin, G.: The importance of marketing segmentation. Am. J. Bus. Educ. (AJBE) 4(6), 15–18 (2011)

Melo, A., Neves, M.: Communication design within social innovation. In: Advances in Design, Music and Arts: 7th Meeting of Research in Music, Arts and Design, EIMAD 2020, 14–15 May 2020, pp. 519–533. Springer, Cham (2021)

Melo, A., Neves, M.: Communication design playing a role in social innovation. In: Perspectives on Design II: Research, Education and Practice, pp. 217–232 (2022)

Mulgan, G.: Social Innovation: How Societies Find the Power to Change. Policy press (2019)

Murray, R., Caulier-Grice, J., Mulgan, G.: The open book of social innovation. Young Foundation, NESTA (2010)

Nielsen, J.: Iterative user-interface design. Computer 26(11), 32–41 (1993)

Nielsen, J., Landauer, T.K.: A mathematical model of the finding of usability problems. In: Arnold, B., van der Veer, G., White T. (eds.) Proceedings of the INTERACT '93 and CHI '93 Conference on Human Factors in Computing Systems, pp. 206–213. Association for Computing Machinery (1993)

Neumeier, S.: Why do social innovations in rural development matter and should they be considered more seriously in rural development research? proposal for a stronger focus on social innovations in rural development research. Sociol. Rural. 52(1), 48–69 (2012)

Neves, M.: Printed interactivity towards a new understanding of graphic design. Iridescent 2(2), 22–37 (2012)

Oliván. R., Horrillo. P.: Innovación abierta y cooperación anfibia en Frena la Curva. Frena La Curva (2020). https://festival.frenalacurva.net/innovacion-abierta-y-cooperacion-anfibia-en-frena-la-curva/

Parente, M., Sedini, C.: Design for territories as practice and theoretical field of study. Des. J. 20(sup1), S3047–S3058 (2017)

Parente, M., Sedini, C.: Design as mediator between local resources and global visions: experiences of design for territories. In: Moret, O. (ed.) Back to the Future/The Future in the Past: Conference Proceedings Book, pp. 125–129. Universitat de Barcelona Edicions, Barcelona (2018)

Penin, L., Forlano, L., Staszowski E., Tonkinwise C.: Amplifying CREATIVE COMMUNITIES NEW YORK CITY. In: Penin L., Kobori M., Forlano L., (eds.) Parsons DESIS LAB, Design for Social Innovation and Sustainability Lab, The New School (2009)

Plataforma Lugar (n.d.). https://plataformalugar.pt/

Projeto Queijeiras (n.d.). https://queijeiras.pt/

Rafael, S.: Multimodality, naturalness and transparency in affective computing for HCI. In: Marcus, A., Rosenzweig, E. (eds.) HCII 2020. LNCS, vol. 12200, pp. 521–531. Springer, Cham (2020). https://doi.org/10.1007/978-3-030-49713-2_36

Ruiz-Muzquiz P.: Frena la curva Maps, conectando hispano-hablantes con recursos críticos en su entorno. Frena la Curva (2020

Salazar, K.: Evaluate Interface Learnability with Cognitive Walkthroughs. Nielsen Norman Group (2022). https://www.nngroup.com/articles/cognitive-walkthroughs/

Schoder, D.: Introduction to the Internet of Things. In: Hassan, Q.F. (ed.) Internet of Things A to Z: Technologies and Applications, pp. 1–50. John Wiley & Sons, Hoboken (2018)

Sechi, L., Moscarelli, R., Pileri, P.: Planning tourist infrastructures to regenerate marginalised territories: the study case of North Sardinia, Italy. City Territory Arch. **7**(1), 1–12 (2020)

Schwab, K.: The Fourth Industrial Revolution—What It Means and How to Respond. Foreign Affair (2015). https://www.foreignaffairs.com/world/fourth-industrial-revolution

Stickdorn, M., Hormess, M., Lawrence, A., Schneider J. (eds.): This is Service Design Doing. O'Reilly, Newton (2018)

Swann, C.: Action research and the practice of design. Des. Issues **18**(1), 49–61 (2002)

UMVI. Programa Nacional para a Coesão Territorial. República Portuguesa, Unidade de Missão para a Valorização do Interior (2016)

Viñas, C.D.: Depopulation processes in European rural areas: a case study of Cantabria (Spain). Eur. Countryside **11**(3), 341–369 (2019)

Zuber-Skerritt, O.: Introduction: new directions in action research. In: Zuber-Skerritt, O. (ed.) New Directions in Action Research, pp. 12–17. Routledge, Abingdon (2003)

Looking Through an Ethical and Equitable Lens at the Constructive Disruption of Design Interventions

Lisa Elzey Mercer(⊠)

University of Illinois, Urbana-Champaign, IL 80260, USA
lemercer@illinois.edu

Abstract. The design research process is a powerful tool for effecting positive social change. Still, it must be recognized that it does not, by default, ensure the development of ethical and equitable design outcomes. Instead, we often see design be used to perpetuate the status quo. The pressure to "move fast and break things" or the assumption that good intentions are good enough are catalysts to perpetuate an oppressive design process. Designers can dismantle this false narrative by examining the inherent assumptions and values in a collaborative design process. There is a growing community of designers focused on framing ethical and equitable methodologies, epistemologies, and ontologies in design. As designers collaborate with the community, the design research process needs a recalibration to develop ethical and equitable outcomes. This paper will discuss the impact of design interventions on testimonial injustice in the design process, the value of developing nuanced design interventions, and the efficacy of determining if a design outcome is ethical and equitable. The leading question for this paper is, how can the enactors of human-centered design implement design interventions at the foundation of the design research process that would facilitate the outcome of ethical and equitable design? We must collaborate to develop and implement constructive ways to pause and constructively disrupt the design research process.

Keywords: Ethics · Equity · Design Interventions · Testimonial Injustice

1 Introduction

The design research process is often a powerful methodology for affecting positive social change when enacted collaboratively and applied to reimagine complex social issues. With that stated, engaging in the design research process does not, by default, ensure the development of ethical and equitable design outcomes that benefit the groups they were intended to benefit when they were initiated. All too often, we see the outcomes of design approaches and methodologies perpetuate the typical status quo, and these outcomes often reinforce social, cultural, political, technological, and economic divisions that sustain one or more inequitable cultural norms. The pressure to "move fast and break things" (Zuckerberg 2014) created a culture where enacting methodologies and ways of working disregarded the impact of the designed outcomes. The assumption that good

© The Author(s), under exclusive license to Springer Nature Switzerland AG 2024
A. Marcus et al. (Eds.): HCII 2024, LNCS 14716, pp. 174–180, 2024.
https://doi.org/10.1007/978-3-031-61362-3_13

intentions are good enough yields undesirable outcomes and are catalysts that too often perpetuate a design process that oppresses historically marginalized groups who have been ignored, disregarded, and misrepresented.

Designers have the agency to dismantle, or at the very least question, this biased and myopically informed approach through a critical and rigorous examination of the socio-culturally, socio-politically, and socio-economically informed assumptions and values that may guide the enactment of any given collaborative design process. A growing community of designers, across the design disciplines, are focused on the contemporary practice of design and intentionally emphasize ethical and equitable methodologies, epistemologies, and ontologies. These efforts ensure that a broader perspective of design is acknowledged and moves the discipline away from a monolithic and homogenous narrative that shapes the pedagogy and practice of design. As designers strive to collaborate, they must engage with stakeholders to develop, recalibrate, and implement constructive ways to pause and constructively disrupt the design research process to develop ethical and equitable design outcomes.

Many different definitions of design illuminate the many different processes and ways of working practitioners enact to develop design outcomes. Practitioners can earn an academic designation that gives them the authority to identify as a designer; some have implemented processes and ways of working that also place them in the role of a designer. We all are designers (Manzini 2015). Practitioners who enact a more contemporary design practice would argue that design is not relegated to the elite few. It is a process that benefits from a collaborative and participatory effort. In this paper, ethical and equitable design is the implementation of methodologies, epistemologies, and ontologies in collaborative spaces that result in purposely designed interventions and outcomes focused on impact over intention.

In light of all of this, deploying strategic design interventions in many of these design processes is warranted and could provide design outcomes with a positive impact. Specifically, this paper will discuss:

- the impact of design interventions on testimonial injustices in particular manifestations of the design process;
- the value of developing and deploying nuanced design interventions;
- the efficacy of determining if any given design research process, in terms of how it affects the needs and aspirations of a particular group, is ethical and equitable.

The primary research question that has guided the development of this paper is how could enactors of the human-centered design process implement design interventions, from the inception to outcome, that have the best chance of facilitating outcomes that satisfy the parameters for ethical and equitable design? This paper will argue that we must collaborate with project partners whose knowledge and understandings are informed by disciplines outside design to develop, implement, and sustain constructive ways to pause and constructively disrupt the design research process. The interconnectedness of ethical and equitable methodologies for enactors of the design research process in the design field allows practitioners the opportunity to address complex social issues in a co-design and collaborative space.

2   The Impact of Design Interventions on Testimonial Injustice

Integrating design interventions in the design research process provides designers with a more ethical and equitable way of designing. The interventions instill an ethical and empirical form of interaction and experiences, individually and collectively (Fricker 2007). It is an opportunity to allow for a more elastic and reflexive perspective in a collaborative group dynamic if they work effectively with community members (Harris 2015). Testimonial injustice is the injustice of not knowing; it is the capacity of not knowing to know when a person or group of people are being wronged (Fricker 2006, p. 295). How are we to know what we do not know? Interventions provide a pause to exchange cognitive work with our collaborators, "exchanges of experiences, assessment of struggles (their own and others'), and careful examination of the knowledge that the dominant social groups mobilize to isolate or disarm the oppressed. The work of intercultural translation does have a dimension of curiosity, that is to say, it encourages opening up to new experiences..." (de Sousa Santos 2018, p. 33). One example is an activity focused on positionality, and the knowledge of positionality can have on a collective, collaborative space. Positionality is how our social identities are situated in the broader context of oppression and other socio-cultural constructs. The context of positionality supports their understanding of how we perpetuate and uphold systems of oppression that shape the everyday lives of people who have been historically marginalized (Mercer and Moses 2023). Power dynamics affect(s) group dynamics and are often overlooked in the design research process.

Integrating design interventions that provide enactors of the design research process with an understanding of positionality could result in a more ethical and equitable way of designing. The positive dynamics of positionality and the intersection of those identities shape the lens of liberation, restoration, and transformation. If enactors of the design research process were aware of the positionality from which they work, it could significantly affect design outcomes; this lens is essential to design research. "This socially situated conception puts questions of social identity and power centre stage, and it is the prerequisite for the revelation of a certain ethical dimension to epistemic life-the dimension of justice and injustice" (Fricker 2013, p. 22). Since the pandemic, it has become even more apparent how we comprise a global community, how our actions significantly affect one another, and the emerging globally situated sense of identity. The value of speaking about the globalization of identity further emphasizes the effects of Westernization with the rise of "hegemonic value systems" (Gunn 2013, p. 245).

According to Arturo Escobar, a theorist focused on decolonizing Eurocentric methodologies, the importance of enactors in a co-design process is understanding their positionality. "The realization of this radical potential, to continue with this design theorist, requires a profound relational sensibility that links materiality, visuality, and empathy (via practice) in creating novel assemblages of infrastructures and devices, skills and know-how, and meanings and identities. Finally, there is a shared emphasis on the need to imbue design education with the tools for ontological reflection in ways that make designers conscious of their situatedness in the ecologies for which they design" (Escobar 2017, p. 206). Understanding the variables in determining if the outcomes are ethical and responsible is also essential. Could they be evaluated by developing a benchmark of success and pre-determining what success would look like per project?

Design Interventions provide a reflective space where educators and practitioners can "support a commitment to understanding the relationships among theory, designed artifacts, and practice" while contributing to a more responsible design process in academia and industry (Design-Based Research Collective 2003, p. 6).

We are born into an existing system with sociocultural constructs that we need to make sense of and contextualize geographically and culturally. This regard for identity provides a lens for orientation; as researchers, educators, and practitioners, it affects how we work, create questions, and collect and analyze data. "...we are all born into a world of meaning bestowed upon us by our culture. Thus, qualitative researchers seek to understand the context or setting of the participants through visiting this context and gathering information personally" (Creswell 2018, p. 8). The interconnectedness of positionality and empathy illuminates ethical and responsible methodologies for enactors in the design field to address complex social issues in a co-design space. Designers engage with empathy in the design process when working with the community to design an artifact, system, or experience.

3 Nuanced Design Interventions

Design interventions are tools that prompt critical reflection and analysis of a way of thinking or action. The potential to allow a nuanced set of design interventions to positively affect a particular design endeavor would depend greatly on the project's focus and stated goals. What design interventions could be integrated to ensure practitioners reflect on their choices at each step? The enactors of the design research process are guiding the experience through the development of a designed outcome. They could focus on working with stakeholders from a specific population to ensure that impact is valued over intentions. Design interventions that are formulated and operationalized ensure that reflective choices are made with and on behalf of the population we are designing. The impact of implementing design interventions into the design research process could result in disruptions that dismantle power dynamics baked into the formulation and operation of the design research process. The determined design interventions implemented should broadly inform discourse and consistently open communication between the enactors of the design research process at different junctures in its evolution. In turn, this would encourage critical reflection among each member of the collaborative process (Lambe and Osborne 2019).

In 2013 Jon Kolko, from the Austin Center for Design, opened the LEAP dialogues with a challenging statement, "while designers are typically well-intentioned, many lack the ethical framework to guide their practice" (Amatullo. The Art Center College of Design organized the LEAP dialogues: The New Professional Frontier in Design for Social Innovation. It intended to focus on career trajectories for designers interested in working toward social innovation and the development of design interventions. One track at the event was titled Multi/Cross-Disciplinary Engagement: Partnerships and Collaborations. It focused on comprehensive proposals, "in which the implications of how and where a design intervention or design process may be situated and carried out within various forms of collaboration" (Amatullo 2014). Winterhouse Institute and co-developed, with feedback from hundreds of designers and educators, started the matrix that resulted from the track.

The matrix considers the range of expertise (x-axis: individual, interdisciplinary, and cross-sector) to the scale of engagement (y-axis: project, system, and culture). They defined these as 1) the range of expertise, a group of experts and collaborators focused on a problem, and 2) the scale of engagement, which is for the reader to understand the level and scale of the design intervention hoping to affect change. They further explain that this work could be done at different levels: project, system, and/or cultural (Winterhouse 2020). The matrix guided designers in determining potential areas within the design research process to integrate design interventions. It also provided an intervention into the different collaborations and partnerships that could develop and implement interventions. This matrix assists practitioner(s) in questioning the status quo of the design research process, actively working to dismantle systems of oppression, and working collaboratively to solve complex social issues. The process must be ethical and equitable to develop a design outcome that takes into account the effects of its impact. Understanding the variables in determining if the process's outcomes are ethical and equitable is essential.

4 Ethical and Equitable Processes

It is the conviction in the existence of numerous ethical and equitable ways of working that designers must consider the efficacy of the design research process in terms of how it affects the needs and aspirations of particular groups of people and if the process is ethical and equitable. We must critically consider the numerous and varied ways ethics, equity, values, and morals find meaning in the design discipline. Our "professional responsibility" is to resist a single narrative or homogenous and monolithic lens of how values are perceived. Instead, we should engage in the design process in ways that require us to consciously produce ethical and equitable design outcomes (Friere 2012, p.187). When we work to understand, unlearn, and take pause in the processes we enact, then we begin to understand how "the failures of the past may be seen not as errors of practice but rather as errors of the thinking behind the practice" (de Sousa Santos 2018, p. 264).

Vikram Patel shares in his 2012 TedTalk his frustration with the lack of mental healthcare resources available to people in India. He was trained in mental healthcare models that utilized specialized professionals. However, he quickly realized that the number of professionals needed was lacking in India. He learned about task shifting to provide "mental health interventions, empowering ordinary people to care for others" (Patel 2012). In this context, the term intervention refers "to the task that is shifted or shared… Interventions in this context may be preventive, curative, therapeutic, diagnostic, or another health action" (Orkin 2021, p. 4). Training "ordinary people," people who have not had specialized health care education, to diagnose and support people in the areas of mental health provided rural spaces in developing countries with an intervention and a new mindset around the structural support for mental healthcare.

"Now, for me, task shifting is an idea with truly global significance because even though it has arisen out of the situation of the lack of resources that you find in developing countries, I think it has a lot of significance for better-resourced countries as well. Why is that? Well, in part, because health care in the developed world, the health care costs in the [developed] world, are rapidly spiraling out of control, and a huge chunk of those costs are human resource costs. But equally important is because health care has become so incredibly professionalized that it's become very remote and removed from local communities" (Patel 2012, min. 9:27).

Patel points out strong evidence that supports how interventions can impact medical, psychological, and social differences. Even with this evidence, he acknowledges the injustice in bridging the gulf between knowing how to transform the lives of people who are affected by mental illness and how we can apply that knowledge in supporting people with mental health needs and those in their everyday circle of care.

The types of interventions Patel incorporates into the healthcare system are from a pluralistic perspective and a social approach. The plurality of this approach broke down the false dichotomy of having or not having access to specialists trained in mental health illnesses. The interventions Patel introduced are strong examples of ethical and equitable approaches to mental healthcare in developing and better-resourced countries. Donald Schön, an American philosopher and professor in urban planning at the Massachusetts Institute of Technology, explores the idea of conflicting paradigms in professional practice when approaching a problem. It requires multiple ways of framing and a critical inquiry that falls outside of a professional's technical expertise; he termed this technical rationality (Schön 1991). He highlights the gap between people with professional technical rationality and everyday problems.

"Whether you're a designer, product manager, or engineer, we should all have an appetite to break down the siloes that prevent us from communicating, collaborating, and garnering strategic alignment together (Bethune 2022, p. 161). We can develop generative and innovative design outcomes when considering ethical implications by working in collaborative and co-participatory spaces. A space where we can focus on developing alternative solutions to everyday current situations (Sanders 2008).

5   Points for Further Understanding

The design research process is an iterative design process that could be more ethical at its foundation and requires its enactors to consider the impact of their developed outcomes. Many educators are interested in embedding the study of ethical design into their curricula and programs. As a field, we are trying to create a better understanding of the paradox of choice, design processes, and interconnectedness for the development of ethical and equitable outcomes. As designers, we are responsible for the work we develop and place in the public domain. Designers develop, implement, and iterate design interventions specific to the communities they are working with.

These interventions are stronger when developed in collaboration with community members specific to the complex social issue. While there is clear evidence of the value of design interventions, the next step is to determine what is at the foundation of an intervention that has been a successful change agent toward a complex social issue. Further clarifying the ways of working in the different collaborative groups and the projects being developed. The work discussed in the chapter outlines an effective and positive way of working. However, it requires further analysis and interviews with more designers and collaborative partners interested in developing interventions that question the status quo.

Designers are working to determine ways of working ethically, and we need to continue questioning the role of ethics in the design research process. The process needs to be reflexive and consider the role of design interventions in order to work collaboratively with community members. At its foundation, the human-centered design process does not ultimately develop an equitable space for all. It perpetuates the status quo. We need to work with students and emerging designers to develop interventions that require designers to stop at certain steps of the process to determine what we are trying to achieve and who we are trying to achieve it with if the design outcome is developed in an equitable space. Implementing design interventions into the design research process could result in a more responsible way of designing at the very foundation of how designers work.

References

Bartunek, J.M., Moch, M.K.: First-order, second-order, and third-order change and organization development design interventions: a cognitive approach. J. Appl. Behav. Sci. **23**(4), 483–500 (1987)

Bethune, K.G.: Reimagining Design (Simplicity: Design, Technology, Business, Life). The MIT Press, Cambridge (2022)

Creswell, J.W., Creswell, J.D.: Research Design. SAGE Publications, Thousands Oaks (2018)

Design-Based Research Collective: Design-based research: an emerging paradigm for educational inquiry. Educ. Res. **32**(1), 5–8 (2003)

de Sousa Santos, B.: The End of the Cognitive Empire the Coming of Age of Epistemologies of the South. Duke University Press, Durham (2018)

Escobar, A.: Designs for the Pluriverse: Radical Interdependence, Autonomy, and the Making of Worlds. Duke University Press, Durham (2017)

Fricker, M.: Epistemic Injustice: Power and the Ethics of Knowing. Oxford University Press, Oxford (2007)

Freire, P.: Pedagogy of the Oppressed 50th Anniversary Edition. First published in 2000 by the Continuum International Publishing, Bloomsbury Academic Publishing, New (2018)

Gunn, W., Otto, T., Smith, R.C.: Design Anthropology. Bloomsbury, New York (2013)

Harris, M.: "Harvey B. Gantt Center - Introduction to AfriCOBRA & AfriCOBRA NOW. YouTube, min. 4:10 (2015). https://www.youtube.com/watch?v=7XegxlZ1Qqg

Lambe, F., Osborne, M.: Designing transformative development design interventions. Stockholm Environment Institute (2019). https://doi.org/10.2307/resrep22972

Manzini, E.: Design, When Everybody Designs: An Introduction to Design for Social Innovation. The MIT Press, Cambridge (2015)

Mercer, L., Moses, T.: Racism Untaught Revealing and Unlearning Racialized Design. The MIT Press, Cambridge (2023)

Orkin, A.M., Rao, S., Venugopal, J., et al.: Conceptual framework for task shifting and task sharing: an international Delphi study. Hum. Resour. Health **19**, 61 (2021). https://doi.org/10.1186/s12960-021-00605-z

Sanders, L.: ON MODELING An evolving map of design practice and design research. Interactions **15**, 13–17 (2008)

Schön, D.A.: The Reflective Practitioner. Ashgate Publishing, Farnham (1991)

Zuckerberg, M. Move Fast and Break Things. Facebook Motto until (2014)

Navigating the Generation Z Wave: Transforming Digital Assistants into Dream Companions with a Touch of Luxury, Hedonism, and Excitement

Weizhu Pan[1], Yunxuan Xing[1], Siwen Ge[1], Lubing He[1], Zhuoyi Sha[1], Ziwen Chen[1], Chengka Wong[1], Wenyuan Jiang[1], Yang Li[1], Xiaotian Ma[1], Guoxuan Xie[1], Yutong Zhai[1], Qi Zhang[1], Yiyang Liu[1], Ruilu Yu[1], Bowen Li[1], Ruonan Huang[1], Mengmeng Xu[2(✉)], Yang Guo[2(✉)], and Wei Liu[1(✉)]

[1] Beijing Key Laboratory of Applied Experimental Psychology, National Demonstration Center for Experimental Psychology Education (Beijing Normal University), Faculty of Psychology, Beijing Normal University, Beijing 100875, China
wei.liu@bnu.edu.cn
[2] Chapter of User Experience, Porsche Digital China, Shanghai 200120, China

Abstract. Individuals born between 1995 and 2009 are referred to as the Generation Z population, characterized by their pursuit of pleasure, innovation, and interaction. As the driving force behind automotive purchases in the next two to three decades, the automotive industry needs to understand their core requirements for in-car intelligent assistants. In this study, we collaborated with Porsche, a brand synonymous with luxury, hedonism, and excitement, to complete three task design briefs based on different user groups. Throughout the model development process, we employed evaluation methods such as heuristic assessment, user testing, and expert reviews, ensuring our models provide personalized services for specific demographics. This not only enhances the driving experience by making it more intelligent, enjoyable, and comfortable but also aligns with the growing expectations of the Generation Z population towards automotive technology. This collaboration offers valuable insights for the future development of the automotive industry, enabling it to better adapt to the digital age and meet the evolving needs of users.

Keywords: Human-Centered Design · Generation Z · Digital Assistants · Luxury · Hedonism · Excitement · Interaction Design

1 Introduction

1.1 Generation Z

With the development of the times and advancements in technology, the internet and smart devices have gradually become ubiquitous in people's lives. Generation Z, born between 1995 and 2009, is a generation that grew up in such an environment, often

A. Marcus et al. (Eds.): HCII 2024, LNCS 14716, pp. 181–192, 2024.
https://doi.org/10.1007/978-3-031-61362-3_14

referred to as the generation raised alongside digital technology [1, 2]. Their lifestyle habits and behaviors show significant differences from their predecessors. For instance, studies have found that Generation Z spends an average of over 5 h per day on smartphones, with shorter attention spans compared to the preceding Generation Y (born between 1980 and 1995). This further shapes their unique values and consumer concepts.

Firstly, they prioritize the satisfaction of personal interests, enjoying engaging with and adopting emerging technologies. Secondly, they prefer expressive freedom, using social media to discuss real-life experiences and evaluate purchased items. Additionally, they emphasize timely communication and feedback, considering interaction between themselves and others as crucial. It is evident that Generation Z places a greater emphasis on self-experience in consumption and highlights the quality of interaction between products and users. Based on this, research has summarized six interaction qualities that Generation Z focuses on: instant, enjoyable, collaborative, expressive, novelty-seeking, and self-pleasing [3].

From a brand perspective, these findings can offer valuable insights for product design. Considering that Generation Z has become the predominant consumer group today, studying their consumption patterns is highly beneficial for a brand's revenue growth and sustainable development. In various fields, many brands have conducted in-depth investigations and research on the characteristics of Generation Z. They have used the results to enhance the interaction quality of their products, making them more aligned with the needs of Generation Z users and seizing the initiative in the consumer market.

1.2 Digital Assistants (DA)

In recent years, the emergence of in-car DA has had a significant impact on the Chinese consumer market, creating a profound influence, especially among the younger Generation Z. As highly intelligent and interactive digital products, in-car DA have garnered increasing attention from the younger generation.

The development of in-car DA has undergone a lengthy process. In the early stages of automotive development, vehicles primarily consisted of mechanical and electrical systems, with limited application of digital technology. It wasn't until the late 1990s and early 2000s that the development of in-car digital systems led to the rise of in-car entertainment and navigation systems. These systems utilized global positioning systems (GPS) and digital map technology to provide navigation, audio, and video entertainment functions [4, 5]. With the rise of the internet, in-car DA became more connected to external networks, enabling vehicles to communicate with the internet, supporting real-time information updates, remote monitoring, and remote control.

By the mid-2010s, the emergence of autonomous driving technology propelled the development of in-car DA, with advanced driver assistance systems (ADAS) becoming mainstream. These systems included functions such as automatic emergency braking, lane-keeping assistance, and adaptive cruise control. Subsequently, the design and application of DA continued to evolve, with researchers exploring various approaches and technologies for the digitization of vehicles [6, 7].

In 2007, at the Tokyo Motor Show, Nissan unveiled the microelectric concept car PIVO2, featuring a "built-in robotic companion," presenting an early prototype of an in-car intelligent robot. In 2009, the MIT SENSEable City Laboratory and Volkswagen jointly developed the AIDA emotional intelligent driving assistant. In 2017, Toyota introduced the in-car intelligent robot Kirobo Mini. In 2018, NIO, an OEM manufacturer with an internet background in China, applied the NOMI robot, an in-car AI (Artificial Intelligence) system, to mass-produced cars, evolving from a simple robot to a companion and friend during the driving process. Chinese new energy vehicle manufacturer, NIO, unveiled the ideal family technology day, releasing the new ideal companion, equipped with the self-developed Mind GPT. It is known that Mind GPT has undergone training with a base model of 13 trillion tokens, meticulously filtered and deduplicated from tens of terabytes of raw training data, equivalent to possessing a comprehensive sum of high-quality human knowledge. The new ideal companion supports voice recognition, content recognition, dialect recognition, travel planning, and even AI drawing, story writing, AI calculation, logical reasoning, and programming. In summary, as an emerging phenomenon in recent years, DA have rapidly iterated, with increasing computing power and rapid development.

1.3 Research Objectives

As evident from the preceding discussion, the development, design, and evolution of DA have primarily been approached from a scientific and technological standpoint, overlooking the crucial importance of a user-centric focus. This study aims to depart from this convention by starting with user needs, integrating a psychological background, and undertaking a user-centric design to offer fresh insights into DA design. The focus of this research is the predominant demographic in the current consumer market—the Generation Z. Specific user segments within Generation Z were meticulously analyzed to identify their distinct needs and expectations regarding in-car DA, aligning human-machine interactions with the characteristics of Generation Z. Additionally, this study explores the multimodal interaction design of DA in the vehicular environment, encompassing aspects such as voice, gestures, and touch. This approach aims to provide a more flexible and convenient user interaction experience, meeting the diverse interactive requirements of Generation Z users. The Porsche company, which this study serves, has relatively slow progress in the development of DA, and its technology is comparatively lagging. Consequently, this research has the potential to offer recommendations for the development of DA, not only for Porsche but also for similar brands, to a certain extent.

2   Methodology

In the autumn semester of 2023, 15 undergraduate psychology students, organized into five groups, completed three task design projects for Porsche in the Engineering Psychology classroom. From introducing Porsche's concepts in class to students autonomously creating low-fidelity models, the process involved two rounds of user testing and one expert review, collectively refining three models tailored to different user groups.

2.1 Practice and Collaboration-Based Classroom

Unlike conventional classrooms, this was a hands-on and collaborative learning experience. The teaching model focused on providing students with in-depth knowledge of engineering psychology through practical applications and delivering creative solutions to collaborating companies [8–11]. The practice and collaboration-based classroom comprised five essential elements: (1) Positive interdependence, (2) Face-to-face promotive interaction, (3) Individual accountability/personal responsibility, (4) Teamwork skills, and (5) Group processing. This project not only offered students practical opportunities but also encouraged them to apply their knowledge of engineering psychology in real-world scenarios, presenting innovative and practical solutions to the collaborating company.

2.2 Collaborative Partners

The collaboration took place with the luxury car brand Porsche. Its sleek design and unique brand values have attracted numerous consumers. However, in today's fiercely competitive automotive market, many brands have successfully integrated DA into their systems, leaving Porsche somewhat behind in this area. Recognizing this, Porsche sought solutions from us. Before commencing the project, Porsche presented their current intelligent assistant—Blue Hole. This shape-shifting voice assistant engages in conversations with passengers, offering features such as navigation, vehicle assistance information, weather updates, and more. However, during the heuristic evaluation in class, students unanimously suggested that while this design partially meets user needs, it might lack distinctiveness and face challenges in error correction. The goal is, therefore, to design an intelligent assistant model that aligns with the expectations of Generation Z users based on the concept of Blue Hole. Through this collaboration, we aim to enhance the user experience of the intelligent assistant, address potential issues, and give Porsche a competitive edge in the digital era.

2.3 Evaluation Tools

Our design underwent an evolution from the initial low-fidelity model to the final design model, including two rounds of user testing and one expert review. The objective of user testing was to assess the model comprehensively from the perspective of real users, while the expert review focused on evaluating the operability and suitability of design concepts from a professional standpoint. In the first round of user testing, we utilized a simplified scale (UEQ-S) with eight questions on a 7-point rating system, covering aspects from "obtrusive" to "helpful" (scores ranging from 1 to 7) [12]. Subsequently, experts were invited for a review, emphasizing professional aspects like "whether users attempt to achieve the correct results," providing four key criteria. The final round of user testing employed a more comprehensive scale (UEQ) with 26 questions, again using a 7-point rating system, encompassing aspects from "annoying" to "pleasant" (scores ranging from 1 to 7). This series of testing and evaluation processes ensured a thorough examination of our design in terms of user experience and professional standards, laying a solid foundation for the final design model. Based on the results of user testing and expert review, each group iteratively refined their design, resulting in the following achievements.

3   Results

3.1   Wealthy Second Generation

The target users for this group are the wealthy second generation of Generation Z. They enjoy superior living conditions, are enthusiastic about socializing, exhibit a higher-than-average spending capacity, have a keen interest in entertainment activities, and seek luxury and exceptional experiences. They value customizable designs to showcase their uniqueness. Often found in high-end shopping malls, clubs, and exclusive venues, these individuals may also engage in regular business negotiations and serious work, especially if they have inherited family businesses. As one of the primary purchasing groups for Porsche, the wealthy second generation considers Porsche not just a symbol of noble status but also expects the in-car intelligent assistant to enhance their overall driving experience. Current intelligent assistants focus more on meeting basic functional needs, lacking emphasis on customizable, diverse interactions preferred by high-end customers. Therefore, our design primarily addresses the core needs of this group, aiming to improve existing designs.

Our story revolves around a young female member of the wealthy second generation (see Fig. 1). Before setting off each day, the Blue Hole system authorizes access to the user's daily schedule and adjusts in-car settings such as temperature and seat height based on the owner's preferences. While driving to the mall, the Blue Hole system can match information about friends with similar itineraries and, with the owner's consent, decide whether to inform the owner if they would like to join (privacy mode is also an option). Ten minutes before reaching the mall, the radar system in the car notifies the store staff that an important customer is about to arrive, prompting them to prepare for an ultimate service experience. It's worth noting that the scenarios for schedule matching and radar system use are versatile, covering various locations such as clubs, stadiums, hotels, etc., meeting the personalized needs of each customer. The intelligent assistant ensures thorough preparation for daily needs. If the wealthy second-generation owner needs to attend a meeting but can't be there in person, the in-car projection system activates when the vehicle is completely stationary, simulating a real meeting scene and initiating privacy-protected glass. When there's a passenger in the front seat, the Blue Hole can recognize passengers through facial recognition, adjusting the seat automatically based on their previous preferences. While the front seat passenger is doing makeup, the Blue Hole activates ambient lighting, signals the car to decelerate, and pushes relevant beauty tutorial videos based on the passenger's request. When the front seat passenger is watching a video on the tablet in front of them, the screen enters privacy mode to avoid disturbing the driver, providing a safer driving environment.

Twelve users participated in the usability test, and the scores for this model were consistently above average, with practicality scores higher than enjoyment scores. Users acknowledged that this intelligent assistant enhanced their overall experience. Expert reviews focused on the need to consider the relationship between users and the intelligent assistant: whether users perceive it as a machine, or a friend might affect their evaluation of the system. Additionally, the operability of this model received positive affirmation. The model presented above is a synthesis of opinions from various perspectives.

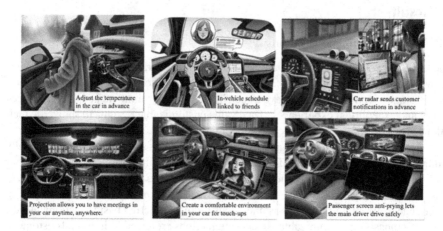

Fig. 1. The user scenario.

3.2 Rental Customer

As digital natives of the internet era, Generation Z places a strong emphasis on self-expression and personal presentation in front of others. They aspire to showcase themselves in a perfect and outstanding manner, leaning towards fashion and luxury. However, for those who have just entered the workforce, their economic income often cannot support their desire for luxury items such as luxury cars. Faced with the inability to afford their preferred items, they often choose the option of renting.

Our story focuses on a social-loving white-collar rental customer (see Fig. 2). The rental customer opens the rental app on their phone and selects a Porsche as their ride. After placing the order, within a few minutes, a self-driving Porsche arrives, already adjusted to the most comfortable driving seat mode based on the customer's preferences in the app. Upon getting into the car, the in-car DA immediately flashes different parts of the car, introducing various features and functions. This intelligent assistant understands natural language and provides various services based on the customer's needs. Additionally, the intelligent assistant offers a "Welcome Mode," with the car's cool lighting system and a projected message on the car window saying, "Welcome" making the entire car look more technological and stylish, helping others instantly recognize the customer's vehicle. On the road, the rental customer wants to take some photos to share on social media. The DA, by analyzing their needs, automatically selects some optimal shooting locations. These photos are not only rich in color but also visually impactful, making the rental customer's friends envious. Upon reaching the destination, the rental customer informs the DA via the mobile app to park the car in the restaurant's parking lot, eliminating the need to drive manually. The DA accurately finds a parking space and helps park the vehicle. During the meal, the rental customer enjoys the ultimate service provided by the DA. They inform the DA via the mobile app to have the car wait near the restaurant, and after finishing the meal, the DA automatically brings the car to the restaurant's entrance, saving the rental customer the trouble of finding the car. At the end of the journey, the rental customer is ready to return the car. The DA conducts a full scan of the car, checking for any damage or missing items, ensuring the customer has no worries. After returning the car, the DA deletes all privacy information about the customer and their girlfriend, ensuring the customer's privacy.

According to the UEQ-8 data analysis, the overall score is good, the pragmatic quality is mediocre, and the hedonic quality is excellent, with the hedonic quality significantly higher than the pragmatic quality. According to the UEQ-26 data analysis, attractiveness and hedonic quality received positive evaluations from users, while pragmatic quality received neutral evaluations. Thus, it is concluded that there is room for improvement in the design related to practical aspects of the task.

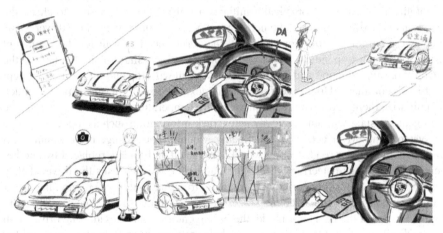

Fig. 2. The user scenario.

3.3 Racing Enthusiast

For amateur racing enthusiasts, their demands for the DA are closely tied to their passion for speed, performance, and precise control. These enthusiasts seek the ultimate driving experience, placing high demands on the vehicle's performance parameters, track information, and real-time data feedback. Additionally, they may desire quick access to racing-related news, events, or other social functions through voice commands to stay closely connected with the racing community. Unlike professional racers, the DA needs of racing enthusiasts may extend beyond racing scenarios, encompassing both daily driving and racing situations. Therefore, they expect the DA to have a broader range of applications while providing assistance in terms of safety. However, current in-car DA fall short in meeting the specific needs of racing enthusiasts. Firstly, existing DA may lack precision in handling complex, specialized racing terminology and user commands, failing to provide professional-level data analysis and advice. Secondly, racing enthusiasts demand high-quality information processing during driving, and the noise in racing environments may disrupt the accuracy of the voice recognition system, leading to command execution errors. Lastly, racing enthusiasts often require more advanced customization services, such as adjusting in-car system settings based on personal preferences or providing track strategy advice. Existing DA systems often have limited functionality in personalized services. Therefore, to better serve this unique user group, significant improvements in voice recognition technology, real-time data processing capabilities, personalized services, and integration of professional racing knowledge are needed for in-car DA. Through these optimizations, the DA will be able to provide more accurate, fast, and personalized services, greatly enhancing the driving experience and satisfaction of racing enthusiasts.

To address the needs of the target audience and the current shortcomings of intelligent assistants, we have set the following scenarios to highlight the features of the Porsche Intelligent Assistant designed by our team. Upon sensing the driver getting into the car, the intelligent assistant automatically initiates a full vehicle safety scan to check the condition of the tires, engine, and other safety aspects. While driving, if the driver wants to change a command after completing it, they don't need to wait for the intelligent assistant to finish responding. They can simply press the "Shut up" button next to the touchpad or say, "shut up," and the intelligent assistant will stop outputting and re-accept the driver's command. Upon reaching the racetrack, the driver will run a lap on the track to familiarize themselves with it and increase tire temperature. During this process, the intelligent assistant will automatically enter track information such as topography into the system. The driver activates the "Racing Mode" through fingerprint scanning. In this mode, the regular road steering wheel is retracted and folded, replaced by another racing-specific square steering wheel. The intelligent assistant asks the driver if they want to activate the "navigator mode," where a virtual navigator will remind the driver of things to note during the upcoming race. Once everything is ready, the race officially begins. Firstly, in the navigator mode, the intelligent assistant provides the driver with rich track information. On one hand, it verbally reports the current standings and lap time information on the field; on the other hand, it uses projection technology to display real-time track maps, track temperature, tire grip, and other parameters on the bottom right corner of the car windshield. Secondly, the intelligent assistant also plays a role in safety assistance. In terms of hearing, the intelligent assistant provides the driver with information about upcoming bends, ensuring that the driver can decelerate into the bend in a timely manner. In terms of vision, it calculates the optimal line for the vehicle based on real-time track scanning and displays it on the car windshield through a projector. In terms of touch, the steering wheel continuously monitors the driver's heart rate and blood pressure. If both are abnormal, indicating that the driver is likely in a dangerous state, the vehicle will enter autopilot mode and park the vehicle in a safe area to ensure the driver's safety. In addition, to provide a more immersive racing experience for the driver, when the vehicle speed exceeds a certain value, the intelligent assistant will activate the "Immersive Mode." Using augmented reality (AR) technology, the engine roar resonates fully inside the car, enhancing the thrill of the race. During the race, both interior and exterior cameras will promptly record the exciting moments of the race. The intelligent assistant will upload these photos to the in-car screen and the driver's mobile device for viewing and saving after the race. Additionally, the race video will be recorded by the intelligent assistant. If the driver does not have time to go to the racetrack, they can simulate the track conditions through the in-car projector, allowing the driver to enjoy the fun of racing without leaving home.

We presented the above concepts through low-fidelity cardboard prototypes and recruited 25 participants for product testing. Based on user feedback, we iterated and improved the prototype twice. Twelve participants conducted usability testing using an 8-question UEQ and low-fidelity user interface (UI). The results showed that pragmatic dimension, hedonic dimension, and overall scores were all at an excellent level, with particularly high scores in the hedonic dimension. This indicates that our design meets users' psychological needs for enjoying and passionate quality. Additionally, some participants provided personalized evaluations based on their own experiences. Based on this subjective feedback, we made the first round of improvements to the product, such as adding car safety scanning and changing the button position on the steering wheel to prevent accidental touches. Subsequently, 13 target users conducted usability testing using a 26-question UEQ and low-fidelity UI. The results showed that scores for all dimensions were above the average. From the user's subjective feedback, they accepted the current product design and provided some innovative improvement suggestions. Based on this, we made final improvements and optimizations to the UI design, enriching the interaction methods of human-computer interaction, monitoring the driver's physiological state to ensure safety, and adding online sharing functions for racing modes with others (Fig. 3).

Fig. 3. The user scenario.

4   Discussion and Reflection

4.1   Achievements and Contributions

Firstly, this course provided an opportunity for psychology students to engage in communication and collaboration with brands, offering a unique classroom experience. In this course, students dived into the theoretical knowledge of human-computer interaction, focusing on "enhancing overall design" and considering how to balance human factors, context, and emotions. Under various themes, the challenge was to imbue the intelligent assistant with excitement, high-tech appeal, and luxury. Traditionally, students primarily learn theoretical knowledge, but this course allowed them to apply psychology in a practical setting. Psychology in the classroom finally moved beyond theoretical frameworks and into real-world applications.

Secondly, this course focused on Generation Z, bringing innovative thinking to Porsche. Porsche, with its long history and high-end positioning, has seen a shift in its primary consumer base towards a younger demographic. To stay relevant, automotive brands need to understand what young people like in cars and what functionalities they expect from intelligent assistants. In this course, six groups targeted Generation Z, focusing on six specific user groups. The perspectives were novel and diverse, and each group developed targeted features. Through user evaluations, expert reviews, and multiple iterations, each group's design ideas matured. Porsche can directly consider these designs as inspiration for the development of new products.

Finally, the outcomes of this course also serve as a reference for future trends in intelligent assistant technology. Throughout the entire cycle of creating their works, students continuously consulted materials, analyzed the development of intelligent assistants, and conducted competitor analyses. The functionalities designed by students were not arbitrary; some technologically advanced companies have already implemented parts of these functionalities. Generation Z is the first generation born in the digital world and will be the main user group for intelligent assistants in the future. As designers of Generation Z, students have thought from the perspectives of both the brand and consumers. Their creativity will, to a certain extent, guide the future development of intelligent assistants.

4.2   Deviations in User Needs Estimation

Due to the more individual interest-focused approach in selecting personas by the three research groups, the actual needs analysis during user profiling relied more on limited cases and stereotypes. Therefore, the envisioned functionalities based on these assumptions may not align with the actual needs of users. Additionally, although these considerations match the current ideas of young people in Generation Z, the age range of the target personas may not necessarily align with this restriction. When the age and economic levels of Generation Z align with the target personas, do they still possess these traits? Existing research and analysis cannot predict the answer to this question.

4.3   Insufficient Understanding of Existing Technology

The research groups mainly designed the intelligent assistant based on meeting user interaction needs, combining conceptual design with existing technology. However, core technologies, including precise voice recognition, input feedback, and real-time correction, still need further fine-tuning to align with design goals. Additionally, some functionalities need to be used in conjunction with in-car hardware, such as holographic projection on the windshield and intelligent privacy design. Achieving these features still requires further technological breakthroughs.

4.4 Prospects

Building on the existing design, research groups and other course members will pay more attention to direct communication with the brand in the future. This approach will not only align design thinking more closely with brand needs but also enable students to transition from theoretical classroom knowledge to practical application, mastering application skills more effectively. For the brand, this collaborative exchange provides insights unique to Generation Z. In the future, when improving the intelligent assistant and functionalities of vehicles, they may analyze the required features from the research groups' designs to meet diverse targets. Looking at the overall field development, this research design can serve as a reference for the development of more human-centered intelligent assistant services in the future.

References

1. Hernandez-de-Menendez, M., Escobar Díaz, C.A., Morales-Menendez, R.: Educational experiences with Generation Z. Int. J. Interact. Des. Manuf. **14**, 847–859 (2020)
2. Fan, A., Shin, H.W., Shi, J., Wu, L.: Young people share, but do So differently: an empirical comparison of peer-to-peer accommodation consumption between millennials and generation Z. Cornell Hosp. Q. **64**(3), 322–337 (2023)
3. Xin, X., et al.: X thinking in the experience economy era: 23 personas that identify generation Z interaction qualities. Creat. Innov. Entrepre. **74**, 86–94 (2023)
4. Maedche, A., et al.: AI-based digital assistants: opportunities, threats, and research perspectives. Bus. Inf. Syst. Eng. **61**, 535–544 (2019)
5. Sachdev, S., Macwan, J., Patel, C., Doshi, N.: Voice-controlled autonomous vehicle using IoT. Procedia Comput. Sci. **160**, 712–717 (2019)
6. Mahajan, K., Large, D.R., Burnett, G., Velaga, N.R.: Exploring the benefits of conversing with a digital voice assistant during automated driving: a parametric duration model of takeover time. Transport. Res. F: Traffic Psychol. Behav. **80**, 104–126 (2021)
7. Chattaraman, V., Kwon, W.S., Gilbert, J.E., Ross, K.: Should AI-Based, conversational digital assistants employ social-or task-oriented interaction style? a task-competency and reciprocity perspective for older adults. Comput. Hum. Behav. **90**, 315–330 (2019)
8. Visser, F.S., Stappers, P.J., Van der Lugt, R., Sanders, E.B.: Contextmapping: experiences from practice. CoDesign **1**(2), 119–149 (2005)
9. Liu, W., Lee, K.P., Gray, C.M., Toombs, A.L., Chen, K.H., Leifer, L.: Transdisciplinary teaching and learning in UX design: a program review and AR case studies. Appl. Sci. **11**(22), 10648 (2021)
10. Kokotsaki, D., Menzies, V., Wiggins, A.: Project-based learning: a review of the literature. Improv. Sch. **19**(3), 267–277 (2016)

11. Desmet, P.M., Xue, H., Xin, X., Liu, W.: Demystifying emotion for designers: a five-day course based on seven fundamental principles. Adv. Des. Res. 1(1), 50–62 (2023)
12. Schrepp, M., Hinderks, A., Thomaschewski, J.: Design and evaluation of a short version of the user experience questionnaire (UEQ-S). Int. J. Interact. Multimedia Artif. Intell. 4(6), 103–108 (2017)

Discovering Unanticipated Uses of Interactive Applications to Improve Usability and Enhance Functionality

Yonglei Tao and Jagdeesh Nandigam[✉]

Grand Valley State University, Allendale, MI, USA
`nandigaj@gvsu.edu`

Abstract. As users use an interactive application, they may, deliberately or inadvertently, use it in ways not anticipated by the developer. Unanticipated use of an application is considered an important and positive phenomenon. It reveals clues to improve usability and enhance functionality, which were not conceived of in the initial design phase. However, developers often fail to benefit from such an opportunity due to the lack of sufficient knowledge about user behavior with respect to task completion. We propose an approach to discovering unexpected uses of an interactive application. In our approach, we choose aspect-oriented instrumentation to capture user interface events across architectural boundaries of an interactive application, perform model-based analysis to identify tasks and task sequences from preprocessed event traces, and conduct criteria-guided evaluation to discover unanticipated uses. Our goal is to provide tool support that is adaptable to an evolving application.

Keywords: Unanticipated Use of Interactive Applications · Tool Support for Usability Evolution · Reusable Software Design

1 Introduction

An interactive application evolves during its lifetime due to changes in functional requirements, user profiles, interaction technologies, as well as contexts of use. Changes for an evolving application are mostly adaptive, rather than corrective [5]. Hence, systematic observation of application use, particularly where it is not used as the developer anticipated, is beneficial in assisting effective application evolution to occur [1].

When users choose to use an interactive application, they also choose how to interact with it. They may, deliberately or inadvertently, use it in ways that are not anticipated by the developer [3]. Unanticipated use of an application is considered an important and positive phenomenon [9]. In many cases, unanticipated uses appear as creative workarounds by users to better fit their tasks, for example, carrying out certain tasks in a more efficient way [1]. Moreover, an application can afford a certain degree of flexibility; users who were never targeted by the developer can explore its functionality and find an alternative way to meet their needs even though the application was not

A. Marcus et al. (Eds.): HCII 2024, LNCS 14716, pp. 193–202, 2024.
https://doi.org/10.1007/978-3-031-61362-3_15

designed with such needs in mind [2]. Attempts that lead to unanticipated uses are not accidental. In response to needs that arise in an evolving context, user perceptions of the overall value of an application persuade them to seek solutions with its assistance. Users often find alternative ways to use an application by reconstructing a usual sequence of basic operations to match their actual work process [12]. Discovering unanticipated uses and understanding ways that users interact with an application can reveal clues for developers to improve usability and enhance functionality, which were not conceived of in the initial design phase [1, 2]. However, application developers often fail to benefit from such an opportunity due to the lack of sufficient knowledge about user behavior with respect to task completion.

In this paper, we describe an approach to discovering unanticipated uses of an interactive application. Briefly, user interface events are generated as users interact with an application via its user interface. Event traces, as they unfold during application execution, provide valuable information about what users do to achieve their objectives [6]. We use aspect-oriented instrumentation to capture user interface events that occur across architectural boundaries of an interactive application, perform model-based analysis to identify tasks and task sequences from preprocessed event traces, and conduct criteria-guided evaluation to discover unanticipated ways the target application was used. Our goal is to provide tool support that is adaptable to changes in the target application as it evolves.

The rest of this paper is organized as follows. Section 2 covers related work. Section 3 addresses issues in unanticipated use of an interactive application via a practical example. Section 4 describes our approach to discovering unanticipated uses with the intent to help developers improve usability and enhance functionality. Section 5 discusses a proof-of-concept experiment to investigate the feasibility of our approach. Finally, Sect. 6 concludes this paper.

2 Related Work

Interactive applications, as social artifacts, are open to interpretation during their use, creating opportunities for individuals to use them in unexpected ways to better fit their tasks [1]. Unanticipated uses are application uses that diverge from the intended, prescribed forms [10]. In the literature, the process as to how users adapt to IT and how IT use evolves over time as users adapt it to their own evolving contexts is referred to as appropriation [3, 11]. A well-known case for appropriation is Internet use. Abbate describes how it evolved from a research-focus network between universities and government labs to include many kinds of activities by users who saw that it could fulfill needs unrelated to research [4]. Quinones et al. demonstrate that users who were never targeted by developers were able to interpret an application in ways that allowed them to appropriate it because the application itself afforded both interpretive flexibility and flexibility of audience [2]. Issues on appropriation have been studied extensively as shown in reports referenced above; however, the lack of tool support for discovering and analyzing cases of appropriation for an interactive application makes it difficult to realize their potential benefits.

Lew addresses issues in unanticipated uses from a much broader perspective, including those that are negative or produce adverse effects [10]. She stresses the need to examine applications beyond the intended uses and users during design or post-design evaluations and points out that early identification of unanticipated uses is critical to determine whether they produce adverse outcomes or not. Apparently, tool support for early identification is indispensable, a key point of our work. In this paper, we restrict ourselves to recurrent unanticipated uses with useful outcomes as most reports referenced above do.

Interactive applications evolve along one or more dimensions, including functionality, architecture, code, and user interface. Changes in one dimension often affect, interact, and impact others [20]. Obviously, tool support for such an application must be able to accommodate continuous changes in the target application. Aspect-oriented programming languages provide useful mechanisms to modularize crosscutting concerns [21]. It is an effective way to develop tool support as separate modules with a loosely coupled connection with the target application [19]. In recent years, context-oriented programming languages emerged as a powerful alternative to accomplish similar objectives [13].

User interface events occur in an interactive application and its run-time environment when user-application interaction takes place [6]. Several reports in the literature describe potential benefits with using aspect-oriented techniques to capture user interface events [8, 14, 19]. While user interface events are identifiable with an appropriate means, they tend to include a lot of data that reflect low-level activities within the target application. Our approach is to focus on events that result from inter-component communication within an interactive application, which are more relevant to user-level activities and therefore more amenable to analyze.

User activities with respect to a user interface are task centered. It is essential to have the ability to identify user tasks from event traces [15]. As a matter of fact, event traces can be analyzed according to observable patterns of application use [18]. Since task models describe expected user activities, they can be used as a basis to interpret event traces and discover tasks the user performed [16]. Moreover, a grammatical version of task models enables a convenient way to map event traces into user tasks [17]. We take a similar approach to achieve our objectives.

3   Issues in Unanticipated Use of an Application

Users use an interactive application to achieve their objectives. In user interface design, tasks are considered as the basic unit of user activities. By definition, a task is a sequence of actions a user performs to interact with an application, which yields an observable result of value. A basic premise for User-Centered Design (UCD), one of the best practices in this field, is that user interface design should emerge from tasks with the focus on user needs and task performance. Guidelines and principles for user interface design are often devoted to making tasks easy to learn and efficient to perform. Users can then avoid routine, tedious, and error-prone actions and concentrate on making key decisions.

In application development process, developers create task models, such as HTA (Hierarchical Task Analysis) models, to specify user tasks the intended application is required to support, including goals users intend to accomplish, actions users need to perform, and action sequences users can walk through. Primarily, task models serve as the basis for user interface design; they can also be used to map a sequence of user actions to the task that users intend to achieve. Action sequences that fall outside of what the underlying task models specify can be viewed as unanticipated use of the target application.

We take a course schedule application as an example to explore issues in unanticipated use of an application. A course schedule application is built to assist users, including students, professors, and administrative staff, to search for information about a university's course schedule. Information that users are allowed to access usually depends on their status. Students can locate courses they plan to take, along with their own schedules. Professors can see courses they are assigned to teach, plus associated class lists. Administrative staff can obtain information relevant to their responsibilities.

In an investigation on user experience with the course schedule application in our institute, we noticed a few interesting scenarios of application use, which reflect usability issues not perceived by the developer when the application was designed.

One scenario showed that users applied creative shortcuts to optimize repetitive activities. For example, users often need to perform the "Search for a Course" task multiple times to meet their objectives. As guided by the user interface, a user navigates through several screens and chooses appropriate options along the way to complete the task. Once the user reaches the final screen, one can click the "Continue to Search" button to do it again for a new search. As a matter of fact, several searches a user performs in succession are very likely to share a common prefix in their navigation paths, such as finding several courses for the same major in the same semester. In other words, the user must carry out a few identical actions to start each repetitive search, but the number of screens involved in the common prefix varies dependent on the context of use. Some users apparently were bothered by redundant efforts. Instead of clicking the "Continue to Search" button when a search is done, they simply hit the "Back" button in the browser for a few times to start a new search without having to repeat the common prefix. Clearly, such knowledge is beneficial for the developer to improve the user interface. In this case, for example, a simple yet flexible solution in user interface redesign is to add a breadcrumb control with descriptive captions on the final screen, allowing the user to return to any preceding screen with one click.

In another scenario, a user puts together a sequence of tasks to achieve a single objective. Such a scenario often arose in an unusual context; for example, finding professors for classes that a given student is enrolled in and then locating his classmates from relevant class lists with those professors for contact tracing purposes at the beginning of the COVID-19 pandemic. It reflects a user need that was not conceived of in the initial design phase; hence, no dedicated task is provided to fulfill such a need, even though the needed information is available. Because of data dependency between adjacent tasks in such a sequence, data transfer from one task to the next must be done manually. As a result, the user can accomplish what the application was not designed to support. A scenario like this may lead to a new version of a prescribed task or a new task. It may also suggest a new function to be considered, for example, sending an email notification to all concerned. Obviously, changes along these lines would offer better experience for the user.

While the above scenarios indicate that users adapt an application to their needs even though the application was not designed with such needs in mind. Lew refers unanticipated use to the use of applications in ways that were not intended, anticipated, or uncovered during their design and development [10]. Unanticipated use of an application arises due to a growing number of users and a shifting context of use. Systematic observation of application use is beneficial for effective application evolution [1]. Obviously, it would be difficult to accomplish without appropriate tool support.

4 An Adaptable Approach to Tool Support

User interface events are generated as natural products of an application's normal operations [6], including user actions (e.g., clicking a button or pressing a key) as well as system responses (e.g., updating the screen display or bringing up a message box); whereas the former are observable actions users perform, the latter correspond to cognitive actions users take to perceive the application's state change. Obviously, traces of user interface events represent sequences of actions that users perform to complete their tasks.

Event traces provide insight into user behavior with respect to the user interface of an application. Since they are extremely voluminous and rich in detail, user interface events must be captured and analyzed in an automatic manner for practical purposes. In our case, tool support should be effective for collecting relevant data and identifying user activities at the task level. It also should be adaptable to an evolving application. Partially based on our previous work [7], we describe below an adaptable approach to discovering unexpected uses of an interactive application.

4.1 Aspect-Oriented Instrumentation to Capture User Interface Events

Instrumentation is a common technique for event tracing. It requires the developer to insert code at specific locations in the target application to capture information of interest at runtime. Instrumentation code tends to be distributed throughout the target application and intimate knowledge about its implementation details is required to develop the code. Scattered code is incredibly difficult to modify when changes in the target application occur. Obviously, manual instrumentation is not desirable for our purposes. Collecting internal events is a cross-cutting concern. By encapsulating cross-cutting concerns into a separate unit called an aspect, aspect-oriented programming languages provide an effective way to modularize instrumentation code in a non-intrusive manner [19].

Interactive applications are often structured according to the Model-View-Controller (MVC) architecture. By encapsulating the three abstractions into separate components, MVC minimizes the impact of user interface redesign and increases the reusability of domain objects. Separating the three abstractions also exposes user interface events within an application. Specifically, the three components in an application must notify each other to collaborate in response to user actions. We use aspects to trace notification events that occur across boundaries of the MVC architecture. Ignoring low-level events (such as those between the application and its run-time environment) effectively reduces the amount of analytical effort without loss of crucial information.

Furthermore, aspects defined to capture notification events are adaptable. In a Java GUI program, a user action triggers an event, which in turn notifies its handler that implements a built-in interface. Here, Java-style interfaces play an essential role for adaptability. An interface provides a uniform way to cope with common behavior of multiple classes. If an interface specifies a method of an event handler to be responsible for a particular event from an event source, invoking that method is to notify the handler of an occurrence of such an event. It works for any event source provided that its event handler implements the same interface. Hence, if an aspect is defined to capture a notification event as such, it will not be affected by changes of the user interface, for example, adding or removing an event source. As regards adaptability, user defined abstract classes can serve the same role as interfaces.

All the above make it possible to develop modular code that is loosely coupled with the target application in addition to tracing relevant user interface events.

4.2   Model-Based Analysis to Identify User Tasks from Event Traces

While allowing to identify individual user actions, the information carried within user interface events themselves is insufficient to allow their meanings to be appropriately interpreted due to the lack of contextual information [6]. Since contextual information spreads across multiple events, it is necessary to analyze event traces at a higher level of abstraction, that is, the level of user task.

In development of an interactive application, task models specify tasks that the application is designed to support and actions that users perform to achieve their objectives; they serve as the basis for user interface design, and in many cases, also serve as the basis for usability evaluation. Hence, event traces can be analyzed at the abstract level as the underlying task models define. Even though individual events do not carry sufficient information on their own, their roles in user tasks can be correctly recognized within the context of relevant task models.

User actions with respect to an application's user interface are grammatical in nature [17]. Parsing event traces into user tasks involves two levels of grammar, lexical (such as regular expressions) and syntactic (such as Backus-Naur Form grammars). While the former splits an input event stream into tokens that correspond to user actions, the latter identifies a sequence of tokens that make up a task. In our case, regular expressions and BNF (Backus-Naur Form) grammars can be derived from HTA models in a systematic manner. As a result, they make it possible to identify user tasks and sequences of user tasks as well as separate them from unexpected occurrences.

Using both grammars to identify user tasks offers a few significant benefits. It is a precise way to specify the syntactic structures of event traces and quite convenient to implement event trace analysis with assistance of open-source components. As stated below, the two grammars are taken as input for event trace analysis; therefore, tool support for event trace analysis is adaptable.

4.3   Criteria-Guided Evaluation to Discover Unanticipated Uses

As stated above, model-based analysis of event traces not only identifies tasks from sequences of user actions but also delivers sequences of tasks. Sequences of user actions and tasks reflect paths users navigate through an application. By analyzing navigation paths, the developer can examine what the user had done to meet one's objectives, including both specified and unspecified navigation behaviors.

In our investigation of user experience with the course schedule application as described earlier, we noticed scenarios in which the target application was not used as expected. Based on our observations, we define two criteria as guidance to evaluate results from event trace analysis and discover instances of unanticipated use.

- Unspecified sequences of user actions to access specified functionality.

    An instance of unspecified action sequence shows that the user could achieve a prescribed task via a path that is not specified in the underlying task model; for example, taking a shortcut to complete a repetitive task. It is natural that the user chose an alternative path over a specified one simply because the former was more efficient. Obviously, such an instance provides clues for the developer to improve an application's usability with respect to user navigation. Regardless of what changes need to be made, it is beneficial for the developer to be informed of such an instance.
- Sequences of user tasks with manual data transfer from one to the next.

    A typical instance is that a user performs two or more tasks sequentially in which the user transfers the output from one task to the successive one as its input. We assume the initial user interface design is adequate with respect to basic usability considerations; that is, every task is carried out in an efficient way with useful results for the user; in other words, users can achieve their objectives without having to do anything unnecessary. If users must do what can be done by a piece of code, for example, it is likely to indicate something that users find value in, but the target application was not intended to support. An instance like this usually emerges as the target application evolves; that is, new needs arise in a shifting context. Evidently, it would persuade the developer to enhance the application's functionality to meet user needs.

Instances that fall under either criterion above can be automatically detected. Unanticipated uses reveal potential usability issues with respect to the target application, enabling the developer to redesign the user interface for better user experience. In addition, tool support for rule-based decision making should be adaptable in the sense that existing criteria can be revised, and new criteria can be added as they become available.

5 Feasibility Experiment

We conducted a proof-of-concept experiment to investigate the feasibility of our approach. Major steps of our experiment, including development tools used in the process, are described as follows.

AspectJ is an aspect-oriented extension to the Java programming language. It is a convenient tool to cope with cross-cutting concerns [21]. AspectJ offers aspect as a basic construct, which consists of pointcuts and advice. While pointcuts refer to well-defined points (with relevant values) in a program, advice defines actions at the associated pointcuts. With an aspect present, additional behavior is introduced at specified points in the target application during its execution. For example, if an aspect is declared to record relevant data in occurrence of a call to the ActionPerformed method for any event handler that implements the ActionListener interface, then the specified action is carried out whenever a user action triggers such a call. We declared aspects to capture notification events across boundaries of the MVC architecture. In our experiment, they were applied to extract event streams from a relatively comprehensive application.

Event streams captured by aspect-oriented instrumentation are not immediately usable because they contain unnecessary details. We created a preprocessor to extract relevant information from event streams and deliver it as an input event streams for analysis.

Event trace analysis is the process of analyzing an input event stream to determine its grammatical structure with respect to user tasks. It involves two steps. The first step is token generation, by which an input event stream is split into meaningful tokens defined by a grammar of regular expressions. And the next step is parsing, which identifies user tasks from a sequence of tokens with reference to a BNF grammar. In our case, tokens denote user actions and token sequences indicate tasks. We used two open-source programs, Lex and Yacc [22], as the basic components to implement event trace analysis. We specified the lexical structure of event traces using regular expressions and the syntactic structure of token sequences with BNF grammars. Both grammars were derived from the underlying HTA models. We developed a script to generate code for token generation and parsing with Lex and Yass respectively and combined them to carry out the analysis process.

In the post-analysis phase, we evaluated results from event trace analysis to discover instances of unanticipated use according to our guiding criteria. It was done manually in our experiment, but automatic tool support is possible due to the nature of our criteria.

Our experiment was largely satisfactory. Even though the experiment scope was limited, it has demonstrated that aspect-oriented instrumentation, model-based analysis, and criteria-guided evaluation together provide an effective way to build adaptable tool support.

6 Summary

Most reports found in the literature implicitly focus on using an interactive application in ways as expected. However, with a growing number of users and a shifting context, it becomes more likely that an application is used by unexpected users and/or in an unexpected way [2]. Early discovery of unanticipated uses can reveal valuable opportunities for developers to improve usability and enhance functionality. Here, systematic observation of application use with appropriate tool support is the key to success.

Unanticipated use is a recurrent phenomenon in application evolution. Our objectives are to provide tool support for discovering unanticipated uses with the ability to adapt to an evolving application. As stated above, a proof-of-concept experiment successfully demonstrated the feasibility of our approach. It is worth noting that although we used programming languages such as Java and AspectJ in this experiment, our approach, based on the notions of HTA, MVC, interfaces/abstract classes, and aspects, is language independent in its design and implementation.

At the same time, we recognize that more research needs to be done due to the limitations of our current work. Our guiding criteria for unanticipated uses originated from observations on user experience with a specific information system; they might not be sufficient in terms of both scope and applicability for a broader category of interactive applications. In addition, more comprehensive evaluation needs to be done on event trace analysis with a large set of realistic data. Obviously, all of these will be the focus of our future research effort.

References

1. Wilkin, C.L., Davern, M.J.: Acceptance of post-adoption unanticipated is usage: towards a taxonomy. DATA BASE Adv. Inf. Syst. **43**(3), 9–25 (2012)
2. Quinones, P.A., Teasley, S.D., Lonn S.: Appropriation by unanticipated users: looking beyond design intent and expected use. In: ACM Computer-Supported Cooperative Work (CSCW), San Antono, Texas, USA (2013)
3. Orliknowski, W.J.: Learning from notes: organizational issues in groupware implementation. In: ACM Computer-Supported Cooperative Work (1992)
4. Abbate, J.: Inventing the Internet. MIT Press, Cambridge (1999)
5. Ernst, N. A., Borgida, A., Jureta, I.: Finding incremental solutions for evolving requirements. In: IEEE 19th International Requirements Engineering Conference (2011)
6. Hilbert, D.M., Redmiles, D.F.: Extracting usability information from user interface events. Comput. Surv. **32**(4), 384–421 (2000)
7. Tao, Y.: Grammatical analysis of user interface events for task identification. In: Marcus, A. (ed.) DUXU 2014. LNCS, vol. 8517, pp. 197–205. Springer, Cham (2014). https://doi.org/10.1007/978-3-319-07668-3_20
8. Tao, Y.: Toward computer-aided usability evaluation for evolving interactive software. In Proceedings of the International Workshop on Reflection, AOP and Meta-Data for Software Evolution, ECOOP, Berlin, Germany (2007)
9. Dix, A.: Designing for appropriation. In: The 21st BCS HCI Group Conference, vol. 2. Lancaster University, UK (2007)
10. Lew, A.: Flipping the script: a sociotechnical approach to platforms and unanticipated uses. IEEE Computer, April, pp. 35–44 (2021)
11. Dourish, P.: The appropriation of interactive technologies: some lessons from placeless documents. ACM Comput. Supp. Cooper. Work (CSCW). **12**(4), 465–490 (2003)
12. Pekkola, S.: Designed for Unanticipated use: common artefacts as design principle for CSCW applications. In: GROUP, Sanibel Island, Florida, USA, 9–12 November 2003 (2003)
13. Taking, N., Wutzler, M., Springer, T., Cardozo, N., Schill, A.: Consistent unanticipated adaptation for context-dependent applications. In: The 8th International Workshop on Context-Oriented Programming (ACM COP), Rome Italy (2016)
14. Bateman, S., Gutwin, C., Osgood, N., McCalla, G.: Interactive usability instrumentation. In: SIGCHI Symposium on Engineering Interactive Computing Systems, Pittsburgh, USA, pp. 45–54, ACM Press (2009)
15. Ivory, M., Hearst, M.: The state of the art in automating usability evaluation of user interfaces. Comput. Surv. **33**(4), 470–516 (2001)
16. Lecerof, A., Paternò, F.: Automatic support for usability evaluation. IEEE Trans. Softw. Eng. **24**(10), 863–888 (1998)
17. Asimakopoulos, S., Dix, A., Fildes, R.: Using hierarchical task decomposition as a grammar to map actions in context: application to forecasting systems in supply chain planning. Int. J. Hum.-Comput. Stud. **69**(4), 234–250 (2011)
18. Olson, G.M., Herbsleb, J.D., Rueter, H.H.: Characterizing the sequential structure of interactive behaviors through statistical and grammatical techniques. Hum.-Comput. Interact. Special Issue ESDA **9**, 427–472 (1994)

19. Shekh S. and Tyerman, S.: An aspect-oriented framework for event capturing and usability evaluation. In: ENASE 2008/2009. CCIS 69, pp.107–119. Springer, Heidelberg (2010)
20. Lehman, M., Ramil, J.: Evolution in software and related areas. In Proceedings of the International Workshop on Principles of Software Evolution (IWPSE), Vienna, Austria (2001)
21. Lieberherr, K., Orleans, D., Ovlinger, J.: Aspect-oriented programming with adaptive methods. Commun. ACM **44**(10), 39–41 (2001)
22. Niemann, T.: Lex & Yacc Tutorial. ePaperPress. http://epaperpress.com/lexandyacc/. Accessed 21 Dec 2023

Affective TV: Concepts of Affective Computing Applied to Digital Television

Pedro Valentim(✉) and Débora Muchaluat-Saade

MídiaCom Lab, Institute of Computing, Niterói 24210-310, Brazil
{pedroalvesvalentim,debora}@midiacom.uff.br

Abstract. The traditional broadcast TV viewing experience has barely evolved since its inception, remaining mostly static despite many technical advances. Smart TVs show attempts of filling this gap, but present challenges, such as limiting functionalities to specific models and lack of standardization. Privacy concerns arise as smart TVs connect to advertising and monitoring services. In the spectrum of interactivity, an option that stands out is affective computing, an interdisciplinary field that seeks to develop systems capable of recognizing, expressing and responding to human emotions. This work proposes the incorporation of affective computing techniques and concepts to improve the experience and interactivity with digital TV, naming it "Affective TV". The work presents a modular architecture, recognition modules developed for multiple modes of interaction and a fully operational implementation of the architecture, developed for the standard digital TV middleware in Brazil, Ginga. Affective TV uses audio and video capturing devices and allows users to set up their environments. Recognition modules capture and classify data, communicating directly to the TV middleware. Proof-of-concept applications, incorporating voice and hand pose interactions with facial expression recognition, were evaluated using the GQM. UEQ-S and TAM questionnaires were employed. Very positive results were obtained, including an excellent UEQ rating, showcasing technical feasibility, attractiveness, user experience, perceived usefulness, and ease of use. The proposal enriches the digital TV experience, providing a novel, interactive model with user-centric customization and emotion-driven responses.

Keywords: Artificial Intelligence (AI) · Human-Centered AI · Emotion Motivation · Persuasion Design

1 Introduction

In the broad spectrum of interactivity with digital systems, affective computing has been proposed [17,18]. Affective computing is a field of computing that focuses on developing systems capable of recognizing, expressing and responding to human emotions. It is an interdisciplinary area that involves knowledge from psychology, computer science and artificial intelligence. The goal of affective computing is to create systems that can identify human emotion and behave

A. Marcus et al. (Eds.): HCII 2024, LNCS 14716, pp. 203–220, 2024.
https://doi.org/10.1007/978-3-031-61362-3_16

accordingly. This can be done using sensors that measure vital signs — such as heart rate and respiratory rate —, using machine learning algorithms that analyze speech or body language to identify emotions, and various other techniques. Affective computing has great potential for improving human-computer interaction and creating more natural and intuitive experiences. For example, it can be used to create virtual assistants that are capable of recognizing and responding to emotions of users, or to develop health systems that can detect signs of stress and mental illnesses.

As TV has become an interactive media over time — with the most recent trend being smart TVs —, it is not far-fetched to also employ concepts from media that have been traditionally interactive, such as computers. By combining interactivity with the capacity of identifying human emotion, the present work proposes the concept of Affective TV [25], the incorporation of affective computing concepts for digital TV (DTV). The intention is to enrich the viewer's experience with interactive digital TV through techniques that can increase their immersion with the system. To this end, the interpretation of the viewer's emotional state during content consumption is understood as positive and desired. To capture the viewer's emotional state, we propose modular components to be integrated to the TV. Those new modules offer voice recognition, facial expression recognition and hand pose recognition. It is worth mentioning that modules of other interaction types can also be integrated in the future, such as capturing the eye gaze, cardiac monitoring, and several others. To evaluate the proposed components, these modules were implemented to work alongside the Ginga DTV middleware [22] and used in a proof-of-concept application, with which tests were conducted with users. The Goal Question Metric (GQM) paradigm [1] was used to plan the experiments. User Experience Questionnaire (UEQ-S) [10] and Technology Acceptance Model (TAM) [5] were employed. The evaluation of the Affective TV proposal, based on these tests, obtained very positive results from the perspectives of technical viability, attractiveness, user experience, perceived usefulness and perceived ease of use.

2   Related Work

In literature there are works related to this one in several aspects. This section discusses them, grouped thematically. In the first group are works about facial expression recognition and the possibility of infer user emotion from this processing. In the second group are works about the collecting and processing of data — from the user or from the environment — without user input, in the context of audiovisual content.

2.1   Emotion Evaluation Based by Facial Expression Recognition

The present work proposes multiple ways of recognizing users' emotional state. However, one of main ways to do this, traditionally, is through the analysis of facial expressions. Naturally, this requires facial recognition. A multitude of challenges, then, follows from this. There are the challenges of determining what is a face [21], identifying a face [9, 24, 26], and the specific challenges of recognizing facial expressions — how to identify which elements of a face define an expression and what expression it is [12, 13, 16].

Research on facial analysis for affective computing is vast. In 2005, Joseph Bullington published a paper discussing affective computing for surveillance systems [2]. This work also discusses the ethical implications of such a concept, such as, for example, whether the people observed would have the freedom to deactivate the function during private meetings or telephone calls, or who would have access to the data produced by the system, or how this data would be stored. In [23], multiple studies are presented regarding affective computing, which includes a long section called "Affective Face and Gesture Processing". This section presents various works that use facial and gesture processing for emotion analysis.

The work in [4] concludes by saying that automated face analysis is mature enough to be employed in real-world solutions for problems of affective computing, entertainment and other areas, despite the space for a lot of basic research. In [14], there is the presentation of AFFDEX SDK, demonstrating that the relationship between affective computing and facial expression recognition was unquestionable. In fact, that work proposes that this relationship was already ready for the market.

More recently, in 2021, the work [19] consists of an evaluation of facial expression recognition techniques.

2.2 Involuntary Feedback for Audiovisual Content

A theme that is adjacent to the present work is the automated collection of opinions and preferences. That is, data for content watching pattern and behavioral profiling. The main problem arises from the fact that this type of data processing can — from a strictly technical point of view — be carried out without the knowledge of the user holding the data.

In [8], the result of sentiment analysis based on Twitch.tv emotes[1,2] is called "implicit feedback". That work, however, focuses on exploring the technical aspect of performing sentiment analysis on emotes.

On the other hand, the work of [15] aims to collect and analyze data from program viewers to adapt television content in real time. The authors propose doing this in an automated way, through machine learning.

It is evident that such work is close to the present proposal. There are some fundamental differences, however. One of them is that, in the work presented here, the user is aware of the data capture. This is due, among other things, to the solution itself, which requires the users to configure their environment.

---

[1] https://twitch.tv.

[2] Twitch.tv emotes are images used by the streamers and their audience to express emotions on the chat. Emotes are comparable to emojis, although many of them are personalized.

Another difference is that the collected data is not stored, but only exists while the TV application is running.

3   Affective TV: Multimodal Interaction and User Emotion

Based on our previous work [25], this work proposes Affective TV to incorporate affective computing concepts into digital TV. To this end, a modular architecture is proposed around the DTV middleware that runs on the TV receiver, so that other devices can communicate directly with it. This way, the architecture as a whole represents an interactive digital TV model capable of recognizing different interaction types and emotions, and responding according to viewers' emotions.

For a viewer to have an Affective TV system at home, they must have physical audio and video capture devices. These devices are associated with modules that recognize and analyze the captured data. Such programs will be called recognition modules in this text. Figure 1 shows an example of an Affective TV environment.

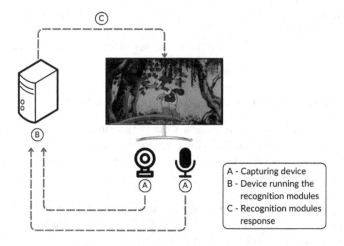

Fig. 1. Example of Affective TV environment. A webcam and a microphone capture image and sound from the viewer, send it to a computer that runs the recognition modules, produces the results of the hand pose, facial expression and voice recognition modules, and sends them to the TV.

The proposed architecture gives the viewer the freedom to configure their environment as they wish, both in terms of physical equipment (whether to use or not a camera, to use or not a microphone, to choose which model, etc.) and recognition modules. Figure 2 illustrates an environment with the same functionalities as that shown in Fig. 1, but using only a smartphone for capturing input and doing recognition.

Detailed descriptions of the components of this system are given in the following subsections.

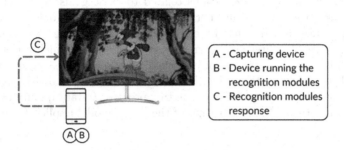

A - Capturing device
B - Device running the recognition modules
C - Recognition modules response

Fig. 2. Example of a minimalist Affective TV environment. The smartphone captures image and audio from the viewer, runs the recognition modules, produces the results for hand pose, facial expression and voice recognition modules, and sends them to the TV.

3.1   Recognition Modules

Recognition modules are programs that must run in parallel with the TV application. They are used to capture, classify and communicate data related to the user to the middleware. To be fast and strictly local, the communication of data from the recognition modules to the middleware, which runs on the TV receiver, is done using the MQTT protocol [7] in our implementation. The middleware runs an MQTT broker in which each topic corresponds to a recognition module.

By definition of the proposed architecture, recognition modules can effectively perform any data processing. The only requirement, conceptually, is that they bridge the gap between the capture device and the middleware. Recognition modules are responsible for perceiving the environment and the user for the TV.

Although countless recognition modules can be imagined, the ones that we implemented are for voice recognition, hand pose recognition and facial expression recognition. In our proposal, what identifies the recognition type a recognition module corresponds to is the topic in the MQTT broker in which it publishes. For example, for voice recognition the module must publish the recognized data in the `voice_recog` topic. This way, the middleware interprets that voice recognition data and fires a `VoiceRecognitionEvent` with it.

4   Evaluation

To evaluate our proposal of Affective TV, experiments were carried out for subjective answers from users. These experiments were planned using the GQM (Goal Question Metric) paradigm [1]. To prepare the questionnaires, the UEQ (User Experience Questionnaire) [10] and the TAM model (Technology Acceptance Model) [5] were used.

4.1   Methodology

GQM is a software metrics paradigm. It is an approach that helps define quality goals, formulate specific questions related to these goals, and then develop metrics to measure progress and performance against these goals [3].

GQM produces a hierarchical model at three levels: conceptual, operational and quantitative. The first level corresponds to the goals, which are what is to be achieved in terms of quality. For each goal, specific and measurable questions are defined that quantify them. Finally, questions are refined to objective or subjective metrics that are capable of evaluating progress toward quality objectives.

Figure 3 illustrates the structuring of the GQM model applied for this work.

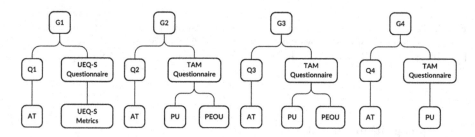

Fig. 3. Structuring of the GQM approach used in this work.

Table 1 presents the goals defined for the evaluation of Affective TV. The sections that follow discuss the questions and metrics regarding each goal.

Table 1. Established goals for the experiments conducted.

Goal	Description
G1	To analyze the concept of Affective TV with the purpose of evaluating user experience.
G2	To analyze voice interaction with digital TV with the purpose of evaluating the acceptance of this technology from the users' point of view.
G3	To analyze hand pose interaction with digital TV with the purpose of evaluating the acceptance of this technology from the users' point of view.
G4	To analyze the recognition of facial expressions for identifying emotions with digital TV with the purpose of evaluating the acceptance of this technology from the users' point of view.

G1 — Questions and Metrics. To evaluate goal G1, the question described in Table 2 and the questionnaire UEQ-S (short version of UEQ) [20], illustrated

Table 2. Goal G1 questions.

Question	Description
Q1	How would you rate your experience with the system?

Table 3. Formulário UEQ-S.

Obstructive	o o o o o o o	Supportive
Complicated	o o o o o o o	Easy
Inefficient	o o o o o o o	Efficient
Confusing	o o o o o o o	Clear
Boring	o o o o o o o	Exciting
Not interesting	o o o o o o o	Interesting
Conventional	o o o o o o o	Inventive
Usual	o o o o o o o	Leading edge

in Table 3, were used. Question Q1 was presented using the Likert scale [11], which indicates the level of agreement with the statement on a line of discrete values.

Table 4 presents the metric corresponding to question Q1. The attractiveness metric (AT) is used to evaluate question Q1.

Table 4. Metrics for the questions of goal G1.

Metric	Description	Questions
AT	Attractiveness [20]. How attractive and enjoyable the technology is to the user. Measured with a Likert scale from 1 to 7.	Q1

The UEQ-S was also used as a set of questions for goal G1. The UEQ aims to be a quick and direct assessment of the user experience [10]. The UEQ-S is a shortened variant of the original UEQ. It was designed by the same authors as the UEQ, in an effort to meet specific scenarios for which the original 26-item questionnaire would be too extensive to be used [20].

As shown in Table 3, the questionnaire corresponds to 8 pairs of antonyms in which, for each pair, there is a scale from 1 to 7. The scale represents the interval [-3, 3] in which, intuitively, negative values indicate agreement with the negative term and positive values indicate agreement with the positive term. For example, a participant who marks 7 — which translates to the value 3 — in the item "Complicated/Easy" expresses complete agreement with the term "Easy".

Naturally, the shortened variant does not come without setbacks. The UEQ-S consists of only 8 items out of the 26 present in the UEQ. One half of these items represents the pragmatic quality metric and the other represents the hedonic quality metric. In addition to these two metrics, UEQ also evaluates an attractiveness metric. To keep the UEQ-S cohesive as in the authors' construction and have some data on this metric, it was decided to measure, for goal G1, attractiveness as a separate question from the UEQ-S, which is covered by question Q1.

G2 and G3 — Questions and Metrics. The goals G2, "To analyze voice interaction with digital TV with the purpose of evaluating the acceptance of this technology from the users' point of view." and G3, "To analyze hand pose interaction with digital TV with the purpose of evaluating the acceptance of this technology from the users' point of view.", are analogous to each other, for voice and hand pose interactions. To evaluate them, questions Q2 and Q3 were used, for goals G2 and G3 respectively, and the questions described in Table 5 and Table 6, prepared from TAM.

TAM is a model for measuring whether or not a technology will be accepted and used by target users. Such measurement is based on the intention of use, affected by the parameters of perceived usefulness and perceived ease of use [5]. The questions were adapted from the questionnaires constructed and discussed in [5] and [6].

The model does not establish standard metrics for evaluating the questions created. As the questions are grouped into perceived usefulness (PU) and perceived ease of use (PEOU), the metrics were based on this. For questions Q2 and Q3, the attractiveness metric (AT) is used. Metrics for questions from goals G2 and G3 are described in Table 7.

G4 — Questions and Metrics. Goal G4, "To analyze the recognition of facial expressions for identifying emotions with digital TV with the purpose of evaluating the acceptance of this technology from the users' point of view.", as indicated in Table 1, is similar to goals G2 and G3. The difference is that the object of analysis is not a voluntary interaction (such as voice or hand poses), but facial expressions. For the purposes of the evaluation, this difference, naturally, makes the issues of perceived ease of use (PEOU) meaningless. Therefore, to evaluate goal G4, question Q4 and perceived usefulness (PU) questions were used. Table 8 presents these questions.

As with goals G2 and G3, in the absence of standard metrics for evaluating the questions created, the metrics for goal G4 will be based on the TAM notions of perceived usefulness (PU) and perceived ease of use (PEOU). As previously discussed, for goal G4 the notion of perceived ease of use does not apply and, therefore, the metric for TAM questions will only be perceived usefulness (PU). For question Q4, the attractiveness metric (AT) is used. Table 9 presents the metrics for the questions in goal G4.

Table 5. Goal G2 questions.

Question	Description
Q2	I enjoyed interacting with the TV using voice recognition.
Perceived Usefulness (PU)	
Question	Description
PU1	Interacting by voice with digital TV applications would allow me to interact more quickly.
PU2	Interacting by voice would worsen my performance when interacting with digital TV applications.
PU3	Interacting by voice could make my interaction with digital TV applications more effective.
PU4	Interacting by voice would make my use of digital TV applications easier.
PU5	Interacting by voice would not be useful for my use of digital TV applications.
PU6	Interacting by voice would help me use digital TV applications.
Perceived Ease of Use (PEOU)	
Question	Description
PEOU1	Learning to interact with digital TV applications by voice would be easy for me.
PEOU2	It would not be easy to interact with digital TV applications by voice.
PEOU3	I consider voice interaction flexible for use in digital TV applications.
PEOU4	It wouldn't be easy to become skilled in voice interaction with digital TV applications.
PEOU5	Interacting by voice would require little physical effort when using digital TV.
PEOU6	Interacting by voice would require little mental effort when using digital TV.

4.2 Procedure

The procedure consists of two applications: one for voice interactions and another one for hand pose interactions. The applications are analogous. Both start with a screen with instruction. To start the voice interaction application, the participant must say "Start". To start the hand pose interaction application, the participant must raise their hand with their thumb up.

Once the application has started, whether through voice or hand pose interaction, the participant is presented with four scenes from classic cartoons (from "Looney Tunes" and "Tom and Jerry"). Under the video, a horizontal bar is displayed with the commands available to the participant. Figure 4 shows to the applications during the presentation of the clips.

The controls, for both applications, are to pause and resume the playing clip. In the voice interaction application, the commands to pause and resume

Table 6. Goal G3 questions.

Question	Description
Q3	I enjoyed interacting with the TV using hand pose recognition.
Perceived Usefulnes (PU)	
Question	Description
PU7	Interacting by hand poses with digital TV applications would allow me to interact more quickly.
PU8	Interacting by hand poses would worsen my performance when interacting with digital TV applications.
PU9	Interacting by hand poses could make my interaction with digital TV applications more effective.
PU10	Interacting by hand poses would make my use of digital TV applications easier.
PU11	Interacting by hand poses would not be useful for my use of digital TV applications.
PU12	Interacting by hand poses would help me use digital TV applications.
Perceived Ease of Use (PEOU)	
Question	Description
PEOU7	Learning to interact with digital TV applications by hand poses would be easy for me.
PEOU8	It would not be easy to interact with digital TV applications by hand poses.
PEOU9	I consider hand pose interaction flexible for use in digital TV applications.
PEOU10	It wouldn't be easy to become skilled in hand pose interaction with digital TV applications.
PEOU11	Interacting by hand poses would require little physical effort when using digital TV.
PEOU12	Interacting by hand poses would require little mental effort when using digital TV.

Table 7. Metrics for questions of goals G2 and G3.

Metric	Description	Questions
AT	Attractiveness [20]. How attractive and enjoyable the technology is to the user. Measured on a Likert scale from 1 to 5.	Q2 and Q3
PU	Perceived Usefulness [5]. How much the user believes that the tested technology will improve their performance in an activity. Measured on a Likert scale from 1 to 5.	PU1 to PU12
PEOU	Perceived Ease of Use [5]. How easy the user believes it would be to use the tested technology. Measured on a Likert scale from 1 to 5.	PEOU1 to PEOU12

Table 8. Goal G4 questions.

Question	Description
Q4	I would like to use digital TV applications that recognize my facial expressions to identify emotions.
Perceived Usefulness (PU)	
Question	Description
PU13	Having facial expressions recognized to identify emotions would improve my use of TV.
PU14	Having facial expressions recognized for emotion identification would not be useful for my use of TV applications.
PU15	Having facial expressions recognized to identify emotions would make my use of TV easier.

Table 9. Metrics for the questions of goal G4.

Metric	Description	Questions
AT	Attractiveness [20]. How attractive and enjoyable the technology is to the user. Measured on a Likert scale from 1 to 5.	Q4
PU	Perceived Usefulness [5]. How much the user believes that the tested technology will improve their performance in an activity. Measured on a Likert scale from 1 to 5.	PU13, PU14 and PU15

(a) Clip presentation in the application of voice interaction.

(b) Clip presentation in the application of hand pose interaction.

Fig. 4. Application screens during clip presentation.

are, respectively and naturally, saying "pause" and "resume". In the hand pose interaction application, the commands are three (the index, middle and ring) fingers raised to pause, and two (the index and middle) fingers raised to resume. These poses were chosen over others that would be more intuitive — such as an open hand and a closed hand — as they are poses that are less likely to be performed unintendedly.

During the presentation of each clip, the application captures, in addition to voice or hand pose interaction data, the user's facial expression. The application then evaluates whether the participant smiles at any point during the scene presentation. If they do, a smiling emoji, mirroring this reaction, is displayed for 3 s, on the bottom right corner of the screen.

At the end of each scene, if at least one smile from the participant is identified during its presentation, a confirmation screen is displayed. On this screen, the participant is prompted to confirm or deny whether they liked the presented scene. This confirmation is made through the interaction corresponding to the application. For the voice interaction application, the participant responds by saying "I liked it" or "I didn't like it". For the hand pose interaction application, the participant responds by showing the hand pose with an extended thumb up or down. After that interaction, the next scene starts. If no smile is identified during the scene, the confirmation screen is not displayed and the next scene starts immediately.

At the end of the last confirmation — or of the last scene — a thanks screen is displayed marking the end of the application. To every participant both applications are played.

4.3   Participants

The experiment was conducted with 24 participants, from the ages 19 to 59. The median for the ages is of 21. 75% of them were male and 25% were female. 87.5% participants had incomplete or were currently undergraduate and 12.5% had complete higher education.

On a scale of 1 to 5, ranging from "Never" to "Always", for frequency of using voice recognition features in systems, 50% of participants marked 2. The other participants responses were spread over the other options.

On a similar scale, for the hand pose recognition feature, 50% of participants marked 1 ("Never"). 25% marked 2, 12.5% marked 3 and 12.5% marked 4. No participant marked 5 ("Always").

For the question "Which one did you like the most?", among the options "Voice interaction", "Hand pose interaction" and "Indifferent", 50% of participants marked "Hand pose interaction", 29.2% marked "Voice interaction" and 20.8% marked "Indifferent". It is worth mentioning that, with the implemented modules, voice interaction presents a delay between interaction and recognition that is significantly greater than hand pose interaction. Although this was not measured in this work, hand pose interaction is recognized in the order of milliseconds and voice interaction is recognized in approximately 1 to 2 s.

4.4   Results and Discussion

For computing metrics results for questions Q1, Q2, Q3, Q4 and TAM questions, the median values of participants' answers were used. For UEQ-S, the official data analysis tool[3] was used.

G1 — Results Analysis. For goal G1, "To analyze the concept of Affective TV with the purpose of evaluating user experience.", question Q1 "How would you rate your experience with the system?" was given and the UEQ-S questionnaire was used. As a metric for question Q1, attractiveness (AT) was defined. This metric was measured by calculating the median of Q1 responses, given on a Likert scale. The obtained median was 7, the maximum degree on the scale presented, which represents an extremely positive result.

For the other questions of goal G1, the UEQ-S does not produce an overall score. As a metric, its scales within pragmatic and hedonic qualities are used. The total range of the scales is [-3, 3], where -3 means terribly bad and 3 means extremely good. Values in the range [-0.8, 0.8] can be interpreted as a neutral result. Values greater than 0.8 present a positive result and values less than -0.8 represent a negative result [20]. Table 10 provides the average value, variance and standard deviation (σ) for each UEQ-S item, and to which quality it corresponds.

Table 10. UEQ-S results.

Item	Average	Variance	σ	Antonyms	Quality
1	1.6	1.8	1.3	Obstructive / Supportive	Pragmatic
2	2.8	0.4	0.6	Complicated / Easy	Pragmatic
3	2.3	0.8	0.9	Inefficient / Efficient	Pragmatic
4	2.8	0.2	0.5	Confusing / Clear	Pragmatic
5	2.3	1.0	1.0	Boring / Exciting	Hedonic
6	2.6	0.4	0.7	Not interesting / Interesting	Hedonic
7	2.2	0.5	0.7	Conventional / Inventive	Hedonic
8	1.7	1.4	1.2	Usual / Leading edge	Hedonic

In addition to the results per item in Table 10, the UEQ-S analysis also provides grouping and calculation of averages by quality. In addition to the analysis of survey data, a comparative benchmark of the results of these data against more than 400 product evaluation results that used that questionnaire is created. The data results from our work obtained a value considered excellent by the benchmark, being within 10% of the best results among the studies that comprise it. The results were of 2.4 for pragmatic quality, 2.18 for hedonic quality and 2.29 overall, on a scale between -3 and 3. Figure 5 presents these results.

---

[3] https://www.ueq-online.org/Material/Short_UEQ_Data_Analysis_Tool.xlsx.

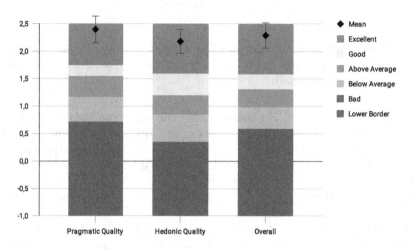

Fig. 5. UEQ-S results compared to the UEQ benchmark.

G2 and G3 — Results Analysis. For goals G2 and G3, "To analyze voice interaction with digital TV with the purpose of evaluating the acceptance of this technology from the users' point of view." and "To analyze hand pose interaction with digital TV with the purpose of evaluating the acceptance of this technology from the users' point of view.", respectively, questions Q2 and Q3 were prepared and TAM questionnaires were used. As a metric for questions Q2 and Q3, attractiveness (AT) was defined. This metric was measured by calculating the median of the responses, given on a Likert scale in the interval [1, 5], obtained by questions Q2 and Q3.

Both question Q2 and question Q3 obtained a median of 5, the maximum degree on the scale presented, which represents extremely positive results.

The remaining questions for goals G2 and G3 correspond to the TAM questionnaire and are grouped into perceived usefulness (PU) and perceived ease of use (PEOU), with both groups being metrics for those goals.

Figure 6 presents the median responses obtained of perceived usefulness and perceived ease of use questions for goal G2, presented in Table 5. Figure 7 presents the median responses obtained of perceived usefulness and perceived ease of use questions for goal G3, presented in Table 6.

Considering that value 1 means "totally disagree" and value 5 means "totally agree" and that questions PU2, PU5, PU8, PU11, PEOU2, PEOU4, PEOU8 and PEOU10 are negative — see Tables 5 and 6 —, the results for perceived usefulness (PU) and perception of ease of use (PEOU) for goals G2 and G3 were very positive.

G4 — Result Analysis. For goal G4, "To analyze the recognition of facial expressions for identifying emotions with digital TV with the purpose of evaluating the acceptance of this technology from the users' point of view", question Q4 was prepared and a questionnaire based on TAM was used. As a metric for

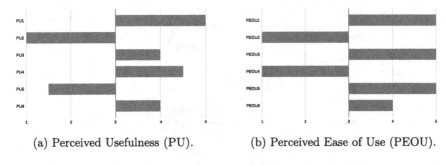

(a) Perceived Usefulness (PU).   (b) Perceived Ease of Use (PEOU).

Fig. 6. Results for goal G2.

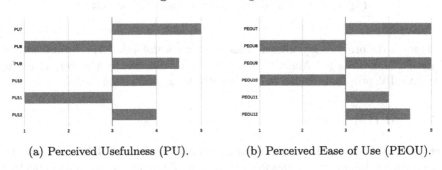

(a) Perceived Usefulness (PU).   (b) Perceived Ease of Use (PEOU).

Fig. 7. Results for goal G3.

question Q4, attractiveness (AT) was defined. This metric was measured by calculating the median of responses, given on a Likert scale in the interval [1, 5]. Question Q4 had a median of 4, a positive result.

The other questions in goal G4 correspond to the TAM and only deal with perceived usefulness (PU). The medians of the responses of questions PU13, PU14 and PU15, presented in Table 8, were calculated. Figure 8 shows the median results. As PU14 is a negative question for perceived usefulness (PU), all results were very positive from the users' point of view for goal G4.

4.5   Limitations

A limitation of the present work, with regard to evaluation, is the punctuality of the procedures carried out with users, as opposed to carrying out continuous procedures arranged in multiple meetings. Another limitation, still within the scope of the evaluation, is that almost all participants were Computer Science students. This profile, naturally, implies some familiarity with the concepts and the system, which may have led to biases in answers.

This work used facial expressions for emotion recognition. In works dealing with affective computing, there is a vast literature on the limitations of taking data like this as a complete indication of [27] emotions.

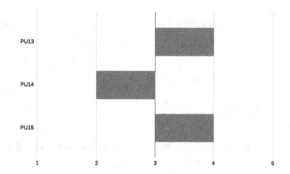

Fig. 8. Perceived usefulness (PU) results for goal G4.

Due to its preliminary nature, this work does not cover the establishment of design standards for Affective TV. This does not mean, however, that the Affective TV proposal cannot benefit greatly from standardization.

5   Final Remarks

The goal of this work was to propose and evaluate the concept of Affective TV. To this end, a modular architecture was designed to allow the application of affective computing concepts to interact with digital TV and multimodal interactivity. In addition to the architecture, this work also presented an implementation as a proof of concept for the proposed architecture. This implementation has voice, hand pose and facial expression recognition modules in an ecosystem operating in Ginga-NCL DTV middleware.

In order to validate the proposal of this work, a qualitative evaluation was carried out with 24 users of different ages and genders. For the purposes of this evaluation, the results were mostly positive.

Privacy within the proposal presented was outside the scope of this work. However, this aspect cannot be neglected. In Brazil, there is the General Data Protection Law (LGPD) and around the world there is vast legislation that regulates the manipulation of user data. Work that assesses viewers' concerns about having their data captured in this way is essential. Privacy and data protection need to be explored in future work on Affective TV.

The ethical limits and impacts of an Affective TV environment need to be assessed. It is a direct consequence of the proposed concept that information from the environment is captured during TV use. In addition to privacy issues, it is worth evaluating the purpose. In other words, determining to what extent this promotes interaction and what would just become a way to collect more data from users.

As future work, it is necessary to work on evolving the capabilities of recognition modules. For example, the voice recognition module, which can be extended to not only do speech-to-text conversion, but also to differentiate speakers and recognize emotions by voice.

Acknowledgements. The authors would like to thank CAPES, CAPES PRINT, CNPq and FAPERJ for the partial financial support of this work.

Disclosure of Interests. The authors have no competing interests to declare that are relevant to the content of this article.

References

1. Basili, V.R.: Goal, question, metric paradigm. Encycl. Softw. Eng. **1**, 528–532 (1994)
2. Bullington, J.: Affective computing and emotion recognition systems: the future of biometric surveillance? In: Proceedings of the 2nd Annual Conference On Information Security Curriculum Development, pp. 95–99 (2005)
3. Caldiera, V.R.B.G., Rombach, H.D.: The goal question metric approach. Encycl. Softw. Eng., 528–532 (1994)
4. Cohn, J.F., De la Torre, F.: Automated face analysis for affective computing (2015)
5. Davis, F.D.: Perceived usefulness, perceived ease of use, and user acceptance of information technology. MIS Q., 319–340 (1989)
6. Hu, P.J., Chau, P.Y., Sheng, O.R.L., Tam, K.Y.: Examining the technology acceptance model using physician acceptance of telemedicine technology. J. Manage. Inf. Syst. **16**(2), 91–112 (1999)
7. Hunkeler, U., Truong, H.L., Stanford-Clark, A.: MQTT-S-a publish/subscribe protocol for wireless sensor networks. In: 2008 3rd International Conference on Communication Systems Software and Middleware and Workshops (COMSWARE'08), pp. 791–798. IEEE (2008)
8. Kobs, et al.: Emote-controlled: obtaining implicit viewer feedback through emote-based sentiment analysis on comments of popular twitch.tv channels. Trans. Soc. Comput. **3**(2) (2020). https://doi.org/10.1145/3365523
9. Kukula, E.P., Elliott, S.J.: Evaluation of a facial recognition algorithm across three illumination conditions. IEEE Aerosp. Electron. Syst. Mag. **19**(9), 19–23 (2004)
10. Laugwitz, B., Held, T., Schrepp, M.: Construction and evaluation of a user experience questionnaire. In: Holzinger, A. (ed.) USAB 2008. LNCS, vol. 5298, pp. 63–76. Springer, Heidelberg (2008). https://doi.org/10.1007/978-3-540-89350-9_6
11. Likert, R.: A technique for the measurement of attitudes. Arch. Psychol., 136–165 (1932). https://books.google.com.br/books?id=9rotAAAAYAAJ
12. Lisetti, C.L., Rumelhart, D.E.: Facial expression recognition using a neural network. In: FLAIRS Conference, pp. 328–332 (1998)
13. Ma, L., Khorasani, K.: Facial expression recognition using constructive feedforward neural networks. IEEE Trans. Syst. Man Cybern. Part B Cybern. **34**(3), 1588–1595 (2004)
14. McDuff, D., et al.: Affdex SDK: a cross-platform real-time multi-face expression recognition toolkit. In: Proceedings of the 2016 CHI Conference Extended Abstracts on Human Factors in Computing Systems, pp. 3723–3726 (2016)
15. Mondragon, V.M., García-Díaz, V., Porcel, C., Crespo, R.G.: Adaptive contents for interactive tv guided by machine learning based on predictive sentiment analysis of data. Soft. Comput. **22**(8), 2731–2752 (2018)
16. Mpiperis, I., Malassiotis, S., Strintzis, M.G.: Bilinear models for 3-D face and facial expression recognition. IEEE Trans. Inf. Forensics Secur. **3**(3), 498–511 (2008)
17. Picard, R.W.: Affective Computing. MIT Press, Cambridge, MA, USA (1997)

18. Picard, R.W.: Affective computing for HCI. In: HCI, vol. 1, pp. 829–833. Citeseer (1999)
19. Revina, I., Emmanuel, W.S.: A survey on human face expression recognition techniques. J. King Saud Univ. Comput. Info. Sci. **33**(6), 619–628 (2021). https://doi.org/10.1016/j.jksuci.2018.09.002
20. Schrepp, M., Hinderks, A., Thomaschewski, J.: Design and evaluation of a short version of the user experience questionnaire (UEQ-s). Int. J. Interact. Multimedia Artif. Intell. **4**(6), 103–108 (2017)
21. Sirovich, L., Kirby, M.: Low-dimensional procedure for the characterization of human faces. J. Optical Soc. Am. A **4**(3), 519–524 (1987)
22. Soares, L.F.G., Rodrigues, R.F., Moreno, M.F.: Ginga-NCL: the declarative environment of the Brazilian digital tv system. J. Braz. Comput. Soc. **13**, 37–46 (2007)
23. Luo, J. (ed.): Affective Computing and Intelligent Interaction. AISC, vol. 137. Springer, Heidelberg (2012). https://doi.org/10.1007/978-3-642-27866-2
24. Turk, M.A., Pentland, A.P.: Face recognition using eigenfaces. In: Proceedings. 1991 IEEE Computer Society Conference On Computer Vision And Pattern Recognition, pp. 586–587. IEEE Computer Society (1991)
25. Valentim, P.A., Barreto, F., Muchaluat-Saade, D.C.: Towards affective tv with facial expression recognition. In: Proceedings of the 1st Life Improvement in Quality by Ubiquitous Experiences Workshop. SBC (2021)
26. Vasilescu, M.A.O., Terzopoulos, D.: Multilinear image analysis for facial recognition. In: Object Recognition Supported By User Interaction For Service Robots, vol. 2, pp. 511–514 (2002)
27. Zhang, P.: The affective response model: a theoretical framework of affective concepts and their relationships in the ICT context. MIS Q., 247–274 (2013)

Research on the Application Trend of Scenario Theory in the Field of Intelligent Product Innovation

Wei Wei[✉]

China Academy of Art, SID, 218 Nanshan Road, Hangzhou, Zhejiang, China
75256442@qq.com

Abstract. The topic aims to thoroughly explore the application potential, trends, and value of scenario theory in the field of intelligent creation, focusing on the innovative talent development path in the track of intelligent creation within an interdisciplinary context. The entire topic is divided into three key stages. Firstly, through literature review and practical case assessments of scenario theory, it deeply analyzes the practical application and future trends of this theory in the field of intelligent creation. Secondly, it proposes an innovative path for intelligent product innovation based on scenario theory. Finally, this methodology is validated through typical teaching cases. In the three main parts of the research, combining with the background of the AIGC (Artificial Intelligence Generation and Creation) era, scenario theory is reinterpreted and understood. At the same time, based on the characteristics of intelligent technology, innovative ideas for human-machine collaboration are explored. This article summarizes the results of the first phase of the research, including literature review, technical interpretation, and case analysis. Adopting a multidimensional research approach ensures the objectivity, authenticity, and effectiveness of the research. It is mainly divided into three parts: trends and insights of scenarios, the intelligent expression of scenarios, and new trends in intelligent scenario creation. This provides a beneficial theoretical framework and methodology for in-depth research on intelligent creation. The research results indicate that the application of scenario theory in intelligent creation plays a crucial role. Designers can use scenario theory to analyze user needs in different scenarios and translate these needs into design guidelines for intelligent machines, thereby achieving a good intelligent experience. Additionally, scenario theory has guiding significance for design education, guiding students to focus on the relationship between products and users, the environment, and interaction, as well as the performance and adaptability of products in specific scenarios. In innovative design education, teachers can guide students to consider product design from multiple perspectives, cultivate students' comprehensive abilities, and help them design products that better meet user expectations and adapt to scenarios.

Keywords: Scenario Theory · Application Trend · Intelligent Product · Innovative Design Education

A. Marcus et al. (Eds.): HCII 2024, LNCS 14716, pp. 221–236, 2024.
https://doi.org/10.1007/978-3-031-61362-3_17

1 Insights and Inspirations from Scenarios

When discussing scenarios, one cannot help but think of various classic paintings, with the most notable being "Guernica." Through the organization of the canvas, Picasso vividly presents the cruelty of the Spanish Civil War in 1937. From the dead horse, the woman holding a lamp, and the burning house to the screaming woman, bull, women, and her deceased son, it feels as if we have personally experienced everything after the bombing destruction of the city of Guernica. Traditional painting skillfully allows us to feel the vastness of the stars, the expansiveness of the universe, and the impermanence of human society through the arrangement of scenes.

In academia, it is generally believed that the formal proposal of scenario theory originated in the field of sociology. Sociologist Erving Goffman, in "The Presentation of Self in Everyday Life," introduced the dramaturgical theory and defined scenarios as "places to some extent set off from the rest of the world." Merleau-Ponty extended the concept of "scenes" from Goffman's theory, and Scobell proposed the "Five Forces of Scenarios" in the era of upcoming scenes in the mobile internet, including mobile devices, social media, big data, sensors, and positioning systems, among others. Scenario theory has undergone development and transformation in different periods, gradually evolving new connotations.

"Scenarios" and related theories are widely applied in various fields, with each field emphasizing its own focus on research content, purpose, and methods. For example, in the field of communication, researchers use scenario theory to analyze the process of information dissemination, while in the field of human-computer interaction research, scenario theory focuses on understanding the relationship between users and devices as well as the user experience. This paper, combining the design innovation of the artificial intelligence era, interdisciplinary and cross-disciplinary aspects, takes the research trends of scenarios in the fields of communication, architecture, marketing, and design as the theoretical basis for the study of intelligent creation scenarios.

1.1 Insights into Communication Scenarios

The study of scenarios in communication comes from the "dramaturgical theory" proposed by sociologist Erving Goffman. It primarily examines the relationship between people in face-to-face encounters and the limited physical space within organizations from the perspective of social science. Erving Goffman defines "scenarios" as "any place that feels to some extent set off from the rest of the world" [1]. Building on Goffman's research, communication scholar Erwin G. M. Merlauwitz studied the impact of scenarios on social behavior. Merlauwitz's scenario theory reflects on the characteristics of the media itself, referring to an environmental atmosphere formed by the media information environment that influences behavior and psychology [2], such as the news communication scenario and today's mobile interactive media communication scenario. In 1987, Walter R. Fisher proposed "Narrative and the Roots of Human Communication," emphasizing the importance of storytelling in human communication scenarios and viewing the communication process as constructing reality through storytelling within specific scenarios.

Integrating intelligent design with narrative communication in the field of communication provides crucial guidance for design teams. Engaging narratives evoke user emotions, strengthen product connections, enhance engagement, and foster loyalty. Coherent storytelling builds a consistent user experience, including interface, interaction, and feedback, improving usability. Infusing meaningful narratives communicates brand stories, establishes brand awareness, and connects with users. Narrative design encourages user co-creation, enhances personalized experiences and satisfaction, explains product value, and increases adoption rates. The narrative paradigm provides a powerful framework for modern design, boosting competitiveness.

1.2 Insights into Spatial Planning Scenarios

In the field of spatial planning and design, scenario theory is widely applied to help designers better understand user needs, spatial utilization, and the architectural environment. The New Chicago School, led by Terry Clark and Daniel Silver, established the scenario theory, which is the first international theoretical tool to analyze the role of cultural styles and aesthetic features in urban development. The Clark team explicitly states in the book "Scenes: How Qualities of Space Shape Social Life" that scenes are redefining urban economies, residential life, political activities, and public policies. The so-called scenario theory refers to the overall cultural style or aesthetic features of a place, derived from the combination of various comfortable elements. Different combinations of comfortable elements result in different external manifestations of the scenario, leading to a wide range of effects [4]. In the paper "Research on Digital Exhibition Design Based on Scenario Interaction," the author views intelligent exhibition systems as digital spatial scenarios and explores the importance of value relationships in the context of scenario-based interactions. It discusses how the concept of scenario interaction affects the balance of value relationships between the main and secondary subjects in modern exhibition design. Additionally, the paper combines the concept of scenario interaction to conduct a case study on the design of a new generation of digital exhibition systems, exploring the possibilities of their application [5].

Intelligent design and comprehensive intelligent spaces shape new lifestyles. Scenario theory has become a key tool for designers, supporting the creation of functional, aesthetically pleasing, and human-centric spaces. In-depth research into user activities and experiences guides experience design, optimizes layouts, and enhances user satisfaction. Viewing space as a narrative scene creates interaction, strengthens the connection between users and spaces, making them more attractive. Scenario analysis helps designers adapt to environmental needs, guiding the design of spatial sequences and flow to improve the user experience. Scenario theory plays a crucial role in community engagement and cultural identity, ensuring that architectural projects better meet community needs. Scenario theory provides intelligent creators with a more comprehensive means to create more appealing intelligent spaces.

1.3 Insights into Business Service Scenarios

The academic definition of scenarios in the field of business services originated from Kenny and Marshall, emphasizing the correlation between specific situations, behaviors, and needs during the customer shopping process [6]. Wu Sheng, in "The Scenario Revolution," believes that the traditional internet era based on traffic is coming to an end, and the construction of scenarios has become a key tool for traditional industries to transform through the internet. He proposed the five characteristics of the scenario revolution and constructed a methodology for enterprise transformation based on scenarios [7]. In "The Upcoming Scenario Era," American authors Robert Scoble and Shel Israel identified the five elements of scenarios, defining them as the "Five Forces of Scenarios" that will disrupt future business and life [8].

It can be seen that the application of scenario theory in the field of business services mainly focuses on the value creation of scenarios for consumer experiences and business model innovation from a business perspective. It drives the upgrade of consumer experiences and innovation in service models. By conducting in-depth research on user activities and needs in service scenarios, it optimizes service processes, interfaces, and interactions to enhance user satisfaction. Scenario theory promotes service innovation and the introduction of design thinking, allowing for a deep understanding of the challenges and opportunities users face in specific contexts through scenario analysis. This, in turn, drives innovative service solutions. In terms of multichannel experience design, employee experience, and personalized services, scenario theory provides multidimensional tools for designers, promoting innovation, improving user experiences, and optimizing service models.

1.4 Insights into Modern Design Scenarios

In the field of design, the concept of scenario-based design was initially proposed by Carroll, a scholar in the field of human-computer interaction. He applied scenario theory and introduced the Scenario-Based Design (SBD) method, applying it to the usability engineering of interactive products. This method includes analysis based on problem scenarios, design based on real scenarios, and prototyping and evaluation based on actual scenarios [9]. Suri and Marsh introduced scenario construction into household product design research, using it as a human-computer engineering method by creating a series of fictional stories that include specific roles, events, and product and service spaces [10]. In the book "Design for Experience: Where Technology Meets Design and Strategy," Rosmannis proposed a design method based on scenario theory to help designers better understand user experience requirements and incorporate user contexts and psychological factors into product design [11]. Yu Conggang believes that design scenarios are spaces to solve design problems. Based on the regularities of design activities, he constructed three key scenarios, namely "Prototype Design Scenario," "Creative Design Scenario," and "Brand Design Scenario," for problem-solving, and proposed the composition of design scenarios [12].

At the same time, scholars have begun to delve into the driving role of artificial intelligence scenarios in modern design innovation. In "From Physical Logic to Behavioral Logic," Xin Xiangyang explained the scenario logic of intelligent systems from the perspective of behavioral logic [13]. Building on Yu Conggang's research, Huang Biao proposed a scenario-driven model for intelligent product design, outlining operational processes for requirements mining based on user scenarios, product design based on conceptual scenarios, and product validation and feedback based on real scenarios [14]. These studies indicate that scenario-based design thinking provides important theoretical support and practical guidance in areas such as human-computer interaction, product innovation, and aesthetics, semantics, and interaction design for intelligent products.

1.5 Application Trends and Insights

Scene innovation thinking, as an important design empowerment tool, is increasingly valued in the field of industrial design research and widely applied, especially in the field of the Internet of Things (IoT). In the IoT industry, scenario theory begins to guide the construction of the design and manufacturing ecosystem. The following explores several viewpoints related to scenario theory under various application perspectives, connecting with the cultivation of talents in design innovation.

Combining the Perspective of User Research Applications: Scenario Theory Emphasizes that Designers Need to Gain in-Depth Insights into Users' Needs and Usage Environments. By observing and analyzing users' behaviors, emotions, and needs in specific scenarios, a better understanding of users' real experiences and expectations can be achieved, guiding product design and innovation more effectively.

In the design of the iPhone, the team utilized scenario analysis to simulate and understand users' mobile phone usage needs in different life scenarios. This method shifted the focus of design towards users' real experiences rather than just product features. Through scenario studies, the team comprehensively understood user needs, optimized the phone design, and successfully adapted the iPhone to users' daily lives, providing an expected user experience. This case illustrates that scenario theory in industrial design offers crucial guidance for in-depth user research, ensuring that products meet user needs in real-world scenarios.

Similarly, in the process of cultivating talents for design innovation, teaching relevant knowledge and methods of scenario theory can help students develop sensitivity and insight into user needs.

Connecting with the Perspective of Human-Computer Interaction Applications, Scenario Theory is a Framework Used to Describe and Analyze Human Behavior, Widely Applied in the Field of Human-computer Interaction. It emphasizes people's behaviors in specific contexts and how these behaviors are influenced by the environment and other factors. (see Fig. 1) scenario theory can be utilized to enhance our understanding of human-computer interaction from six dimensions: the importance of scenarios, goal-oriented behavior, the dynamics of behavior, the influence of the environment, cooperation and sociability, and cognitive processes.

Firstly, scenario theory posits that human behavior occurs in specific contexts. This context can include physical environments, social environments, cultural backgrounds, etc. In human-computer interaction, this may involve the user's surroundings, the nature of tasks, and the specific conditions for interacting with a computer system. Secondly, scenario theory emphasizes that human behavior is often goal-oriented, meaning people pursue certain goals or complete specific tasks in specific contexts. In human-computer interaction, users typically engage with computer systems to achieve specific goals, such as obtaining information, completing tasks, or entertainment. Thirdly, scenario theory highlights that human behavior is dynamic and changes with time and context. In human-computer interaction, the interaction between users and computer systems is also a dynamic process, involving different stages and multiple steps. Simultaneously, scenario theory recognizes the significant impact of the environment on human behavior. In human-computer interaction, the environment includes factors such as user interfaces, system feedback, and device performance, influencing how users interact with the system and its effectiveness. Additionally, scenario theory considers humans as social animals, emphasizing behaviors in cooperation and social interaction. In human-computer interaction, this may involve aspects such as multi-user collaboration and social media interaction. Lastly, scenario theory focuses on human cognitive processes, i.e., how people understand and process information. In human-computer interaction, this includes aspects such as user cognitive load, information presentation methods, and the learning process. By considering users' behaviors and needs in different scenarios, designers can optimize product interface layouts, interaction processes, and feedback mechanisms, enhancing user experience and usability.

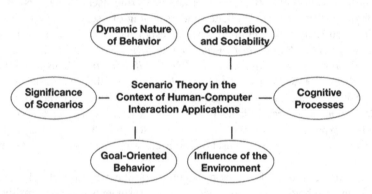

Fig. 1. Scenario Theory in the Context of Human-Computer Interaction Applications

In 1980, Apple Commissioned the Design Firm IDEO to Develop a Mouse Adapted to Its Computer System. Utilizing scenario theory, the design team conducted in-depth research into the actual scenarios of users using the mouse in office environments, focusing on different usage contexts such as on office desks, movement on various surfaces, as well as tasks like graphic design and text editing. Through observing and analyzing these scenarios, the design team understood users' habits and expectations, ultimately innovating the design of the distinctive oval-shaped Apple mouse. This successful case highlights the practical value of a design approach centered around user scenarios in the field of human-computer interaction, laying the foundation for subsequent mouse designs.

From the perspective of product design applications, scenario theory encompasses the relationships among products, users, environments, and interactions. It can guide designers to focus on the relationships between products and users, environments, and interactions, as well as the performance and adaptability of products in specific scenarios.

The CELL Intelligent Travel System is a New Travel Logic Designed for Future IoT Cities. The design team conducted in-depth research into various scenarios of future urban intelligent travel to understand the potential needs of users in these scenarios. Using methods such as user research, observation, and interviews, the design team constructed user profiles for different scenarios. Based on these profiles, a brand-new intelligent travel system based on rail transportation was developed. This system can cater to the future urban travel needs in different scenarios, providing a more person-alized and user-centric intelligent experience.

In innovative design education, teachers can guide students to consider product design from multiple perspectives, fostering students' comprehensive abilities and helping them create products that better align with user expectations and adapt to various scenarios.

Integrating the Service Design Perspective, Scenario Theory Can Help Designers Understand the Needs and Expectations of Users in the Service Interaction Process. By analyzing users' service experiences in different scenarios, designers can optimize service processes, interface designs, and communication methods to provide a better service experience.

Airbnb is an online short-term rental service platform. By thoroughly exploring the needs of travelers and hosts in different scenarios, the design team optimized the interface, search, and booking functions, reinforcing communication and support with hosts. By applying scenario theory, Airbnb successfully created a service system that aligns with user expectations, emphasizing the crucial aspect of understanding user needs in different scenarios in service design. Its success stems from a profound understanding of user scenarios, ensuring that the product meets user expectations.

Focusing on the Perspective of Brand Experience Design, Scenario Theory Can Assist Designers in Considering Users' Perceptions and Emotional Experiences in Different Scenarios During Brand Design. By designing brand elements and experiences relat-ed to specific scenarios, designers can enhance brand consistency and emotional resonance, thereby increasing user awareness and loyalty to the brand. In innovative design education, teachers can guide students to incorporate user experience into the design process by emphasizing the usability and emotional resonance of the product, ultimately enhancing the product's attractiveness and user satisfaction through lec-tures and demonstrations of real cases.

Starbucks has created a diverse brand experience by crafting unique coffee shop environments. Beyond offering fast service and convenient coffee choices, it has culti-vated a social and relaxed atmosphere. Elements such as store layout, seating, and coffee cup design work together to create an enjoyable experience. The mobile app and mem-bership program provide personalized customer service, successfully utilizing scenario theory to create a brand image closely aligned with customers' lives. This highlights the importance of focusing on user needs and expectations in different scenarios in brand design.

In general, the application of scenario theory in various fields provides compre-hensive tools for modern designers, driving innovation, enhancing user experiences, and facilitating the integration of design thinking. The use of scenario-based design in industrial design exhibits multidimensional and multi-perspective characteristics, positively impacting the understanding of user needs, optimization of product and service design, and the enhancement of brand awareness and user loyalty. Through research, it is also noted that the current application of scenario theory is predominantly focused on the internet business domain, and there is still a need for further development in the theoretical and applied research for innovative design in the realm of smart hardware products.

2 Scene's Intelligent Expression

Since 2022, AI technology has rapidly advanced, with iterations accelerating for large models like ChatGPT and others in the text-to-image, image-to-image, and language domains. In 2023, the AI platform layer gradually solidifies, and the emergence of applications heralds the realization of intelligent scenes. Intelligent scenes integrate advanced technologies to create environments with perception, learning, adaptability, and interactive capabilities. Focusing on the research of intelligent scenes has a profound impact on design innovation, not only driving the development of the design field but also providing new possibilities and challenges. How to use the intelligent features of scenes to drive innovative creations is a significant proposition for the cultivation of industrial design innovation talents in the context of the AIGC era. This chapter will systematically interpret intelligent scenes from four aspects: content, composition, features, and impact. It will explore the application trends of scene theory in the field of intelligent creation and the direction of cultivating innovative talents.

2.1 The Essence and Composition of Intelligent Scenes

In the four-dimensional space of social activities, scenes embody intrinsic life logic and are endowed with rich connotations. Scenes, akin to containers, represent the fundamental process of our social activities, transitioning from one scene container to another. The composition of intelligent scenes typically involves a variety of technologies and elements that collaborate to create an intelligent, adaptive, and highly interconnected environment. Elements considered essential for technology-driven intelligent scenes generally include sensor technology, IoT connectivity, artificial intelligence and machine learning, cloud computing, smart devices and terminals, edge computing, human-computer interaction, security and privacy considerations, as well as sustainability. These elements synergistically merge to form the foundation of intelligent scenes, enabling environments to become more intelligent, interconnected, and adaptive to user needs.

However, as we delve deeper into our understanding of the AI-driven society, we realize that deconstructing intelligent scenes solely from a technological perspective is incomplete. Renowned design and art philosopher Professor Sun Zhouxing, when discussing design in the era of AIGC, believes that in the latter part of the Anthropocene, under the new technological landscape of ubiquitous algorithms and general intelligence, human technology is unfolding human existence into a dual style of "embodied existence" and "digital existence." He sharply points out the issue of technological optimism in modern design, stating that design is the most technologically advanced among all art styles, and in the age of ubiquitous algorithms and general intelligence today, design's scientific optimism, with the blessing of new technologies, has made designers arrogant and conceited. Furthermore, from the perspective of the future responsibility of design, he proposes two points of view. Firstly, the duality of art and technology; Professor Sun suggests that future intelligent design should adopt a "dual/differentiated" intermediate strategy between art and technology. Secondly, based on the traditional constructive entropy design, he introduces the concept of "deconstructive negative entropy," aiming to find an ideal balance between human "embodied existence" and "digital existence," thereby achieving the reconstruction of a new life world [16].

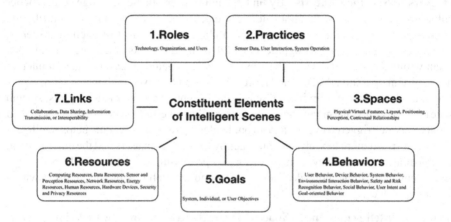

Fig. 2. Constituent Elements of Intelligent Scenes

So, the connotation of intelligent scenes is further expanded, and human understanding of their own "embodied existence" is reexamined. The inherent connecting features of scenes are further strengthened, and the structural reorganization between different scene elements constitutes the intelligent social scenes of the future human. As predicted by Robert Scoble and Shel Israel in the era of scenes, "big data, mobile devices, social media, sensors, and positioning systems together constitute scenes, and with intelligent products as the core, they complete scene tasks and realize scene value" [8]. Scenes represent real-time perception and interpretation of relevant data information in typical situations and, more importantly, signify a completely new human-computer interaction, interface feedback, and user experience. Therefore, the research on intelligent scenes from the perspective of innovative design is essentially a study of the core elements and their new ecological environment that constitute intelligent scenes, including roles, events, spaces, behaviors, goals, resources, connections, etc. (see Fig. 2), understanding the significance of roles, events, spaces, behaviors, goals, resources, and links to intelligent scenes is crucial, as these elements together form a rich and organic intelligent environment.

Roles: Roles in Intelligent Scenes Can be Divided into Multiple Levels, Including Technical, Organizational, and User Roles. These roles collaborate in intelligent scenes, collectively driving the application and development of intelligent technologies to achieve benefits for organizations and society. User roles, in particular, are a key focus in the design phase. For example, when studying an intelligent system, attention is often given to the end-user roles who use the intelligent system for services, the business roles within the organization that use intelligent systems to support business decision-making and execution, and the backend administrators responsible for managing and monitoring the system to ensure its proper functioning, as well as performing necessary configurations and maintenance. Exploring requirements from different perspectives and dimensions supports design innovation.

Practices: In Traditional Design Logic, Practices Refer to the Behaviors and Habits of Users in Specific Contexts. By understanding user practices, designers can better tailor product systems to accommodate users' daily routines and workflows, contributing to increased user acceptance and system usability. In the context of intelligent scenes, "practices" typically refer to significant and meaningful events or changes in state that occur within a system or device. These events may be related to sensor data, user interactions, system operational status, and more. In a comprehensive intelligent system, events may include, but are not limited to, sensor data events, user interaction events, system state change events, alarms and anomalies, user behavior events, scheduled events, linked events, service-triggered events, and so on. Understanding these events helps intelligent systems respond more flexibly and intelligently to changes in users and the environment. Establishing appropriate event monitoring and processing mechanisms allows the system to enhance autonomous decision-making and adaptability, providing users with a better experience.

Spaces: In Intelligent Scenes, "Spaces" Typically Refer to Specific Locations, Areas, or Places in Physical or Virtual Environments. Understanding spaces is crucial for designing and implementing the functionality of intelligent systems because the behavior and functionality of many intelligent systems are influenced by specific spaces. Therefore, designers need to consider various elements of spaces, including not only the characteristics, layout, and perception of spaces but also understanding the contextual relationships and interactions within spaces. This ensures that intelligent systems can adapt to different environmental requirements, contributing to the delivery of more intelligent, personalized, and precise services.

Behaviors: In Intelligent Scenes, "Behaviors" Typically Refer to the Actions, Activities, or Reactions of Individuals or Systems in a Specific Environment. In the research field of intelligent scenes, behavior data, including user behavior, device behavior, system behavior, environmental interaction behavior, safety and risk identification behavior, social behavior, user intent, and goal-oriented behavior, can be obtained through sensor data, user interaction records, environmental monitoring, and other methods. Understanding behavior forms the basis for intelligent systems to make more targeted and adaptive decisions. By comprehending user behavior, designers can anticipate user needs and provide a more intelligent, responsive system.

Goals: In Intelligent Scenes, "Goals" Typically Refer to the Specific Outcomes or Desired States that a System, Individual, or User Aims to Achieve During a Specific Period. Understanding goals is crucial for the design and decision-making of intelligent systems. Knowing the goals of users helps designers determine the behavior, planning, resource allocation, functionality, and priorities of intelligent systems. This ensures that intelligent systems better understand user expectations, plan their actions, and adopt appropriate strategies to achieve these goals.

Resources: Resources Include Tools, Equipment, and Information Available for Achieving Goals. In intelligent scenes, "resources" typically refer to various elements or assets that can be utilized to complete tasks, support system operation, or achieve objectives. This encompasses computing resources, data resources, sensors and perceptual resources, network resources, energy resources, human resources, hardware devices, security and privacy resources, and more. Understanding and effectively managing these resources are crucial for the performance, reliability, and user satisfaction of intelligent systems. When designing and developing intelligent systems, careful assessment and planning of resource utilization are necessary to ensure optimal system performance in specific scenarios.

Links: Links Refer to the Connections and Relationships Between Elements. In intelligent scenes, "links" typically refer to the interactive relationships that connect different components, devices, systems, or entities to achieve collaboration, data sharing, information transmission, or interoperability. Understanding links is a crucial factor in intelligent system design, as it involves information flow, data exchange, and collaborative operations between systems. It also helps achieve collaborative work in intelligent systems, optimize resource utilization, and provide more flexible and efficient services.

These elements are interwoven, collectively shaping the overall picture of intelligent scenes. By understanding and delving into these elements, designers can better meet user needs and create scenes that are more intelligent and closely aligned with actual requirements.

2.2 Characteristics of Intelligent Scenes

John McCarthy defined "intelligence" as making a machine's reactions similar to those of a person in action [17]. The technological characteristics of intelligent scenes with intelligent products at the core are manifested through the Internet, big data, and cloud computing. Essentially, it relies on the rapid development of the Internet, big data, and sensor technology to establish multi-dimensional interactive relationships among roles, events, spaces, behaviors, goals, resources, and links. This enables people to be perceived, and products proactively provide services for specific occasions.

For example, Amazon Alexa, Google Assistant, or Apple's Siri. These voice assistants provide more intelligent and personalized services by continuously learning and adapting to user needs. Alexa, through advanced voice recognition and natural language processing technologies, can understand users' verbal commands and inquiries, even grasping context to make conversations more coherent. It also learns users' habits, preferences, and needs gradually. Utilizing data from interactions with devices, user history queries, and device usage patterns, Alexa can understand personalized user requirements. Moreover, Alexa goes beyond personalizing services based solely on static user data; it possesses adaptive learning capabilities. Through continuous interaction, it dynamically adjusts responses and suggestions, enhancing the overall user experience.

Whether it's Amazon Alexa, Google Assistant, or Apple's Siri, it's easy to see that intelligent scenes exhibit a series of prominent features, as illustrated in Figs. 1 and 2. These characteristics reflect the intelligence, adaptability, and interactivity inherent in environments that integrate advanced technologies. In summary, these features can be roughly categorized into the following ten points:

Perceptiveness: Intelligent Scenarios Possess the Ability to Perceive the Environment and Users. Through various sensors, cameras, sound recognition, and other technologies, the system can real-time acquire and comprehend information about the surrounding environment, including user behavior, environmental changes, etc. Based on the development of sensing technology, the scenario can achieve self-perception of information and respond to needs. This is also the core difference that distinguishes intelligent scenarios from traditional demand discovery methods. Machines can perceive complex external environments, and the development of robotics and mechanics enables machines to perform various actions in response to external environments.

For example, Tesla's Full Self-Driving (FSD) system version 11.4.2, updated in May 2023, in addition to easily recognizing obstacles, pedestrians, license plates, and road traffic signs, is specifically optimized for diverse road network facilities such as China's urban overpasses, main and auxiliary roads, congested traffic conditions, complex types of vehicles, and more intricate traffic light systems. It also considers the differences in driving habits, providing optimized road scenes for Chinese urban smart travel scenarios. This significantly enhances the safety, convenience, and comfort of travel.

Learning: Intelligent Scenarios Possess the Capability to Learn and Adapt. The system can continuously accumulate experience by analyzing user behavior, preferences, and feedback, enhancing its understanding of user needs and making more intelligent decisions.

Automation: Intelligent Scenarios Emphasize the Ability to Automatically Execute Tasks. The system can automatically perform tasks based on preset rules or learned patterns, reducing the workload for users and improving efficiency.

Interactivity: Intelligent Scenarios Focus on Interaction with Users. Through Natural Interaction Methods such as Voice, Gestures, Touch, etc., Users can communicate with and control the system more intuitively, enhancing the user experience. The development of mobile internet allows people to interact with machines anytime, anywhere, leading to the fusion of human and machine, where machines begin to think more like humans.

Adaptability: Intelligent Scenarios Possess Adaptability, Allowing them to Automatically Adjust Based on Changes in the Environment and User Preferences. The system can flexibly adapt to different scenarios, needs, and preferences, providing more personalized and user-centric services that align with user expectations.

Context Awareness: Intelligent Scenarios not only Focus on Specific Situations but also Possess the Capability of Full-scene Coverage. The system can perceive and interact across various scenarios such as home, work, and city environments. IoT (Internet of Things) technology enables machines to exchange information with each other, forming an ecosystem where common household items like light bulbs, medical assets such as healthcare devices, wearable devices, smart appliances, and even smart cities can connect to the internet. These devices can receive and transmit data through wireless networks with minimal human intervention, creating a network of interconnected physical systems.

Multimodal Integration: Intelligent Scenarios Integrate Multiple Perceptual Modalities and Interaction Methods. Various modes such as voice, images, sensors, and more can collaborate, enabling the system to comprehensively perceive and understand users and the environment.

Data-Driven: Intelligent Scenarios are Driven by Data A large volume of real-time data is collected, analyzed, and applied to the system's decision-making and optimization processes, thereby enhancing system performance and user experience.

Real-time Responsiveness: Intelligent Scenarios Emphasize Real-time Responsiveness, Enabling Swift Responses to User Needs and Environmental Changes The system possesses timely feedback and execution capabilities, enhancing real-time user experience.

Security and Privacy: Intelligent Scenarios Feature Security and Privacy Protection Mechanisms The system must ensure the security of user data and provide clear privacy settings to establish user trust in the system.

These characteristics collectively constitute the essence of intelligent scenarios, making systems more intelligent, flexible, and adaptive to user needs and environmental changes. The integration and optimization of these features are crucial for the successful creation of intelligent scenarios.

2.3 The Impact of Intelligent Scenes

"The Impact of Intelligent Scenes on Design Innovation. Scene theory emphasizes a thorough understanding of user needs and goals. In the context of intelligent scenes, design should focus on the interaction between users and intelligent technologies to achieve a personalized user experience. Adaptive design requires products to possess strong contextual awareness, integrating IoT (Internet of Things) technology to create intelligent, interactive, and adaptive environments. In terms of user participation and collaboration, the innovation of new interaction methods prompts designers to reconsider the interaction between users and products, services, or environments, providing intelligent and natural interactive experiences.

Concerning the overall user experience, there is an emphasis on data-driven design decisions and holistic service experiences across various scenarios. Attention is given to the entire user journey, providing integrated, coherent, and intelligent experiences. The iteration and evolution of intelligent systems demand design flexibility. In terms of social impact and ethical considerations, intelligent scenes give rise to new business models. Designers need to consider the societal impact of innovative product delivery methods, including privacy, security, and data ethics.

Overall, intelligent scenes drive innovation in the design field, requiring designers to pay more attention to user experience, data-driven design, holistic service, sustainability, and more. To adapt to the continually evolving intelligent environment, continuous learning and innovation are necessary to better meet the needs of users and the market."

3 Intelligent Scene Creation: Emerging Trends

In Henrik von Scheel's concept of Industry 4.0, he emphasizes the importance of focusing on values rather than technology, and on humanity rather than tools in the development of the manufacturing industry. Over the past 12 years, since the concept of Industrie 4.0 was first introduced at the Hanover Industrial Fair in 2011, we have witnessed the rapid emergence of intelligent technologies, including artificial intelligence, big data, the Internet of Things, edge computing, cloud computing, blockchain, digital twins, 5G, and more. The emergence of these technologies has sparked a transformation in design thinking, driving the upgrading of the manufacturing industry.

In December 2023, the 2023 China Design and Artificial Intelligence Liangzhu Summit was held at the Liangzhu Campus of the China Academy of Art. Nearly 150 scholars, experts, and guests from 8 countries and regions gathered in Liangzhu to discuss the theme of "Design Leadership in the Era of AIGC." Centered around the dialogue between Chinese design and artificial intelligence, the summit actively engaged in fruitful discussions on the emerging trends in intelligent scene creation.

Liu Ning, the President of the China Industrial Design Association and Deputy Director of the Committee of Instruction for National Design Professional Degree Graduates, pointed out that facing the rapidly evolving technological revolution and industrial changes, the new industrialization represented by artificial intelligence, digitalization, information, green energy, and industrial internet is dramatically transforming this era. He believes that under the new trend of intelligent scene creation, exploring how to build harmonious and symbiotic development relationships among humans, society, nature, and digital spaces will become a significant exploration area for the major design forces, including academic institutions, corporate entities, and design companies, in the era of artificial intelligence.

During the discussion on the topic "AI and Design Thinking Prospects - Technology and Ethics," Professor Qin Jingyan from Beijing University of Science and Technology emphasized the deep relationship between technology and ethics, asserting that it has now evolved into a question of how natural ecological civilization and digital ecological civilization can coexist. She emphasized the need to consider the balance between the ultimate values and meanings that humanity relies on for survival. Technology should be contemplated from ethical, philosophical, and aesthetic perspectives to truly achieve a beautiful, healthy, and sustainable future.

Dr. Wu Jiyi, Committee Member of the Zhejiang Association for Science and Technology and Deputy Chairman cum Secretary-General of the Zhejiang Artificial Intelligence Society, discussed the contradictory nature between AI development and ethics. From a long-term perspective, he believes that the series of issues arising from the interaction between AI and ethics can be gradually resolved, ultimately leading human society to a new balance, a state of new collaboration, and harmony.

In addition, at the academic forum "Humans and the New Ecology System" during this summit, Professor Han Ting from the School of Design at Shanghai Jiao Tong University presented on "Design Thinking and Innovative Design for Human-Intelligence-Machine Systems," showcasing innovative paths and cases of intelligent scene creation through the collaborative efforts of carbon-based and silicon-based intelligence in intelligent ecological scenarios, expanding the cognitive boundaries of intelligent scenes.

The evolution of intelligent scenes is driving the transformation of products from "objects" to "systems" and further to "ecosystems." These scenes are not only ecological but also extend the ecosystem of intelligent creation to encompass society, humanity, and the natural environment, spreading throughout various aspects of human existence and life. The symbiotic relationship between humans and the ecosystem has become a contemplative theme in intelligent creation. It is foreseeable that artificial intelligence plays a role here, but equally important are human care, insights, and expectations for themselves within this context.

4   Conclusion

As the wave of innovation is sparked by intelligent products, scenario theory is emerging as a powerful tool in the field of design, profoundly shaping the landscape of product innovation. Firstly, the rise of scenario theory calls for a reexamination of the essence of user experience. By focusing on user behaviors and needs in intelligent scenes, designers can go beyond abstract functional technology stacking and truly delve into the users' hearts, thereby leading the forefront of innovation in intelligent product design. However, this deeply integrated design approach also imposes higher demands on design education. Traditional curriculum frameworks and methods may struggle to adapt to this trend. Design education needs a transformation, not only fostering students with solid technical skills but also igniting their sensitivity to various fields such as sociology, psychology, culture, technology, and philosophy. Such speculative education will help designers better understand and address the complex challenges in the rapidly evolving advanced technological environment.

Simultaneously, scenario theory opens a window for designers, bringing them closer to the everyday lives of users and allowing insights into subtle changes. However, this also requires designers to find a delicate balance between innovation and practical needs. Design education needs to cultivate students' critical thinking, enabling them to pursue uniqueness and foresight while maintaining a clear understanding of the complexity of real-world scenarios.

In this era full of possibilities and challenges, scenario theory is not just a methodology for product design but also a reflection on design philosophy. Design education needs to transcend traditional boundaries, fostering students with an exploratory spirit towards the unknown and complexity, making them capable of becoming innovative designers who can lead the future. Only through scenario-based design thinking education can we better embrace the possibilities and challenges brought by the wave of intelligent creation.

Acknowledgments. This study was funded by China Academy of Art, school-level scientific research project - general project, research on application trends of scene theory in the field of intelligent product innovation, YB2022003.

Disclosure of Interests. It is now necessary to declare any competing interests or to specifically state that the authors have no competing interests.

References

1. Goffman, E.: The Presentation of Self in Everyday Life. Translated by Feng Gang, p. 102. Peking University Press, Beijing (2008)
2. Meyrowitz, J.: No Sense of Place: The Impact of Electronic Media on Social Behavior. Translated by Xiao Zhijun, p. 33. Tsinghua University Press, Beijing (2002)
3. Fisher, W.R.: The Narrative Paradigm: In the Beginning. J. Commun. **35**(4), 74–89 (1985)
4. Silver, D.A., Clark, T.N.: Scenes: How Spaces Shape Social Life. Translated by Qi, S. Social Science Literature Press, Beijing (2019)
5. Wei, W.: Research on digital exhibition design based on scene-based interaction. Design **17**, 46–48 (2018)
6. Kenny, D., Marshall, J.F.: Contextual marketing. Harv. Bus. Rev. **78**(6), 119–25 (2000)
7. Sheng, W.: Scene Revolution: Reconstructing the Connection between People and Business. Beijing United Publishing Company, Beijing
8. Schaefer, I.: The Coming Age of Scenius. Beijing United Publishing Company, Beijing
9. Scenarios, C.J.M.: Requirements engineering. In: Proceedings of IEEE Joint International Conference on Design Cognition, pp. 3–5. IEEE (2002) (2002)
10. Suri, J.F., Marsh, M.: Scenario building as an ergonomics method in consumer product design. Appl. Ergon. **31**(2), 151–157 (2000)
11. Kim, J.: Design for Experience: Where Technology Meets Design and Strategy. Springer, USA (2019). https://doi.org/10.1007/978-3-319-14304-0
12. Yu, C.: Problem Solving in Data-Driven Design. Ph.D. dissertation, Hunan University, Hunan (2017)
13. Xin, X.: Interaction design: from physical logic to behavioral logic. Decoration **01**, 58–62 (2015)
14. Huang, B.: Methodology and Practice of Scene-Driven Intelligent Product Design. Master's thesis. Xiangtan University, Hunan (2018)
15. Bai, X., Li, P.: Application of situated cognition theory in industrial design education model. J. North China Elect. Power Univ. **41**(4), 87–90 (2014)
16. ACC Homepage. https://www.baijiahao.baidu.com/s?id=1785281641696873683
17. McCarthy, J.: Commentary on World, US, and scientific affairs. 2007–03–07 [2008–02–01]

From Theory to Practice: Bridging the Gap in Future Kitchen Design for the Chinese Generation Z

Fan Yang, Wenwen Yang[✉], Xiaojing Huang, and Shihao Cao

Guangzhou Academy of Fine Arts, Haizhu District, No. 257, Changgang East Road, Guangzhou, China
fanyang@gzarts.edu.cn, 1508145057@qq.com

Abstract. This paper delves into the intricate nexus of kitchen design and the unique characteristics of Chinese Generation Z, a cohort immersed in digital technologies. Building upon prior research, the study scrutinizes the applicability of existing user research methods in shaping kitchen appliance innovations tailored to the Chinese Generation Z. Through triangulating the methods of questionnaire, in-depth interview, and behavioral observation, this research identified distinct lifestyle archetypes within this demographic. These included the 'social cooking group', 'extreme dual-sided lifestyle group', 'high-quality and efficient lifestyle group' and 'health-conscious and sustainable lifestyle group'. Each group exhibited varied preferences and behaviors, posing challenges and opportunities for appliance design. Leveraging the Kano analysis method, the study prioritized the determining factors for user satisfaction. This led to the creation of a new design research model, specifically for the Chinese Generation Z. This model served as a blueprint for future kitchen appliance innovations, aiming to bridge the gap between user expectations and product performance.

Keywords: Kitchen Appliances · Generation Z · User Research Methods · Chinese Market

1 Background

The kitchen is often regarded as the core of the home and plays a crucial role in meeting the diverse needs and desires of residents. Currently, the kitchen appliance market is in a rapid development stage. The global smart kitchen appliance market reached a scale of approximately \$12 billion in 2019, and it is expected to grow at a Compound Annual Growth Rate (CAGR) of 14.12% from 2023 to 2028 [1]. The Chinese kitchen appliance market reached a scale of approximately 120 billion yuan in 2019, and it is expected to grow at a Compound Annual Growth Rate (CAGR) of 7.5% from 2023 to 2028 [2]. In the era marked by advanced digital technology, the "Z generation" is a unique and important consumer group in the field of kitchen appliances. They are individuals who have grown up in a technology-driven environment and they are full of confidence in the future.

A. Marcus et al. (Eds.): HCII 2024, LNCS 14716, pp. 237–257, 2024.
https://doi.org/10.1007/978-3-031-61362-3_18

They have high standards for quality of life and show a strong interest in and expectations for smart kitchen appliances. From the perspective of consumer characteristics and behaviors, the Z generation exhibits unique trends in impulse consumption, brand loyalty, omnichannel shopping, technological sense, and cooking interests. According to a report from McKinsey China Consumer Special Issue, the Z generation is confident about the future, possess strong self-awareness and expression desires. They are more concerned about the quality, safety, and environmental friendliness of products rather than just the price [3]. They have higher expectations and demands for smart kitchen appliances. These unique characteristics bring opportunities and challenges for the design of kitchen appliances. As pointed out by many scholars Bennett et al.; Wang et al. Akçayır et al. [4–6], brands need to refine their value propositions, provide personalized and intelligent product services, strengthen the integration of online and offline channels, and use social media and Key Opinion Leaders (KOLs) to attract and retain young consumers. At the same time, in-depth user research and innovative design have become particularly important in order to meet the diversified and personalized needs of the Z generation and enhance their kitchen experience and quality of life.

In the face of challenges in kitchen appliance design, scholars and practitioners have proposed various research methods, emphasizing the importance of a comprehensive understanding of residents' needs and expectations. However, we found that existing research is inadequate in exploring how to meet the real needs of residents. Therefore, we conducted a joint research project with the support of leading manufacturers. This research explored the characteristics of the Chinese Z generation and assessed the applicability and practicality of general theoretical user research methods in guiding kitchen appliance innovations for this group in the next 3–5 years. Finally, a new model was proposed which helps apply general methods in the implementation of new kitchen appliance innovations. In terms of methodology, we comprehensively understood the dining and cooking habits of the local Z generation through multi-level methods such as questionnaires, in-depth interviews, and behavioral observations. Extensive data collection included distributing WeChat and phone questionnaires, as well as conducting in-depth interviews with 30 Z generation participants using snowball sampling. These interviews aimed to collect daily activity information and opinions of participants in a group format, while behavioral observation methods provided more detailed information about the cooking processes and other related activities of the interviewees on weekdays and weekends. Subsequently, we used Kano analysis to quantify the collected data and determine the prioritized key features of design satisfaction. The research results revealed that Z generation participants can be divided into five lifestyle groups, each displaying unique preferences and interests. These findings revealed the challenges faced by the design of usable and functional kitchen appliances, laying a foundation for the development of a new design research model specifically targeting the Chinese Z generation to drive product innovations in this field. The new model provides preliminary guidance for the user performance of future kitchen appliances.

2 Methods

We conducted in-depth research on the dining and cooking habits of Generation Z in China through various data collection methods, including surveys, in-depth interviews, and behavioral observations. Data analysis utilized the Kano model to quantitatively evaluate user needs and designed a survey questionnaire based on the attributes of this model. The experimental design went through comprehensive evaluations by designers, engineers, business representatives, and Generation Z users, and the evaluation results were analyzed using the Likert scale satisfaction test.

2.1 Data Collection

We employed a multi-level data collection approach, including surveys, in-depth interviews, and behavioral observations, to fully understand the dining and cooking habits of Generation Z in China. By using Kano analysis to quantify the data, we identified the priority of key features for designing satisfying kitchen products.

Survey. To Gain Deeper Insights into the Needs and Experiences of Generation Z Users in Kitchen Product Design and Usage, We Conducted an Initial Survey Targeting 300 Generation Z Users Through Two Channels: WeChat and Phone Calls. We Successfully Collected 280 Valid Questionnaires, Achieving a Response Rate of 93%. We Focused on the Frequency of Users' Cooking Activities, Analyzed Their Motivations for Cooking, and Identified the Inconveniences They Encounter When Using Current Kitchen Products. The Results of This Survey Will Provide Us with Profound Insights to Guide the Future Design and Improvement of Kitchen Products, Better Meeting the Expectations and Needs of Generation Z Users.

From the perspective of users' cooking frequency, it can be categorized into four groups within a week: 1–2 times, 3–4 times, rarely or never, and every day. Among them, the majority falls into the categories of 1–2 times and 3–4 times, accounting for 45% and 36% respectively, while the categories of rarely or never and every day are in the minority, accounting for only 15% and 4%. In terms of cooking motivations, they can be divided into three categories: improving cooking skills and enjoying food, social activities, and improving healthy eating habits. 45% cook to improve their cooking skills and enjoy food, 30% for social activities, and 20% to improve their healthy eating habits by cooking themselves. Users' current issues with kitchen product usage can be classified into six categories: safety hazards, failure to meet personal needs and preferences, unsuitability for specific kitchen layouts, difficulty in cleaning, inconvenient operation, and lack of smart and connected functions. Among them, the proportion of difficulty in cleaning is as high as 75%, while inconvenient operation and lack of smart and connected functions account for 45% and 40% respectively. The proportions for failure to meet personal needs and preferences, unsuitability for specific kitchen layouts, and safety hazards are 30%, 15%, and 10% respectively.

User Interviews. Snowball sampling is a non-probability sampling technique where researchers first identify and interview a small group of participants who meet the research criteria, and then ask these participants to recommend other potential participants. This process continues, gradually expanding the sample size like a rolling snowball Goodman [7]. Through the implementation of snowball sampling, we initially selected a small group of preliminary participants from the identified population of young Generation Z users who met the research criteria. With the recommendations from our company partners, we chose representative participants and contacted them through phone or online channels after obtaining their consent. The in-depth interviews involved 30 Generation Z users from Guangdong Province, China. We explored their personal information, family status, future expectations, daily kitchen usage, and their expectations for future innovative kitchen designs. Participants were encouraged to recommend others who fit the criteria, gradually expanding the interview sample to ensure diversity and representativeness. The interviews were recorded in writing, capturing participants' exact words to ensure the validity and authenticity of the interview content, based on users' ultimate needs.

To explore the expectations of Generation Z users for future kitchen appliance innovation design and understand their understanding of real kitchen needs, we conducted in-depth interviews and questionnaires to design the interview content around three core purposes: user types, user needs in both working and non-working situations, and analysis of user behavior processes. The scope of the interview content includes the following four aspects: 1) understanding the basic information of Generation Z users, such as gender, age, occupation, family living arrangement, and cooking frequency in daily life; 2) understanding the daily use of the kitchen by Generation Z users, such as cooking situations on weekdays, cooking methods (cooking by themselves or with family or friends), awareness of cooking socialization, and physical and mental health conditions; 3) understanding the relevant issues encountered by Generation Z users in the process of daily kitchen use, such as the functionality of kitchen facilities, kitchen space layout, the usage of operators, emotional kitchen design, dietary health issues, safety conditions, and how they solve these problems; 4) understanding the expectations of Generation Z users for future kitchens, such as expectations for innovative designs and new features in future kitchen appliances.

We contacted preliminary participants through phone calls or online channels, introduced the purpose and content of the research, and obtained their consent to participate in in-depth interviews. A total of 30 users (14 males and 16 females) participated in the interviews, covering different ages, educational backgrounds, cooking experiences, and levels of digital technology use to ensure coverage of different household situations.

We adopted a semi-structured interview questioning method, emphasizing freedom during the interview to obtain users' genuine attitudes towards kitchen appliances. The interview process consists of a preparation stage (10 min), transition stage (15 min), and in-depth stage (20 min). Through progressively deepening question design, the aim is to reduce user discomfort during the interview and truly understand their thoughts. The interview outline focused on kitchen life, cooking needs, and the use of kitchen appliances, in order to gain a deeper understanding of users' lifestyles, consumption habits, and expectations for kitchen products. In the initial stage of the interview, the warm-up stage aims to eliminate potential interview nerves and gather information about users' lives, interests, consumption patterns, concerns, home life philosophies, and criteria for choosing home appliances. The question outline revolves around weekend activities and preferences during weekdays. The purpose of the transition stage is to gain a deeper understanding of users' needs for cooking attitude and kitchen space, gathering information about cooking frequency, motivation, and time arrangements through question outlines. The final in-depth stage aims to obtain detailed information about users' actual use of kitchen products and potential problems. The question outline focuses on the frequency of kitchen appliance use, functional preferences, cleaning methods, and considerations during actual cooking processes, in order to comprehensively understand users' real needs and expectations.

2.2 Data Analysis

By analyzing users' behaviors regarding kitchen product use, we can identify a set of demands that users have for kitchen products. In order to determine the priority of these demands and focus on addressing the ones that users are most concerned about, quantitative analysis of these demands is necessary. In the 1980s, Japanese scholar Noriaki Kano proposed the Kano model, which constructs targeted product quality factors to address the challenge of quantifying user needs in the process of product innovation design and development [8]. In the Kano model, product functionalities/needs and the characteristics of services are divided into five types of attributes: Must-be attributes (M), One-dimensional attributes (O), Attractive attributes (A), Indifferent attributes (I), and Reverse attributes (R). These attribute classifications are related to user satisfaction [9]. Based on these five attribute classifications, we designed the questionnaire samples. Each demand factor includes questions on both positive and negative aspects, with five options for each question: naturally, very like, indifferent, can tolerate, and dislike. The survey adopts a 5-point scale, where users rate based on personal perception, with scores increasing from 1 to 5. Based on the survey results, we established a Kano evaluation result comparison table (see Table 2).

Table 1. Analysis of the results of the Kano questionnaires

		Negative questions				
		like (5)	naturally (4)	indifferent (3)	can tolerate (2)	dislike (1)
Positive questions	like (5)	Q	A	A	A	O
	naturally (4)	R	I	I	I	M
	indifferent (3)	R	I	I	I	M
	can tolerate (2)	R	I	I	I	M
	dislike (1)	R	R	R	R	Q

When designing the Kano questionnaire for kitchen product development, it is necessary to ask positive and negative questions for each demand factor, and then calculate the frequencies of each attribute category. The most frequently occurring attribute category in the statistical results is used as the quality attribute for that demand factor [10]. Let's take the demand for cooking step teaching in kitchen products as an example to design the Kano questionnaire (see Table 2).

Table 2. Kano questionnaire

Step-by-step instruction for cooking kitchen products	Very like	naturally	indifferent	marginally accept	dislike
When highlighted for consideration					
When not considered at all					

We distributed the designed Kano questionnaire on kitchen product user demands to a target group of newly emerging middle-class individuals online, with a total of 120 questionnaires distributed. We received 100 valid responses, resulting in an effective questionnaire response rate of 83%. The Kano survey results were statistically analyzed and entered into the Kano model investigation result analysis table to determine the attribute types for each demand (see Table 3).

Table 3. Summary of kitchen product functions

Sensory needs	A1. The product design style is consistent with the home decoration style
	A2. The product features a combination of multiple materials
	A3. The product provides intelligent voice feedback according to user requirements
Interaction needs	B1. There is visual representation of functional status (current operating mode, temperature, wind power, power)
	B2. There is cooking step instruction
	B3. There is a one-key cooking process recording and sharing feature
	B4. The product can be awakened without contact (e.g., through gestures/voice)
	B5. The product's functions can be adjusted through touch-sensitive controls without physical buttons
	B6. The product automatically folds/hides after cooking is finished

(*continued*)

Table 3. (*continued*)

	B7. There is a self-cleaning function after cooking is finished
	B8. The product can be connected to a mobile phone for remote control
	B9. There are pots and pans that can be matched with different cooktop surfaces
	B10. There is a convenient visual flame
	B11. There is intelligent recommendation of daily recipes
Emotional needs	C1. There is provision of a healthy and safe cooking environment
	C2. There is provision of a cooking environment for family interaction
	C3. There is provision of a high-quality sensory experience

2.3 Testing Plan

The product design was comprehensively evaluated by inviting industrial designers, engineers, company representatives, and Generation Z users to obtain multi-perspective feedback on the product concept. The evaluation dimensions mainly included usability, reliability, ease of use, efficiency, diversity, convenience, pleasure, and feasibility based on the product's characteristics, usage scenarios, and design positioning. Through satisfaction testing of the product, the goal is to reveal any potential issues in the design, gain a deep understanding of its shortcomings, and provide targeted modifications and feedback. The evaluation involved a total of 30 participants, including 4 designers, 4 engineers, 4 company representatives, and 18 Generation Z users. The evaluation method used a Likert scale satisfaction testing questionnaire (see Fig. 1). A score of 5 indicates "strongly agree," while a score of 1 indicates "strongly disagree." Other scores decrease or increase accordingly, with 3 representing a neutral feeling Chen [11]. This method aims to quantitatively measure the satisfaction of the evaluation subjects across various dimensions, thus providing an overall assessment of the design concept.

Op- tions	stron gly disagree	disa- gree	indif- ferent	agr ee	stron gly agree	High est total score	Low est total score
Scor e	1	2	3	4	5	150	30
P.S.	Higher scores indicate that users tend to "strongly agree" and vice versa for "strongly disagree".						

Fig. 1. Likert Scale Satisfaction Test Statistical Table

3 Results

Among the 30 Generation Z users, 25 indicated a preference for flexible dining options such as snacks, takeout, and fast food in their daily lives, while only 5 adhered to traditional three-meal schedules. Additionally, 21 users stated a tendency to choose convenient food options like frozen foods or ready-to-eat meals on busy work or study days. On weekends or when they have free time, 90% of the users expressed a willingness to try new recipes or cook by themselves.

Based on the interview results, 28 users mentioned that the main reason they purchased kitchen appliances is to improve cooking efficiency and convenience. Furthermore, 24 users indicated that they also consider the technological and smart features when buying kitchen appliances, as they appreciate technologically advanced products that enhance the kitchen experience.

During the interviews, 18 users mentioned a certain learning curve associated with complex appliance interfaces. They expressed a desire for future kitchen appliances to have simpler and more intuitive operation interfaces, making it easier for them to master the use of appliances.

Summary of the interviews with users revealed four different user types. The Social Cooking Type consists of 7 users, who are usually singles or young couples. They engage in cooking activities together with friends 2–3 times a week and prioritize multi-functional and convenient kitchen appliances, such as juicers, rice cookers, and innovative products related to social interaction. High-quality and efficient lifestyle: There are 8 users in total, most of them are professional singles or young couples in the workplace. They have cooking activities 3–4 times a week, pursuing quality and efficiency. They like high-end, intelligent kitchen appliances such as smart ovens and mixers. The extreme dual-sided lifestyle group consists of 9 users who are successful professionals or young families. They only have cooking activities 1–2 times a week and prefer dining out. They value diverse lifestyles and have relatively low frequency of using kitchen appliances. The health-conscious and sustainable lifestyle group consists of 6 users who are young couples or families with children. They have cooking activities more than 4 times a week because they pay more attention to ingredient selection and dietary healthiness. They have certain demand for environmentally friendly and healthy kitchen appliances (see Table 4).

Specific data on each requirement of the Kano questionnaire were summarized, and the data was quantitatively analyzed to determine the attribute types of each requirement (see Table 5). The final Kano positioning result for each requirement refers to the category with the largest proportion, typically prioritized as: Must-be attributes > One-dimensional attributes > Attractive attributes > Indifferent attributes. The improved satisfaction coefficient (Better coefficient) $= (A + O)/(A + O + M + I)$, where Better coefficient values are usually positive, and the larger or closer to 100%, the more the user satisfaction improves when providing a certain attribute. The eliminated dissatisfaction coefficient (Worse coefficient) $= -(O + M)/(A + O + M + I)$, where Worse coefficient values are usually negative, and the smaller or closer to -100%, the larger the decrease in user satisfaction when not providing a certain attribute.

The positioning of product features is intuitively presented through a matrix diagram, which is beneficial for determining the priority of product development functions. Based

Table 4. User classification

User Type	No	Family structure	Cooking frequency	Cooking motivation	Utilization of kitchen products	User description
Social Cooking Type	7	singles or young couples	engage in cooking activities together with friends 2–3 times a week	loves to enhance relationships and share unique food experiences through cooking	prioritize multi-functional and convenient kitchen appliances, such as juicers, rice cookers, and innovative products related to social interaction	These users have an open-minded personality, enjoy trying new things, and consider the kitchen as an extension of social activities. They like cooking with friends and sharing unique cooking skills and culinary experiences
High-quality and efficient lifestyle	8	professional singles or young couples in the workplace	cooking 3–4 times a week, with a tendency to create delicate cuisine in a limited time	seeker of quality and efficiency who wants to enhance the quality of life through cooking	like high-end, intelligent kitchen appliances such as smart ovens and mixers	focused on time management, value efficient cooking process but unwilling to compromise on taste. Have high demands on kitchen appliances
extreme dual-sided lifestyle	9	successful professionals or young families	cooking 1–2 times a week and prefer dining out	value diverse lifestyle, kitchen is an entertainment and enjoyment for them	focusing on design and technology, they may choose stylish kitchen appliances that are used relatively infrequently	low cooking ability and preference for multiple dietary flavors and tastes shift from relying on instructions to relying on one's own experience
health-conscious and sustainable lifestyle	6	young couples or families with children	cooking more than 4 times a week because they pay more attention to ingredient selection and dietary healthiness	emphasizes health and sustainability and wants to take control of their diet through cooking	focus on eco-friendly and healthy kitchen appliances such as slow cookers and mixers, as well as sustainable products	have certain demand for environmentally friendly and healthy kitchen appliances

on the Better-Worse coefficient values (where Worse is taken in absolute value), the scatter plot is divided into four quadrants. The first quadrant (top-right quadrant: One-dimensional attributes) represents a situation where the Better coefficient value is high and the absolute value of the Worse coefficient is also high. This indicates that if the product provides this feature, user satisfaction will increase, but if this feature is not provided, user satisfaction will decrease. These are competitive quality attributes, and efforts should be made to meet users' expectations. By providing additional services

Table 5. Results of the Kano questionnaire for each requirement factor

Product function	percentage						Kano Positioning	Better coefficient	Worse coefficient
	A (Attractive attribute)	O (One-dimensional attribute)	M (Must-be attribute)	I (Indifferent attribute)	R (Reverse attribute)	Q (Questioning result)			
A1 (positive) &A1reverse (negative)	42.0%	0.0%	0.0%	53.0%	3.0%	2.0%	I (Indifferent attributes)	44.211%	-0.0%
A2 (positive) &A2 reverse (negative)	73.0%	18.0%	1.0%	4.0%	1.0%	3.0%	A (Attractive attributes)	94.792%	-19.792%
A3 (positive) &A3 reverse (negative)	72.0%	17.0%	2.0%	5.0%	1.0%	3.0%	A (Attractive attributes)	92.708%	-19.792%
B1 (positive) &B1 reverse (negative)	67.0%	21.0%	3.0%	4.0%	2.0%	3.0%	A (Attractive attributes)	92.632%	-25.263%
B2 (positive) &B2 reverse (negative)	73.0%	19.0%	0.0%	4.0%	1.0%	3.0%	A (Attractive attributes)	95.833%	-19.792%
B3 (positive) &B3 reverse (negative)	4.0%	16.0%	45.0%	20.0%	6.0%	9.0%	M (Must-be attributes)	23.529%	-71.765%
B4 (positive) &B4 reverse (negative)	54.0%	6.0%	11.0%	12.0%	14.0%	3.0%	A (Attractive attributes)	72.289%	-20.482%
B5 (positive) &B5 reverse (negative)	15.0%	5.0%	15.0%	46.0%	19.0%	0.0%	I (Indifferent attributes)	24.691%	-24.691%
B6 (positive) &B6 reverse (negative)	54.0%	6.0%	11.0%	12.0%	14.0%	3.0%	A (Attractive attributes)	72.289%	-20.482%
B7 (positive) &B7reverse (negative)	15.0%	5.0%	15.0%	60.0%	5.0%	0.0%	I (Indifferent attributes)	21.053%	-21.053%
B8 (positive) &B8 reverse (negative)	54.0%	6.0%	11.0%	12.0%	14.0%	3.0%	A (Attractive attributes)	72.289%	-20.482%
B9 (positive) &B9 reverse (negative)	0.0%	0.0%	3.0%	58.0%	34.0%	5.0%	I (Indifferent attributes)	0.0%	-4.918%
B10 (positive) &B10 reverse (negative)	54.0%	6.0%	11.0%	21.0%	5.0%	3.0%	A (Attractive attributes)	65.217%	-18.478%
B11 (positive) &B11 reverse (negative)	16.0%	40.0%	11.0%	33.0%	0.0%	0.0%	O (One-dimensional attributes)	86.0%	77.0%

(*continued*)

Table 5. (*continued*)

Product function	percentage						Kano Positioning	Better coefficient	Worse coefficient
	A (Attractive attribute)	O (One-dimensional attribute)	M (Must-be attribute)	I (Indifferent attribute)	R (Reverse attribute)	Q (Questioning result)			
C1 (positive) &C1 reverse (negative)	57.0%	8.0%	9.0%	9.0%	14.0%	3.0%	A (Attractive attributes)	78.313%	-20.482%
C2 (positive) &C2 reverse (negative)	32.0%	8.0%	12.0%	29.0%	19.0%	0.0%	A (Attractive attributes)	49.383%	-24.691%
C3 (positive) &C3 reverse (negative)	65.0%	6.0%	11.0%	12.0%	1.0%	5.0%	A (Attractive attributes)	75.532%	-18.085%

or product features that users like, this product and service can surpass competitors and stand out, leading to a stronger positive impression from users. The second quadrant (top-left quadrant: Attractive attributes) represents a situation where the Better coefficient value is high and the absolute value of the Worse coefficient is low. This indicates that if this feature is not provided, user satisfaction will not decrease, but if this feature is provided, user satisfaction and loyalty will greatly increase. The third quadrant (bottom-left quadrant: Indifferent attributes) represents a situation where the Better coefficient value is low and the absolute value of the Worse coefficient is also low. This means that whether these features are provided or not, user satisfaction will not change. These are features that users do not care about. The fourth quadrant (bottom-right quadrant: Must-be attributes) represents a situation where the Better coefficient value is low and the absolute value of the Worse coefficient is high. This indicates that if the product provides this feature, user satisfaction will not increase, but if this feature is not provided, user satisfaction will significantly decrease. This implies that the functions in this quadrant are the most basic ones, and these requirements are what users believe we have an obligation to fulfill. Typically, the priority of product development requirements is: Must-be attributes > One-dimensional attributes > Attractive attributes > Indifferent attributes. (see Fig. 2).

Among the 17 extracted user requirements, there are no reverse attributes. Among them, requirements A2, A3, B1, B2, B4, B6, B8, B10, and B11 belong to the indifferent category. This means that whether these 9 requirements are provided or not, they will not affect user satisfaction because they are not important to users. However, the attributes of Must-be, Attractive, and One-dimensional attributes should be met in the design process (see Table 6).

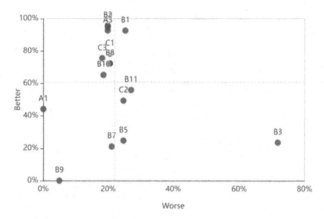

Fig. 2. Better-Worse Matrix Analysis Chart

Table 6. Steam Oven User Requirement Prioritization Level

Must-be attributes	B3
One-dimensional attributes	B11
Attractive attributes	A1, B5, B7, B9
Indifferent attributes	A2, A3, B1, B2, B4, B6, B8, B10, B11

4 Discussion and Conclusion

4.1 A New User Needs Model for Designing New Household Kitchen Appliances

This study's user requirement model helps reveal the diverse and personalized needs of China's Z generation users for household kitchen appliances, reflecting their differences and characteristics in cooking habits and lifestyle. This study divides users into four types: Social Cooking Type, High-quality and Efficient Lifestyle, Extreme Dual-sided Lifestyle, and Health-conscious Sustainable Lifestyle. These four types of users have different core demands for household kitchen appliances in both working days and non-working days (see Table 7).

Social Cooking Type, including singles or young couples, attach importance to cooking and sharing with friends, emphasizing social interaction, and have high demand for multi-functional and convenient kitchen appliances. High-quality and Efficient Lifestyle group is mainly career-oriented singles or working couples who pursue making exquisite dishes in limited time, emphasizing quality and efficiency, and have high expectations for high-end smart kitchen appliances. Extreme Dual-sided Lifestyle group is successful professionals or young families who view the kitchen as a place for entertainment and enjoyment. They prefer stylish kitchen appliances with a strong design sense, even though the frequency of use is relatively low, they value the diversity of life. Health-conscious Sustainable Lifestyle advocates include young couples or families with children, emphasizing health and sustainability. They control their diet through cooking and have high attention to environmentally friendly and healthy kitchen appliances.

Based on the behavioral process of using kitchen products for cooking by the four typical user groups, their behavior activities are analyzed. Firstly, the four user groups are compared and analyzed in terms of working days and non-working days, and their core demands show significant characteristics under different usage scenarios. In the context of working days, Social Cooking Type pursue efficient and quick cooking methods so that they can share food with friends after work. High-quality and Efficient Lifestyle emphasize an efficient lifestyle, including quickly preparing high-quality meals and efficient time management. Extreme Dual-sided Lifestyle strive to balance between work and life, focusing on efficient working and cooking methods to better manage their dual roles. Health-conscious Sustainable Lifestyle Advocates expect healthy and convenient food choices on working days and may pursue simple and healthy dietary habits, emphasizing obtaining nutrition within limited time.

In the context of non-working days, Social Cooking Type users expect to turn social cooking into a more relaxed and enjoyable experience, with a focus on creative cooking. High-quality and Efficient Lifestyle users are more willing to spend time experiencing deeply and enjoying unique cooking experiences. The Extreme Dual-sided Lifestyle users will experience a more diversified life and may integrate cooking with social activities. Users who value a Health-conscious Sustainable Lifestyle pursue more complex and health-oriented cooking methods on non-working days, paying more attention to using organic and local ingredients, and experiencing more meaningful dining. These characteristics help understand the core needs of different users in specific contexts of kitchen experience, providing targeted guidance for product design.

We further explore users' behavior and related needs at different stages of cooking. Firstly, during the pre-cooking stage, users need to deal with moisture issues when handling ingredients. During the cooking process, users may feel that it takes a long time when using small kitchen appliances (such as steaming cookers), and they also hope to be able to carry out other cooking steps simultaneously, such as stir-frying. In addition, during the cleaning stage after cooking, users need to deal with kitchen cleaning tasks, such as cleaning range hoods, wiping stoves, and arranging food storage in the refrigerator. Users expect kitchen cleaning tools to provide more efficient, easy-to-clean, and maintain characteristics, thus enhancing the overall enjoyment of kitchen work.

The important points of user needs include solving moisture problems in ingredient handling, improving the cooking efficiency of small kitchen appliances and enhancing user experience, addressing cleaning challenges of range hoods, stoves, and other equipment, optimizing food storage in the refrigerator, and providing more efficient and labor-saving kitchen cleaning tools. These needs reflect the focus of users on the kitchen experience, providing valuable guidance for the design and improvement of kitchen appliances (see Table 8).

In this user requirement model, we not only consider the diverse needs of China's Generation Z users, but also conduct in-depth research on user behavior and preferences in different contexts. Through questionnaires, we understand users' expectations and

Table 7. Comparison of core needs of four groups of users in two situations

Usage Context	Core requirement description			
	Social Cooking Type	High-quality and Efficient lifestyle	Extreme dual-sided lifestyle	Health-conscious Sustainable Lifestyle
Working Days	pursuing efficient and quick cooking, convenient for sharing food with friends after work	efficient lifestyle, including preparing high-quality meals quickly and efficient time management	striving for a balance between career and life, efficient work and cooking methods to better balance dual roles	healthy and convenient food choices, may pursue simple and healthy dietary methods, emphasizing obtaining nutrients within limited time
Non-working Days	expects to transform social cooking into a more relaxing and enjoyable experience, with a focus on creative cooking	more willing to spend time experiencing deeply and enjoying unique cooking experiences	will experience a more diversified life, may integrate cooking with social activities	pursuing more complex, health and sustainability-oriented cooking methods, emphasizing the use of organic and local ingredients, and experiencing more meaningful dining

Table 8. User behavior process analysis

Task Stage	Task Subdivision	Usage Phenomenon, Product Factors	User Needs
Pre-cooking Stage	1.Handling ingredients 2.Preparing kitchen utensils and seasonings 3. Cleaning the dining table	1. Take beef out of the refrigerator in advance to thaw, wash vegetables, chop them, and shred potatoes 2. Handle beef, squeeze out excess moisture, season with pepper 3. Prepare dumplings and wash them, ready to put into the steamer	Need to solve moisture issues in the process of handling ingredients Effective way of garbage disposal

(*continued*)

Table 8. (*continued*)

Task Stage	Task Subdivision	Usage Phenomenon, Product Factors	User Needs
During Cooking Stage	1. Preparing for cooking 2. Using kitchen appliances for cooking 3. Viewing cooking tutorials	1. Limited functionality on the stove 2. Using small appliances like steaming cookers takes a long time, and also wishing to serve stir-fried dishes simultaneously, needing a fan for cooling 3. Conveniently washing utensils used for preparations	1. Oil fume issues 2. Heat control issues 3. Safety concerns 4. Food taste issues 5. Appliance functionality issues
After Cooking Stage	1. Washing dishes and sink 2. Putting dishes into the disinfection cabinet 3. Wiping the stove 4. Robotic cleaner cleaning the floor 5. Packing leftover food and putting it in the refrigerator	1. Accumulated grease on the range hood affecting effectiveness and safety, requiring regular cleaning 2. Difficulties in cleaning greasy stains on stoves affecting aesthetics and sanitation, requiring timely wiping 3. Improper food storage in the refrigerator leading to spoilage and contamination, needing separate storage and cleaning 4. Improper use of dishwasher affecting dishwashing effectiveness and equipment lifespan, requiring rinsing tableware and cleaning equipment	1. Hoping for more efficient and labor-saving kitchen cleaning tools 2. Expecting range hoods, stoves, and other equipment to be easy to clean and maintain, reducing post-cleaning tasks 3. Aiming for a more humanized kitchen cleaning process, enhancing the overall enjoyment of kitchen work

concerns about kitchen appliances, while in-depth interviews help us gain a deeper understanding of their lifestyles and usage habits. Behavior observation provides direct observation of users using kitchen appliances in real environments, further validating the effectiveness of our model.

In terms of sensory needs, we not only consider the appearance design of products, but also pay attention to the coordination with home decoration. Users hope that kitchen appliances are not only functional but also blend into the home environment and match the overall style. Providing a variety of material combination options is also expected by users because different users have different aesthetic preferences. Smart voice feedback is aimed at improving the usability and intelligence of products, allowing users to easily control kitchen appliances through voice commands and improve convenience in use.

In terms of interaction needs, we found that users have a strong demand for functional status visualization and cooking step guidance. They want to have a clear understanding of the working status of products and receive detailed cooking guidance to ensure delicious dishes. One-click cooking process recording and sharing is an important function to meet users' social needs, allowing users to share their cooking achievements with others and increase the fun of social interaction. Contactless activation of products is aimed at providing a more convenient user experience, where users can activate the product without touching it, reducing operational complexity.

In terms of emotional needs, we emphasize a healthy and safe cooking environment, as users have a high level of concern for food safety and health. Promoting family interaction is also what users expect, and they hope that kitchen appliances can become a platform for communication and interaction among family members, enhancing family cohesion. Providing a high-quality user experience is the overall expectation of users for kitchen appliances. They hope that products are not only practical tools, but also improve their quality of life and bring enjoyable experiences.

In addition to the above core elements, we also noticed that users may need to consider other factors in specific situations. For example, in kitchens with limited space, automatic folding/hiding functions and self-cleaning functions will be particularly welcomed by users. The function of remote control connected to mobile phones meets the needs of users who want to control kitchen appliances while they are away from home.

Our user requirement model provides a structured approach for designing innovative household kitchen appliances that cater to the specific preferences and lifestyles of China's Generation Z users. Manufacturers can enhance the usability, functionality, and attractiveness of products by integrating the insights we have obtained, thus achieving higher user satisfaction (see Table 9).

4.2 Applying the New User Needs Model in a Design Experiment

To validate and apply our optimized user requirement model, we conducted a series of design experiments. These experiments aim to translate user needs into specific product designs and evaluate whether the design solutions can meet users' expectations and needs.

Based on the user requirement set, convert the requirement set into a functional set, conduct functional analysis and definition, form a functional collection, map the

Table 9. User requirement model.

Sensory	The product design style is unified with the home decoration style	The product features a combination of multiple materials	Provides intelligent voice feedback according to user needs
Interaction	Visualizes the functional status	Automatically folds/hides after cooking is finished	Contactless wake-up of the product
	Convenient visual inspection of flames	Teaching of cooking steps	Self-cleaning function after cooking is finished
	Touch sensing without physical buttons	One-click recording and sharing of cooking processes	The product can be connected to a mobile phone for remote control
	Matches different pot surfaces	Intelligently recommends daily recipes	
Emotion	Provides a healthy and safe cooking environment	Provides a cooking environment for family members to interact with each other	Provides a high-quality sensory experience

functions to user behaviors, perform behavior analysis and validation, and complete the output of design concepts.

Based on the user research, we classified the user requirements according to their attribute characteristics and conducted an importance analysis of each requirement. During the mapping process of requirement set to function definition, we sorted the mapping according to the importance values. We highlighted the demand factors that are highly important to improve the user satisfaction of new products. Due to the particularity of kitchen products, where demands and functions do not have a simple one-to-one mapping relationship, there are cross-interactions during the mapping process. Therefore, when carrying out actual demand mapping, various types of demands cannot be mapped separately.

In the "requirement-function" mapping diagram, the 14 user requirements were translated into 14 conceptual functions. From the diagram, it can be seen that one requirement may require multiple functional modules to achieve. By mapping the user requirements to conceptual function definitions, we prepared for the subsequent functional analysis (see Fig. 3).

In terms of kitchen appliance linkage, the screen of the range hood allows users to view the status of other kitchen appliances. This enables users to quickly understand the cooking status of other dishes, making kitchen operations more intelligent and efficient. This design concept aims to provide users with a comprehensive intelligent cooking experience, making cooking easier, convenient, and enjoyable (see Fig. 4).

The appearance design aims to blend into modern homes and break through the traditional design of range hoods, transforming them into home artworks. The appearance adopts elegant and simple lines, and the overall shape uses a noble metallic texture,

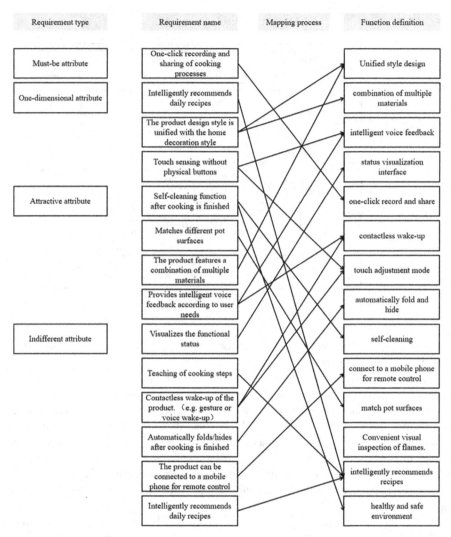

Fig. 3. "Requirement-Function" Mapping Diagram

making it a beautiful landscape in the kitchen. The surface of the range hood uses easy-to-clean and high-temperature-resistant materials to ensure a long service life and easy maintenance (see Figs. 5 and 6).

Classify and calculate the average scores of the evaluated objects and calculate the final average value to generate the design scheme evaluation result chart From the figure, it can be seen that the four types of evaluators, including designers, engineers, company representatives, and Generation Z users, generally have consistent scoring patterns for each evaluation dimension. On one hand, all evaluators have a relatively high recognition of the usefulness, diversity, and feasibility of this design scheme, believing that it meets

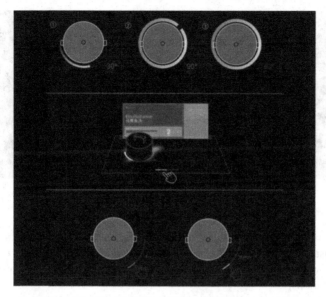

Fig. 4. Interactive Functions

Fig. 5. Usage Scenario

the needs of the new middle-class consumers and aligns with the company's design goals.

On the other hand, there are significant differences among the four types of evaluators in terms of convenience. Engineers gave the lowest score with an average of 3.9, while Generation Z users gave an average of 4.6 (see Fig. 7). Apart from convenience, all

Fig. 6. Product Usage Scenario

four types of evaluators believe that the design of the steam oven product scheme does not excel in usability. Therefore, in the subsequent design process, further research will be conducted on the convenience and usability of kitchen products to propose more optimized solutions.

Overall, the comprehensive average values of each evaluation dimension of this design scheme are above 3.8, indicating a generally satisfactory evaluation of the final design scheme for the steam oven product.

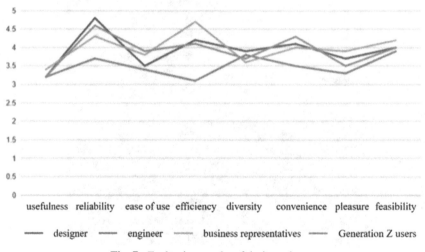

Fig. 7. Evaluation results of design scheme

Acknowledgments. This study was supported by Guangdong Planning Office of Philosophy and Social Science (Grant No. GD24CYS41); and the Department of Education of Guangdong Province (Grant No. 2023WTSCX052, and Grant No. 2023GXJK347).

References

1. Mordor Intelligence: Smart Kitchen Appliances Market: Size, Share, Analysis - Growth, Trends, and Forecast (2023). https://www.mordorintelligence.com/zh-CN/industry-reports/smart-kitchen-appliances-market
2. Mordor Intelligence: China Kitchen Appliances Product Market: Size, Share, Analysis - Growth, Trends, and Forecast (2023). https://www.mordorintelligence.com/zh-CN/industry-reports/china-kitchen-appliances-product-market
3. McKinsey China: China's Generation Z comes of age: How to capture their hearts. McKinsey China Consumer Insights [PDF file] (2023)
4. Bennett, S., Maton, K., Kervin, L.: The 'digital natives' debate: a critical review of the evidence. Br. J. Edu. Technol. 39(5), 775–786 (2008)
5. Wang, S.K., Hsu, H.Y., Campbell, T., Coster, D.C., Longhurst, M.: An investigation of middle school science teachers and students' use of technology inside and outside of classrooms: considering whether digital natives are more technology savvy than their teachers. Educ. Tech. Res. Dev. 62(6), 637–662 (2014)
6. Akçayır, M., Dündar, H., Akçayır, G.: What makes you a digital native? Is it enough to be born after 1980? Comput. Hum. Behav. 60, 435–440 (2016)
7. Goodman, L.A.: Snowball sampling. Ann. Math. Stat. 32(1), 148–170 (1961)
8. Chang, Y., Tang, L., Li, X.: Research on the shape design of plant protection UAVs based on the kano model. J. Mach. 36(1), 139–144 (2019). (Chinese)
9. Zhang, L., Wang, L., Yan, L.: Research on the Design of Household Washing Machines Based on the UCD-Kano Model. J. Mach. 35(12), 110–115 (2018). (Chinese)
10. Matzler, K., Hinterhuber, H.H.: How to make product development projects more successful by integrating Kano's model of customer satisfaction into quality function deployment. Technovation 18(1), 25–38 (1998). (Chinese)
11. Chen, Y.: Design and Research of Smart Furniture Based on User Experience. Doctoral dissertation. South China University of Technology (2016). (Chinese)

Research on the Application Software Design of University Campus Friend-Making Needs Based on Kano Model

Guanqun Zhang[1], Boqian He[1], Yanfei Zhu[2], Zhuoxin Li[1], Chenxiao Yin[1], Ying Li[3], and Yuhua Zhang[1(✉)]

[1] Beijing University of Chemical Technology, Changping District, Beijing, China
2022210960@buct.edu.cn
[2] Southeast University, Nanjing, Jiangsu Province, China
[3] Beijing University of Technology, Beijing, China

Abstract. On university campuses, there are limited channels through which students can access information, leading to limited group activities and, in severe cases, even a lack of friendship. From this, social application software is necessary among college students. This article applies the Kano model to analyze user needs for university campus dating and campus dating application software. It explores the prioritization of design elements and designs dating software functions and interfaces based on user needs. After conducting a Kano model demand survey, refined 13 demand attributes through user demand analysis and Better-Worse coefficient analysis. Finally, the 13 demand attributes were in divided as one Must-be Quality, four One-dimensional Quality, five Attractive Quality, two Indifferent Quality, and one Reverse Quality. The functional direction design includes the privacy function, autonomous function, positioning function, and design of the interface direction from color settings and interface framework. This approach aims to further enhance the design of the application software for university campus dating, effectively meeting users' needs to improve campus dating behavior, promote campus dating, and cultivate a positive campus dating environment.

Keywords: University Campus Social Application · User Requirements · Kano Model

1 Research Background

1.1 The Current Situation of Social Networking Applications

The widespread application of network technology has greatly influenced various aspects of people's lives, work, and education, bringing about the emergence of social networking applications that rely on the internet. Scholars have observed that individuals experiencing loneliness and depression in real life tend to prefer online interactions [1]. Currently, social networking applications such as Coffee Meets Bagel and Bumble dominate the majority of the market. However, due to the lack of constraints on user groups, the unregulated nature of user behavior has led to safety issues. The higher the user's trust in the social network platform, the greater the willingness to disclose personal information [2].

A. Marcus et al. (Eds.): HCII 2024, LNCS 14716, pp. 258–268, 2024.
https://doi.org/10.1007/978-3-031-61362-3_19

1.2 The Current Situation of Social Networking Applications

In modern society, college students constitute an emerging consumer group with significant social needs, giving rise to challenges in university campus social networking. Friendship constitutes an important facet of human behavior [3]. One dimension of Maslow's hierarchy of needs, reflecting human values after evolution, is characterized as high-level needs, emphasizing love, a sense of belonging, respect, and being respected [4]. Consequently, social interaction is deemed necessary. However, for individuals seeking social connections, there may not be a suitable opportunity to interact with those they wish to meet. Likewise, individuals with common interests may lack a platform to gather. Those confined to limited social circles may lack a platform to connect with friends from other disciplines. In summary, within the university campus, students face limitations in information channels, resulting in insufficient group activities and, in severe cases, a loss of friendships. Therefore, the necessity of social networking applications among college students is evident.

1.3 The Current Situation of Modern Campus Social Networking Applications

The Chinese smart campus market surpassed 20 billion yuan in 2012 and reached 62.1 billion yuan in 2018, indicating the continuous growth in demand for campus application software in the market. Surveys show that 90% of students believe campus application software brings convenience to their studies and daily lives, with nearly 80% expressing a desire for comprehensive campus applications. It is evident that social networking applications have high acceptance and wide usage among university students, leading to the rapid development of current campus application software. These applications aim to better serve students' diverse needs and enrich campus life.

However, campus data is only digital, not informatized [5]. Existing campus application software faces several challenges, such as limited communication methods in our campus application and the lack of privacy protection. Importantly, providing a safe and secure environment becomes the responsibility of campus management [6]. For instance, while PU Pocket Campus offers rich content, it does not prioritize social networking. On the other hand, the Ivy Love application focuses on romantic relationships, limiting its target audience to those interested in such connections. Consequently, current campus social networking applications suffer from issues like monotonous content, insufficient privacy protection mechanisms, and an inability to meet diverse socializing needs. Based on this analysis, this paper proposes a research on the design of university campus social networking applications based on user demands.

2   Research Methods

2.1 Kano Model

The Kano model, developed by Professor Noriaki Kano in 1984, serves as a framework for assessing user requirements. It provides a comprehensive understanding of user satisfaction with products or services. By utilizing this model to evaluate user needs, we can gain insight into demand characteristics, establish demand priorities for product design and development, and facilitate developers in making informed design trade-offs. Kano's model is constructed according to customers' requirements, which evolve over time and situation [7]. It divides the attributes of user needs into five categories: Must-be Quality(M), One-dimensional Quality (O), Attractive Quality (A), Indifferent Quality (I) and Reverse Quality (R) [8]. Must-be Quality represents the essential requirements that must be fulfilled to meet the users' needs. Failure to meet these requirements will result in decreased user satisfaction. One-dimensional Quality refers to users' basic needs and expectations from the products. Higher satisfaction among users in this category contributes significantly to overall satisfaction, making this a critical factor to consider during the design phase. Attractive Quality encompasses the product features that users are not consciously aware of. While their absence may not impact satisfaction, their presence can significantly increase it, making it an area of innovation in the design process. Indifferent Quality pertains to the product requirements that users tend to overlook. When designing, it is important to consider the proportion of these requirements. Lastly, Reverse Quality represents the unnecessary requirements that, if fulfilled, would decrease user satisfaction (Fig. 1).

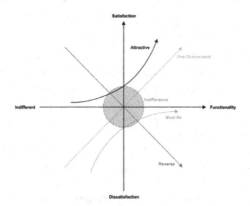

Fig. 1. Kano model

2.2 Application Steps of Kano Model Requirement Survey

After conducting a survey based on the basic user requirements obtained through user behavior research, the Kano model questionnaire is designed to categorize user needs into positive and negative aspects. Each question is set with five dimensions: Like, Should be, Indifferent, Reluctantly accept, and Dislike. After collecting the questionnaires, invalid data is filtered out, and the feedback is categorized into user needs. The analysis of whether there is a linear relationship in bidirectional questions helps determine the attribution of needs, thereby identifying user pain points, interests, and concerns. The Better-Worse coefficient is calculated from the questionnaire feedback data, and a four-quadrant scatter plot is generated to provide a clearer understanding of user needs during the design process (Fig. 2).

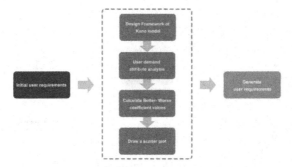

Fig. 2. Application steps of Kano model

Therefore, based on the Kano model, the user requirements for designing a university campus social application need to undergo requirement classification and prioritization of design elements. The application of the Kano model aids in elucidating the pain points, interests, and concerns of college students during the process of making friends on campus. This precision in design positioning for a university campus social networking app aims to enhance satisfaction in meeting the socializing needs of college students, thereby, fostering a positive campus atmosphere.

3   Requirements Investigation Based on the Kano Model

3.1   Acquisition of Initial User Requirements for University Campus Social Networking App

To better understand the social networking needs of students on university campuses, this survey targeted students aged 18–25 who have a desire for social connections in university life. Ten university students were selected for interviews, comprising 5 individuals with more than one year of experience using social networking apps on campus and 5 with over three years of experience using various social networking apps. The interview questions included: "Can the social networking apps you have used meet your socializing needs on university campuses? What functionalities would you like to see added to university campus social networking apps? What shortcomings do you think exist in the interface of the social networking apps you use?".

Based on the interview results, it was concluded that in terms of interface functionality, the color and style aspects lack sufficient distinctiveness. Regarding users' psychological needs, there is a desire to integrate features from other messaging apps, and the current apps lack proactive measures in protecting privacy, especially for those unwilling to engage in social interactions. Analyzing the opportunities in meeting university campus social networking needs, certain features were identified through the analysis of existing functionalities in popular apps. Additionally, user requirements for functionalities in university campus social networking apps were obtained through in-depth interviews, considering both aesthetic and psychological needs of the users (Fig. 3).

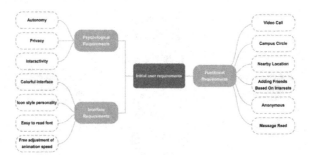

Fig. 3. User initial needs

3.2 Kano Questionnaire Design and Research

Questionnaire Design. Based on the initial user demand elements obtained, a Kano questionnaire design survey was conducted. This Kano questionnaire employs a dual-questioning approach, with each question structured across five dimensions: "Like," "Should be," "Indifferent," "Reluctantly accept," and "Dislike." The survey measures users' reactions to each of the 13 requirements when faced with the presence or absence of a particular feature. User selection explanations are included to ensure accuracy in user responses (Table 1).

Questionnaire Survey. This Study Designed an Online Questionnaire Using the Questionnaire Star Platform and Distributed It to a Target Group of University Students Aged Between 18 and 25, Living on Campus, with a Desire for Social Networking and the Use of Apps for Making Friends. The Survey Included 51% Female and 49% Male Respondents. A Total of 101 Questionnaires Were Distributed, with 12 Invalid Ones Excluded Due to Significant Contradictions or Omissions. The Final Valid Response Rate Was 88.12%, with 89 Valid Questionnaires Collected. The Cronbach's A Coefficient Analyzed Through SPSS Was 0.808, Indicating High Reliability and Demonstrating that the Responses to the Questionnaire Were Reliable and Consistent.

Table 1. Questionnaire design of the Kano model

Demand factors	Question	Like	Should be	Indifferent	Reluctantly accept	Dislike
How do you feel about the following functions of campus dating apps?	**Having** the Video call function					
	Not Having the Video call function					
	…					

4 User Requirements Analysis Based on the Kano Model

4.1 Classification of User Requirements Based on the Kano Model

According to the Kano model user demand classification table, the collected survey data are statistically analyzed. Cross-analysis is performed for each set of data comprising positive and reverse questions. The attribute with the highest proportion after evaluation is considered the Kano attribute for that specific requirement element (Table 2).

Table 2. The Kano model categorizes user requirements

Features/Services		Reverse questions				
		Like	Should be	Indifferent	Reluctantly accept	Dislike
Forward questions	Like	Q	A	A	A	O
	Should be	R	I	I	I	M
	Indifferent	R	I	I	I	M
	Reluctantly accept	R	I	I	I	M
	Dislike	R	R	R	R	Q

4.2 KANO Model Requirement Assessment Analysis

Kano Model User Requirements Analysis. Fill in the Kano questionnaire user demand analysis table with the bidirectional survey results data to obtain classified demand element attributes (Table 3).

Consumer Satisfaction Analysis Based on the Better-Worse Coefficient Method. The Better-Worse coefficient represents the impact of product demand categories on user satisfaction, and the Better-Worse coefficient method is used to explore consumer satisfaction coefficients based on the Kano model for the auxiliary identification of demand types. The following is the formula for calculating the Better-Worse satisfaction coefficient (Table 4):

$$Better = (A + O)/(A + O + M + I) \qquad (1)$$

$$Worse = -(O + M)/(A + O + M + I) \qquad (2)$$

After the above analysis, a Better-Worse quadrant diagram is drawn, with the horizontal axis representing the absolute value of Worse and the vertical axis representing

Table 3. Kano Questionnaire User Needs Analysis Table

Requirement Category	A	O	M	I	R	Q	Requirement attributes
Interest-Based Friend Addition Feature	47	6	5	31	0	0	A
Requirement Category	A	O	M	I	R	Q	Requirement attributes
Rich Color UI Interface	29	28	5	23	4	0	A
Proximity-based Location Functionality	12	38	9	29	0	1	O
Friend Interaction Functionality	11	37	15	25	1	0	O
Campus Circle Dynamic Posting Functionality	17	34	8	29	1	0	O
Flexible Room Creation Capability	14	46	17	12	0	0	O
Anonymous Functionality	20	31	6	28	4	0	O
Privacy Display Range Selection Feature	16	41	9	22	1	0	O
The user interface employs easily readable font sizes	3	5	62	18	0	1	M
Video Call Capability	3	2	34	45	3	2	I
Use personalized style for UI icons	22	21	7	35	4	0	I
Freely Adjustable UI Animation Speed Functionality	14	17	6	43	6	3	I
Read Receipt Functionality	0	0	0	12	77	0	R

Better values. This diagram provides a visual representation of all the demand attributes. The first quadrant represents One-dimensional Quality, and user demands in this quadrant should be prioritized. The second quadrant represents Attractive Quality, and user demands in this quadrant should also be prioritized. The third quadrant represents Indifferent Quality, and user demands in this quadrant are usually not provided. The fourth quadrant represents Must be Quality, and user demands in this quadrant must be fulfilled. In summary, the hierarchy of user demand attributes is as follows: Must-be Quality > One-dimensional Quality > Attractive Quality > Indifferent Quality (Fig. 4).

Result Analysis. Based on the above analysis of requirements, it can be concluded that A11 is Must-be Quality. Therefore, attention should be paid to the font size in the UI interface design. A4, A9, A10, and A7 are One-dimensional Quality, and priority should be given to satisfying them in the design. A5, A2, A8, A3, and A6 are Attractive Quality and during the design process, efforts should be made to address them as they contribute to increasing satisfaction. A12, A1 as an Indifferent Quality, and their design can be based on specific circumstances. As a Reverse Quality, A13 should be avoided when designing.

Table 4. User demand impact analysis

Serial Number	Requirement Category	Better	Worse
A1	Video Call Capability	5.95%	−42.86%
A2	Proximity-based Location Functionality	56.82%	−53.41%
A3	Friend Interaction Functionality	54.55%	−59.09%
A4	Interest-Based Friend Addition Feature	59.55%	−12.36%
A5	Campus Circle Dynamic Posting Functionality	57.95%	−47.73%
Serial Number	Requirement Category	Better	Worse
A6	Flexible Room Creation Capability	67.42%	−70.79%
A7	Anonymous Functionality	60.00%	−43.53%
A8	Privacy Display Range Selection Feature	64.77%	−56.82%
A9	Rich Color UI Interface	67.06%	−38.82%
A10	Use personalized style for UI icons	50.59%	−32.94%
A11	The user interface employs easily readable font sizes	9.09%	−76.14%
A12	Freely Adjustable UI Animation Speed Functionality	38.75%	−28.75%
A13	Read Receipt Functionality	0.00%	−0.00%

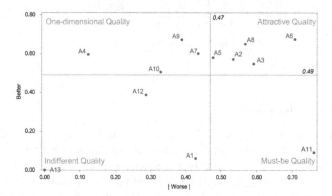

Fig. 4. Quadrant chart

Hence, when designing a campus social networking application, it is crucial to prioritize elements based on their significance. Subsequently, strategically plan and analyze various design aspects of the app in accordance with the hierarchical needs identified during the results analysis.

5 Design Practice of Social Networking Applications for University Campus Socializing Needs

5.1 Design Specifications

For the issues existing in campus social networking applications, such as the inability to address safety concerns, the need for multifunctional socializing, and the desire for free-form connections, we aimed to uncover the genuine needs and pain points of college student users. Utilizing the Kano model, we identified the core requirements for campus social networking applications and designed the "Gorgeous Campus" application. We initiated the process with the construction of a low-fidelity model, exploring design elements for preliminary interface design (Fig. 5).

Fig. 5. Low-fidelity model

5.2 Function Configuration

The software design includes the following functions: The application offers nearby positioning, allowing users to communicate and meet offline, making it more convenient to forge new connections. Additionally, the application provides a range of features, including dynamic shooting, adding friends based on shared interests, campus circle, and custom room creation, which add functional diversity and enhance the interactivity of social interactions. Users can communicate, learn, and collaborate based on their hobbies and interests for overall improvement. The application prioritizes security and autonomy, as users can set preferences such as selecting their preferred crowd range, displaying their daily lives, and remaining anonymous in chat rooms, which provides a secure and autonomous environment. The design aims to address the core needs of campus dating applications and provide a comprehensive and secure platform for college students to make friends and connect (Fig. 6).

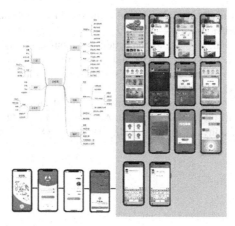

Fig. 6. "Gorgeous Campus" application flow chart and UI interface

5.3 Interface Configuration

In UI design, vibrant colors such as pink, orange, and blue are utilized to convey a lively and energetic atmosphere, enhancing the vibrancy of campus life. Additionally, personalized icon designs have been implemented for simplicity and clarity, incorporating distinctive campus-themed styles.

6 Conclusion

The design of the "Gorgeous Campus" app is a comprehensive application based on Kano analysis, integrating various functional requirements. Through design elements such as functionality, interface, and color, the app aims to provide users with a platform for social networking on university campuses. This paper aspires to design a campus application that offers comprehensive services, with the hope that it will be widely utilized and become an integral part of daily life. The design is not only derived from life but also aims to better serve life by meeting the diverse needs of students on campus. The objective is to enhance social interactions, promote multifaceted socialization on campus, and not only provide convenience in students' lives but also foster friendships among peers. This approach significantly facilitates student life and emotions, contributing to the creation of a positive campus environment.

References

1. Caplan, S.E.: Preference for online social interaction: a theory of problematic internet use and psychosocial well-being. Commun. Res. **30**(6), 625–648 (2003)
2. Li, H., Sarathy, R., Xu, H.: The role of affect and cognition on online consumers' decision to disclose personal 14 information to unfamiliar online vendors. Decis. Support Syst. **51**(3), 434–445 (2011)
3. Maslow, A.H.A.: Theory Human Motivation Psychologic Review (1973)

4. Apostolou, M., Keramari, D., Kagialis, A., Sullman, M.: Why people make friends: the nature of friendship. Pers. Relationsh. **28**, 4–18 (2021)

5. Amoatemaa, D.K., Arthur, Y.: Students perception of campus safety: a case of Kumasi campus of university of education, Winneba, GHA, Asian. Res. J. Arts Soc. Sci. **3**(1), 1–9 (2017)

6. Li, W.: Design of smart campus management system based on Internet of Things technology. J. Intell. Fuzzy Syst. **40**, 3159–3168 (2021)

7. Basfirinci, C., Mitra, A.: A cross cultural investigation of airlines service quality through integration of Servqual and the Kano model. J. Air Transp. Manag. **42**, 239–248 (2015)

8. Kano, N.: Attractive quality and must-be quality. Hinshitsu (Qual. J. Jpn. Soc. Qual. Control) **14**, 39–48 (1984)

Research on Emotional Perception of Game Characters Based on Semantic Network Analysis

Shiyuan Zhu, Ruonan Wu$^{(\boxtimes)}$, and Jiahao Sun

School of Design Art, Changsha University of Science and Technology, Changsha, China
wrnlinn@163.com

Abstract. The objective of this study is to analyze the influencing factors of game users' emotional perception of game character design through a case study of online reviews of game characters, to provide a reference for improving character design. The pycharm development tool was used to crawl the text data about character design in online comments on the Bilibili platform (a cultural community and video website with a high concentration of young generation in China) as data samples, and after software deduplication and data cleaning, the text analysis method and ROST CM 6.0 software were used to formulate a custom chart for word segmentation, and the influencing factors of character design emotional perception were analyzed by word frequency analysis, semantic network construction, and sentiment analysis were carried out afterword segmentation. The results showed that the high-frequency words that game users paid attention to included the character's modeling elements, personality traits, Peking Opera culture, voice choice, etc. The semantic web of online reviews presents a "core-periphery" hierarchy. The content of user reviews is dominated by positive emotions, followed by neutral emotions, and the least negative emotions. The aesthetic beauty, temperament and charm, cultural expression and career shaping of game characters are the most significant influencing factors of game users' emotional perception. Designers of game characters should consider aspects such as appearance design, character building, cultural integration, and professional embodiment, and design the characters that can most resonate with users and be most conducive to cultural inheritance.

Keywords: Semantic Network · Game Characters · Emotional Perception · Online Reviews · Text Analysis

1 Introduction

According to the data from China Internet Network Information Center [1], the market size of cloud gaming is gradually expanding, and the industry is in a stage of rapid growth. The Internet penetration rate has increased year by year, and the number of Internet users in China has increased from 688.26 million in 2015 to 103195 in 2021, with an average annual growth rate of 6.98%. The year-on-year increase in game users provides a good environment for the development of games, which has created a rapid development of the game industry.

A. Marcus et al. (Eds.): HCII 2024, LNCS 14716, pp. 269–281, 2024.
https://doi.org/10.1007/978-3-031-61362-3_20

According to TalkingData's data, the age of mobile game users is mostly female, with 56.6% of female users, of which 80.2% are 18–39 years old, which is the main audience group of mobile games.

In the list of popular cloud games in China in 2022, the number of role-playing games has reached the first. Game-related research has become an important research field, and there are many role-playing studies, character design is closely related to role-playing game design, so game character design research should also follow suit. According to the "2022 China Game Industry Report" released on the official website of the China Audio-video and Digital Publishing Association, the largest number of the top 100 mobile game products in terms of revenue is original IP, accounting for 53%. As a typical case of cultural integration and dissemination, the characters of "Genshin Impact" Yun Jin integrate traditional opera elements and skillfully bring opera culture into the game. Nowadays, in the era of rapid iteration of information, the design of new characters is still a key proposition, and how to integrate culture with game characters and let game users have an emotional resonance with game characters is a problem we need to think about. This paper captures and analyzes the online comment data of the character Yun Jin through a case study, studies the emotional tendency of game users toward game characters, and summarizes the design factors that can best affect the emotions of game users, which has certain reference value for emotional resonance, cultural inheritance, and dissemination in-game character design.

2 Conceptual Interpretation and Literature Review

2.1 Semantic Network

The semantic network was first proposed by Quillian [2] in 1967 to apply the network format to human knowledge construction, which can use the structure of a graph to represent the overall relationship between information nodes and the relationship between a pair of information nodes, and it can simply and directly express the conceptual relationship between semantics, including causality, juxtaposition, condition, progression, etc. The biggest feature of a semantic network is that it is structural, using logical terms to deal with various facts and rules, and is a deep inference network of knowledge. Semantic networks have made achievements in various fields, such as Benedek et al. [3] in 2016, who combined semantic networks and medicine to study the relationship between semantic memory structure and individual creative thinking, and Byambasuren et al. [4] in 2018, who created a localized bilingual semantic network based on Chinese-English vocabulary and CELK-Net through automatic mapping algorithms, Fadigas et al. [5] Combined with semantic networks, the Louvain algorithm was used to study the title of the Brazilian mathematics master's thesis from both qualitative and quantitative perspectives, and the semantic network is also related to emoji perception [6]. Horan [7] used the semantic web to analyze the communication information on social media Twitter and concluded that there was a biased tendency between soft and hard news information. Nowadays, semantic networks are widely used in computer science, medicine, communication, education, literature, architecture, art, and other fields, and have a strong interdisciplinary nature [8]. Although the research on character design has already begun, and the semantic network has also had a profound influence in the study of emotional perception, it has not yet been applied to character design, this paper studies the user's emotional tendency to the game character through the semantic network, and analyzes the user's emotional perception design factors, which can clearly and intuitively see the interrelationship between the factors and the factors, which is conducive to the design of the game character.

2.2 Emotional Perception

Emotion is a psychological experience, a person's response to an objective attitude, with the ability to promote or disrupt constructive functioning, and the extent of this ability depends on the degree to which the individual monitors, evaluates, and controls emotional arousal [9]. Emotional perception (emotional perception) is a feeling or emotional state of objective things, and some media, such as pictures, convey feelings that guide people's emotional perception by affecting endocrine changes in the nerves [10]. In the field of emotion perception, Diemer et al. [11] conducted a review of virtual reality (VR) and showed that fear and anxiety are important emotions in the VR environment. Neesha Desai et al. [12] found that the gender of game characters is one of the factors that affect user behavior and emotion, and female users have a higher appreciation for the complex behavior of the characters than male users. Johnson et al. [13] found that age differences were associated with emotional perception. At the same time, visual attributes [14] are also one of the important factors influencing aesthetic preferences and emotional perception. In the field of nutrition, deficits in emotional perception also contribute to eating disorders (ED) [15]. The research on emotional perception is particularly in-depth in the field of psychology, but there is little research in the field of art in foreign countries, and it has also received some attention in the field of art in China, where characters can connect emotionally with users and transmit emotional energy, and the game type with the longest playing time in many games is role-playing games (RPGs) [1] From the perspective of semantic network analysis, this paper studies the emotional perception factors of users on game characters, and integrates cultural connotations into game characters, hoping to achieve the cultivation of good values and the improvement of cultural literacy through the contact between users and game characters, which is also of constructive significance for the inheritance and development of culture.

3   Data Sources and Research Methods

3.1 Data Sources

This paper analyzes the case and selects Yun Jin, a game character in the Genshin Impact game that integrates traditional drama elements, as shown in Fig. 1 (the picture is taken from the official account of Genshin Impact bilibili), which has caused huge repercussions at home and abroad, has strong IP attributes, and has a large number of users, a stable fan base, and a large player base, and the research sample will not be too single and cause a strong deviation in the results.

Select the comments of the game promotion video posted by the official account of the game company on Bilibili as the data source. The bilibili website (www.bilibili.

com, abbreviated as bilibili) is a well-known gathering place for ACG network culture in China, actively developing the user-generated content (UGC) ecology, aiming to create two-dimensional platform content with rich game attributes [16]. Among the new media platforms, bilibili users aged 24 and below, 25–30, and 31–35 have all reached first place, becoming the most popular new media platform for the younger generation. Among the typical new media platforms, bilibili's user penetration rate and platform interaction reached the top five levels, among which the proportion of games published and the proportion of interactions ranked first among all content types [17]. From the above network data, we know that games are one of the favorite entertainment methods of the younger generation, and most of the young people get first-hand game information on the website bilibili.

dramatic archetype   character setting   Actual installation screen

Fig. 1. " Red Chanjuan · Yun Jin" drama prototype, character set, and actual picture.

This article uses pycharm development tools, Python language, requests, pandas, os, time, random, and other tool libraries to automatically crawl the online comment data of the "Genshin Impact" character demo - "Yun Jin: Hongzhangshu True Meaning" video released by the official account of Genshin Impact on Bilibili. As of November 3, 2023, the total number of comments on the video is 26,508, a total of 13,470 first-level comments have been crawled, and the number of comments after automatic deduplication is 13,163. At this time, the quality of the data is still slightly poor, and manual data cleaning is required. Firstly, the words that are irrelevant to the video content are excluded, secondly, the emoji codes with interfering properties such as [detaching single doge], [defending radish_crying], [Tibetan fox], and other interfering emoji codes are deleted, and finally the simple sentences such as unclear meanings and single mood words are deleted, and the final number of comments obtained after manual data cleaning is 2929, see Table 1.

Table 1. Source and number of comments.

The name of the role	Data source	Total number of first-level comments	Number of comments after deduplication	Number of reviews after screening
Red Chanjuan · Yun Jin	Bilibili	13470	13163	2929

3.2 Research Methods

Textual analytics is a method that uses computer algorithms and natural language processing technology to quantitatively describe non-systematic and non-quantitative text data. Its goal is to extract meaningful and valuable information from large amounts of textual data, helping researchers understand the characteristics, sentiments, themes, and trends of texts. ROST CM 6.0 software was used to deeply mine the semantics of the commented data after data cleaning, firstly, a custom chart for word segmentation was formulated, word frequency analysis was carried out afterword segmentation, a semantic network was constructed, a sentiment analysis was carried out and a visual word cloud was generated. Textual analysis can play an important role in character design research. By analyzing the online review text data related to the game character Yun Jin, we can understand the feedback and evaluation of players' emotional perception and character image shaping of the character.

The word frequency analysis counts the frequency of relevant keywords in the published online comments, which can see the hot events at that time and the core content that users pay attention to, and summarize the user-specific speech rules from a small point of view. The higher the frequency, the more the gamer cares about the element, which is one of the most important elements of the character, and the more important it is for the character designer to focus on using these elements.

Semantic network analysis can be used to understand and explain the relationship between concepts, weaving keywords into a network model composed of a node (concept) and an edge (the relationship between concepts), which can effectively help researchers clarify the complex relationships between concepts. Establishing the relationship between the character's characteristics, behaviors, backgrounds, and other concepts, drawing conclusions, and applying them to a specific practice, is conducive to creating characters that are more relatable, more attractive, and more vivid and sound in storytelling.

Sentiment analysis obtains and summarizes the emotional feedback of different players on the same character through emotional color analysis of players' comments and discussions on game characters on social media, game forums, and other platforms. For example, by analyzing the player's comments, you can understand how the player is attracted by the character's appearance, expression, voice, cultural elements, action design, etc., and what weight the player is attracted to by which element, or why the player hates the character, etc. Summarizing these reasons, it is concluded that there are three types of emotional bias of the player, which are divided into positive emotions, neutral emotions, and negative emotions, and the player's emotional perception of the game character is also revealed.

After importing the final filtered review data into ROST CM 6.0, the custom vocabulary was edited, a custom dictionary containing keywords such as "Peking Opera", "Wanyu", "Voice" and "Personality" was set, words with the same meaning were merged, meaningless words were filtered, and high-frequency words were screened, and finally a semantic network graph was constructed through semantic network analysis, and sentiment analysis was performed on the online review data to identify the emotional perception results of game players on game characters, as shown in Fig. 2.

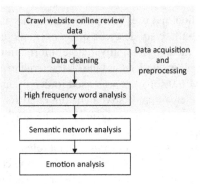

Fig. 2. Research process

4   Results and Analysis

4.1   High-Frequency Word Analysis of Game Characters

Counting the high-frequency words with the top 300 vocabulary frequencies, removing the words with low relevance (such as "simply", "down", "instead"), and merging the words with the same meaning (such as "crazy", "fantastic", "absolute"), a total of 86 high-frequency words were obtained, and a total of 71 words with a frequency of ≥ 20 were finally retained, as shown in Table 2. Statistical analysis of high-frequency words can be divided into the following categories:

The Importance of the Character Name.   First of all, the top two high-frequency words, "Yun Jin" and "Mr. Yun" are the names of the characters, and the frequent mention of the character names is one of the reasons for the attractiveness of the characters, which can smoothly arouse the discussion of users.

The Combination of Role and Culture.   The association of characters with cultural elements, such as "Peking Opera", "Chinese Opera", and "Chinese Culture", is frequently mentioned in online reviews, showing that the characters are rooted in a specific cultural context. This combination not only adds depth and complexity to the character but may also enhance the character's uniqueness and appeal. In the context of globalization, this culturally distinctive character design may have aroused the interest and curiosity of audiences from different cultural backgrounds, thus promoting cross-cultural communication and understanding.

Sound and Musical Expression.   The discussion of artistic expressions such as "background music", "sound", and "singing" shows their centrality in character design. This focus reveals the importance of sound and music in creating an emotional atmosphere, deepening the storyline, and shaping the character's personality. Especially in works that represent a particular culture or era, the choice and application of background music and sound are essential to create a sense of realism and a deep experience.

The Combination of Sight and Hearing.   The discussion of elements such as "drama", "singing", "picture", and "vertical painting" revealed how the combination of visual and sound arts affects the audience experience. This combination not only enhances the overall aesthetic of the artwork but also increases the expressiveness and immersion of the work. In the interaction between visual and sound art, the audience can experience the storyline and character emotions more deeply, thus enhancing the overall artistic enjoyment.

Professional Technical Details.   The high frequency of voice acting ("Chinese", "Japanese", "And English") and lines reflects the importance of technical execution in the popularity of the work. Good voice acting can significantly enhance the vividness of the characters and the appeal of the story, while the right lines can enhance the coherence and depth of the plot, which directly affects the overall quality and audience acceptance of the work.

Cultural Diversity and Depth.   Discussing traditional Chinese culture and the context of the times shows the importance of cultural elements in building stories and characters. This discussion reveals the audience's awareness and appreciation of the deep cultural value of the work. For example, the appearance of terms such as "Peking Opera" and "Xun School" reflects the character's profound discussion and presentation of traditional culture. This depth not only enriches the background of the story but also adds layers and realism to the characters, allowing the audience to experience and understand the cultural connotations more deeply.

The Fusion of History and Modernity.   The combination of historical legends, traditional elements, and modern elements (e.g., games, and foreign cultures) shows the reviewer's focus on cultural integration. This fusion embodies an innovative artistic approach that creates new narratives and visual experiences by combining ancient stories with modern elements. This approach not only appeals to a wide audience but also promotes communication and understanding between different cultures. For example, combining elements of traditional Chinese culture with foreign cultures may make the work more internationally appealing, while also providing the viewer with a new way to experience culture.

Expression of Emotions and Feelings.   The use of words such as "gentle", "touching", and "comfortable" reveals the audience's emotional response to the work. These words indicate that the viewer experienced a deep emotional experience while watching the work, which may be due to factors such as storyline, character development, and other factors. For example, the "tenderness" of a character's personality may evoke sympathy and empathy from the audience, while the "touched" may be a strong emotional response to the storyline or the character's behavior. The expression of these emotions not only reflects the emotional depth of the work but may also increase the emotional connection between the viewer and the work.

Positive Comments and Responses. Expressions such as "so good", "fantastic" and so on show the positive reviews that the work has caused in the audience. This expression usually indicates a high level of praise and satisfaction with the work, which may be related to aspects such as the artistic quality of the work, the content of the story, or the design of the characters. For example, "so good" might refer to the quality of the music or sound, while "fantastic" might be a comprehensive evaluation of the overall work. This positive feedback not only shows the popularity of the work among viewers but may also encourage more people to see and experience it.

4.2   Semantic Network Analysis of Online Reviews

By constructing a semantic network and co-occurrence matrix vocabulary, we dig deep into online review data. Degree centrality can be used to express the degree of correlation between a node and other nodes in a network, and the degree centrality of a node in a semantic network diagram (Fig. 3) can be calculated according to Eq. 1 [18]. *DegreeCentrality* represents the degree centrality of a node, N_{degree} represents the degree of the node, and n represents the number of nodes in the semantic network diagram. The degree centrality of the word "Yun Jin" was the largest, which was 0.675, the degree centrality of "role", "voice" and "medium matching" was 0.325 or 0.225, the degree centrality of "dubbing", "Mr. Yun" and "gentle" was between 0.175 ~ 0.125, and the degree centrality of the other words was 0.100 or below. It can be concluded that the semantic network of online review data presents a "core-periphery" hierarchy.

$$Degree\ centrality = \frac{N_{degree}}{n-1} \tag{1}$$

The first layer is the core layer, which is the "cloud pansy". As the core of user discussions, the name of the character is the most important keyword to be mentioned, and the character name is closely related to the character itself and plays an important role in the storytelling. For example, the comment "I listen to Yun Jin sing Liyue Opera every day!" has 11,035 likes, indicating that the character name is the most likely keyword to spark discussion among users. The second layer is the sub-core layer, which is composed of "role", "voice", and "medium dubbing", which is a further expansion of the role of "Yun Jin", and users pay more attention to the overall design of the role, dubbing language, voice selection, actor interpretation, etc., such as "The middle dubbing is so good, there is a kind of little girl's brittle immaturity, but she has grasped the calm and old way of the drama bones" These three elements are described in detail in the comments. The third layer is the transition layer, where "Mr. Yun", "Xiqu", "Dubbing", "Gentle", "Yingduing", "Riduing", and "Liyue" are the components of this layer, which mainly reflect the user's perception of the character's title, professional characteristics, personality, voice actors, and regional background culture. The fourth layer is the marginal layer,

Table 2. The frequency of high-frequency words and occurrences of online reviews

High-frequency words	Frequency	High-frequency words	Frequency	High-frequency words	Frequency	High-frequency words	Frequency
Yun Jin	741	Lifetime	140	Demonstrate	59	Immortal	39
Mr. Yun	446	Story	139	Poke me	59	Foreign	38
Background Music	429	Gentle	131	Clothing	57	Tradition	36
Sound	353	Singing opera	127	Personality	55	Comfortable	33
Chinese dubbing	351	Peking opera	126	Action	54	spoken parts of a Chinese opera	31
Sounds Amazing	335	Liyue	122	Aria	54	Translate	29
Marvelous	330	Flags up	107	Poetry	53	Feel	28
Dubbing	306	Lovely	107	Combine	52	Looking back	27
Culture	245	Era	105	The Divine damsel of devastation	51	Quercus rubra	25
Character	232	China	98	Picture	49	So sweet	25
Lines	229	Four countries dubbing	97	Historical legend	49	Loop Playback	24
Japanese dubbing	198	Music	86	Life mirrors opera	48	Element	23
Let's go (走了)	180	Game	84	Cute	47	Opera reflects life	22
Drama	170	Opera tune	82	Style	44	Too hasty	22
Move	167	Strike as one	73	Weapon	44	Read it every time	22
Listening to traditional Chinese opera	161	Heroic	70	Girl	43	Actor	20
Stunning	146	Make up one's mind	68	Observe	41	Stage	20
English dubbing	141	Korean dubbing	64	Character portrait	39		

which is composed of words such as "listening to opera", "tradition", "Peking opera", "story", "language", "demonstration", "the hearts of the world" and so on, which is a further extension of the character's occupation, growth environment, cultural tradition, language charm, and character display, and is the embodiment of various details in the character building.

4.3 Sentiment Analysis of Online Reviews

Implicit in online reviews is the emotional tendencies of game users towards game characters. Positive emotions can awaken the user's pursuit of the good elements embodied in the character, while negative emotions can increase the user's stress, causing the user

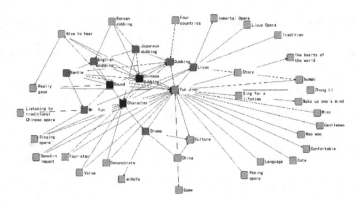

Fig. 3. Review Data Semantic Web Online

to hate the character and give up playing the game. The sentiment analysis results of online reviews are shown in Fig. 4 below.

Proportion/%

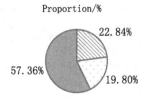

22. 84%

57. 36%

19. 80%

■Positive emotion comments □Neutral sentiment review □Negative emotional comments

Fig. 4. Online review sentiment analysis

Positive Emotions. Positive emotions were the dominant part of online reviews, accounting for 57.36% of the total number of comments, and words such as "very good", "fantastic" and "amazing" that indicated satisfaction with the game characters appeared more frequently. Words such as "historical charm", "exquisite", and "jewel-like" mainly refer to the appearance of the game character, indicating that the beauty of the character is one of the important elements that affect the user's emotions. Words such as "knowledgeable", "serious", and "pure" describe the character of the game, indicating that a character with positive emotional energy will bring positive emotions to the user. "Opera Troupe", "Master", "Peking Opera" and "Classical Chinese" belong to the professional shaping of characters, and the relevant design of game characters and traditional culture is the focus of character shaping and the focus of users' attention. Words such as "life is like a play", "a lifetime", and "advancing with the times" highlights the cultural inheritance and the user's perception of life, and the closeness of the role and life can trigger the user's imagination and the pursuit of beautiful things.

Neutral Emotion. Neutral emotions accounted for 22.84% of the comments. Neutral emotional comments are not very tendentious to the character's emotional expression, and only state objective facts, popular science, etc. For example, "Mr. Yun's head is called loyalty and courage, not a ball of yarn", "traditional culture is not far from us" and so on.

Negative Emotions. The number of negative emotions accounted for 19.80%. Negative emotions are more expressed by users' dissatisfaction with the speed of lines and translation, such as "Why don't you have more scenes in the demonstration", and "there are too many lines, and there are few gaps in the middle and matching, let alone Japanese". In addition, the evaluation of the proportion of traditional elements in clothing design, whether the sound and painting are synchronized, etc., are also mixed.

5 Discussion and Suggestions

Based on the above data analysis, it is concluded that game users are more concerned about the beauty of the character's shape, temperament, cultural performance, and career-shaping, which is the most significant influencing factor of game users' emotional perception. Among them, the beauty of modeling is the most discussed topic among users. The discussion is as follows:

5.1 Optimized the Aesthetics of Character Modeling

Meticulous Visual Design. Noting that users rate the character's appearance and costume design highly, designers should aim to create detailed and memorable visuals. For example, by using unique colors or patterns such as pattern designs, or clothing styles to express a character's personality and story.

Integration of Cultural Elements. Incorporating cultural elements into the design, such as traditional costume details, traditional symbols, or mythological clues, can further deepen the user's impression of the game character and enhance the character's attractiveness. Designers should consider how to integrate these elements naturally into the overall design of the game character while maintaining their original aesthetic and recognizability.

5.2 The Expression of Temperament and Charm

The Choice of Sound. Users have a strong emotional response to background sounds and speech. The right timbre is not only about shaping the character's personality but also about the emotional output of the story and the fit of the character with the background.

Diversity of Personalities. Designing a character with a multi-layered personality can make it more three-dimensional and realistic. Starting the character's growth experience and regional culture, makes it more realistic and attractive. For example, Yun Jin often goes to rock music concerts in her spare time, and increasing the sense of contrast is also a key point to enrich her personality.

5.3 Deepening of Cultural Expression

Emphasis on Cultural Background. Users have expressed a strong interest in the cultural background of the character. Designers can shape game characters through their dialogues, costumes, behavior habits, etc., to show their cultural characteristics. For example, it is possible to incorporate specific dialects or cultural habits into the dialogues of game characters.

The Exploration of Modern Interpretations. Combine traditional culture with modern elements to create a new character design that meets the modern aesthetic. This combination not only appeals to younger players but also creates memory points that enhance the character's sense of the times and appeal.

5.4 Career-Shaping Innovation

Refinement of Occupational Characteristics. Profession is an important part of a character's identity. Designers should work on the character's skills, costumes, props, and action design to reflect the character's professional characteristics. For example, the pompoms, cloud shoulders, streamers, and patterns on the clothes in Yun Jin's costumes reflect the characteristics of traditional opera costumes, the gentle conversation temperament refers to the way of speaking of famous singers, the action design reflects a sense of lightness, and the appearance of the main design of the action and the play of flower guns all show the relevance of the game characters and professional characteristics.

Integration with Personal Stories. Combining a character's professional life with his or her personal story can make the character more three-dimensional and in-depth. For example, Yun Jin not only loves to sing, but also likes to write new plays, and she wrote the story she experienced with the protagonist as a new play "The Goddess Splitting Views", which immediately became a sensation.

6 Conclusion

By discussing the emotional perception of game users of game characters in online reviews, it is concluded that the most significant influencing factors of game users' emotional perception are the beauty of game characters, temperament and charm, cultural performance, and career-shaping. Designers should consider designing game characters from the aspects of appearance design, character building, cultural integration, and professional embodiment, so as to export traditional culture to the younger generation, arouse users' resonance with the characters, and then inherit and carry forward traditional culture.

Fund Projects. The project is a key project of the Hunan Provincial Department of Education, "Research on the Integrated Development Mechanism and Countermeasures of Hunan Video Cultural and Creative Industry", and the project number is 22A0203.

References

1. China Internet Network Information Center. https://www.cnnic.net.cn. Accessed 13 Dec 2023
2. Quillian, M.R.: Word concepts: a theory and simulation of some basic semantic capabilities. Behav. Sci. **12**(5), 410–430 (1967)
3. Benedek, M., Kenett, Y.N., Umdasch, K., et al.: How semantic memory structure and intelligence contribute to creative thought: a network science approach. Think. Reason. **23**(2), 158–183 (2017)
4. Byambasuren, O., Sui, Z., Chang, B.: A research on construction of knowledge fusion network in Chinese and English languages. In: Hong, J.F., Su, Q., Wu, J.S. (eds.) Chinese Lexical Semantics. CLSW 2018. LNCS, vol. 11173, pp. 698–704. Springer, Cham (2018). https://doi.org/10.1007/978-3-030-04015-4_61
5. de Sousa Fadigas, I., Casas, T.H.P., Rosa, M.G., et al.: Programas de mestrado em Matemática no Brasil: uma aplicação de redes para caracterizar seus títulos. Obra digital. Revista de comunicación, estudios mediáticos y procesos sociales. **18**, 103–118 (2020)
6. Shardlow, M., Gerber, L., Nawaz, R.: One emoji, many meanings: a corpus for the prediction and disambiguation of emoji sense. Expert Syst. Appl. **198**, 116862 (2022)
7. Horan, T.J.: 'Soft'versus 'hard'news on microblogging networks: semantic analysis of twitter produsage. Inf. Commun. Soc. **16**(1), 43–60 (2013)
8. de Barros, P.H.B., Grilo, M., de Sousa, F.I., et al.: Systematic review of the "semantic network" definitions. Expert Syst. Appl. **2022**, 118455 (2022)
9. Thompson, R.A.: Emotional regulation and emotional development. Educ. Psychol. Rev. **3**, 269–307 (1991)
10. Codispoti, M., Gerra, G., Montebarocci, O., et al.: Emotional perception and neuroendocrine changes. Psychophysiology **40**(6), 863–868 (2003)
11. Diemer, J., Alpers, G.W., Peperkorn, H.M., et al.: The impact of perception and presence on emotional reactions: a review of research in virtual reality. Front. Psychol. **6**, 26 (2015)
12. Desai, N., Zhao, R., Szafron, D.: Effects of gender on perception and interpretation of video game character behavior and emotion. IEEE Trans. Comput. Intell. AI Games **9**(4), 333–341 (2016)
13. Johnson, D.R., Whiting, W.L.: Detecting subtle expressions: older adults demonstrate automatic and controlled positive response bias in emotional perception. Psychol. Aging **28**(1), 172 (2013)
14. Zhuang, J., Qiao, L., Zhang, X., et al.: Effects of visual attributes of flower borders in urban vegetation landscapes on aesthetic preference and emotional perception. Int. J. Environ. Res. Public Health **18**(17), 9318 (2021)
15. Joos, A.A.B., Cabrillac, E., Hartmann, A., et al.: Emotional perception in eating disorders. Int. J. Eat. Disord. **42**(4), 318–325 (2009)
16. QUESTMOBILE. https://www.questmobile.com.cn/research/report/1719277873330753538. Accessed 13 Dec 2023
17. QUESTMOBILE. https://www.questmobile.com.cn/research/report/1726888249161519105. Accessed 13 Dec 2023
18. Freeman, L.C.: Centrality in social networks conceptual clarification. Soc. Netw. **1**(3), 215–239 (1978)

Innovations in Product and Service Design

Research on the Influence Factors of Live Streaming Experience on College Students' Purchase Intention of Beauty Products-Take Taobao Live Streaming as an Example

Yiwen Cui[✉], Youxi Zhou, and Sihan Cheng

Guangzhou City University of Technology, Guangzhou 510800, People's Republic of China
cuiyiwencj@qq.com

Abstract. This study focuses on the live e-commerce environment, especially in the field of beauty products, and explores how the elements of the live streaming experience affect college students' purchase intention. The college student population has a strong sensitivity to new things and plays a key role in the beauty live streaming market. The mediating roles of perceived value and perceived trust in purchase decision were analyzed using perceived value theory and S-O-R model, and the questionnaire data were analyzed through structural equation modelling (SEM), as well as SPSS and AMOS software, and it was found that the professionalism, popularity, interactivity and attractiveness of the anchors significantly increased the perceived value and trust, and that the transparency and availability of the product information, as well as the scene's atmosphere also had a significant impact on consumers' purchase intention. Transparency and accessibility of product information, as well as a sense of presence in the scene, also had a significant impact on consumers' purchase intention. The results of this study provide empirical evidence on how brands can effectively use live streaming platforms to attract and influence college students, and enrich the theoretical research in the field of e-commerce live streaming.

Keywords: live streaming experience · perceived value · perceived trust · S-O-R model · Taobao live streaming · purchase intention

1 Introduction

In today's rapid development of digital economy, live e-commerce is rapidly emerging as an innovative online marketing method, which integrates the characteristics of social media and e-commerce, bringing consumers a new shopping experience. According to the 52nd China Internet Network Information Centre (CNNIC) "China Internet Development Statistics Report", as of June 2023, China's Internet users reached 1.079 billion, of which 765 million users of live webcasting, while the scale of live e-commerce users is as high as 526 million, accounting for nearly half of all Internet users [1]. The statistics of the Ministry of Commerce also depicted the prosperous scene of live e-commerce:

© The Author(s), under exclusive license to Springer Nature Switzerland AG 2024
A. Marcus et al. (Eds.): HCII 2024, LNCS 14716, pp. 285–306, 2024.
https://doi.org/10.1007/978-3-031-61362-3_21

the total sales of live broadcast in the first half of 2023 exceeded 1.27 trillion yuan, the number of live broadcasts exceeded 110 million, the variety of goods also exceeded 70 million, and the number of active anchors reached 2.7 million []. With the expansion of the audience base and the rise in sales, live e-commerce has brought about disruptive changes in the industry, and has become a powerful tool for many businesses to broaden their markets and attract customers.

Among many commodity sectors, beauty products are particularly suitable for display and sales through live streaming as they are highly dependent on visual effects and live experience. Live streaming allows consumers to instantly see product effects and interact with sellers, an immersive shopping experience that greatly facilitates consumers' purchasing decisions. The college student population, in particular, has become an important target and potential consumer for beauty live streaming due to its high sensitivity to fashion trends and wide acceptance of novelty, and its consumption preferences and behaviors have gradually become a weathervane that guides market trends. This study takes Taobao live streaming platform, which has a significant market share and wide influence, as an example, and builds an analytical framework of how Taobao live streaming experience affects college students' intention to purchase beauty products based on the theory of perceived value and the environment-organism-response (S-O-R) model. It is expected to provide theoretical guidance on how to better design live interactive scenarios and enhance college students' user experience for beauty live e-commerce platforms, which is also of some reference significance for academic research and practical application of live e-commerce.

2 Literature Review

2.1 Review of Research on Purchase Intention and Influencing Factors

The term "intention" comes from the field of psychology, which refers to the individual's idea of things under certain conditions, a certain motivation before reaching a certain behavior, usually the higher the intention, the higher the degree of achievement of the behavior. Eagly (1993) subjective intention to think is not only the individual's attitude towards objective facts, but also involves the individual's conscious thinking with autonomous motivation and purpose before carrying out a behavior [2]. Mullet et al. (1997) viewed consumers' intention to buy as an individual decision based on self-perceived brand identity and influenced by external conditions, which has been widely accepted by academics and used as a key indicator for predicting consumer behavior [3]. According to Feng Jianying et al. (2006), consumers' intention to buy is a true reflection of consumers' psychological state and activities during a specific period of time, which shows the possibility of consumer behavior during a certain period of time [4]. In summary, various studies have shown that consumers' intention to buy is a complex internal process, subject to a combination of factors such as personal attitudes, external environment and social influence, and is an important concept for understanding and predicting consumer decision-making (Table 1).

Most scholars explore and analyse consumers' Purchase Intention from the perspective of perceived value, and believe that consumers consider the functionality and emotional satisfaction of products, as well as IWOM and social influence when facing product

Table 1. Factors influencing Purchase Intention

Scholars	Time	Factors influencing Purchase Intention
Amn, S	2002	Service quality, additional services [5]
Lu HP & Hsiao KL	2010	Perceived value as a mediating variable in the shopping process is an important factor influencing purchase intentions [6]
Gogoi	2013	Price, perceived value [7]
Li Chenyang	2019	Individual Characteristics, Product Attributes, Perceived Ease of Use, Perceived Riskiness of Online Shopping, Perceived Import Risks [8]
Yuan Yuan	2020	Functional value, perceived value, emotional value, IWOM [9]
Siyue Wang	2021	Anchor Factor, Shop Factor, Professionalism Factor, Review Factor, Product Factor, Live Streaming Factor [10]
Tao Rui, Yang Yu, Huang Lidong	2022	Perceived usefulness, perceived ease of use, perceived pleasantness, perceived risk [11]
Yang Weimin, Zheng Yuzhu, Dao Ri Na	2022	Functional value, emotional value, cognitive value, social value, conditional value [12]

selection. In addition, factors such as trust, anchor interaction, and live atmosphere in the live e-commerce environment are also considered important factors influencing purchase intention. Chinese scholars' research on purchase intention reflects the combined role of individual characteristics, product evaluation, network-wide reputation, and live streaming marketing strategies in the consumer decision-making process.

2.2 Review of the Study of Live Streaming of e-commerce

E-commerce live streaming combines interactivity, communication and entertainment, bringing innovation to modern e-commerce. As described by Wu Bing and Gong Chunyu (2017), it is a form of live network video content based on the social e-commerce model, incorporating network social elements to provide consumers with rich and comprehensive information about goods [13]. Yang Jie and Wang Lu (2021) further pointed out that e-commerce live streaming platform is a product of the integration of live streaming and e-commerce business, and the traditional e-commerce model is experiencing technological upgrading and innovation with the application of 5G and cloud technology [14].

Table 2. A review of research on live streaming

Researcher	Key Elements	Main Findings
Zhi Xuan Liang (2019)	Communicator, form of communication activities, content of communication interactions	Live streaming mainly relies on the output of commodity information, to enhance the interactive form of the anchor user group, to solve the problem of coupon issuance and the decline in the attractiveness of the anchor [15]
Qin Jiayi (2020)	Anchor, other viewers, live streaming content and mode, target audience, communication effect	Propose a model of e-commerce live streaming communication mode, including five key elements, and provide the research direction of e-commerce live streaming [16]
Huang Minxue et al. (2021)	Internet celebrity anchors, consumption type products, social impact	Celebrities increase purchase intention through webcasting and may promote the feedback mechanism of new product consumption awareness and increase commodity sales [17]
Xiao Xijun (2021)	Opinion leaders, Information quality, Brand trust	Information quality and brand trust are key to purchase intention, professionalism and celebrity popularity influence consumer trust and purchase intention [18]
Tan Lijiao (2022)	Social relationship, professionalism, social influence, entertainment atmosphere, preferential environment, perceived value	Social relationships, live streaming professionalism, social influence, and preferential environment and the value of the product and live streaming reputation all positively affect purchase intention [19]

In summary, e-commerce live streaming enhances the shopping experience of consumers, and through the real-time interaction of the anchor, it enhances the user's understanding of the product and confidence in purchasing. Merchants use live streaming to attract traffic and quickly convert it into sales, while consumers get a more intuitive, social and interactive way to shop. With the progress of technology, e-commerce live streaming is continuing to promote the upgrading and reform of e-commerce business, showing great development potential and market value.

Chinese scholars mainly explore live streaming from two dimensions, namely, communication and purchase intention, as shown in Table 2. Under the perspective of communication, attention is paid to the role of the subject in live streaming, the information transfer mechanism, audience feedback and communication effectiveness. And from the analysis of purchase intention, the specific role of the anchor's influence, information quality and social elements on purchase intention is examined in depth.

2.3 Review of Theories of Perceived Value

Table 3. Definition of perceived value

Scholars	Time	Definition of perceived value
Monroe	1990	Customer perceived value is a trade-off between the benefits that the customer receives and the costs incurred in the transaction process, emphasising the relative nature of customer perceived value [20]
Dodds et al	1991	Perceived value is a trade-off between the get and the give of a product to the consumer [21]
Woodruff	1997	The outcome preferences and evaluations that users form about the image, performance, and use of a product in a given context that may facilitate or hinder their consumption intentions [22]
Anderson, Jain & Chintagunta	1993	A perceived benefit of a product relative to the purchase price, in terms of service, technical, economic and social benefits [23]
Dong, Da Hai	1999	Comparison of the utility obtained and the cost paid by the customer during the whole process of purchasing and using a product [24]
Yao Zhonghua	2002	The ratio of the total benefits that a customer obtains from a product or service to the total costs paid; the greater the ratio, the greater the value obtained by the customer, i.e., the customer's needs are consistent with the value of the product [25]

As can be seen from Tables 2, 3 and 4, scholars have conducted rich research on the definition and theoretical development of perceived value, resulting in a variety of theoretical perspectives. Monroe (1990) and Dodds et al. (1991) argue that perceived value is a trade-off between benefits and costs, and is part of the trade-off value theory. While Woodruff (1997) and Fan Xiucheng (2003) suggest that perceived value is hierarchical, including the dimensions of consumption context, product expectations and customer goals. This suggests that perceived value not only involves economic dimensions, but is also closely related to customers' personal goals and consumption context. Subsequently, Chang HH and Wang HW (2011) focused on the role of emotional value in their research in the field of online shopping, emphasizing that perceived value is a combined experience of consumers in both rational and emotional dimensions [26]. This suggests that the understanding of perceived value is expanding and the importance of emotional dimensions in current consumer experiences is increasing.

In summary, this paper defines perceived value as consumers' subjective feelings about the anchor and the product in watching beauty live streaming. Specifically, it is the outcome preferences and evaluations that consumers form after comparing the total benefits (e.g., utility, service assurance, and pleasure, etc.) they receive from live streaming and products with the costs they pay (money and time, etc.), which may facilitate or hinder their consumption intentions. This study will build on the existing literature to explore how functional and emotional values influence purchase intentions, taking into account the characteristics of live shopping contexts and consumers' emotional engagement.

2.4 Review of S-O-R Model Research

John Watson (1913) was the first to establish the Stimulus-Response Theory, or S-R theory, which states that human behavior is a response to a stimulus, which includes both internal and external stimuli [27]. Mehrabian (1962) and Russell (1974) modified the S-R theoretical model and proposed Stimulus Stimulus-Organism-Organism (physiological, psychological)-Response, which is used to investigate the influence of the environment on human behavior []. In S-O-R theory, S stands for Stimulus, O stands for Organism, and R stands for Response, which suggests that stimuli from the external environment will affect the physiological and psychological responses of the individual and thus influence the individual's behavior [28]. Eroglu (2001) firstly introduced the S-O-R model into the context of online shopping, and the model has been widely used in the study of consumer purchasing behaviors in the field of e-commerce in the ensuing researches [29]. Liu Junyue, Liu Wanxin et al. (2020) based on the SOR model to study the influence of online opinion leaders on consumers' purchase intention, and he argued that online opinion leaders (S) indirectly influence consumers' purchase intention (R) through trust, perceived risk and perceived value (O) [30]. Li Yuxi, Ye Li (2020) empirically investigated the effect of live e-commerce streaming on consumers' purchase intention based on the SOR model by taking interactivity, preferential treatment, and authenticity of live e-commerce streaming as stimulus (S), trust and demand release as organism (O), and purchase intention as response (R) [31].

In summary, purchase intention, as an individual's psychological tendency to take action on specific goods or services, is deeply influenced by a variety of factors, including individual consumer characteristics, market environment, product attributes, and live streaming elements. Scholars have conducted a large number of studies on Purchase Intention, focusing on analyzing the intrinsic psychological components such as product functionality, emotional value, and social identity, as well as the purchase motives constituted by the interactivity of the live streaming experience, the quality of information, and the credibility of the host. However, fewer studies have distinguished between product categories to explore the impact of live streaming e-commerce. Considering college students' fashion sensitivity and acceptance of new things, they become key consumers of live beauty broadcasts and indicate market trends. In view of this, this study takes Taobao live streaming as an example to target how different elements of the live streaming experience play a role in college students' purchase decision-making process of beauty products. Adhering to a more nuanced theoretical perspective and research methodology, it provides valuable insights into college students' consumption psychology and behavior for beauty brands. The results of the study are not only expected to provide a theoretical basis for academics to further understand consumer behaviors, but also provide practical references for the beauty industry's live streaming marketing strategies targeting high-potential consumer segments.

3 Model Construction and Research Design

3.1 Model Construction and Variable Definition

Combined with the above research, based on the S-O-R model and the perceived value theory, a conceptual model is constructed with consumer purchase intention as the dependent variable, 10 variables in the three dimensions of anchor, merchandise and scene atmosphere as the independent variables, and consumer trust and perceived value as the mediator variables, as shown in Figs. 1, 2, 3.

In this paper, the independent variables are divided into three dimensions, which are anchor dimension, commodity dimension, and scene atmosphere. Anchor dimension contains anchor's own professionalism, popularity, interactivity and attractiveness; commodity dimension contains commodity information accessibility, information quality, promotional activities and purchasing limitations; and scene atmosphere contains spatial proximity and social proximity. The definition of each variable is shown in Tables 1, 2, 3.

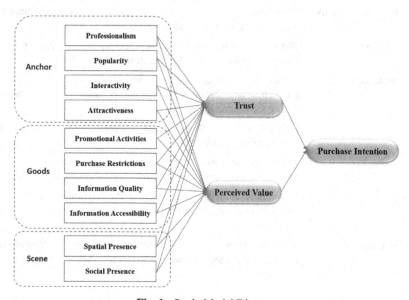

Fig. 1. Study Model Diagram

Table 4. Definitions of Observation Variables

Variable name	Specific definition
Professionalism	Anchor's level of knowledge and skills of beauty products and professionalism of live presentation
Popularity	The degree of recognition of the anchor among potential consumer groups, including the number and activity of fans and brand recognition
Interactivity	The frequency, depth and breadth of the anchor's interaction with the audience, as well as its ability to promote user participation
Attractiveness	Attractiveness of the anchor's personal charisma, including values, language expression and style, etc., to the target audience
Promotional activities	The attractiveness and purchase-inducing ability of promotional measures such as time-limited offers, discounts, and free gifts
Purchase restrictions	Limiting the quantity, frequency or conditions of consumers' purchase of goods or services
Information quality	The accuracy and completeness of the product information delivered in the live broadcast and its influence on consumer decisions
Information accessibility	The convenience of consumers in obtaining product information, including the visibility and comprehension of the information
Spatial presence	The sense of immersion consumers feel when using the live streaming platform as if they are in the scene
Social Presence	The degree of authenticity and intimacy of social connection and interaction with the anchor or others experienced by consumers during the interaction process
Trust	Consumers' trust in the reliability and integrity of the host and the live streaming platform
Functional value	The subjective value of the emotional and entertainment experience that consumers get in the live broadcast interaction
Hedonic value	Consumers' subjective assessment of the performance and functional satisfaction of the product promoted by the live streaming
Purchase Intention	The intensity of consumers' intention to repurchase, recommend or share the products recommended by the anchor in the future

3.2 Research Hypotheses

Anchor Dimension. Anchors have a significant impact on consumers' purchase intention, which is key to their professionalism, popularity, interactivity and attractiveness. A study by Liu, Zhongyu & Zhao, Xianghao (2020) found that professional anchors earned consumer trust and enhanced purchase intention. Qiaoxian Fu (2020) emphasised the role of Popularity and professionalism in building consumer knowledge and trust. Interactivity, especially for young consumers seeking a social experience, such as college students, plays an important role. The personal charisma of the anchors, including their appearance and behaviour, is key to maintaining the long-term attention of young consumers (Tables 4 ands 5). Therefore, the following hypotheses are proposed:

Ha1/Ha2: Beauty anchors' professionalism positively affects college consumers' trust/ perceived value.

Ha3/ Ha4: Beauty anchors' popularity positively affects college consumers' trust/ perceived value.

Ha5/ Ha6: Interactivity of beauty anchors positively affects college consumers' trust/ perceived value.

Ha7/ Ha8: Attractiveness of beauty anchors positively affects college consumers' trust/ perceived value.

Goods Dimension. The live e-commerce format omits multiple intermediate stages of traditional retailing, reduces supply chain costs, and provides merchants and consumers with price advantages and attractive promotions. The limited promotional strategy enhances user engagement and deepens consumer trust in the anchor. Studies have shown that price promotions are associated with consumers' perceived functional and hedonic benefits, which affects purchase intentions; limited quantity purchases and discounts may induce impulse purchases (Chandon et al., 2000; Biswas & Burton, 1993; Lin Jianhuang et al., 2005). In the live streaming environment, detailed and high-quality product information increases consumers' product knowledge and enhances purchase intention; easy-to-access information also enhances trust in the anchor and the live streaming platform.

Therefore, the following hypothesis is proposed:

Ha9/ Ha10: Promotional activities of goods positively affect college consumers' trust/ perceived value.

Ha11/ Ha12: Purchase restriction of goods positively affects college consumers' trust/ perceived value.

Ha13/ Ha14: Information quality of goods positively affects college consumers' trust/ perceived value.

Ha15/ Ha16: Information accessibility of goods positively affects college consumers' trust/ perceived value.

Scene Atmosphere. Spatial and social presence play a crucial role in digital shopping environments in terms of users' purchase intention. Spatial presence is the degree to which users feel as if they are experiencing the digital environment, as Song et al. (2007) found that it significantly enhances users' mental imagery during the shopping process, stimulates pleasure, and enhances trust in the website. Social presence, on the other hand, reflects the degree of users' social interactions with anchors and other online users, reflecting their perception of others who are not present, and enhancing the sense of interaction and trust (Lu et al., 2016). Zhao Hongxia et al. (2015) also confirmed that spatial presence enhances trust in product quality, while social presence promotes trust in merchant integrity.

Ha17 /Ha18: Live streaming spatial proximity positively affects college consumers' trust/ perceived value.

Ha19/Ha20: Live streaming social presence positively affects college consumers' trust/ perceived value.

Trust. Live e-commerce is an activity with high intensity of social interaction, in which the trust relationship between the anchor and the audience plays a crucial role. When consumers have a high level of trust in the anchor, they are more inclined to believe that the information provided by the anchor is credible, that the recommended products are valuable, and that the anchor's advice takes into account the interests of consumers and helps them to obtain the value of product use, social acceptance, and a sense of fulfilment, among other things. This trust has a direct and positive effect on increasing consumers' purchase intention. The studies of Cheng Zhenyu (2013) and Zhou Shouliang et al. (2019) emphasised the importance of trust on purchase intention and supported the view that trust acts as a mediating variable, and the empirical study of Hsiao et al. verified the significant role of trust. Based on this, this study considers consumers' trust in anchors as a mediating variable and proposes the following hypotheses:

Ha21: Trust in the anchor positively influences college consumers' intention to purchase beauty products.

Hb1 /Hb3/ Hb5 /Hb7: Trust acts as a mediating variable between the professionalism/ the popularity/ the interactivity/the attractiveness of beauty anchors and purchase intention.

Hb9/ Hb11/ Hb13/ Hb15: Trust acts as a mediating variable between promotional activities / purchase restrictions /information quality/ information accessibility of live-streamed goods and purchase intention.

Hb17/ Hb19: Trust acts as a mediator between spatial presence/ social presence and Purchase Intention in the live streaming room.

Perceived Value. Perceived value plays a key role in consumer purchase intention in live e-commerce. It consists of perceived costs and perceived benefits, the latter subdivided into functional, emotional and social values. Together, these factors shape the overall evaluation of a product. Studies by Zeithaml (1988), Chang (1994) and Wang et al. (2019) show that there is a significant positive relationship between perceived value and purchase intention. Consumers' perceived value includes time savings, reduced shopping effort and money costs, and related practical and economic benefits from live streaming. Meanwhile, the products promoted by the anchors can provide emotional satisfaction and social identity, enhancing the perceived value. Accordingly, this study takes perceived value as a mediating variable and proposes the following hypotheses:

Ha22: Perceived value of live e-commerce positively affects college consumers' purchase intention.

Hb2/ Hb4/ Hb6/ Hb8: Perceived value acts as a mediating variable between the professionalism/ the popularity/ the interactivity/the attractiveness of beauty anchors and purchase intention.

Hb10/ Hb12/ Hb14/ Hb16: Perceived value acts as a mediating variable between promotional activities / purchase restrictions /information quality/ information accessibility of live-streamed goods and purchase intention.

Hb18/Hb20: Perceived value acts as a mediator between spatial presence/ social presence and Purchase Intention in the live streaming room.

3.3 Data Collection and Sample Characteristics

In this empirical study, we lasted six weeks to conduct a questionnaire survey, which was conducted through the Questionnaire Star platform for data collection, and utilized social media platforms such as Weibo, Douban, Beili Beili (B station), QQ and Xiaohongshu for the release and dissemination of the questionnaire. The content of the survey can be divided into two main parts: The first part mainly collected the basic information of the participants and investigated and analyzed the beauty consumption behavior of college students as well as their habit of participating in live e-commerce activities. In order to improve the reliability and accuracy of the data, specific screening questions were designed in the questionnaire. After screening, 378 valid questionnaires were collected in this part, 370 valid questionnaires were obtained in the analysis for beauty consumption behavior and 345 valid questionnaires were obtained in the analysis for e-commerce live streaming behavioral habits. The second part is the scale survey part, based on the Likert five-level scale design (ranging from "Strongly Disagree" to "Strongly Agree"), combined with the theoretical model, we designed a total of 39 survey entries around the six dimensions of anchor traits, product information, scene atmosphere, trust, perceived value and purchase intention. A total of 321 valid questionnaire data were collected from a survey of a group of college students who have already watched Taobao beauty live broadcasts. The data collected above provide empirical support for further quantitative analysis to ensure the scientific validity and effectiveness of the research results.

Table 5. Sample Characteristics

Name	Options	Frequency	Percentage
Gender	Female	243	75.7%
	Male	78	24.3%
Education	Junior college student	53	16.5%
	Undergraduate	175	54.5%
	Master's Degree Students	64	20%
	Doctoral students	29	9%
Monthly disposable income	0–1000	17	5.3%
	1001–2000	161	50.2%
	2001–3000	86	26.8%
	3001–4000	46	14.3%
	4000 or more	11	3.4%

4 Empirical Research

4.1 Reliability and Validity Analysis

This paper uses SPSS27 to analyse the reliability of the scales, and Table 6 shows that the Cronbach's Alpha coefficients for most of the first-level latent variables are significantly higher than 0.7, and that there are first-level latent variables that define second-level latent variables with a minimum of 0.78 or more, and that the Cronbach's Alpha coefficient value of the overall scales is 0.975, which is significantly higher than 0.9, proving that the internal consistency of the questionnaire's scales is strong and that there is generally good reliability among the scales.

Table 6. Reliability Tests

Level 1 latent variable	Cronbach's Alpha	Cronbach's Alpha (secondary latent variable)	Cronbach's Alpha (total scale)
Professionalism	0.781	0.924	0.975
Popularity	0.753		
Interactivity	0.745		
Attractiveness	0.782		
Promotionactivities	0.760	0.892	
Purchase restrictions	0.719		
Information quality	0.697		
Information accessibility	0.692		
Spatial presence	0.687	0.79	
Social Presence	0.65		
Functional value	0.841	0.902	
Hedonic value	0.791		
Trust	0.775		
Purchase Intention	0.878		

In this paper, validity was assessed using validated factor analysis. Before conducting validity analysis, the data needs to be unfolded with KMO test to determine whether the data is suitable for validity analysis, as can be seen in Table 7, KMO value = 0.979 > 0.9, meanwhile, significance = 0 < 0.05, which proves that the scales are suitable for factor analysis among each other.

Table 7. KMO test

KMO Quantity of Sampling Suitability	--	0.979
Bartlett's test of sphericity	Approximate chi-square	8358.324
--	Degrees of freedom	741
--	Significance	0

Table 8 shows the structural validity of this scale, in general, the chi-square degrees of freedom ratio is required to be in [1, 2], the chi-square degrees of freedom ratio of this model is closer to 1, the IFI, CFI, TLI are required to be greater than 0.9, the three indexes of this model are much greater than 0.9, the RESEA is generally required to be less than 0.05, this model also meets the requirements of the model, the model of these five indexes are higher than the acceptable standard to a certain extent The five indicators of this model are all higher than the acceptable standard by a certain degree, indicating that the overall fit of the established model is better.

Table 8. Structural Validity

Indicators of model fit (structural validity)					
	chi-square ratio of degrees of freedom $\chi 2$/df	IFI	CFI	TLI	RMSEA
numerical value	1.375	0.969	0.968	0.965	0.034

4.2 Hypothesis Path Test Results

As shown in Fig. 2, attractiveness, professionalism, popularity, and interactivity in the anchor dimension have a significant positive effect on the perceived value dimension, with path coefficients of 0.4, 0.14, 0.08, and 0.03, respectively; social proximity in the scene dimension has a significant positive effect on the perceived value dimension, with path coefficients of 0.08; and promotional activities, purchasing restrictions, information quality, and information accessibility have significant positive effects on the perceived value dimension with path coefficients of 0.14, 0.09, 0.11, and 0.22.

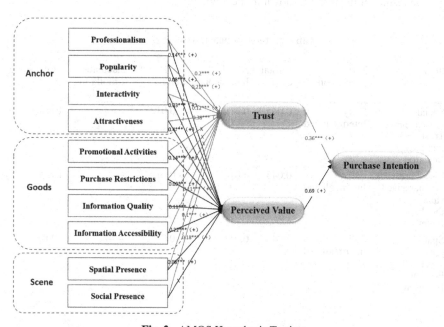

Fig. 2. AMOS Hypothesis Testing

In the anchor dimension, attractiveness, professionalism, popularity, and interactivity have a significant positive effect on the trust dimension, with path coefficients of 0.38, 0.2, 0.21, and 0.12, respectively; social presence and spatial presence in the scene dimension also have a significant positive effect on the trust dimension, with path coefficients of 0.18 and 0.1, respectively; and the information accessibility in the goods dimension has a significant positive effect on the trust dimension, with path coefficients of 0.18 and 0.1, respectively. Positive effect on the trust dimension, with a path coefficient of 0.11.

The perceived value dimension has a significant positive effect on purchase intention with a path coefficient of 0.69, while the trust dimension has a significant positive effect on purchase intention with a path coefficient of 0.36. This means that both the perceived value and trust dimensions have a positive effect on purchase intention, but the former has a greater effect.

4.3 Mediated Effects Test

According to the above analysis, the independent variables and the dependent variable all have correlations and are significant, combined with the previous hypothesis testing, a total of four hypotheses Ha9, Ha11, Ha13, Ha18 are not valid, i.e., the four hypotheses corresponding to the independent variables and the mediating variables do not have a correlation between them and do not satisfy the prerequisite relationship of the test of mediating variables, and it is decided that the four hypotheses of Hb9, Hb11, Hb13, Hb18 are also not valid. Hypotheses are also not valid. After eliminating the variables that did not satisfy the prerequisite relationships, SPSS was used to conduct the mediator test on the scale.

The results of the test are shown in the Table 9:

Table 9. Intermediate test effect sizes

Item	Test conclusion	c Total effect	a*b Intermediary effect	c' Direct effect	Calculation formula for effect share	Effect share
Social Presence => Trust => Purchase Intention	Fully Intermediated	0.045	0.019	0.012	——	100%
Social presence => perceived value => Purchase Intention	Fully Intermediated	0.045	0.014	0.012	——	100%
Spatial presence => Trust => Purchase Intention	Fully Intermediated	0.043	0.011	0.021	——	100%

(*continued*)

Table 9. (*continued*)

Item	Test conclusion	c Total effect	a*b Intermediary effect	c' Direct effect	Calculation formula for effect share	Effect share
Information accessibility => trust => Purchase Intention	Partially intermediary	0.122	0.004	0.079	a * b / c	3.28%
Information accessibility => perceived value => Purchase Intention	Partially intermediary	0.122	0.039	0.079	a * b / c	31.928%
Information quality => perceived value => Purchase Intention	Fully intermediary	0.065	0.032	0.015	——	100%
Promotional activities => Perceived value => Purchase Intention	Fully intermediary	0.088	0.033	0.062	——	100%
Purchase Restrictions => Perceived Value => Purchase Intention	Fully intermediary	0.066	0.034	0.025	——	100%
Expertise => Trust => Purchase Intention	Fully Intermediary	0.066	0.03	-0.012	——	100%
Expertise => Perceived Value => Purchase Intention	Fully intermediated	0.066	0.049	-0.012	——	100%
Attractiveness => Trust => Purchase Intention	Partially intermediary	0.292	0.034	0.199	a * b / c	11.725%
Attractiveness => Perceived Value => Purchase Intention	Partially Intermediary	0.292	0.059	0.199	a * b / c	20.261%

(*continued*)

Table 9. (*continued*)

Item	Test conclusion	c Total effect	a*b Intermediary effect	c' Direct effect	Calculation formula for effect share	Effect share
Interactivity => Trust => Purchase Intention	Fully intermediary	0.139	0.012	0.093	——	100%
Interactivity => Perceived Value => Purchase Intention	Fully intermediary	0.139	0.034	0.093	——	100%
Popularity => Trust => Purchase Intention	Fully intermediary	0.105	0.024	0.065	——	100%
Popularity => Perceived value => Purchase Intention	Fully intermediary	0.105	0.016	0.065	——	100%

4.4 Model Revision

From the results of data analysis in the summary Table 10, it can be concluded that out of the 42 hypotheses proposed in this study, a total of 34 hypotheses are valid and 8 hypotheses are not valid, and the specific results of hypothesis testing are shown in the Table 10:

Table 10. Summary table of hypothesis testing results

No	Assumptions	Results
Ha1	Professionalism → Trust	Valid
Ha2	Professionalism → Perceived value	Valid
Ha3	Popularity → Trust	Valid
Ha4	Popularity → Perceived value	Valid
Ha5	Interactivity → Trust	Valid
Ha6	Interactivity → Perceived value	Valid
Ha7	Attractiveness → Trust	Valid
Ha8	Attractiveness → Perceived value	Valid
Ha9	Purchase constraints → Trust	Not valid
Ha10	Purchase restrictions → Perceived value	Valid
Ha11	Promotional activities → Trust	Not valid

(*continued*)

Table 10. (*continued*)

No	Assumptions	Results
Ha12	Promotional activities → Perceived value	Valid
Ha13	Information quality → Trust	Not valid
Ha14	Information quality → Perceived value	Valid
Ha15	Information accessibility → Trust	Valid
Ha16	Information accessibility → Perceived value	Valid
Ha17	Spatial proximity → Trust	Valid
Ha18	Spatial proximity → Perceived value	Not valid
Ha19	Social presence → Trust	Valid
Ha20	Social proximity → Perceived value	Valid
Ha21	Trust → Purchase Intention	Valid
Ha22	Perceived value → Purchase Intention	Valid
Hb1	Professionalism => Trust => Purchase Intention	Valid
Hb2	Professionalism => Perceived value => Purchase Intention	Valid
Hb3	Popularity => Trust => Purchase Intention	Valid
Hb4	Popularity => Perceived Value => Purchase Intention	Valid
Hb5	Interactivity => Trust => Purchase Intention	Valid
Hb6	Interactivity => Perceived Value => Purchase Intention	Valid
Hb7	Attractiveness => Trust => Purchase Intention	Valid
Hb8	Attractiveness => Perceived value => Purchase Intention	Valid
Hb9	Purchase Restrictions => Trust => Purchase Intention	Not valid
Hb10	Purchase Restrictions => Perceived Value => Purchase Intention	Valid
Hb11	Promotional activities => Trust => Purchase Intention	Not valid
Hb12	Promotional activities => Perceived value => Purchase Intention	Valid
Hb13	Information quality => Trust => Purchase Intention	Not valid
Hb14	Information Quality => Perceived Value => Purchase Intention	Valid
Hb15	Information accessibility => Trust => Purchase Intention	Valid
Hb16	Information accessibility => Perceived value => Purchase Intention	Valid
Hb17	Spatial presence => Trust => Purchase Intention	Valid
Hb18	Spatial presence => Perceived value => Purchase Intention	Not valid
Hb19	Social Presence => Trust => Purchase Intention	Valid
Hb20	Social Presence => Perceived Value => Purchase Intention	Valid

Table 11. Map of concluding recommendations

Recommended for	Influencing factors	Suggestions
Anchor	Professionalism	Strengthen make-up and skincare knowledge, attend professional training, pay attention to product background and applicability, and enhance professionalism to attract student consumers
	Interactivity, Social presence	Increase interactive links, such as themed cosplay, to improve audience participation and conversion rate in the live streaming room
	Attractiveness	Build up correct outlook on life and values, and read literary books corresponding to the audience group
	Popularity	Promote the product through multiple channels and platforms, and design explosive marketing methods
	Information quality, Information accessibility	Simplify the presentation of product information, ensure quality, and provide timely feedback on consumer evaluations to enhance trust
	Promotional activities	Fully interface with the company and operation, back-tune the brand in advance, get enough benefits for fans, and increase fan enthusiasm
Brand Merchants	Professionalism, Attractiveness	Select anchors that match the positioning of the products promoted by the brand and the user groups; strengthen product quality control
	Interactivity	Reward and incentives; according to the atmosphere of the live streaming room, interaction, etc., should modify the product homepage related introduction

(*continued*)

Table 11. (*continued*)

Recommended for	Influencing factors	Suggestions
Platform Expertise	Professionalism	Strengthen the content screening mechanism to improve the quality of content; actively expand the self-built anchor
	Interactivity	Traffic incentives, home page recommendations
	Spatial presence	Optimize the Taobao live interface, optimize the HAR make-up trial function

According to the above table, the spatial proximity in the scene dimension has no significant effect on the perceived value dimension, and the promotional activities, purchasing restrictions, and information quality in the goods dimension have no significant effect on the information dimension, therefore, these four corresponding paths should be deleted in the model diagram, and the original model should be corrected, and the corrected model is shown in the following Fig. 3.

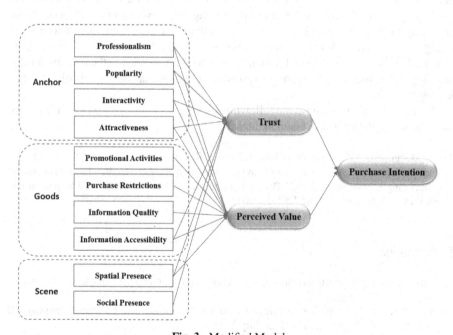

Fig. 3. Modified Model

5   Conclusions and Recommendations

The following conclusions are drawn from the empirical analysis: (1) The professionalism, popularity, interactivity and attractiveness of beauty anchors have a significant positive impact on the perceived value and trust of college students' consumers, which in turn affects the purchase intention. This suggests that beauty anchors have great influence on college students' consumers during live streaming, where attractiveness, such as personal qualities and values, are the elements that college students' consumers pay primary attention to. Secondly, the professionalism of beauty anchors is also one of the key concerns of college students' consumers. While interactivity and popularity are relatively secondary factors of concern for college consumers. Therefore, it is recommended to develop relevant strategies around the professionalism and attractiveness of beauty anchors. (2) The information quality, information accessibility, purchase restrictions and promotional activities of commodity information all have a significant positive impact on the perceived value of college students' consumers, while information accessibility also has a significant positive impact on college students' trust. This suggests that in the live streaming process, both the information level and information accessibility of the goods affect the degree of emotional experience of college students' consumers, which promotes the formation of perceived value and thus increases purchase intention. In addition, information accessibility also affects perceived value and further influences the accessibility of commodity information. Therefore, emphasizing the accessibility of commodity information is the key to improving the conversion rate. (3) The spatial proximity of the scene atmosphere positively affects the perceived value and trust of college consumers, while the social proximity positively affects the trust of college consumers. This suggests that spatial proximity is crucial for increasing the perceived value of college consumers, while social proximity is more important after establishing closer fan relationships.

Based on the above findings the following recommendations are made from anchors, merchants and platforms as shown in Table 11:

Acknowledgments. The research is funded by Key Research Base of Humanities and Social Sciences in Universities of Guangdong Province: Research Base for Digital Transformation of Manufacturing Enterprises(2023WZJD012) & Principles of Marketing Course Ideological and Political Demonstration Course(57-S23120001).

References

1. China Internet Network Information Centre (cnnic). https://www.cnnic.cn/n4/2023/0828/c88-10829.html. 28 August 2023
2. Commerce of the People's Republic of China. http://www.mofcom.gov.cn/article/tj/tjsj/202307/20230703424499.shtml2023. 26 July 2023
3. Eagly, A.H., Chaiken, S.: The Psychology of Attitudes. Harcourt Brace Jovanovich College Publishers, vol. 45(7), pp. 213–215 (1993)
4. Zellweger, P.: Web-based sales: defining the cognitive buyer. Elect. Mark. **7**(3), 10–16 (1997)
5. Feng, J.Y., Mu, W.S., Fu, Z.T.: A review of research on consumers' willingness to buy. Mod. Manage. Sci. **11**, 7–9 (2006)

6. Arun, S.: Trends in internet-based business-to-business marketing. Ind. Mark. Manage. **31**, 77–84 (2002)
7. Lu, H.P., Hsiao, K.L.: The influence of extro/introversion on the intention to pay for social networking sites. Inf. Manage. **47**(3), 150–157 (2010)
8. Gogoi, B.: Study of antecedents of purchase intention and its effect on brand loyalty of private label brand of apparel. Int. J. Sales Mark. **3**(2), 73–86 (2013)
9. Li, C.: Research on consumers' willingness to purchase imported fresh fruits online and its influencing factors. Hunan Agricultural University (2019)
10. Yuan, Y.: Study on the Influencing Factors of Purchase Intention of Household Sweeping Robot. Beijing Jiaotong University (2020)
11. Wang, S-Y.: Study on the Influencing Factors of Consumers' Purchase Intention in E-commerce Live Streaming. Southwest University of Finance and Economics (2021)
12. Rui, T., Yang, Y., Lidong, H.: Rationality and pleasure: an empirical study on the driving factors of consumers' purchase behavior in live streaming with goods. Bus. Econ. **08**, 64–67 (2022)
13. Yang, W., Zheng, Y., Dao, R.: Research on yoghurt purchase intention based on consumer value theory and marketing insights. China Dairy Indus. **06**, 18–27 (2022)
14. Bing, W.U., Chunyu, G.O.N.G.: Research on e-commerce live streaming based on information system success model-taking Taobao e-commerce live streaming as an example. Bus. Glob. **3**, 37–45 (2017)
15. Jier, Y., Wang, L.: Influencing factors of consumers' repurchase intention under the mode of "live streaming + e-commerce". China Circ. Econ. **11**, 56–66 (2021)
16. Liang, Z.: Research on communication characteristics, problems and countermeasures of e-commerce live streaming. Lanzhou University of Finance and Economics (2019)
17. Qin, J.: Research on e-commerce live marketing communication mode. East China Normal University (2020)
18. Huang, M., Ye, Y., Wang, W.: The influence of live streaming anchor type on consumers' purchase intention and behavior under different types of products. Nankai Manage. Rev. 1–21
19. Xiao, X.: Research on the influence of opinion leaders on consumers' purchase intention under e-commerce live mode. Hunan University (2021)
20. Tan, L.: Study on the Influence Factors of Consumers' Purchase Intention in the Context of E-commerce Live Streaming. Changchun University of Technology (2022)
21. Monroe, K.B.: Pricing-Making Profitable Decisions, pp. 25–27. McGraw Hill, New York (1991)
22. Dodds, W.B., Monroe, K.B., Grewal, D.: Effects of price, brand, and store information on buyers' product evaluations. J. Mark. Res. 307–319 (1991)
23. Woodruff, R.B.: Customer value: the next source for competitive advantage. J. Acad. Market. Sci. **25**(2), 139–153 (1997)
24. Anderson, J.C., Jain, C., Chintagunta, P.K.: Customer value assessment in business markets. J. Bus. Bus. Mark. **1**(1), 3–30 (1993)
25. Dahai, D., Quan X.: Customer value and its composition. J. Dalian Univ. Tech. **20**(4), 18–20 (1999)
26. Zhonghua, Y.: Customer value analysis of enterprises' core competitiveness. Jiangxi Soc. Sci. **2**, 145–146 (2002)
27. Chang, H.H., Wang, H.W.: The moderating effect of customer perceived value on online shopping behavior. Online Inf. Rev. **35**(3), 333–359 (2011)
28. Watson, J.B.: Psychology as the behaviorist views it. Psychol. Rev. **20**, 158–177 (1913)
29. Zeithaml, V.A.: Consumer perceptions of price, quality and value: a means-end model and synthesis of evidence. J. Mark. **52**(3), 2–22 (1988)
30. Eroglu, S.A., Machleit, K.A., Davis, L.M.: Atmospheric qualities of online retailing: a conceptual model and implications. J. Bus. Res. **54**(2), 177–184 (2001)

31. Junyue, L., Wanxin, L., Junfeng, L., et al.: A study on the impact of online opinion leaders on consumers' purchase intention based on the SOR model. J. Chongqing Univ. Technol. (Soc. Sci.) **6**, 70–79 (2020)
32. Yuxi, L., Li, Y.: The influence of e-commerce live streaming on consumers' purchase intention - an empirical analysis based on the iceberg model and SOR model. Bus. Res. **12**, 5–8 (2020)

A Service Design Method Based on Digitalization and Componentization Service Blueprint Construction

Xiong Ding[✉] and Xiangming Zeng

Guangzhou Academy of Fine Arts, Guangzhou 510006, China
dingxiong@gzarts.edu.cn

Abstract. As a visual expression tool for service concept models, Service Blueprint directly affect the efficiency and sharing level of multi-party cooperation in service design, service management, and service deliver. Based on the research and analysis of multiple cases, this article provides an optimized service design innovation framework: 1) Using digital transformation to standardize Service Blueprint tools; 2) In the digital Service Blueprint, a universal component library and business middle platform (which called Middle-stage) are constructed based on atomic design theory to achieve the reuse of service components, thereby improving the collaborative efficiency and resource utilization of service design, achieving consistency in service experience, and improving service quality.

Keywords: Service Design · Service Blueprint · Digital Transformation · Componentization · Middle Platform · Middle-stage

1 Introduction

The tertiary industry played a pivotal role in China's economic growth over the past decade. According to the report series released by the National Bureau of Statistics of China [1], the average annual growth rate of the added value of the tertiary industry reached 7.4% from 2013 to 2021, with an average annual contribution rate of 55.6% to economic growth. While the service industry is booming, service design is also emerging in China. From the keyword search results on China National Knowledge Infrastructure (CNKI), it can be seen that the literature with the keyword "service design" has been growing rapidly since 2010, indicating that the application of service design and related modeling research have gained great development in this period."

The development of China's tertiary industry coincides with the rapid development of the Internet. Many design fields, such as interactive design, graphic design and digital media design have realized digital transformation. Both the carriers in these design fields and design methods are digitalized, greatly enhancing the design efficiency and output. Based on the digital transformation of Service Blueprint, an important tool for service design, this study aims to digitalize Service Blueprint to improve the usability of service design tools.

A. Marcus et al. (Eds.): HCII 2024, LNCS 14716, pp. 307–325, 2024.
https://doi.org/10.1007/978-3-031-61362-3_22

2 Evolving Journey and Application Scenario of Service Blueprint

2.1 The Proposal and Development of Service Design Concept

Service Blueprint is a diagram that visualizes the relationships between different service components (people, props, and processes) that are directly related to touch points in a certain customer journey. It systematically depicts the entire service process so that the various stakeholders within an organization can better meet the needs of the customer.

The concept of Service Blueprint was first proposed in 1982 by G. Lynn Shostack, an American management expert [2], who believed that the intangible nature of services makes it impossible to be recognized as physical products. If services cannot be described objectively, it is unable to compare services horizontally, and services cannot be evaluated, planned scientifically and controlled effectively [3]. Therefore, she integrated the structure and basic elements of services by establishing a systematic approach, and depicted the initial Service Blueprint template by taking the example of the street corner shoe-shine service. This Service Blueprint included the processes, time and required elements for standardized execution time, and set up visibility lines, service deviations and overall acceptable expected deviations [4]. Shostack modified the Service Blueprint in her paper published in 1984 by adding elements of customer behavior, customer perception, evidence and employee behavior, and proposed design principles for Service Blueprint.

In 1993, Jane Kingmam Brundage [5] and others expanded the Service Blueprint on the basis of Lynn Shostack's research, put forward the concept of service map, added a top-end customer area to reflect "customer-centered" concept, as well as the support and management area in the bottom. The service for front-line employees is in the middle of the structure to connect the top and bottom ends. The service map systematically and tangibly displays customer behavior, service behavior, support behavior and management behavior, which greatly improves the structured performance of the Service Blueprint.

In 1995, Valarie A. Zeithaml and Mary Jo Bitner, from the Service Leadership Center at Arizona State University, further updated the Service Blueprint [6] by adding tangible displays and removing management behaviors, so that "intangible" services can be tangible and the difficulty of understanding service design can be decreased. The improvement of Service Blueprint by the two scholars enables it to become the most popular Service Blueprint model. Besides using by service designers, it also becomes the main tool for marketing managers to analyze service touch-points and improve service quality. Since then, the basic framework of the Service Blueprint has matured into the version used by most designers (Fig. 1).

2.2 Problems Faced by the Application of Service Design

As China's economy developing, consumers' consumption needs are increasingly upgraded. According to Maslow's demand theory, when the basic physiological demands are satisfied, people will pursue higher-level demands, just like the increased demand on service quality in consumption industry. According to China's National Bureau of

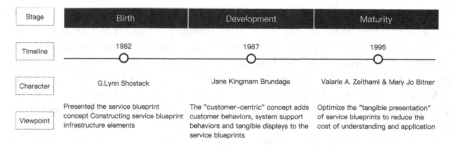

Stage	Birth	Development	Maturity
Timeline	1982	1987	1995
Character	G.Lynn Shostack	Jane Kingmam Brundage	Valarie A. Zeithaml & Mary Jo Bitner
Viewpoint	Presented the service blueprint concept Constructing service blueprint infrastructure elements	The "customer–centric" concept adds customer behaviors, system support behaviors and tangible displays to the service blueprints	Optimize the "tangible presentation" of service blueprints to reduce the cost of understanding and application

Fig. 1. Evolving journey of Service Blueprint

Statistics, the number of legal entities in China's service industry reached 21.66 million in 2022, a year-on-year increase of 14.7%. Meanwhile, the competition in various service industry segments, such as the Internet, automobile and catering, has become increasingly fierce. In such an environment, only companies that provide better quality can stand the test of competition and gain profit. Company will face new requirements on services.

Rapid Service Iteration. Due to the rapid market changes, changing consumer preferences and competitors' innovations, enterprises can only gain advantage by quickly upgrading their services. ByteDance, a well-known Internet company is a good example. When they promote a product, they will have several products plans internally and have A/B test to find out the optimal one for further application, so as to better respond to the customer needs compared with other market players.

Provide Dynamic and High-Quality Services. This is not only about the service itself, but more importantly, to adjust and upgrade the service flexibly base on the different features and needs of customers. Companies can meet diversified and dynamic consumption needs through a flexible and evolving service system. The catering company Haidilao is renowned for its excellent tailored services, such as celebrating birthday for customers and providing companion dolls to customers who dine alone, so as to obtain higher customer loyalty and commercial value.

As an important visual delivery tool in service design, Service Blueprint has been widely applied in all kinds of service design projects since its birth in the 1980s. However, it's drawbacks and limits become obvious during the long-term application and practices.

Driven by Multidisciplinary and Demands, the Presentation and Constituent Elements of Service Blueprint Are not Consistent. On the basis of the final version of Service Blueprint in 1995, the tool has been extended by the practices of different researchers and designers, resulting in numerous variants, which leads to differences in the Service Blueprint adopted in service design projects within the same enterprise. This inconsistency brings barriers to collaboration and communication within the enterprise. Standardized protocols and language systems can facilitate efficient collaboration among different roles within an organization, so the differentiation of tools for Service Blueprint increases the using cost of employee and is not conducive to inter-project and inter-departmental communication. Service Blueprint is an important tool used by enterprises to conceptualize and validate services, which can completely display the service process, help enterprises establish standardized service operation procedures, identify and solve problems in the service. With the increasing participants in the service design process, especially the wide participation of the general public, the understandability and engagement of Service Blueprint have become new issues. The complex and abstract expression of Service Blueprint make it difficult for non-specialized designers to fully understand and participate. Therefore, optimizing the form and interaction of Service Blueprint, lowering the threshold of use, and allowing more participants to understand their roles are important. In addition, the Covid-19 pandemic has made multi-person online collaboration an important office mode, which also requires Service Blueprint to be digital that can support collaboration among participants.

Service Blueprint Cannot Be Managed Over a Long Term. As companies growing and consumer needs changing, the types and complexity of the services that companies provide are constantly increasing. This requires a dynamic and long-term management and optimization of services. However, traditional service design and output Service Blueprint focus more on the service design plan at the current state, and it is difficult to carry out long-term tracking and management. Secondly, service validation mechanisms also focus on short-term service experience, such as the service theater method, and ignore the long-term evaluation of the service after launch, which is unable to measure the long-term impact of the service business revenue, customer satisfaction, and so on.

3   The Impact on Enterprises and Design Industry Brought by Digital Transformation

3.1   The Impact on Enterprises Brought by Digital Transformation

Digital transformation has become a core growth strategy for today's companies. A study conducted by IDC, a leading global research organization in 2018 showed that about 67% of the top 1000 companies in the world take digitalization as a core strategy [7]. Digitalization can significantly improve the operational efficiency of enterprises. The key for enterprises is to gain profit by providing competitive products to users. To that end, enterprises must accurately target users, design differentiated products, provide rational pricing and inventory management [8], in which digitalization provides an important support.

Specifically speaking, during the user-targeting stage, digitalization can help companies with accurate user profiling through big data analysis to fully understand the characteristics and needs of target users, which was not an easy thing in the past. In the product design stage, designers can use big data to identify user preferences, get design inspiration and create differentiated products. In addition, digital design tools (e.g., 3D software, VR/AR) have greatly improved design efficiency and product quality. In terms of pricing and inventory management, digitalization enables real-time data monitoring through cloud technology, which optimizes enterprises' supply chain and inventory management and avoids overproduction. Digital transformation has become an important way for enterprises to gain a competitive advantage. Through digital reconstruction of the entire value chain, enterprises can gain in-depth insight into user needs, realize iterative optimization of product design, and intelligent management of the supply chain, which will significantly improve their key competitiveness and efficiency.

3.2 Digital Transformation Impact on Design

Digital transformation is having a huge impact both on business practice and on the design discipline, which is reflected in shifts of design methodologies, processes, and tools.

Design Methodology. Digitalization breaks the linear thinking of traditional design, creating a new environment of fast-paced and high complexity. The design task has changed from a single product building to complex system problem solving. Design is no longer a fragmented individual behavior. Instead, it requires systematic thinking, multiple interests coordinating, and digital resources integrating. This has led to a shift in methodology from "small design" (single product) to "big design" (system and process).

Design Process. In the past, the design cycle, from concept to product launch, was long and the processes were linear and clear. However, digitalization accelerated product iteration. The design process has become increasingly complex, agile and data-driven. Designers need to identify the needs based on user data survey, create and verify digital prototypes quickly, and launch products with engineers. The whole design cycle is greatly reduced.

Tool Application. Digital design software replaces traditional manual drawing. For example, Photoshop can digitalize image processing, CAD can realize the electronicization engineering drawing, Rhino and SolidWorks virtualizes 3D model design, which significantly improves the design efficiency and quality. Besides, a greater number of new tools such as VR/AR are gradually applied.

3.3 Digital Transformation Bring Two Core Advantages to Companies and Design: Efficiency Improvement and Deep User Insight

Compared with traditional tools, digital tools are more efficient and convenient to handle tasks in batches. 3D printing and other rapid manufacturing technologies have significantly reduced the threshold for product prototyping. In terms of collaboration efficiency, the Internet and cloud technology enable a smooth cross-regional and multi-party online collaboration, and the introduction of big data analysis into intelligent decision-making can optimize whole chain management.

What's more, digital transformation has dramatically improved the company's insight into user needs. Traditional design methods are mostly from a product perspective, but digitalization allows companies to understand users. Big data analysis enables a fine user profile building, which can help companies to identify target group characteristics and consumption preferences, and then implement a demand-driven design process. This is totally opposite to the top-down product design approach in the past. The design which based on user insights is more in line with customer needs.

Although China's service design has developed in the Internet era, its digital transformation is still in the primary stage. First of all, service design is an emerging field in interdisciplinary integration. With the digitalization of other related disciplines, service design is gradually showing digital characteristics. However, at present, it is more related to the design tools, such as outputting design results through digital software. In terms of user research and strategy direction, the traditional way is still dominant. Secondly, Service Blueprint, as one of the core design tools, have only realized a formal digital transformation. Drawing through software can improve the efficiency of carrier conversion, but it is only about expression, which does not really improve the efficiency of the design process or user insights through digital methods. The digitalization of Service Blueprint still remains at the art-creating stage, and does not play the role of supporting companies to enhance their core competitiveness.

4   The Role of Middle Platform in Digital Transformation and Related Cases

In the process of business digitalization, the middle platform has been a powerful driving force to the rapid growth of Internet companies over the past few years. The middle platform is a platform that provides shared data, capabilities and services between the business front-end and the technology back-end. A traditional company is usually divided into a front-end and a back-end. The front-end refers to the interface that has direct interaction with users, and the back-end is the internal management operating system of the company. Under such structure, each business function is either relatively isolated or highly duplicated, forming a Information Silo Architecture. The isolation of each business function leads to the duplication of similar business, and the difficulty of collaboration among teams [9], resulting in a waste of internal resources, hindering the progress of research and development, and ultimately affecting the development of business and user experience. The middle platform, on the other hand, is a platform created to better serve the front-end. It provides some reusable and shareable core capabilities, so that the front-end can meet users demands in a more flexible and efficient manner. Meanwhile, the front-end can break down the Information Island within the system, enabling the comprehensive integration of data, technology, business, operations and organization [10], providing an efficient operation mechanism for business development.

The concept of the middle platform was first introduced by the Chinese Internet company Alibaba. In 2015, Jack Ma led a team of Alibaba executives to visit the Dutch mobile gaming company Supercell. Supercell is an independent game development team of five employees who develop games through agile development and rapid iteration, and quickly conduct public beta testing to gain market response. If the market doesn't respond well, they will quickly abandon the product and move on to a new product development. This model has brought Supercell's pre-tax revenue to $1.5 billion, bringing the company great commercial success. Supercell's business model has given Alibaba's leadership the confidence to adjust its organizational structure. By building a big middle platform and a small front-end, various business center of middle platform within Alibaba have been formed [11].

As an operating idea and methodology for the company, middle platform is an organizational innovation. Although no scholars have proposed the origin of middle platform theory, it can be found that its theoretical foundation integrates management and computer science after the analysis of the nature and technical theory of middle platform. From the organizational design perspective, the construction of middle platform adheres to the concept of building a shared service center of a company, which is the same as the idea of service sharing between modules by defining interfaces in modular organization theory. It can be considered that modular organization theory lays the foundation for the positioning of middle platform. In terms of the implementation pathway, the middle platform carries out technical practice through micro-service architecture to realize the service decoupling of business capabilities. The micro-service theory guides the software architecture scheme of the middle platform construction.

Regarding the classification of the middle platform, data middle platform and business middle platform are the two kinds that have been currently recognized. Meanwhile, other middle platform have emerged gradually such as technology middle platform, AI middle platform, organization middle platform, algorithm middle platform, communication middle platform, security middle platform, etc.. Although there are many kinds of middle platforms, their core value is to improve the efficiency of resource utilization and reduce the threshold of innovation by means of platformization [12]. The construction of the middle platform has been successfully practiced in several leading Internet companies and produced a series of typical cases, proving the important role of the middle platform in improving business agility.

4.1 Dual Middle Platform Strategy of Alibaba

At the end of 2015, Alibaba launched the middle platform strategy to build a more innovative and flexible "big middle platform, small front office" organization and business mechanism, which is suitable for the parallel development of multiple businesses. Through the conclusion and accumulation of general capabilities, the Information Silo Architecture and duplicated construction can be avoided. Through the extraction of the general business capabilities, a unified "knowledge base" is built to form the middle platform of the company. Moreover, as long as the middle platform and the business interact with each other according to the standards and planning, all business can share the ability to reduce production costs, improve efficiency and create an internal closed loop.

At this time, China's Internet companies are experiencing the traffic explosion and scaled development. As businesses are becoming more diversified, how to allocate the internal powers and responsibilities in a more reasonable way, invest more resources into the potential business lines and respond to the front-end needs with the support of back end, the middle platform is particularly important. The concept of the middle platform is spreading rapidly in China since then. The middle platform abstracts and processes common technology, products, data, security and other service capabilities, and outputs them through standardized interfaces, realizing efficient collaboration and co-innovation among various business units within the enterprise. It has also incubated several phenomenal products, such as Freshippo and Taobao specials.

The "Dual Middle Platform" (Fig. 2) has brought tremendous value to Alibaba in the five years since it was proposed, solving the inefficiency and waste of resources caused by duplicated construction and tree structure brought by the expansion of Alibaba

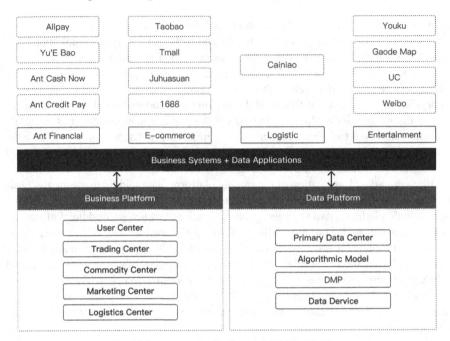

Fig. 2. Structure of Alibaba Dual Middle Platform

business and organization. Alibaba's application of dual middle platform demonstrates the core value of the middle platform in connecting different businesses, supporting business innovation, and improving agility. The middle platform makes it possible to reuse functions in business system, leading to the smooth and efficient communication and collaboration of new businesses. The middle platform provides enterprises with a service-oriented architecture that connects internal and external systems and supports rapid business evolution. These successful cases prove that the middle platform building has become an important way for enterprises to become agile.

4.2 ByteDance Volcano Engine Data Middle Platform

As the fastest growing company in China's Internet in the past decade, ByteDance has established many top apps in a short period of time, such as Tiktok, Xigua Video, Dcar, and TopBuzz, etc. The reason for this is the basic capability brought by the ByteDance's internal Volcano Engine data center. During the initial development of ByteDance, there was not a mature data processing system, nor was there a data middle platform system. Along with the growth of top apps, the data middle platform system was also established.

ByteDance upholds the idea that A/B is a kind of faith, and Aeolus (a data insight platform) is a habit. In 2012, when ByteDance is still at its early stage, they began to apply A/B testing, which is also known as bucket testing, split-run testing, or split testing. These tests are designed to compare the effectiveness of two versions of content, and identify which one is more appealing to visitors or viewers. With a large number of A/B Tests between 2014 and 2018, ByteDance found that having only one result as a reference is not enough to prove the authenticity of the data, and further analysis and supporting judgment of the data is needed. Therefore, they developed the data insight platform Aeolus on the basis of A/B testing, and also formed the ability of data integration, data development, and data governance at this stage.

After 2018, ByteDance embraced its key change. At this time, ByteDance has built its own data middle platform-Volcano Engine to maintain the phenomenal explosion and incubate new businesses (Fig. 3). Because of the involvement of the data middle platform, the rapid access to basic capabilities can be realized besides the new businesses completion. Meanwhile, ByteDance is also actively preparing the "BP team of data middle platform" to realize the BP of the data middle platform (the full name of the BP is Business Partner, which is responsible for connecting the traditional middle and back office with the front-end business). That is, on the basis of centralized organization, the management deployment is unified and execution is distributed into each business.

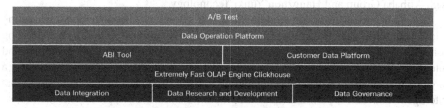

Fig. 3. Structure of ByteDance Volcano Engine

The data middle platform not only enabled ByteDance to gain understanding of data, but also enhanced their understanding of customers. They considered business lines as customers and provide customized needs. After 2020, ByteDance announced that it opened up its Volcano Engine to the public, which also shows that ByteDance middle platform is already serving its internal business well and is starting to think about how to serve its external customers well.

Although more and more enterprises have gone through the process of building to dismantling the middle platform, ByteDance still keeps the middle platform and makes it available to the public, indicting that the middle platform in ByteDance played its role. First of all, the data middle platform BP system can bring excellent support and service to the business continuously; second, the data middle platform built for business value can evaluate the needs of the business, and then provide light tools, and gradually improve more capabilities. The data middle platform needs capacity building periodically. Many companies do not have application scenarios after building the middle platform building, resulting in the useless of the middle platform. Coupled with the lack of organizational safeguards and governance mechanism, middle platform could not be operated sustainably.

In November 2021, Rubo Liang, the new CEO and chairman of ByteDance, announced a new round of organizational adjustments, merging the original business into six business segments, and developing the original general middle platform into an enterprise service business. The idea is to split the big middle platform and merge the small front-end. Changing from the functional structure to a business structure and splitting the middle platform capabilities into business groups indict that the development of the middle platform has moved to a new stage. The original big middle platform and business have been split into small middle platform within each business unit. The middle platform has been further split vertically, making it much lighter and more agile, and closer to the business development.

4.3 Dual Middle Platform Practice by Chang'an Ford

Chang'an Ford Automobile Co., Ltd. was founded in 2001. When the automobile industry experienced downward development in 2018, Ford faced multiple difficulties such as failed marketing model, relatively backward level of informationization, insufficient consumer insights, and fragmentation of internal systems. In order to realize the transformation, Chang'an Ford decided to introduce the middle platform system to reconstruct its marketing model. Against this background, Chang'an Ford entered into a partnership with Alibaba Group and Hangzhou Yunxi Technology.

The three parties utilize the middle platform technology to build a digital marketing middle platform, which can provide Chang'an Ford with new data-driven marketing solutions, WeChat marketing solutions, and dealer marketing campaign solutions, and integrate all required resources. The new platform is based on a public cloud and a large middle platform architecture, including a business service middle platform and an intelligent data middle platform (dual middle platform). In the first phase of construction, a total of eight shared service centers are planned to meet the platform's basic data interconnection requirements (Fig. 4).

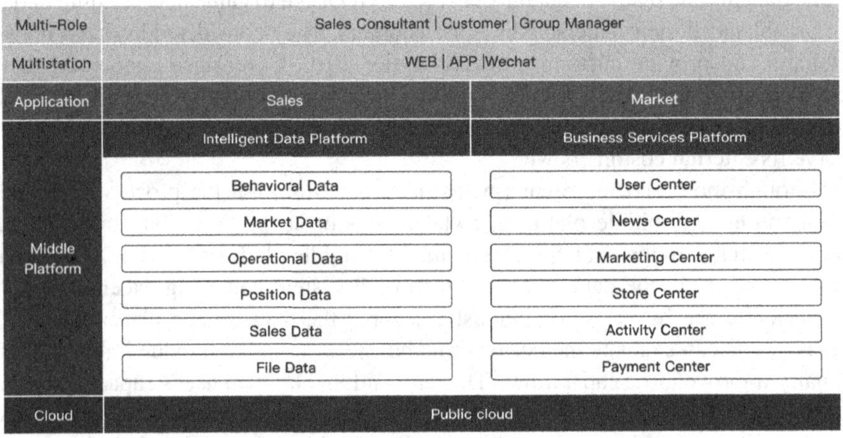

Multi–Role	Sales Consultant | Customer | Group Manager	
Multistation	WEB | APP |Wechat	
Application	Sales	Market
Middle Platform	Intelligent Data Platform	Business Services Platform
	Behavioral Data	User Center
	Market Data	News Center
	Operational Data	Marketing Center
	Position Data	Store Center
	Sales Data	Activity Center
	File Data	Payment Center
Cloud	Public cloud	

Fig. 4. Structure of Ford's Dual Middle Platform

On the user side, the platform has built Chang'an Ford's WeChat Mall "Ford Mall". The functions developed in the first development phase include model inquiry, special car sales, event registration and drive testing booking. Through the deep integration with the capabilities of the middle platform, the WeChat Mall realized the seamless connection of the entire vehicle selling process. This provided a solid foundation for Chang'an Ford to carry out marketing events with deeper user interaction. The digital middle platform building helped Chang'an Ford realize the transformation and upgrading of its marketing model and establish a new retail marketing system that is more intelligent and future-oriented. The digitalized operation empowered by the middle platform will continue to unleash the growth momentum and promote Chang'an Ford's production and sales performance.

4.4 Data Middle Platform Building of R&F Group

Founded in 1994, after more than 20 years of rapid development, R&F Group has grown into a leading comprehensive company in real estate, hotel, commerce, culture and tourism, Internet and other fields. As early as 2015, R&F began the exploration and practice of digital transformation. For example, its self-developed "Self-Community" app provides owners and tenants with a convenient experience by providing services such as household payment, bill payment, parking and community interaction services. The scale of registered users has exceeded 1 million. Against the backdrop of multi-industry development, R&F will promote digital transformation in the following four aspects: a) Platform building. Build a group-level data middle platform and improve data management and analysis capabilities quickly. b) Comprehensive integration. To establish a unified data connection model on the collecting, cleaning and modeling data of different businesses. c) Unified service. Different business data are converged into the big data platform, and services are provided through standard interfaces to realize data sharing and realization. d) Enabling operations. Based on the data middle platform, the data analysis output is fully applied to business operations.

The customer information collected through the data middle platform can be used to analyze the purchasing willingness, providing data support for the sales team's negotiations and conversions. It can also integrate business data from real estate, hotels and football to conduct multi-dimensional analysis and develop targeted marketing strategies. In addition, the establishment of a labeling system for customers, projects, and property consultants helps to improve the refinement of operations. In addition, R&F has launched the solution of "Digital Dual Middle Platform + Digital Marketing Cloud + Operation Service", which builds up the middle platform and operation capability of real estate companies. This can not only help companies with the operation of household stock, but also support the incremental development, realizing a synergy of "stock operation" and "incremental development". It can be seen that the introduction of the digital intelligence middle platform enabled R&F Group to realize the transformation from a "data island" to a "data asset", unleashing the value of data and promoting business collaboration and innovation. The middle platform will also continue to improve R&F's capabilities in customer operation, business operation, and new business incubation, driving R&F's business transformation and the Group's value enhancement.

4.5 Middle Platform Building of BESTORE

As a leading snack company in China, BESTORE's business gained rapid development with its strategic positioning of high-end snacks and a series of brand upgrades. During the 2020 Double 11 (Refers to the large-scale promotional activities of online shopping platforms in China on November 11 every year), BESTORE's omni-channel sales reached 560 million yuan, a significant increase from last year's 400 million yuan. There are several sets of data on customers needs attention. BESTORE Tmall Double 11 card members exceeded 11.3 million, brand awareness rate increased from 32% to 53% with 328,000 new members and 2.39 million times of services for the old users. Behind these achievements, the establishment of the middle platform digital solution should not be ignored.

With the rapid expansion of BESTORE sales network, how to manage tens of millions of members and build a unified digital operation system has become a top priority. Thus, based on the core technology of "business + data" dual middle platform, and innovative membership management and intelligent marketing products, BESTORE has built a new generation of membership middle platform to create a "marketing hub" for Double 11 to better interact with users and enhance the shopping experience.

In September 2023, after the membership platform upgrading, BESTORE realized the efficient operation and unified management of 80 million members across all channels through membership management system. User data collected from various channels are stored and managed in a unified way, forming a company-level "data reservoir". Different engines are used for integration and analysis, then the members labeling and user profile are generated automatically. Digging out the value from massive data and gaining insights to carry out targeted marketing for old customers with strong purchasing intention. The innovation value of the refined, non-stop and digitally-supported member middle platform has been fully demonstrated: a) Faster speed. Based on the middle platform, BESTORE realizes the fastest formulation of million-level marketing strategies within one hour, with all-day response and full coverage, and the reaching rate is 99.7%. The information of Double 11 will be delivered to the members faster, helping the brand to cover the users widely in advance. b) More accurate targeting. In the past, manual labeling was relatively sloppy, but with big data, BESTORE can segment user groups in unlimited dimensions, realizing tailored marketing to different users, reaching users more accurately, and improving the conversion rate. Meanwhile, through OneID technology, the same user in different channels can be recognized, thus avoiding the duplicate pushing and improving the customer experience. c) Better experience. In the past, membership data among multiple systems was isolated, and their card points, card coupons and other benefits were not shared nor connected. At present, the middle platform can enable the inter-connectivity of information, unified management, and automatic allocation of rights and benefits, which significantly improve member's satisfaction.

4.6 Case Summary

The above cases demonstrate that the middle platform can help enterprises handle complex business and data, reduce internal communication costs, improve efficiency, and better serve innovation. Middle platform not only plays an important role in the development of Internet enterprises, but also enables the development of traditional physical enterprises, which indicates that the idea of middle platform can be more agile and applicable to different categories. We can use the advantages of the middle platform to help the Service Blueprint establish digitalization, so that the Service Blueprint can have better usability and scalability, and better meet the service development needs of the Internet era.

5 The Service Blueprint Building Based on the Digitalization and Componentization

Service Blueprint have two major problems in a long-term: first, the form and components are not unified, resulting in increased communication costs between different users and reduced working efficiency; second, Service Blueprint are static, and designers only focus on the short-term results, instead of analyzing users in a deep way. The digital transformation has the advantages of efficiency improvement and in-depth user insight gaining.

Therefore, this study intends to explore how to overcome the above deficiencies of Service Blueprint by digital means. On the one hand, to prove the possibility of service design componentization through atomic design theory, enabling consistency in the internal design collaboration. In addition, through the foundation of componentization, a service middle platform for cross-departmental cooperation is established, which can solve the efficiency obstacles arising from external collaboration of service design and reduce the cost of multi-party use. On the other hand, digital technology such as big data analysis is used to continuously deepen the understanding of user needs, which provides inputs to the design as a means of continuous evaluation (Fig. 5).

Fig. 5. Goals of digitalized Service Blueprint

5.1 The Service Blueprint Componentization Based on Atomic Design

Atomic Design is widely used in user interface design, and its core concept is to modularize and hierarchize interface components. First proposed by Brad Frost, Atomic Design is about decomposing the interface components according to different granularity, forming a clear hierarchical component system. In this system, the atom is the smallest unit of the component, such as buttons, text boxes, icons, etc.. Through the combination of atoms, molecules can form smaller components such as the searching box component. Organism is larger, through the combination of a variety of molecules, a more complex module is formed, such as the navigation bar, card sets, and so on. On this basis, templates determine the layout and content structure of multiple tissue. The page is filled with the actual content and a complete user interface is formulated. Through this bottom-up layering approach, designers can build a systematic component pool, improve component reusability, and make interface design more consistent. It also facilitates collaboration and communication between design teams. Therefore, atomic design has become one of the important methodologies in the field of interface design. Starting from the concept of atomic design, service design can also adopt a layered and componentized approach to modularize the service process and improve the systematicity and reusability of the design (Fig. 6).

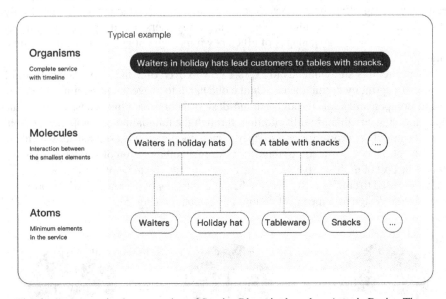

Fig. 6. Componentized construction of Service Blueprint based on Atomic Design Theory

Atoms. The basic elements in a service can be viewed as atoms, such as people, equipment, space, and touch points. Atoms are the smallest independent units. At this stage, the elements have not yet interacted or formed relationships with each other. Triggered from the enterprise resources, these atoms correspond to the various types of resources that the enterprise already has or plans to deploy, such as waiters, holiday hats, tables, snacks, and other people or items, which are still existed as discrete atoms, and have not yet been combined and used. Abstracting service elements into atoms is the first step of componentized service design, which provides the base unit for service assembly and innovation in the enterprise.

Molecules. On the basis of the atomic level, multiple atoms can be combined to form service components according to functional requirements, which is equivalent to the "molecules" in atomic design. For example, a waiter with a specific holiday hat or a table with snacks are simple combinations of service components at the atomic level. These components form a specific behavior or subject matter that provides a particular service, and they are often derived from interactions and combinations of atoms. A service component incorporates multiple atomic elements to realize a more complex service function.

Organisms. Introducing the concept of time between service components enables the stringing of static components, which can form a complete service. A complete service is like a story, a stage play that happens over time. Service components cannot make up a complete service due to the lack of choreography of time. Introducing time into the two service components, the waiter in the holiday hat and the table with the snacks, and adding the object to be served, the customer, generates a complete service: the waiter in the holiday hat takes the customer to the table with snacks.

Through this layered approach, complex service designs can be systematized and modularized. Designers can reuse service components, and different modules are easier to understand and collaborate with each other. Users can standardize the definition and description of service elements among internal designers based on this guideline, enabling the establishment of a unified language system within the design. This is conducive to the design quality improvement and the scalability and continuous optimization of the design.

By analyzing the service flow, reusable business functions are identified and extracted into common business components. These extracted business functions are encapsulated and constructed to form service component products that can be deployed and used independently. Meanwhile, it is supposed to define the access specifications for each service component so that it can be flexibly accessed. In the process of service design, replace the original business function with counterpart component. In the replacement process, attention should be paid to managing the dependencies between components to avoid strong coupling and ensure the flexibility. By introducing this componentized service implementation, Service Blueprint can achieve more agile process iteration and innovation, which can respond to the changing requirements in a better way.

5.2 Service Blueprint Construction Based on Componentized Middle-Stage

The middle platform plays an important role both in the Internet and in the physical industry, helping companies centralize and optimize the allocation of resources. Through the abstract componentization of business management and data, the middle platform realizes the reusability and configurable collocation of resources, reduces work duplication, and improves efficiency. After the componentization of Service Blueprint, it can effectively solve the inconsistent expression. However, in order to realize the effective reuse of service resources, this is not enough. It is also necessary to build the middle stage system(the middle-stage, which is located between the front-stage and the back-stage) of service design on the basis of the componentization and manage it in an unified way to play the role of optimized allocation of resources. The essence of service design also lies in the recombination and interaction of existing resources to create new service value. After component disassembly based on atomic design theory, service elements can be used as reusable "building blocks" that can be flexibly combined according to demand and generate personalized services efficiently, which is highly compatible with the concept of middle stage. For example, for different festivals in the same restaurant, the core service process and service staff scenarios can be reused. The middle-stage can abstract and summarize these core service components, and then quickly combine them into feasible services by adjusting only the components such as decorations, service language, and other elements according to different festivals. In the case of multi-brand operation, the middle stage can also realize that different brands share the same service set, replacing only some visual elements according to brand positioning, which can significantly reduce design costs and improve efficiency.

The middle-stage of a Service Blueprint includes three aspects: the Service Platform(SP), the Business Platform(BP), and the Data Platform(DP) (Fig. 7). The SP forms a library of reusable service components by componentizing and abstracting existing resources so that designers can perform rapid assembly, improve design efficiency, and reduce work duplication. The BP can provide business support that is closely related to service design, such as marketing operations, channel management, and other capabilities, which enables better integration of design output into enterprise business requirements. The DP provides basic data collection, processing, analysis and modeling capabilities, which provide data support for conducting refined user research and service design decisions.

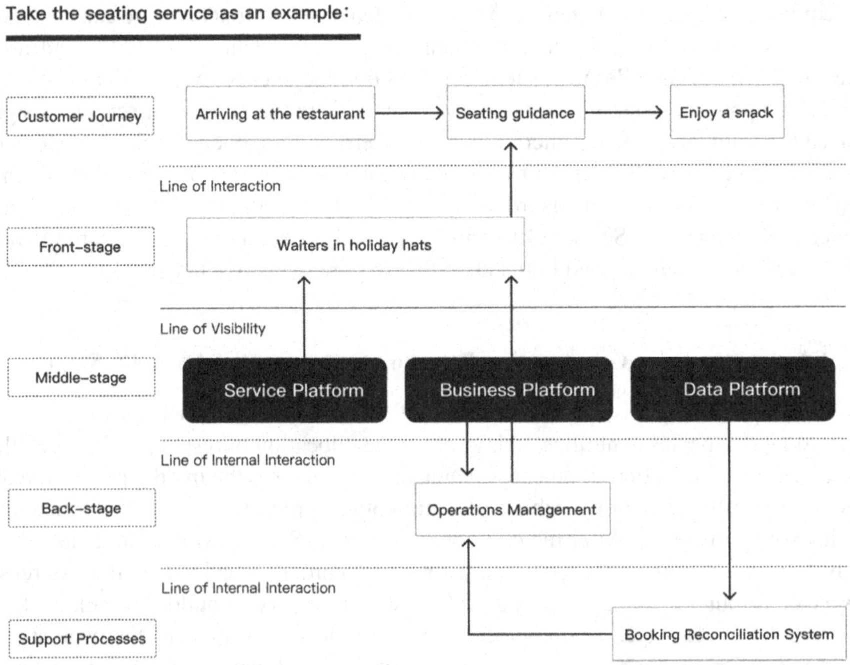

Take the seating service as an example:

Fig. 7. Service Blueprint with middle-stage added

In specific applications, the Service Blueprint does not necessarily have to include all three types of middle platform (service, business, and data) at the same time. Instead, middle-stage should be introduced selectively according to the actual design requirements. For example, only the light optimization of existing service processes needs the establishment of service middle-stage, and process improvement can be accomplished through component rearrangement (Fig. 8). When designing complex cross-departmental services, it may be necessary to introduce a BP to provide support, and to analyze requirements and evaluate results through a DP. If we take the example of the service that "guides customers with holiday hats wearing and provides snacks" mentioned in the previous section, we can find that festivals and holidays are a regular business of the restaurant. Therefore, by componentizing this service function in advance, it can be directly used in the design process without the need to perform the design all over again. In addition, if the new service process does not introduce a new system or department, it can also be supported by allocating existing business processes and departments directly from the BP.

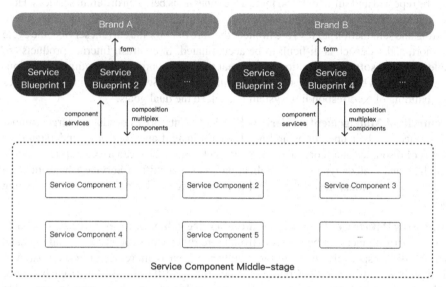

Fig. 8. Different service processes use the componentized service middle-stage

It is worth noting that the value of the middle stage is not limited to supporting Service Blueprint. Through digitalization, it is also possible to continuously monitor the usage data of the middle stage and assess the value contribution of different components. For example, analyzing which service components are more frequently utilized, which data metrics are more effective, and so on. This can be fed back to managers, helping them to dynamically adjust and optimize the middle stage system to ensure the maximum value brought by the middle stage.

Traditional service design tends to treat different services in isolation, and build all required elements from scratch for every service, ignoring the potential reuse value between service modules. This is particularly detrimental when the market is changing fast, as blank designs with a large number of duplicated modules not only reduce design efficiency, but also make it difficult to respond quickly to changing requirements. The construction of service middle stage can improve design resuability and agility. More importantly, the middle stage continues to conclude and enriches the component library, so that the enterprise service design capabilities can upgrade continuously, and gain advantages in fierce competition. During the downward economic status, the advantages of the middle stage become more prominent. Enterprises are more likely to look for innovation from existing resources and capabilities rather than investing heavily in developing new service modules.

5.3 Dynamic Service Management and Monitoring Based on Big Data

The traditional Service Blueprint are mainly used as a tool for designers to express single service scenario by visualizing the overall picture of a particular service, such as the service flow of a festival event in seconds. However, in reality, elements of services can be repeated and sufficient, and there are connections between different services. How do you assess the value of recombining services? Traditional practices such as prototype testing and satisfaction surveys are limited: they are only for the current service, the cycle is short, and feedback is difficult to be accumulated. In contrast, Internet products are able to update software operation data in real time and continuously optimize decision-making through big data analysis, so the digitalization of Service Blueprint also requires the building of a corresponding system to achieve the dual goals.

Centralized Management of Various Services. Enterprises produce a large number of services in their operations and need overall insight and control to understand the status of resources and reorganize the various elements. This can avoid duplication and conflicts and realize synergy. Digitalization enables a shift in Service Blueprint from expressing individual designs to a tool for managing service portfolios on an ongoing basis.

Utilize Big Data to Continuously Monitor Service Value. In addition to user feedback, service performance can be assessed from more dimensions such as financial data and service data, especially the long-term impact, which is more scientific compared to a single satisfaction survey. Continuous monitoring of the data status of each service helps designers to better understand customer needs and corporate goals. By analyzing the service-related indicators through big data, we can provide a more scientific basis for design decisions. This digital transformation is an inevitable trend for the further development of Service Blueprint.

6 Conclusion

As an important visual expression tool for service design, Service Blueprint has undergone many rounds of iteration and optimization over the past forty years. However, against the backdrop of fierce market, its application had certain problems, including: different versions and users lead to inconsistency in the form of expression and components, increasing the cost of communication within the enterprise; it is only for a single service, and the static characteristics lead to the impossibility of real-time monitoring of the service effect. Digital transformation provides improvement ideas for optimizing Service Blueprint, mainly in terms of enhancing efficiency and continuous monitoring.

This research firstly adopts atomic design theory to realize the atomized splitting and modularization of Service Blueprint elements to form reusable components. At the same time, it establishes specifications for the componentized elements and unifies the internal design language system, which improves the communication efficiency. Secondly, building the service middle stage through componentization enables the circulation and reuse of service components between different departments within the enterprise. This can reduce duplication of work and improve efficiency. Meanwhile, the componentized middle stage supports multi-brand differentiated combinations, which can quickly derive personalized services, significantly improve design efficiency and reduce design costs. Finally, a digital platform for service detection and management is constructed. It helps decision makers on overall control and resource deployment, realizing the dynamic adjustment and optimization of services. Through the digital transformation of Service Blueprint, this study provides an optimized service design innovation framework, which solves the pain points of low reuse rate of service components and weak dynamic detection capability, improving the efficiency and sensitivity of enterprise service design, and thus assisting enterprises to gain a competitive advantage in complex environments.

References

1. Xinhua News Agency: National bureau of statistics: the average annual contribution rate of the added value of the tertiary industry to economic growth has reached 55.6% over the past decade (2022). https://www.gov.cn/xinwen/2022-09/28/content_5713452.htm. Accessed 22 Jan 2024
2. Zhan, W.: Research and practice of service design based on service blueprint and design experience. Packaging Eng. **36**(12), 41–44+53 (2015)
3. Shostack, G.L.: Design service that deliver. Harv. Bus. Rev. **62**(1), 133–139 (1984)
4. Jun, F.: Design, Application, and Development of Service Blueprint. Science Press, Beijing (2023)
5. Kingman-Brundage, J.: Technology, design and service quality. Int. J. Serv. Ind. Manag. **2**(3), 47–59 (1991)
6. Valarie, A.Z., et al.: Services Marketing. Machinery Industry Press, Beijing (2002)
7. Dongmei, C., et al.: Digitalization and strategic management theory: review, challenges, and prospects. Manage. World. **36**(5), 220–236+20 (2020)
8. Jian, C., et al.: From empowering to enabling: enterprise operations management in the digital environment. Manage. World. **36**(2), 117–128+222 (2020)
9. Yinghui, L., et al.: Middle platform strategy and architecture design of different enterprises in digital transformation. Telecommun. Sci. **36**(7), 126–135 (2020)
10. Tian, T., Ye, C.: Preliminary exploration of middle platform management in the construction of convergent media. News Enthusiasts. **5**, 42–44 (2023)
11. Yun, L., Ruixuan, L.: Exploration of middle platform architecture system in telecom operators. Telecommun. Eng. Technol. Stand. **33**(11), 13–19+26 (2020)
12. Cong, Z., et al.: Research on the construction path and practice of middle platform in university libraries. Library Work Res. **10**, 5–12 (2022)

Design of Sustainable Fashion APP Based on Perceived Value Theory - Taking "Eco Echo" as an Example

Bailu Guo, Xiaolei Mi, and Wenjing Li[✉]

Art and Design Academy, Beijing City University, Beijing, China
13521505946@163.com

Abstract. While the fashion industry is currently paying increasing attention to environmental pollution, the attention of "Generation Z" consumers to sustainable fashion has not yet reached a high level. Although they vaguely believe that sustainable fashion should be a choice direction of daily consumption, they haven't actually implemented it in their lives, or clearly understand the environmental impact brought by consumption behavior. Based on the theory of perceived value, this study constructs a sustainable fashion application prototype named "Eco Echo". It aims to popularize the knowledge of sustainable fashion to "Generation Z" consumers while guiding them to make environmentally friendly fashion consumption choices and behaviors, thus narrowing the "green gap" in the field of sustainable fashion. Each functional module in "Eco Echo" has specific perceived value attributes, such as green value, social value, educational value, emotional value, and functional value. Users will increase the corresponding points in each module operation, and the points can then be used to unlock the corresponding honor certificate level. In addition to giving users a sense of pride, these certificates will also provide some material benefits. In the final prototype testing stage, the "Eco Echo" application has also been recognized by many consumers. In particular, the tester showed a great deal of enthusiasm by using the function of clothing environmental protection data generated by a virtual device. The educational value, which is also the main focus of our subsequent development, is embodied by this function. We believe that consumers' perceived value in the field of sustainable fashion will help to promote their behavior changes, and "Eco Echo" will contribute to narrowing the "green gap". The limitation of this study is that our project has only developed a prototype and has yet to be put into use in the market. In the future, we intend to establish contact with professional organizations, environmental protection agencies, or industrial partners in related fields in order to gain more in-depth industry opinions and support in putting the prototype into the actual market so that usage data can be gathered and feedback can be given.

Keywords: APP design · Sustainable fashion · Perceived value · Generation Z · Sustainable consumption

A. Marcus et al. (Eds.): HCII 2024, LNCS 14716, pp. 326–337, 2024.
https://doi.org/10.1007/978-3-031-61362-3_23

1 Introduction

When we initially explored the field of sustainable research, we found a lot of connections between environmental pollution and the fashion industry. Even though researchers in the field of sustainability have a clear understanding of these connections, do consumers of "Generation Z", who are similar to us, have the same level of understanding? With such questions, we carried out extensive data research, and the findings confirmed our conjecture. In fact, although the majority of consumers of "Generation Z" realize the importance of environmental protection consumption, they are still unsure about sustainable fashion. There is a gap between the importance of sustainability and actual environmental protection behavior because they are not fully aware of the influence of their consumption behavior on the environment. This phenomenon is called the "green gap" in the field of sustainable research.

Given that "Generation Z" will become the main force of social consumption in the future, their consumption orientation will drive the development trend of future consumption patterns. Therefore, at the consumer level. it is crucial to guide the "Generation Z" to raise their awareness of environmental protection and shape their consumption habits, so as to promote the development of sustainable fashion. To narrow the "green gap" in sustainable fashion, we attempt to solve it by designing applications.

2 Design Goal

2.1 The Core Issues to Be Solved

For the purpose of resolving the issue of the "'green gap" in the field of sustainable fashion, we made a quantitative and qualitative study on the consumer groups of "Generation Z". An application prototype named "Eco Echo" was then developed based on the theory of perceived value. It aims to spread the knowledge of sustainable fashion to consumers of "Generation Z" and guide them to make fashion consumption and behavior that is beneficial to the environment.

2.2 Target User

We have positioned the target users of the application in the "Generation Z" fashion consumer group. The term "Generation Z" is defined differently by different people, and there is no unified year range. In 2017, the word "Generation Z" was officially included in the Oxford Dictionary, and a detailed definition was provided, defining it as a young person born between 1995 and 20091. Yip T2 and PETERSON H3's research results confirm that "Generation Z" consumers like to spend money in food institutions and fashion clothing stores. China Tencent found that "Generation Z" is more inclined to consume the related products of enterprises with public welfare and social responsibility when gaining insight into the consumption tendency of these young people today as well as in the future. As a very large consumer group, it has unlimited consumption potential.

2.3 Data Investigation

We surveyed 200 people of "Generation Z" from some first-tier cities in China, as illustrated in Fig. 1. The data reveals that 44% of consumers are very vague about the concept of sustainable fashion, while 24% of consumers don't even understand the relationship between the fashion industry and environmental pollution. Based on this data, we believe that spreading the knowledge of sustainable fashion to the "Generation Z" is imperative, which is also reflected in our later APP construction. When purchasing fashion items, over 79% of people want to be told by enterprises whether this product is environmentally friendly and sustainable. This shows that even if more than half of "Generation Z" consumers are vague about the concept of sustainable fashion, or even know little about it, the vast majority of consumers are still willing to know whether the goods they buy are environmentally friendly. We require that every commodity sold in "Eco Echo" should show its own sustainable attributes. The system will grade it and show it to users in the form of icons. When a fashionable product is environmentally friendly, 90% of people are willing to pay extra money. About 25% of this amount is in 1–5 RMB, 49% in 5–10 RMB, and women make up slightly more than men in the 5–10 RMB category. This demonstrates that the majority of people are willing to pay more for products or services with environmental protection attributes, but this amount must be within a certain range. Based on this data, we also provide a certain amount of material rewards to help direct environmental consumption and behavior. When asked if they want to get an official certificate to reward their environmental protection behavior when buying sustainable fashion goods, 79% of people gave a positive answer, and 78% of these people want to sign the certificate, indicating that many people want to be rewarded with honor. All behavior in every "Eco Echo" module can be exchanged for points, which can then be used to unlock different grades of honorary certificates. Moreover, different grades of certificates can be exchanged for different material benefits.

We have also constructed user portraits of "Generation Z" consumers in three age stages, as shown in Fig. 2. They represent the "Generation Z" people in high school, college, and working stages respectively.

2.4 Perceived Value Theory

The application of "Eco Echo" is based on the theory of perceived value. Since the publication of Silent Spring in 1962, environmental protection has attracted public attention. Up to now, "fast fashion" has brought a lot of waste of resources and environmental pollution, which has aroused the reflection of fashion industry and consumers.Bridging the "green gap" in sustainable fashion has become particularly important. Many previous studies have confirmed the promotion of perceived value to sustainable fashion. Jung Park4 and Lee Eun-jung have demonstrated that perceived value will affect purchase intention when purchasing environmentally-friendly fashion products. The research of SN Khan5 and M Mohsin shows that functional value and emotional value have a major influence on consumers' attitudes towards environmental protection products. The research of Jeong6 and others confirmed the moderating effect of consumer perceived value on sustainable fashion and purchase intention. According to the research

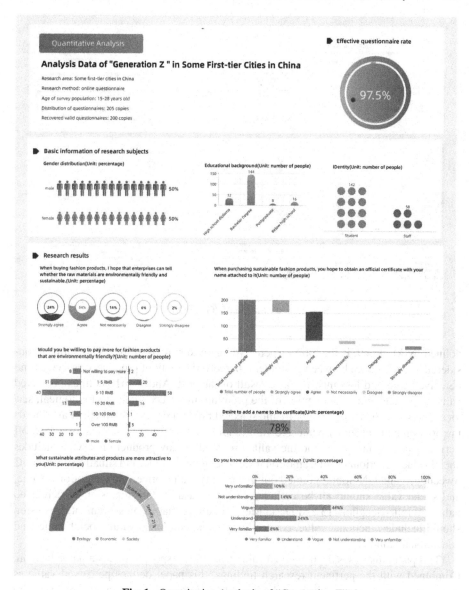

Fig. 1. Quantitative Analysis of "Generation Z"

of Nupur Arora7 and Parul Manchanda, there is a strong correlation between green perceived value and the positive attitude and purchase intention of sustainable clothing.

As Table 1 displays, different scholars have different definitions and measurement dimensions of consumer perceived value. Zeithaml8 believes that consumer perceived value is the overall evaluation of perceived product utility made by consumers based on gains (i.e., perceived benefits) and losses (i.e., perceived costs). Perceived value, as

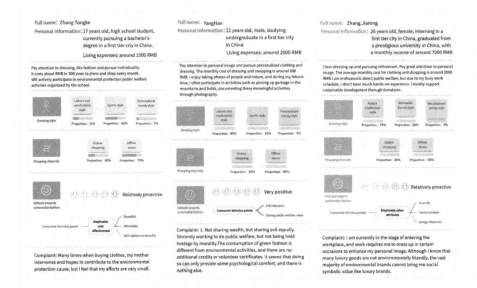

Fig. 2. User Profile of "Generation Z"

defined by Monroe9, is the ratio of perceived gain to perceived loss. This ratio is considered as the balance between customers' perceived benefit of products or services and perceived gain and loss incurred as a result of the cost. Anderson10 defines perceived value as the customer's perception of the premium in the economic, technological, service, and social benefits brought by the selected product or service. Sheth et al11 holds the opinion that consumer perceived value should not be simply regarded as a trade-off between quality and price, and the value provided by any product or service includes social value, functional value, emotional value, cognitive value, and situational value. JC Sweeney12 and GN Soutar pointed out that quality value, price value, emotional value, and social value should all be included in the measurement dimension of perceived value. Aurelio Scaglione13 and Daria Mendol believe that its measurement dimension should include functional value, convenience value, emotional value, social value, and educational value.

This paper discusses the perceived value from the perspective of sustainable fashion. Combined with the pertinent research findings, this paper defines perceived value as the comprehensive comparison of the benefits and costs that consumers receive from fashion products or services. We believe that the measurement dimensions of perceived value should include green value, social value, educational value, emotional value, and functional value, and their proportions are indicated in Fig. 3.

Table 1. Definition and Dividing Dimensions of Perceived Value by Some Scholars

Author	Define
Zeithaml	consumer perceived value is the overall evaluation of perceived product utility made by consumers based on gains (i.e., perceived benefits) and losses (i.e., perceived costs)
Monroe	Perceived value is the ratio of perceived gain to perceived loss. This ratio is considered as the balance between customers' perceived benefit of products or services and perceived gain and loss incurred as a result of the cost
Anderson	perceived value as the customer's perception of the premium in the economic, technological, service, and social benefits brought by the selected product or service
Author	Dividing dimensions
Shethet al	social value, functional value, emotional value, cognitive value, and situational value
JC Sweeney and GN Soutar	quality value, price value, emotional value, social value
Aurelio Scaglione and Daria Mendol	functional value, convenience value, emotional value, social value, educational value

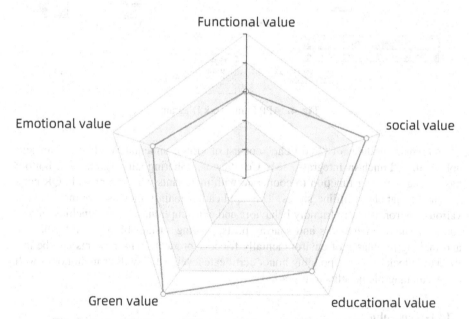

Fig. 3. Radar Distribution of Perceived Value in the Sustainable Fashion Field

3 Build the "Eco Echo" Application

The development of sustainable application programs and the functions assigned to them have a positive effect on guiding people's sustainable consciousness and behavior. First, we described the perceived value in the field of sustainable fashion, and then based on the theory of perceived value, we built the prototype of the "Eco Echo" application with JsDesign software. The overall framework of the APP is depicted in Fig. 4 and the interface is shown in Fig. 5.

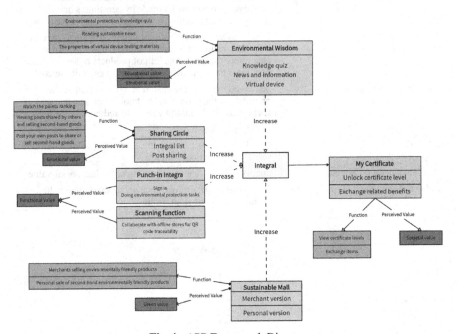

Fig. 4. APP Framework Diagram

The main modules of "Eco Echo" consist of «Environmental Wisdom», «Sustainable Mall", "Punch-in Integral», «My Certificate", "Sharing Circle", etc. The bottom has a code scanning function to cooperate with merchants who can provide QR code traceability labels in offline stores. This application mainly increases points through various environmentally friendly behaviors and consumption, such as punching in personal sustainable behaviors and sharing posts, reading sustainable news information, and making purchases of environmentally friendly products. These points can be utilized to unlock the corresponding honor certificate level, which will bring honor as well as certain tangible benefits to users.

3.1 Green Value

The "Sustainable Mall" module's primary purpose is to sell environmentally friendly goods, which are divided into merchant versions and personal versions. The merchant version is provided to merchants with environmentally-friendly products, and merchants can sell their own environmentally-friendly products in the mall.Personal edition is provided to individual users who need to sell environmental protection products second-hand, in order to cut down on waste and make clothing or other products recyclable. The green value is this module's most prominent feature. Green value was first put forward

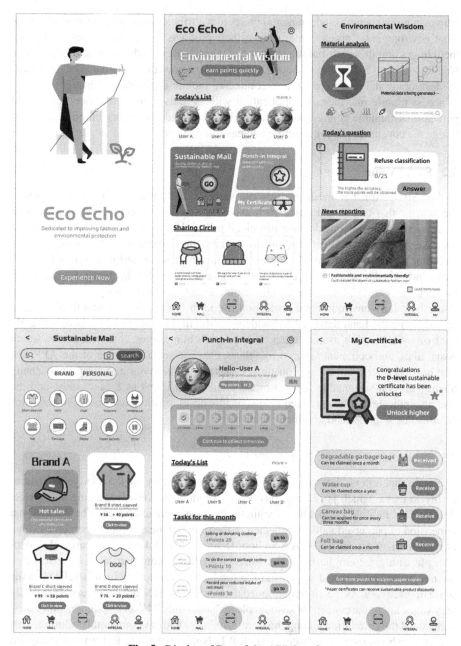

Fig. 5. Display of Part of the APP Interface

by Yu-Shan Chen14, and it was defined as "consumers' overall evaluation of the net income of products or services based on their environmental aspirations, sustainable expectations and green demand". In the "Sustainable Mall", businesses and individuals who own products with environmental protection attributes are required to clearly show what environmental protection attributes their products have. The system will assist them in grading these attributes and showing them to users in the form of icons. Just as Nell Rasmussen15 let millennial consumers know the power of sustainable development by developing the prototype of an e-commerce mobile application. Through an easy-to-access mobile interface, the application will serve as a guide for users looking to purchase sustainable clothes. Additionally, it will provide necessary brand research to bridge the consumer gap with simple and easy-to-consume output.

3.2 Social Value

In the "My Certificate" module, users can view the current certificate level as well as the benefits that can be redeemed with this certificate. This module focuses on social value, which can be considered a perceived utility that is associated with positive or negative stereotyped populations, and socio-economic and cultural ethics groups16. As an honor, the certificate has a certain symbolic significance, and it is a manifestation of the individual's pursuit of social recognition and respect for the group. Furthermore, the "Sharing Circle" module is also the embodiment of social value. In this, users can share their daily environmental protection life in the form of posts, and they can also sell their second-hand sustainable goods in posts. In this interface, users can directly click on other people's avatars, enter other people's homepages, chat with others, watch posts, likes, and comments shared by others, etc. The social function of the APP will also have a positive impact on consumers' sustainable behavior and awareness. Zheng Shen17 takes a sustainable fashion brand named OnTheList as a case study, and the findings indicate that texts related to sustainable development have a positive influence on consumers' praise and comment behavior.

3.3 Educational Value

The main function of "Environmental Wisdom" is to convey the knowledge of sustainability to users, which is realized through two functions: knowledge quiz and virtual device. This module's educational value is its most notable feature. The educational dimension of perceived value is reflected in the research measuring the perceived value of rural tourism conducted by A Scaglione18 and D Mendola. The educational dimension places a great emphasis on the value created by taking part in an experience or the new knowledge gained by consuming products or services, which is related to the sense of discovery. As the aforementioned data indicates, 44% of consumers are actually very vague about the concept of sustainable fashion, while 24% of consumers don't even understand the correlation among the fashion industry and environmental pollution. This module can bring users new discoveries. T. P. L. Nghiem19 and L. R. Carrasco compiled 32 sustainable consumption applications in order to assess their transparency, authority, and whether consumers can understand the connection between consumption and biodiversity impact, and there is almost no connection between consumption and biodiversity protection. For the purpose of addressing these disadvantages, we set up a virtual device in the module of "Environmental Protection Wisdom", and we drag the materials used in commodities into this device, which can display the pollution or beneficial impact of materials per square centimeter on the environment. Provide users with an intuitive experience through data, as this can greatly aid in the dissemination of environmental protection knowledge and let users realize the relationship between buying clothes and sustainable development.

3.4 Emotional Value

Emotional value refers to the utility of customer feelings or emotional state evoked by products or services. Emotional states triggered by mobile phone applications, such as pleasure and empathy, can positively impact their perceived value20. The function of news propaganda in the module of "Environmental Wisdom" can not only play an educational role in environmental propaganda for users but also pique their emotional affinity and empathy for nature. When constructing user portraits based on survey data, it is found that "Generation Z" consumers are more receptive to "positive" news than "negative" news. "Positive" here refers to the environmental benefits brought by sustainable fashion actions. For instance, a school has set an example of recycling old clothes. These clothes reduce 3.6 kg of carbon dioxide emissions per kilogram, save 6,000 L of water, and reduce the use of 0.3 kg of chemical fertilizers and 0.2 kg of pesticides. This kind of positive publicity makes consumers feel proud. Moreover, "negative" news denotes the negative impact of behavior on the environment. For example, how many creatures in the ocean are dying because of excessive human pollution. Although moral emotion is the key factor affecting sustainable behavior, some "Generation Z" consumers hold different views. They think: "I didn't share the wealth; why should I share the sin equally?" They question that their water-saving behavior in the past year may not be able to offset the amount of water consumed by extravagant wasters in one second. "Negative" news is seen by many "Generation Z" consumers as a moral abduction. Therefore, in news propaganda, if we want to touch consumers in an emotional way, we must grasp the scale reasonably.

3.5 Functional Value

The function value of the APP is mainly experienced by the "Punch-in Integral" and the code scanning function at the bottom. Users who successfully complete the current task and sign in daily will get corresponding points from the "Punch-in Integral" module. The code scanning function is used in conjunction with some offline stores. Stores need to provide two-dimensional code traceability labels of products and use "Eco Echo" to check the origin, production, and other environmental attributes of goods. In addition, research into the traceability function of sustainable goods is worthwhile since it can increase trust in products. Strähle J21 and Gräff C discusses the relationship between consumers' perception of sustainability and the application of two-dimensional code in stores, and consumers prefer applications that give two-dimensional code functions. Providing transparent information via a QR code will result in a positive shopping feeling. These participants hold the opinion that origin, production, and quality are of higher importance. These findings reveal that transparency provided by the application of QR codes on the website affects consumers' views on sustainability.

4 Conclusion and Later Work

We tested "Eco Echo" with 169 college students from "Generation Z" in the final proto-type test. The testers provided us with feedback on how to improve the APP's interface and a few of its features. We found that the majority of testers showed great enthusiasm for the virtual devices in the module of "Environmental Wisdom". When it comes to knowledge dissemination, the clothing environmental protection data generated by virtual devices can make consumers accept the concept of sustainable development more easily than just conveying sustainable development news and environmental protection knowledge questions and answers. This is a key concern for us to improve the educational value in the further development of "Eco Echo" in the future.

While our research has yielded some positive results, we equally acknowledge that we have certain shortcomings. The most obvious of which is that our project "Eco Echo" has developed a prototype and has not really put it into the market. In the future, we will build contact with professional organizations, environmental protection agencies, or industrial partners in related fields so as to obtain more in-depth industry opinions and support. We will make every effort to put the prototype into the actual market to collect usage data and provide feedback.

References

1. Zhang, K.: A study on the Recruitment of Generation Z Consumers in Shanghai a Shop-ping Center. Shanghai Foreign Studies University, Shanghai, China (2021). https://doi.org/10.27316/d.cnki.gswyu.2021.000265
2. Yip, T., Chan, K., Poon, E.: Attributes of young consumers' favorite retail shops: a qualitative study. J. Consum. Mark. **29**(6–7), 545–552 (2012)
3. Peterson, H.: Millennials are old news — here's everything you should know about generation Z. Bus. Insider (2014)
4. Park, S.J., Lee, E.J.: Influences of middle-and old-aged shoppers' perceived risk and con-sumption value on purchase intentions of eco-friendly clothing: the mediation effect of risk reduction behaviors. J. Korean Soc. Fashion Des. **15**(1), 51–68 (2015)
5. Khan, S.N., Mohsin, M.: The power of emotional value: exploring the effects of values on green product consumer choice behavior. J. Clean. Prod. **150**(MAY1), 65–74 (2017). https://doi.org/10.1016/j.jclepro.2017.02.187
6. Jeong, D., Ko, E.: The influence of consumers' self-concept and perceived value on sustainable fashion. J. Glob. Scholars Market. Sci. **31**(4), 511–525 (2021)
7. Arora, N., Manchanda, P., Wang, Y.: Green perceived value and intention to purchase sus-tainable apparel among Gen Z: the moderated mediation of attitudes. J. Glob. Fash. Market. **13**(2), 168–185 (2022). https://doi.org/10.1080/20932685.2021.2021435
8. Zeithaml, V.A.: Consumer perceptions of price, quality, and value: a means-end model and synthesis of evidence. J. Mark. **52**(3), 2–22 (1988). https://doi.org/10.1177/002224298805200302
9. Monroe, K.B.: Pricing: Making Profitable Decisions: McGraw-Hill, New York City, New York (1991)
10. Anderson, J.C., Narus, J.A.: Capturing the Value of Supplementary Service. Harvard Bus. Rev. (1995)
11. Daly, J.N.: Why we buy what we buy: a theory of consumption values (1989)

12. Sweeney, J.C., Soutar, G.N.: Consumer perceived value: the development of a multiple item scale. J. Retail. **77**(2), 203–220 (2001). https://doi.org/10.1016/S0022-4359(01)00041-0
13. Scaglione, A., Mendol, D.: Measuring the perceived value of rural tourism: a field survey in the western Sicilian agritourism sector. Qual. Quant. (2016). https://doi.org/10.1007/s11135-016-0437-8
14. Chen, Y.-S.: Towards green loyalty: driving from green perceived value, green satisfaction, and green trust. Sustain. Dev. **21**(5), 294–308 (2013)
15. Rasmussen, N.: 'Clothes' the loop: raising awareness of sustainable fashion among millennial consumers through digital platforms. Boller Rev. **5** (2020)
16. Sánchez-Fernández, R., Iniesta-Bonillo, M.Á.: The concept of perceived value: a systematic review of the research. Mark. Theory **7**(4), 427–451 (2007)
17. Shen, Z.: Mining sustainable fashion e-commerce: social media texts and consumer behaviors. Electron. Commer. Res. **23**(2), 949–971 (2023)
18. Scaglione, A., Mendola, D.: Measuring the perceived value of rural tourism: a field survey in the western Sicilian agritourism sector. Qual. Quant. **51**, 745–763 (2017)
19. Nghiem, T.P.L., Carrasco, L.R.: Mobile applications to link sustainable consumption with impacts on the environment and biodiversity. Bio Sci. **66**(5), 384–392 (2016). https://doi.org/10.1093/biosci/biw016
20. Sweeney, J.C., Soutar, G.N.: Consumer perceived value: the development of a multiple item scale. J. Retail. **77**(2), 203–220 (2001). https://doi.org/10.1016/S0022-4359(01)00041-0
21. Strähle, J., Gräff, C.: The role of social media for a sustainable consumption. In: Strähle, J. (ed.) Green Fashion Retail, pp. 225–247. Springer Singapore, Singapore (2017). https://doi.org/10.1007/978-981-10-2440-5_12

Psychological Service Design: From Consulting Space to Experience Place

Manhai Li[✉], Yiman Wu, Qi Hou, Yingying Sun, and Ming Chen

Chongqing University of Posts and Telecommunications, Chongqing 400065, China
limh@cqupt.edu.cn

Abstract. Through case analysis of changes in mental health counseling methods both domestically and internationally, a multidimensional quadrant model for the design turn of psychological counseling centers is abstracted from philosophy, and a fusion path for the design turn between different quadrants is proposed. At the same time, it is proposed that the design of psychological counseling centers is shifting from traditional counseling spaces to technology based experiential place, and the role of psychological counselors is shifting from providing counseling services to evaluating experiential effects. The positioning of psychological counseling centers is shifting from a space for relieving psychological stress to a place where stories can occur, which is the academic contribution of this study. Based on the service theater model, it is proposed that psychological counseling services as experience venues can be designed from three aspects of service contacts: common goals, service scenarios, and interactive processes. Then, through the transformation of the Psychological Counseling Center of Chongqing University of Posts and Telecommunications, the necessity and feasibility of designing psychological counseling services from consultation spaces to experience venues are verified through the actual design process and effects. This is the practical value of this study.

Keyword: Psychological service; Service design; Experience

1 Emerging Psychological Services

The world's earliest recognition of the value of service design and its application in psychological counseling was achieved by some advanced universities, enterprises, and institutions in developed countries in Europe and America. Especially since entering the 21st century, the environment of the psychological industry has been constantly changing, leading many well-known institutions, enterprises, and universities to actively explore new models and business opportunities of psychological counseling services based on user experience and interactive technology, using innovative thinking and methods of service design, guiding the development trend of the psychological industry.

Taking Google's meditation room as an example, in order to allow employees to experience a surreal atmosphere in their work environment and alleviate their negative emotions at work, Google collaborated with New York's architectural design studio

Office of Things to innovate the traditional office environment in the YouTube office building and the Bay Area Google office [1], introducing an immersive meditation space that creates a breathing outlet between work and meditation. The immersive meditation space launched by Google.

This design focuses on the mental health of employees, providing them with a place to actively acknowledge and restore their mental health. It redefines the relationship between the office environment and people, alleviates negative emotions such as anxiety and tension at work, improves office health, and becomes one of the factors that Google attracts and retains talents to ensure employee health.

In fact, whether it is the psychological industry actively seeking intervention in service design, or relevant institutions, companies, universities, etc. vigorously developing psychological service innovation, all indicate the positive role and widespread influence of service design concepts in foreign psychological service innovation. Especially driven by the Internet, this trend is becoming increasingly evident.

The same is true for the Chinese Psychological Service. China's psychological services have undergone commercialization and market-oriented reforms, and the innovation mechanism is more flexible and the innovation momentum is stronger than ever. More and more universities, enterprises, and institutions have begun to seriously examine the diversity and innovative methods of psychological services, and actively explore new forms of psychological services from the perspective of service design.

Fig.1. Guangzhou WeTBen Psychological Technology Experience Center

Taking Guangzhou WeTBen Psychological Technology Experience Center as an example, in order to better adapt to the changes in people's psychological needs in the Internet era, WeTBen Psychological Technology Experience Center takes "psychology + technology" as the center, and actively explores dynamic psychology, VR psychological experience, and Methods such as intelligent catharsis experience are combined with traditional psychological services. With interactive psychological services as the carrier, traditional psychological services as an extension, combined with the psychological experience of positive psychology, intelligent interactive psychological technology equipment and autonomous psychological service experience, it promotes the interaction between people and psychological services in multiple media and multi-sensory services, so that people can experience a relaxed and pleasant psychological service experience, breaking through the depressing and monotonous style of traditional psychological services. as shown in Fig. 1.

To sum up, many universities and enterprises at home and abroad are particularly active in the service design innovation of psychological services. From the perspective of the demander, from the perspective of service design, they pay attention to people's real psychological needs, emphasize problem-oriented, keenly understand demand planning, give technology a more despicable form, and finally create a free, efficient, useful and willing experience for the demander, create effective and efficient services for the organization, create a good experience, and deliver positive value behaviors [2].

2   Two Kinds of Psychological Services

Today's university system is a typical open and complex system, the core issue is the circular causal relationship between decision-making actions and the environment, psychological counseling is an extremely important link, and students as the most important and active factor, is the starting point and foothold of the design, how to grasp the phenomenon and significance of students, has been an important basis and premise of the design As a design activity to improve experience and service quality, service design is an important development direction of psychological counseling services in colleges and universities [3] Psychological centers in colleges and universities need to shift from traditional counseling to service design, with the goal of creating a humanized service base such as service culture and science It not only meets the functional needs of psychological counseling, but also becomes an important activity space for visitors' psychological exploration and development.

2.1   Psychological Center as Consulting Space

The traditional psychological center is limited to basic counseling and classroom assistance functions, and is limited to relatively independent "mental health education" [4], Often neglecting the autonomy of visitors and the diversity of psychological counseling. The traditional social psychological counseling mainly helps visitors to self-awareness, self-acceptance, and self-regulation through individual counseling, collective counseling, and psychological counseling in education and teaching. However, these contents put visitors in a passive state and are arranged, causing them to have reservations and consideration instead.

In summary, in this situation, psychological counseling in universities urgently needs to change their mindset, consider various forms of psychological counseling from the perspective of visitors, and create more favorable forms of psycho-logical counseling for visitors through design innovation.

2.2   Psychological Center as Experiential Place

The psychological center of the university uses interactive technology, "positive psychology" and psychological services to combine it, adhering to the principle of people-oriented and serving visitors, and starting from the perspective of visitors. The establishment of an interactive psychological counseling room adopts a series of complex interactive systems to create a safe interactive space and "experience place" for visitors, to vent and channel visitors' emotions and relieve learning pressure.

The interactive psychological technology devices that can be widely used now include: VR psychological therapy intervention, which has become the key to further improve the effect of psychological intervention [5] Progressive virtual reality technology (VR) is used to intervene with visitors from visual, auditory and tactile aspects to relieve psychological anxiety and realistic pressure. VR psychotherapy intervention, as shown in Fig. 2.

Fig. 2. VR psychotherapy intervention.

Eye tracking is a detection technique for obtaining eye movement information. Accurate and objective eye movement data can be obtained using eye tracking technology [6]. By analyzing the data obtained by the system and psychological counselors, they can effectively identify the emotions, cognitive effects, and psychological states of visitors, and provide targeted medication and effective psychological counseling.

These new interactive psychological technology devices are maximizing the psychological development of visitors, and their space is to interact with visitors to a certain extent, supplemented by positive psychological experience to fully explore the positive psychological factors of education activities, such as the establishment of positive psychology education model, starting from the classroom and outside the classroom, inside and outside the school, from the classroom teaching Psychological counseling and counseling, peer assistance, campus culture, family and other ways to practice the concept of positive psychology [7] and on this basis, we can also carry out service design in various aspects.

3   Theoretically: Psychological Service Design

3.1   From Consulting to Experiential Place

Service design is a new extension of the traditional design field in the postindustrial era, which comprehensively implements design concepts. Its ontology attribute is the systematic design of the relationships between people, objects, behavior, environment, and society [12]. Since its inception, service design has received widespread attention from different fields internationally and has penetrated into different industries, profoundly affecting the operational mode of modern commerce [13]. The application of service design in the field of psychological services is based on the ontology attribute cognition of traditional psychological services, exploring unmet needs and opportunities with design wisdom, and driving psychological services to better adapt to service transformation as an important practice.

Nowadays, the design of psychological centers has shifted from traditional consulting spaces to technology-based experiential spaces. The role of psychological counselors has also shifted from providing consulting services to evaluating experiential effects. The positioning of psychological centers has shifted from a space for psychological stress relief to a place where stories can occur, and the two complement and integrate each other. Traditional psychological services and interactive psychological services complement each other, and the integrated development is shown in Fig. 3.

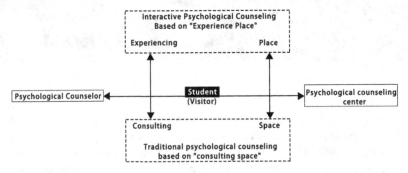

Fig. 3. The design shift of psychological service centers. Photo made by the author.

4   Practically: Psychological Service Design

4.1   Psychological Space Design

In today's era, people of all ages mostly have psychological problems, with students accounting for nearly half of them. According to the 2020 China National Psychological Health Development Report (2019–2020), a blue book on mental health in China, 18.5% of college students have a tendency towards depression, and 4.2% have a high risk of depression; 8.4% have anxiety tendencies.

The psychological problems of college students directly affect their learning and life. Psychological health education for college students is an important way for universities to achieve psychological education, and is also one of the hot topics of concern in the current education industry [14]. Regarding the mental health status of college students, universities have taken relevant actions. The university has taken relevant actions regarding the mental health status of college students. However, psychological counseling in universities, like most psychological institutions in society, has a traditional form. Using counseling to provide psychological counseling has low timeliness and specificity, which is unreasonable for a large number of university students.

The Psychological Counseling Center of Chongqing University of Posts and Telecommunications currently provides students with traditional psychological counseling methods. There are problems such as unreasonable layout and low utilization rate. With the increase of personnel from psychological centers such as office spaces and the number of students visiting, the current psychological counseling centers do not meet the needs of students; Moreover, traditional environmental equipment and colors cannot create a favorable environment and atmosphere for students' psychological counseling [15]; The lack of proper use of light and other factors have led to a lack of timeliness and specificity in student work at the tutoring center.

Through the design and research of traditional and interactive psychological counseling in the previous text, a conceptual design scheme for the integration and development of consultation space and experiential space was ultimately formed. This plan is selected at the original location of the Psychological Counseling Center of Chongqing University of Posts and Telecommunications, and the plan of the counseling center is shown in Fig. 4.

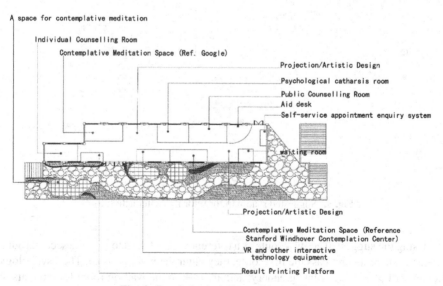

Fig. 4. Psychological Center Layout Plan.

This plan combines indoor space with outdoor space, traditional psychological counseling with interactive psychological counseling, and consulting space with experiential space, creating a trustworthy and trustworthy psychological space for students. In the design space of this plan, three gradual routes were mainly designed to complete the psychological journey of students. The first section of the route mainly consists of a tour guide desk and a self-service reservation inquiry machine. There is a tour guide service desk and a self-service reservation inquiry system at the entrance. After students enter the center, the guidance desk will automatically obtain their latest information, such as grades and past mental health checklists, through facial recognition. This allows staff to conduct a preliminary assessment of students' current psychological status without contact with them. Students can not only use the self-service appointment query system to book a consultation center, but also sign privacy treaties and other instructions through the system, ensuring that students have a clear understanding of their future mental health journey. In this first section of the route, the protagonist is mainly the students and auxiliary staff.

Subsequently, there is the second route composed of various psychological experience projects, in which students become the only protagonists. Students can choose the main project based on their specific needs, and the psychological center provides students with full freedom of choice (Fig. 5).

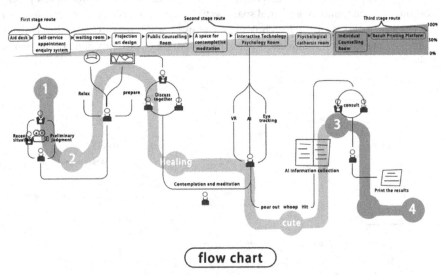

Fig. 5. Suggested roadmap for tutoring center activities.

Using the suggested activity route as a reference, let's take a look at the second route. After the students first pass the first route, they enter the waiting room. The Psychology Center will place lazy sofas, greenery, and artwork in the waiting room for students to relax and reduce anxiety about the unknown counseling journey. In addition to waiting outdoors, lazy sofas and art combinations can be placed in a number of other places to ensure that students feel relaxed, comfortable and unrestrained throughout the visit.

Subsequently, a large number of projection/art designs appeared, and the psychological center created a peaceful atmosphere for students through the projection of sound, light, images, art, etc., which also played a role in relaxing. This is followed by the basic public counseling room and the contemplative meditation space set up by the Counseling Center, which play a complementary role in allowing students to come to the contemplative meditation space to reflect and relax after various activities in the public counseling room, so as to relieve the information received in the public counseling room. Further down is that students enter the interactive psychological space, and a large number of interactive psychological technology equipment is placed in the psychological center, such as VR equipment, eye tracking, etc., and students will be accompanied by AI data systems when using the equipment to provide students with psychological interaction space. The stepwise help and interaction with the students greatly alleviated their sense of uncertainty and negative psychological pressure in this activity, and truly recognized and acknowledged their current psychological state. In addition, the information collection system also transmits the output of students' performance on various devices to the backend of the system. Finally, there is the psychological catharsis room. This psychological venting room is not a traditional form of venting space, and the psychological space planning is equipped with an AI data system and an information collection system. Students can confide, shout, strike, etc. The AI data system will simply ask and judge the student's confidence, while the information collection system can collect the key information confided by the student, facial expressions, decibel and changes in shouting, the degree and change of the hit, and analyze and make preliminary judgments, so as to transmit them to the background of the system. In this route, all the collected information will be integrated in the background of the system.

The AI usage effect is shown in Fig. 6.

4.2 Meditation Place Design

In the above, we mentioned that students can heal themselves through meditation spaces. Let's take a closer look at the relevant content. The first is the outdoor contemplative space, where students can meditate, self-regulate, relieve fatigue, clear their minds, and relax in hidden spaces, lights, architecture, and landscapes. In addition to the outdoor meditation space, the Mind Center plan also creates an indoor meditation space that will take on a small, enveloping image, with comfortable seating inside the space, a screen covering the entire space, and the Mind Center creates an almost illusory and relaxing hidden space for students by utilizing the light and color of the screen. These are all hideaways created for students to think and relax. Renderings of the outdoor and indoor meditation spaces are shown in Fig. 7.

If a student is still unable to resolve their negative emotions and alleviate their poor psychological state through the above process and needs further assistance from a professional teacher, they will enter the third route consisting of an individual psychological counseling center and a self-service result printing platform. The individual psychological counseling room will meet the student's needs, and the psychological counselor will provide one-Mon-one counseling and counseling to the student, At this point, students have gained further interaction and familiarity with the environment of the psychological counseling center, and without the initial strong vigilance and emotional pressure,

Fig. 6. AI usage rendering.

Fig. 7. Outdoor and indoor meditation space renderings

the intervention of psychological counselors has a much stronger effect. Finally, students can obtain their own psychological results reports on the export result printing platform, which includes changes in the student's activity process, system analysis, and advice from a counselor. Through the reports, students can understand their current psychological situation.

In summary, this plan utilizes various elements from the perspective of service design to provide better services for students, focusing on their true psychological needs, and creating a more comfortable, efficient, and useful psychological space for students.

5 Conclusion

Our original intention was to transform the mental health counseling center into a service design. Committed to creating a service-oriented place for immersive experiential exploration. Its form is not limited to traditional consultation and treatment. We will showcase advanced technological means in various forms. Simply put, service design is a design mindset that creates and improves service experiences for individuals. These experiences occur at different touchpoints over time. It emphasizes cooperation to make co creation possible, making services more useful, usable, efficient, effective, and needed. It is a new, holistic, and interdisciplinary comprehensive field. Service design is a design expertise that helps develop and provide excellent services. Service design projects can also improve control, satisfaction, loyalty, and efficiency in areas such as environment, communication, and products.

The research conclusion of this article is that it is feasible to shift from "dedicated spaces that focus on functions" to "people-oriented living spaces" in practice. Designers can achieve a design shift through lifestyle design methods and spatial narrative design methods. They can construct a lifestyle related to urban underground space from three aspects: user behavior, environment, and values, create meaning related to users, and build a harmonious and harmonious relationship between the city, nature, and people. In fact, more and more design practice cases are turning this way.

Acknowledgements. This work was supported by Doctoral startup fund and talent introduction fund project of Chongqing University of Posts and Telecommunications -- Research on the cost and benefit distribution of big data productization (K2020–201) and Chongqing educational science planning project -- Research on the talent training system of "social theme" in Colleges and Universities (2020-GX-284) and Research Center for network social development of Chongqing University of Posts and Telecommunications -- Research on the cost of network big data production (2020SKJD06).

References

1. Fall, A.: Rest, rest immersive office space series. Inter. Des. Decoration **5**, 106–111 (2021)
2. Stickdorn, M., Schneider, J.: This is Service Design Think Ing: Basics, Tools, Cases. Wiley (2011)
3. Ying, G.: Discussing the value of service design from the perspective of public service. New Art **36**(04), 84–90 (2015)
4. Li, P., Meihao, D.: The practical difficulties and breakthroughs faced by psychological education in colleges and universities. Ideological Theor. Edu. **480**(03), 90–94 (2019). https://doi.org/10.16075/j.cnki.cn31-120/g4.2019.03.016
5. Li, M.: Application of virtual reality technology and VR devices in psychological intervention therapy. Comput. Knowl. Technol. **18**(20), 94–95 (2022). https://doi.org/10.14004/j.cnki.ckt.2022.1407
6. Jialu, Y., Yannian, H., Le, Z.: Clinical application progress of eye movement and eye tracking technology. Int. J. Ophthalmol. **23**(01), 90–95 (2023)
7. Jianchun, H.: Construction of a model for mental health education in universities under the concept of positive psychology. Hunan Soc. Sci. **164** (04), 247–250 (2014)

8. Xin, X., Cao, J.: Service design driven public affairs management and organizational innovation. Design (5), 124–128 (2014)
9. Cao, J., Xin, X.: Thinking on service design from physical banking to internet finance. Packag. Eng. **37**(8), 6 (2016)
10. Shu, W., Ning, H., Ningning, C., et al.: Reflections on psychological health education for college students in the new era. China Continuing Med. Edu. **14**(20), 148–152 (2022)
11. Hanqing, D.: Research on the Design of Unmanned Psychological Healing Space for College Students. Beijing Forestry University (2021). https://doi.org/10.26949/dcnki.gblyu.2021.000534

Construction of Double UG Design Model of Product Service System from the Perspective of Media Participation

Yujie Ren and Xiong Ding[✉]

Guangzhou Academy of Fine Arts, Guangzhou 510006, China
dingxiong@gzarts.edu.cn

Abstract. As a new production system that highly integrates tangible products and intangible services, the product service system provides an opportunity for the transformation from discrete production to integrated production. Product Service System Design, proposed on this basis, involves systematic planning and design of related strategies, concepts, products, usage, processes, etc. However, existing literature shows a relative lack of attention on the role of "Media" during product service system design. Hence, this study, grounded in Product Service System design procedures and Uses & Gratifications theory, constructed the Double UG Design Model encompassing four phases - Unearth, Generation, Uses & Gratifications - with reference to the Double Diamond Design Model. The model emphasizes the working mechanism of "Media" across the entire design process, explores more possibilities brought by interdisciplinary research, provides new ideas to subsequent studies on Product Service System Design, and expands the application boundary of media in design research.

Keywords: Product Service System · Uses & Gratifications Theory · Media Participation · Double Diamond Design Model · Double UG Design Model

1 Introduction

The Media represent an intermediary presence that establishes connections between things and can be natural elements, technology, or even humans themselves [1]. As one of the forms of information, media are an important shaper of individual perception, shaping human perception and experience in an expanded way. At the same time, design, as a strategic problem-solving innovation activity, is widespread in various fields and has a profound impact on our daily lives, production systems and ecosystems. Media have always been the main focus of design practice. With the continuous evolution of media forms, from traditional paper media to digital media and online media, design activities continue to be profoundly affected by emerging media forms. The scope of design gradually expands, extending from visual communication design to information design, interaction design, service design and other design branches.

Product Service System Design (PSSD) is a system planning and design path based on integrating tangible products and intangible services in production systems. "Media"

A. Marcus et al. (Eds.): HCII 2024, LNCS 14716, pp. 349–364, 2024.
https://doi.org/10.1007/978-3-031-61362-3_25

plays a crucial role and function as the carrier of "products" and "services" throughout the entire design path. Currently, most of the research in China on PSSD focuses on the practice of design and some academic developments in the field itself, but there has been relatively little research on the intervention of communication studies and the corresponding research from the perspective of "Media" attention. Therefore, studying the role of media in PSS is conducive to expanding the research horizons of PSSD, realizing the effective combination of communication and design, and providing media application guidance for Product Service System (PSS) practice. This paper will be based on the general design process of PSS, taking "Uses & Gratifications Theory (U&G Theory)" as the perspective, and explore more possibilities of PSS from the perspective of communication.

2 U&G Theory and Product Service System

2.1 U&G Theory

Uses & Gratifications (U&G) theory is one of the classic theories in the field of communication. As summarized in the Uses & Gratifications Research co-authored by Katz, Blumler and Gurevitch, the research into U&G is mainly concerned with: (1) social and psychological origins cause (2) needs; needs stimulate (3)mass media and other sources' (4)expectations; expectations result in different types of (5)media exposure, ultimately leading to the (6)gratifications of needs and (7)other non-intended outcomes [2]. Later, Katz briefly summarized media contact as a basic model of "social factors + psychological factors → media expectations → media exposure → need gratifications" [3]. In 2011, Lu Heng of the City University of Hong Kong further refined and summarized the model into five core concepts: Use/Exposure, Gratification, Need, Motive/Motivation, and Expectation, in the work *Uses & Gratifications: A Theory as a Lab*. In U&G empirical studies, key concepts such as Use/Exposure, Gratification, Need, Motive/Motivation, and Expectation evolve with changes in the research context, and there are no strict theoretical or operational definitions [4]. Different scholars have researched different types of media, and U&G Theory has become more and more like a perspective and a path rather than a systematic theory in the strict sense. Based on the more recognized and relatively unified academic views at home and abroad, this paper connects the five elements of U&G Theory in series according to the logic presented in Fig. 1.

Fig. 1. Five elements of U&G Theory

The research on U&G Theory argues that media can provide various gratifications to satisfy the needs of the audience, which determines the significance of media. Media gratify the audience's need for information. Media provide news and information to the audience by selecting and processing information, gratifying their needs to understand local or broader environments [5]. Secondly, the media gratify the audience's need for personal identity and a sense of belonging. Media content reflects the environment in which the audience lives, helping to enhance an individual's social identity [6]. Although this theory has been researched around "Media", the definition of this core concept itself is not clear enough, nor does it fully consider the possible deviations of the word "Media" during translation. As "Media" is one of the core concepts studied in this theory, clearly defining its definition is of great significance for correctly applying the theoretical meaning. Only by clarifying the meaning of "Media" and providing a clear definition can ambiguity be avoided and the research in this paper be advanced. Li Qin pointed out in *Immersive Media: Redefining the Connotation and Extension of Media* that the plural form of medium in English has been in use since about the 1930s. The Latin word for medium is Medius, which means middle or center. Therefore, media can be understood as an Intermediate Agency or Channel of Communication (Online Etymology Dictionary, 2013). In this sense, media is an intermediary presence that enables the establishment of connections between things, which can be natural elements, technology, or even humans themselves. The connections established can be either forces or information. Charles Cooley of the Chicago School [7] defines media sociologically: gesture, speech, writing, printing, letters, telephones, telegraphs, photography, and the means of art and science—all means by which thoughts and emotions can be transmitted from one person to another. In addition, in the Chinese literature on the application of the U&G Theory, "Media" is often translated as Meijie. This paper will also explore and discuss using Meijie as the focus of research.

2.2 Product Service System

The essence of Service Design is to design an effective model for organizing and planning the people, infrastructure, communication and physical components of the service system [8], used to improve the quality of a certain physical product or intangible service. The entire service process is viewed as a system that is constantly iterating from the outside in [9], with obvious characteristics of "core without boundaries" and "core with soft edges" [10]. The development of new services is based on service extensions of existing products. Services gradually replace products, but services must be useful and attractive, which is what Service Design pursues. To achieve this goal, Service Design requires that the service be visible. This is the design for service touchpoints. PSS is a system strategy that uses products as the main touchpoint to provide high-quality services. It is a part of service design [11].

The concept of PSS originated in Europe in the late 1990s. In 1999, Goedkoop et al. first proposed a comprehensive definition of PSS: it is a system composed of products, services, organizer networks, and support facilities, aiming to maintain competitiveness, gratify customer needs, and reduce environmental impacts compared to traditional business models [12]. They further clarified the three key elements of PSS: Product (tangible physical entities manufactured for sale and gratifying user needs), Services (activities performed in business that provide economic benefits to others), and System (a collection of all related elements and element relationships) [13].

With the continuous development of technology and economy, the research on PSS is also evolving. PSS can be subdivided into three categories, including eight implementation methods (Fig. 2): A) Product-Oriented PSS: In this type of PSS, the product is sold to customers while providing some features designed to ensure the normal operation of the product. Additional services. B) Use-Oriented PSS: This type of PSS provides a usage platform rather than the product itself. The product is owned by the service provider, and the functions or services of the product are the objects of sale. The customer uses the product in other ways except for ownership; that is, the ownership of the product is divided. C) Result-Oriented PSS: This type of PSS focuses on delivering the desired outcome instead of specific products. Enterprises provide customized service packages to gratify specific customer needs [14].

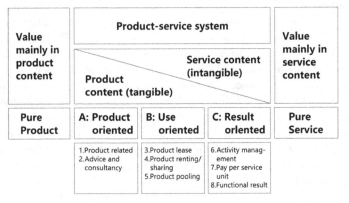

Fig. 2. Classification of Product Service Systems

Unlike traditional product design methods, the Product Service System Design (PSSD) process focuses on integrity and comprehensiveness to meet the requirements of the service experience. Morelli [15] believed that the role of design in PSS is mainly concentrated in the conceptual stage before use. Design methods that can be used for reference include user needs positioning, concept development, testing and iteration. Maussang and others [16] regard the physical product service unit as the basic element of the PSS system, and after the main elements are determined, the operation scenarios are used to describe the system in more depth. While various scholars may emphasize different aspects, this study adopts the five-stage framework for a universal design process as outlined in *Product Service System Design*: Value Proposition, System Architecture, Service Process, Touchpoint Design, and Prototype Testing [17] (Fig. 3).

Fig. 3. General process of Product Service System Design

3 Double UG Design Model Based on U&G Theory and PSS

3.1 Bridging Factor: Media

The U&G Theory consistently emphasizes the importance of "Media". Marshall McLuhan's "the media are the message" and "the media are the extension of humans" affirm the ubiquity and strong connectivity of media [18]. Looking back into the development of media, design is dependent on media. Designers use their own tacit knowledge and coding functions to shape various media objects [19]. The designed object carries a wealth of rich information, and every behavior and experience in daily living space can be a "touchpoint" for its effective communication, which can be understood as the manifestation of media in design. Service Design emphasizes a systematic approach, consisting of behaviors, processes and experiences in tangible and/or intangible means from the perspective of users (service recipients/providers), combined with service environments/scenarios (online and/or offline). The design aims to make services useful, available, and needed, as well as efficient, effective, and distinctive."

For PSS, "tangible and intangible ways" mean "products" and "services", which are necessary components of its entirety. Among them, "Media" is always the intermediary between "humans" and "products and services". Products, services and jointly constructed "experiences" convey stock and incremental value to "humans" through media. In U&G Theory, "Media" consisting of technology, information and consciousness, are regarded as the key object for audience gratifications or fulfilling needs, as well as the intermediate dependency between "humans" and "information" interaction. As the digital age progresses, the boundaries of design are consistently being pushed, and the ultimate manifestation of "products and services" design can also be perceived as a form of media. Design increasingly reflects a shift "from the tangible to the intangible", whereas the study of communication reveals an evolution "from the intangible to the tangible". The two are inextricably linked, ushering in an era where "everything is a medium" (Fig. 4) [20]. Andreas Hepp posits that the media possess a dual nature characterized by both institutionalization, which depends on the habitual actions of the user, and reification, which offers the user a tangible form or materialization [21]. This statement offers a nuanced explanation of the design process, including user research, needs gathering, product definition, user feedback, and product iteration, as well as the adaptable application of design outcomes in practical contexts.

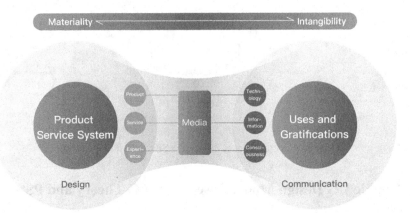

Fig. 4. The bridging role of "Media" in PSS and U&G Theory

3.2 Discussion on the Fitness

The U&G Theory holds that media serve a crucial function in gratifying audience needs [3]. This perspective aligns with the design philosophy of PSS, both emphasizing the pivotal role of "Media" as a bridge [15]. As stated, the five key concepts outlined will vary with the research context, lacking rigid theoretical and operational definitions. Upon comparison, it has been determined that the core factors of PSS and U&G share a degree of consistency. The "needs" stemming from social and psychological origins, as highlighted by U&G, along with the user psychology and behavioral motivations they trigger, exhibit a notable alignment at the theoretical level with the investigation of user roles and the discernment of issues in PSS. This can be interpreted as the research phase focusing on the audience/users' profound needs, challenges, and responses to impulses. Furthermore, U&G's concept of "expectations" drives the audience's behavior and behavioral intention, namely, the aspiration to achieve their objective. In the PSS design process, it is essentially an anticipation of future design. In the PSS design process, design and service developers see this reflected at every stage, from System Architecture and Service Process to Touchpoint Design. Through these stages, the design aim of meeting user expectations—or, put another way, fulfilling audience expectations—is accomplished. Ultimately, "use/exposure" and "gratification" represent the experiences and emotions associated with the previously mentioned connections and elements within the U&G Theory. They are the outcomes of the audience's engagement with and exposure to the media, reflecting their intentions and motivations. Compared to PSS, Prototype Testing represents a crucial phase where users assess the experience of products or services created by developers based on user requirements. They provide feedback on the outcomes, share their experiences, and evaluate the offerings, allowing users to experience the gratifications of their actual needs and the resolution of real-world issues through use or exposure. Thus, following the foundational PSS pathway outlined in this research, the five central concepts have been aligned and refined, yielding the logical framework depicted in Fig. 5: Value Proposition aligns with "need" and "motivation", constituting New Stage 1 (NS1). System Architecture, Service Process, and Touchpoint

Design align with "expectation" to constitute New Phase 2 (NS2). Prototype Testing aligns with "use/exposure" and "gratifications" to constitute New Phase 3 (NS3).

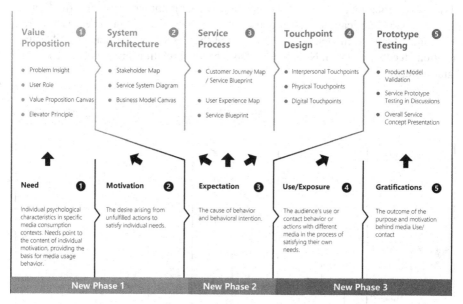

Fig. 5. Correspondence between PSS and U&G Elements

3.3 Architecture Reference: Double Diamond Design Model

The Double Diamond design model, introduced by the British Design Council in 2005, has been widely applied by design practitioners. The crux of this model lies in its approach to identifying and solving problems within design composition. It serves as a practical daily design process, with its fundamental principle being the accurate pinpointing of the issue at hand and the subsequent discovery of an appropriate solution. As a design method that is both widely recognized and extensively disseminated, it holds significant guidance for the construction of the process model in this paper. The Double Diamond design model underscores the dual "divergence-convergence" thought processes, delineated into four distinct phases: Discover, Define, Develop, and Deliver. Based on the foregoing, NS1 denotes a phase dedicated to investigating and defining user "needs". It is also a critical stage for identifying users' exposure to "motivation" and consistently "converging" on these insights. In alignment with the double diamond model, the "exploration" and "definition" phases demonstrate strong alignment with NS1 regarding the ultimate objective and the overarching process, respectively. Consequently, the two are further interconnected. NS2 encompasses the majority of the developmental tasks within the design process and aligns with the "development" phase when paralleled with the double diamond model. NS3 represents the final phase of user/audience "uses" and "gratifications". It also embodies a cycle of testing and iteration where developers, in collaboration with users, align with the Deliver phase of the double diamond model. Figure 6 illustrates that, following the double diamond design model, the framework presented in this paper has been refined into two distinct phases: "User & Need" and "Uses & Gratifications". These phases encompass four granular steps: Unearth, Generation, Use, and Gratification, each aligning with the sophisticated outcomes derived from the double diamond model. It should be noted that, given the presence of a "testing-iteration" feedback loop in NS3, there exists a cyclical relationship between "uses" and "gratifications".

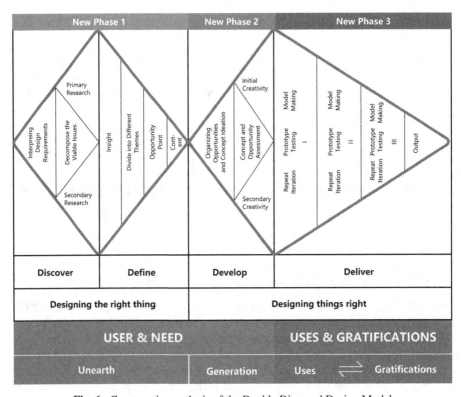

Fig. 6. Comparative analysis of the Double Diamond Design Model

3.4   Double UG Design Model Development

Building on prior research, this study primarily distinguishes between the User & Need stage and the Uses & Gratifications stage. The key cyclical components of Unearth, Generation, Use, and Gratification form the central theoretical innovation of this research. To maintain alignment with the reference models utilized throughout the research process and to further refine the details of each component, this study proceeds with a more in-depth discussion to develop a comprehensive theoretical model.

Unearth. Both PSS and U&G are grounded in the needs of users/audiences, with insights and problem-solving approaches centered on "humans". The "Unearth" stemming from this naturally upholds the legacy of this concept. Given that the emphasis of this study is on "design", the investigation and enhancement of the model's content are also centered more on the examination of theories related to design. Thus, at this stage, the content breakdown primarily leverages the concepts and definitions of user problem insight and needs identification from the general PSS design process. It also integrates the notion of the user's "need source level" from U&G Theory to establish the "Unearth" phase.

Generation. This link primarily targets design and service developers, typically involving the design and development of products and services based on the "needs" identified in the initial phase. Thus, at this phase, user participation is significantly diminished, with emphasis shifting to the developer's contemplation of the overall System Architecture, Service Process, and Touchpoint Design.

Uses. When the appropriate products and services have been designed and developed, it is essential for the "user/audience" to experience and assess whether the outcomes align with their initial needs. This phase aims to give users a full sense of the "target expectations" of the products and services, and to make evaluations and feedback after the experience to provide design developers with iterative reference and improvement directions.

Gratifications. Once users or the audience have interacted with the product or service, they will provide feedback based on their experiences and impressions. If the user experience is positive, the users will naturally transition from "passive recipients" to "active participants", leading them to purchase the product and promote the brand. Should the user experience prove subpar, this feedback can serve as a foundation for highlighting existing issues to the design and development team. Subsequent optimization cycles can then be conducted to refine and enhance products and services, ultimately fostering a superior experience for users.

In the progressive steps of the four stages mentioned above, a complete design chain from "Unearth" to "Gratifications" has been achieved. The process is not simply linear; rather, it is a cyclical loop that encompasses both "service design" and the "service itself" in tandem. The entire model begins with "needs" and progresses to "Gratifications", displaying a clear external cycle. Simultaneously, it loops back to a particular "specific stage" based on varying scenarios. Distinctive internal loops are demonstrated at different stages of Unearth, Generation, Use, and Gratification. The "Unearth" stage's internal loop can be understood as the design or service developer's "divergence-convergence" cycle during the user needs and problem insight process. Clear Unearth of requirements is achieved through effective iteration. The internal loop of the "Generation" phase manifests itself as an exploration of touchpoint design based on early problem definition. At this point, the first two phases constitute the cyclical process of the service design part. The "Uses & Gratifications" phases are embodied in the cycle of service. User feedback on "products and services" is utilized for iterative optimization. This feedback offers essential guidance for enhancing products and services, further refining the quality and efficacy of the service.

Furthermore, the incorporation of U&G Theory has underscored and magnified the media's role, presenting a significant focus within the entire model across all facets of the pathway. This is particularly evident in the "Unearth" stage of discerning insight needs, as well as the "Uses & Gratifications" phases of the user experience. It is worth noting that this model introduces a "media participation curve", offering a fresh perspective on the current design process through the lens of communication studies and investigating the potential for greater interdisciplinarity.

To delve more thoroughly into user needs and uncover underlying issues, the "Unearth" phase reveals that the "media participation curve" performs notably well. This indicates that user or audience potential needs are assessed across various dimensions through the integration of multiple media forms at this stage. Based on this premise, the development of targeted design services is carried out, and then the media intervenes again in the "Uses & Gratifications" stages, showing significant curve fluctuations. Compared to the Double Diamond Design Model and the general PSS design process, the significant feature of the Double UG Model lies in its comprehensive consideration of "Media" and "Communication". The Double Diamond Model centers on defining problems and uncovering solutions, highlighting the openness and universality of design thinking. In contrast, the PSS design process prioritizes the integrated design of products and services. The Double UG Model not only includes these elements, but also introduces a unique media and communication research perspective, broadening the design scope from conventional products and services to the creation of media applications and communication strategies. The design process for this model is thus more inclusive, emphasizing the practical use of products and services, while also addressing effective communication of the design across various media channels and improving user experience via "Media".

Additionally, building on the aforementioned breakdown of "Media" components, the model further delineates the "media type" and "content type" for users to contemplate

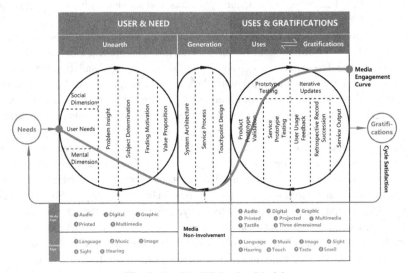

Fig. 7. Double UG Design Model

at each phase of "media participation". This serves as supplementary guidance for user engagement, as depicted in Fig. 7. Various media embody the utilization of distinct scenarios in today's society, and design service developers integrate the assorted media and content types offered by the model to leverage each scene within the design process.

4 Model Validation Based on the Burberry Brand Case

In the previous text, the U&G Theory is applied to analyze the PSS design process from a communication perspective and unearthed the inherent compatibility of the two theories in terms of content and significance. Based on this, the Double UG design model is developed. To further assess the model's practical application, this study performs an initial verification analysis of the Double UG design model using the Burberry brand case study. This unveils the role of media in brand communication and the elements of successful marketing strategies. By analyzing case studies, this paper evaluates the model's real-world applicability in brand design and the viability of converting theoretical concepts into actionable strategies, thereby increasing the professionalism and rigor of brand design.

4.1 Art of the Trench: The Beginnings of Digital Marketing

Brand recognition is not innate; it requires extensive promotion to foster consumer awareness and acceptance. Integrated marketing communication is fundamental to brand promotion. In the information age, the robust interconnectedness of network media has transformed the traditional model of brand promotion. Leveraging big data technology, brands can precisely sift through and analyze complex datasets, thereby delivering more tailored content to consumers and achieving nuanced market segmentation. Likewise, consumer collectives wield greater control over web-based applications, enjoy access to a broader array of communication platforms, and possess amplified influence in discourse, enabling proactive exposure with and targeted selection of brands [22]. In the preliminary phase of the brand service experience, "interaction" has emerged as the primary factor for brands to attract an "audience". In 2009, luxury brand Burberry made the audacious move to position itself as the premier digital luxury fashion brand. Since then, Burberry has launched various social media campaigns, including Facebook, Twitter, Pinterest, Instagram, YouTube and Sina Weibo. It also launched its own website, Art of the Trench, as a platform for communication with consumers. It fosters community engagement through user-generated content, then leverage that community to attract consumers. Users upload and share street-style photos featuring the brand's trench coats on Art of the Trench, garnering comments and likes within the community. Linking to personal social media profiles further amplifies the interaction's reach and engagement. This user-generated content (UGC) strategy meets the user's desire to project their self-image while also supplying Burberry with invaluable insights into product preferences, offering empirical backing for the brand's strategic direction and product development. Art of the Trench has emerged as a trailblazer in incorporating UGC within the luxury sector. Burberry, with its keen insight into the immense impact of media participation, has

Fig. 8. Web page of Burberry - Art of the Trench

successfully implemented high-quality brand marketing and communication before and after the service (Fig. 8).

Burberry's social media strategy not only fortifies the bond between the brand and its users but also markedly showcases the significance of the interplay between media and user needs. This aligns with the central tenet of the Double UG Model. The pursuit of user needs through "media participation" yields richer and more nuanced insights, thereby offering informed direction for the brand's evolution. The case study of Art of the Trench not only underscores the pivotal role of media in broadening brand influence but also showcases the significance of "media participation" in molding and enhancing user experience design. Utilizing social media platforms to encourage UGC not only yields valuable insights from users for brands but also deepens the emotional bond consumers have with the brand. This allows Burberry to better comprehend and fulfill consumer needs, thereby enhancing brand loyalty and market competitiveness.

4.2 Burberry Kisses: Soft Reality Shaping

Anthony Giddens, a contemporary British sociologist, contends that the role of media has undergone a dramatic shift in the new era. Its primary function is no longer to accurately "reflect reality" but rather to "shape reality" in an appropriate manner [23]. This concept communicates a crucial point: in today's world, information is frequently judged not by its substance, but by the manner of its distribution, thus elevating the role of media in the spread of information [24]. In 2013, Burberry launched the daring and innovative Burberry Kisses campaign, featuring kiss-imprinted letters. The initiative melds the brand's core identity with Google's digital revolution to forge an impeccable synergy. In collaboration with Google, Burberry has unveiled a delightful and thoughtful service. Users can easily log into *kisses.burberry.com* through Google's Chrome browser, then press their lips against the screen, and the app will send their affectionate kiss to their loved one (Fig. 9). This flawless and daring marketing innovation deeply resonates with the user's inherent desire to convey their feelings, while the straightforward yet sentimental slogan infuses the product with a sense of warm emotional value, transforming it from cold and impersonal to something more meaningful. Drawing inspiration from real-world products, Burberry has masterfully crafted a gentler, more human-centric approach to its marketing strategies and campaigns. They fully leveraged the new media channel and flawlessly accomplished their objective of "reality shaping". This innovation enables Burberry to connect more deeply with consumers, fostering a sense of warmth and closeness with the brand.

In the "Uses & Gratifications" phase of the Double UG Model, the "media curve" surges, underscoring the significance of "media participation" in fostering robust brand communication and user experience. Burberry Kisses, through its digital strategy, enables users to uniquely express their emotions. This underscores the pivotal role media plays in molding reality and enriching experiences, as well as Burberry's inventive approach to utilizing digital media for interaction and communication. Burberry's digital media strategy moves beyond traditional one-way brand communication by fostering a two-way interactive experience that not only offers users a fresh and creative product experience but also strengthens brand identity. The "media participation curve" ascent signifies a brand's increased media exposure tailored to users, who find gratifications in these innovative interactive experiences, underscoring the varied use of media in contemporary brand strategies.

Fig. 9. Burberry Kisses Campaign

4.3 Connect to Play: Scenario Shaping in the New Media Channel

Scenario communication is the emerging trend in the advertising industry. Unlike the straightforward notion of space, "scenario" leans more toward shaping the audience's psychological model, embodying the ambiance crafted through diverse technical methods or design styles within a particular time and space, transforming the space into a conceived scenario [26]. American scholars Robert Scoble and Shel Israel suggest that the convergence of big data, mobile devices, social media, sensors, and location systems heralds the advent of the "Age of Scenarios" [27]. In a particular scenario, advertising content merges seamlessly with the living environment, intertwining the real and virtual worlds to create a distinct sense of time and space. Unknowingly, this experience molds consumers' identification with the brand. During Christmas 2015, Burberry partnered with Dream Works to lease curved screens at London's Piccadilly Circus. Using 3D technology, passers-by can create personalized scarf designs with their mobile phones. Participants can select their favorite Burberry scarf pattern on their phone and then shake the device to generate a design that will soar across the big screen (Fig. 10). Creating "scenarios" enhances media applications, boosts user engagement and experience, and strengthens brand recognition. In the age of scenario communication, advertising transcends traditional media, utilizing multimedia channels and embracing the concept of "scenario" to engage with audiences—either by leveraging existing scenes or crafting new ones. This approach brings brands into closer proximity to consumers' lives, fostering more profound emotional connections.

Fig. 10. Burberry's interactive event at Piccadilly Circus Square

In the Double UG Model, the "media participation curve" peaks at the end of the process, indicating the media's maximum role in the overall design process. By crafting interactive scenarios, Burberry elevates media utilization, enriches the user's brand experience, and strengthens brand identification among users. This illustrates that within the design process, media serve not merely as a conduit for information dissemination but also as a vital connection in fostering the user experience and their bonds with brands.

Using the curved screen at Piccadilly Circus, Burberry transforms users from passive observers into active participants, enriching and adding depth to brand communication. Within the cycle of "Uses & Gratifications", users consistently find fulfillment, while brands persistently enhance the user experience. This fortifies the interaction between users and the brand, simultaneously boosting brand recognition and a sense of belonging among consumers, thereby forging a more profound emotional bond.

5   Conclusions and Prospects

In the emerging social structure shaped by big data and cloud computing, design has transitioned from a traditional emphasis on the shaping of media objects to a conceptual approach that prioritizes the linking and associating of these objects. It has evolved into an immersive media ecosystem where the center is omnipresent, and the periphery is boundless [28]. In an era where new media reigns supreme and consumer awareness is heightened, brands can no longer claim sole control over communication resources [24]. The paradigm has shifted from a "one-way linear" approach to a "two-way inter-active closed-loop" model. Drawing on the product service system design process and integrating U&G Theory and Double Diamond design model, this study develops a Double UG design model comprising four phases: Unearth, Generation, Uses, and Gratifications. The model underscores the working mechanism of "Media" throughout the design process, delving into the myriad possibilities that interdisciplinary research can offer. It presents fresh perspectives for future product service system design studies and broadens the scope of media's utilization in design research.

As media technology advances, the merging of various media with distinct characteristics and forms has become inevitable. The convergence of media will significantly impact brand communication, presenting a substantial challenge for brands striving to thrive in the new media landscape. Facing this challenge, brands, product, and service developers must cultivate deep, comprehensive insights into consumer needs, leveraging contemporary media and emerging consumer behaviors. This entails a thorough analysis and strategic transformation of both explicit and implicit needs, along with the development of a brand strategy centered on "products and services" with an emphasis on "media participation".

References

1. Qin, L.: Immersive media: redefining the connotation and extension of media. Chin. J. Journalism Commun. **39**(08), 115–139 (2017)
2. Heng, L.: Uses and gratifications: a theory as a label. Chin. J. Int. Commun. **33**(02), 11–18 (2011)
3. Katz, E., Haas, H., Gurevitch, M.: On the use of the mass media for important things. Am. Sociol. Rev. **38**(2), 164 (1973). https://doi.org/10.2307/2094393
4. Yan, Z.: A Study on the use behavior of "TikTok" interest-related group-Based on use and gratification theory. Wuhan: Wuhan University (2018)
5. Katz, E., Blumler, J.G., Gurevitch, M.: Uses and gratifications research. Public Opin. Q. **37**(4), 509–523 (1973)

6. Rubin, A.M.: Uses-and-gratifications perspective on media effects. In: Bryant, J., Oliver, M.B. (eds.) Media Effects: Advances in Theory and Research, pp. 181–200. Routledge (2009). https://doi.org/10.4324/9780203877111-14

7. Cooley, C.: Social Organization: A Study of the Larger Mind, p. 61. Charles Scribner's Sons, New York (1967)

8. Vargo, S.L., Maglio, P.P., Akaka, M.A.: On value and value co-creation: a service systems and service logic perspective. Eur. Manag. J. 26(3), 145–152 (2008)

9. Shi-Jian, L., Wen-Yin, Z.: Status and progress of service design. Packag. Eng. 39(24), 43–53 (2018)

10. Xiong, D., Shan, L.: Redefinition of service design based on typology and psychological field theory. Zhuangshi. 11, 124–125 (2020)

11. Lianqun, F., Guosheng, W.: Service design and product service systems. Industr. Des. 05, 63–64 (2016)

12. Goedkoop, M.J., van Halen, C.J.G., te Riele, H.R.M.: Product service systems, ecological and economic basics. Report for Dutch Ministries of Environment (VROM) and Economic Affairs (EZ) 36(1), 1–122 (1999)

13. Xi, C.: Review of research on product service system and service design. J. Beijing Univ. Posts Telecommun. Soc. Sci. Ed. 22(5), 61–73 (2020)

14. Tukker, A.: Eight types of product–service system: eight ways to sustainability? Experiences from SusProNet. Bus. Strateg. Environ. 13(4), 246–260 (2004)

15. Morelli, N.: Designing product/service systems: A methodological exploration. Des. Issues 18(3), 3–17 (2002)

16. Maussang, N., Zwolinski, P., Brissaud, D.: Product-service system design methodology: from the PSS architecture design to the products specifications. J. Eng. Des. 20(4), 349–366 (2009)

17. Xiong, D., Shan L.: Product Service System Design. China Architecture & Building Press (2022)

18. McLuhan, M.: Understanding Media: The Extensions of Man (Daokuan, H. Trans.). Beijing: The Commercial Press.19 (2000) (1994)

19. Hui, X., Minmin, L.: From shapemaker to enabler: observation of the role of designers in media practice. Art Des. 2(05), 32–34 (2023)

20. Yun, L., Jiacheng, L., Baixi, X.: Institutions, contexts and representations: bike sharing system design in the perspective of mediatization. Zhuangshi 03, 17–23 (2023)

21. Yuchen, D.: Towards a "media-centered" social ontology? - A critical analysis of European "mediatization school". Study Journalism Commun. (05), 53 (2016)

22. Yiqiang, H.: Research on the innovation of enterprise brand promotion model in the context of "Internet+." Bus. Econ. 10, 62–65 (2016)

23. Enqiang, G.: Between "mediatization" and "mediazation": the transformation of communication methods from the perspective of the history of social thought. Mod. Commun. J. Commun. Univ. China 40(8), 67–72 (2018)

24. Qing, L., Zhipeng, Z.: Brand communication strategy and packaging design in the new media era. Packag. Eng. 44(14), 262–269 (2023)

25. Zikai, Z.: Research on brand communication strategies in the new media environment. Trade Fair Econ 08, 59–61 (2023)

26. Shuliang, W., Yaoyao, Z., Yuhua, Z.: Two-way integration of advertising and design from the cross-media perspective in the digital media era. Zhuangshi 07, 28–30 (2020)

27. Scober, R., Israel, S.: The Age of Context: Mobile, Sensors, Data and the Future of Privacy (Qiankun, Z., Baoyao, Z. Trans.), p. 11. Beijing United Publishing Co (2014)

28. Qing, L.: Mediatized Living, p. 306. China Renmin University Press (2019)

Empowering Work-Life Harmony: Introducing a Porsche-Inspired Voice Digital Assistants Tailored for Women

Fenghua Tang[1], Yifang Li[1], Ke Xu[1], Tingting Guo[1], Yuchen Li[1], Jiayao Li[1], Simin Ren[1], Zihan Niu[1], Xingyi Liu[1], Xinyi An[1], Yuxin Miao[1], Xinran Xu[1], Yiqi Chen[1], Lingjun Liu[1], Dan Qiu[1], Jiaqing Xiong[1], Bowen Li[1], Ruonan Huang[1], Mengmeng Xu[2(✉)], Yang Guo[2(✉)], and Wei Liu[1(✉)]

[1] Beijing Key Laboratory of Applied Experimental Psychology, National Demonstration Center for Experimental Psychology Education, Beijing Normal University, Beijing 100875, China
202111061098@mail.bnu.edu.cn, wei.liu@bnu.edu.cn
[2] Porsche Digital China, Shanghai 200120, China

Abstract. With the rapid increase in the personalized demands for in-car voice assistants in the Generation Z era, innovation in digital assistants (DA) becomes crucial to better meet the growing needs of human-vehicle interaction (HVI). Focusing on the women of the new era, our study divides into three groups, targeting specific groups with era-specific characteristics: female fashion designers, white-collar professionals, and beauty and travel bloggers. Through course design, we aim to create products that combine luxury, high-tech, and excitement. The iterative design of our product aims to meet the specific needs of different female groups in unique scenarios, providing a significant reference for the future design of DA. Based on our firsthand experience in the design teaching process, we have identified and reflected on the challenges faced during practical design teaching. Finally, we propose further prospects for future in-car artificial intelligence voice assistants, exploring possibilities for human-centered design (HCD).

Keywords: Human-Centered Design · Human-Vehicle Interaction · Engineering Psychology · Generation Z · Women · Digital Assistants · Work-Life Balance

1 Introduction

The term Generation Z generally refers to individuals born after 1995 [1]. Growing up amidst the rapid evolution of digital technology, including widespread access to the internet, social media, and smartphones, Generation Z has acquired innate digital skills, demonstrating a natural inclination towards information and technology use. Shaped within a backdrop of globalization and multiculturalism, this generation exhibits heightened awareness of social and environmental issues and embraces an open attitude towards innovation and change [2]. Their lifestyle and values are significantly influenced by technology and social media, distinguishing them markedly from preceding generations.

F. Tang, Y. Li, K. Xu, T. Guo and Y. Li—These authors contributed equally.

In comparison to previous generations, Generation Z women possess unique values and consumption habits. As native users of the digital age, they are accustomed to utilizing various online platforms. Research indicates that, compared to men, women typically spend more time presenting their ideal selves on social media. Since the 21st century, with the widespread coverage of Marxist feminist perspectives, an increasing number of women emphasize economic independence and career development, opting for challenging and growth-oriented career paths [3]. They prioritize a balance between work and life and exhibit a strong sense of independence, emphasizing privacy protection and desiring a dedicated personal space. With the rise of feminist consciousness, they focus more on seeking internal satisfaction, self-expression, and self-presentation. In summary, Generation Z women are characterized by openness, independence, and autonomy. Therefore, in selecting vehicles, they place a greater emphasis on personalized and digital driving experiences, preferring interfaces that are both simple and aesthetically pleasing [4]. Additionally, during driving, they have a high demand for communication and social interaction with the external environment. Furthermore, research results show that female users consider vehicle safety as the top priority when purchasing a car, indicating a significant concern for safety and reliability.

This paper focuses on applying human factors engineering (HFE) and HCD principles, combined with engineering psychology, to meet the needs of female drivers for car and DA transformations [5–9]. This approach aims to provide women with a more tailored automotive experience, drive innovation in automotive engineering, and enhance product diversity and inclusivity.

Firstly, we introduce the concept of HFE and its pivotal role in automotive design. HFE focuses on improving the interaction between humans and their environment systems, aiming to optimize user experience, enhance safety, and efficiency. HFE has three fundamental characteristics: (1) HFE adopts a systematic approach; (2) HFE is design-driven; (3) HFE emphasizes two related outcomes: performance and well-being. In our car and DA transformation, HFE principles can enhance control interfaces, seating comfort, accessibility, and other factors related to driving and riding in cars to meet the needs of female drivers. Secondly, HCD is crucial in our design. The core philosophy of HCD is to place the needs, expectations, and experiences of end users at the core of the design process, ensuring that products, services, or systems meet user needs, provide a better user experience, and improve product utility and acceptability. In our car transformation design, HCD can help Porsche better understand the needs of female drivers, thereby creating a more attractive and intelligent product. Lastly, we introduce the concept of engineering psychology and its application in our design. Engineering psychology is an interdisciplinary field that focuses on the intersection of human psychology and engineering, emphasizing the study and application of psychological principles and methods to improve and optimize the interaction between humans and technology, equipment, tools, and systems. The goal of engineering psychology is to design and develop more human-friendly, easy-to-use, and efficient products, systems, and work environments to adapt and enhance human work and life to the maximum extent possible. In our transformation, engineering psychology can provide useful insights into how best to meet the needs of female drivers, including interpersonal interaction, information communication, and user satisfaction.

By combining the principles of human factors engineering, HCD, and engineering psychology, this paper aims to provide a new perspective for Porsche's transformation, meeting the growing demands of the female driver market in Generation Z, promoting the development of automotive engineering, and bringing innovation and competitive advantage to the automotive industry.

2 Methodology

2023 Fall Semester saw the collaboration of 12 undergraduate psychology students in the form of 4–5 person teams to undertake a design task. Applying the fundamental principles of human factors engineering, the teams critically evaluated and contemplated the concept prototype "Blue Hole," a car-mounted voice DA provided by the collaborating company, Porsche. The focus was on designing relevant features of the car-mounted voice DA for different target user groups to enhance innovation and effectiveness. Throughout the process, the teams concentrated on the following research questions:

- What are the characteristics of the target user groups?
- What are the typical user scenarios?
- What are the future trends in HVI?
- What are some new design ideas for future HVI?

2.1 Course Content

Diverging from other theoretical psychology courses, this course is centered around applied psychology, with its primary goal being to teach students research methods and basic processes related to user experience (UX). Focusing on the interaction experience between users and products or services, the course aims to understand the needs, expectations, and behaviors of the target users to optimize the design of products or services, ultimately providing better service to users [10, 11]. In this course, students learn about HFE and HCD principles, understanding and applying basic user research methods such as user testing and expert reviews, practicing in projects, and continuously iterating on design outputs.

2.2 Student Groups

In this course, 12 undergraduate students majoring in psychology collaborated in teams of 4–5 individuals. Before taking this course, they had already completed foundational courses in disciplines such as cognitive psychology, developmental psychology, psychological measurement, and psychological statistics. They possessed a relatively comprehensive knowledge framework of psychological theories and had accumulated some experience related to research interviews and data analysis.

2.3 Collaborative Partner

The course collaborated with Porsche, a German luxury car manufacturer founded in 1931 and headquartered in Stuttgart. Renowned for producing high-performance, high-quality sports cars and SUVs, the company has gained global acclaim for its iconic sports models and unique design style. Porsche cars are known for their outstanding performance, handling, and driving experience. The company has consistently invested significant research and development resources in automotive engineering and technology to ensure its vehicles maintain a leading position in the industry. To enhance the company's competitiveness in car-mounted voice DA, Porsche provided the concept prototype "Blue Hole," expecting students to offer innovative design ideas and inspiration based on the principles of luxury, high-tech, and excitement.

- Luxury: The pursuit of luxury involves a feeling or experience of opulence, high-end quality, and comfort. In the automotive field, the pursuit of luxury may involve luxurious interior design, the use of high-quality materials, comfortable seats, and dashboards. Upholding the principle of luxury in the design aligns with the brand's luxury and high-end identity, adding a unique touch.
- High-Tech: High-tech refers to a feeling or experience related to advanced technology, innovative features, and digital elements. In the automotive field, high technology is usually reflected in advanced in-car technology and intelligent features. This may include advanced driver assistance systems (such as autonomous driving technology and intelligent cruise control), advanced infotainment systems, integration with smartphones, intelligent voice recognition, and interaction. In-car communication technology, real-time data analysis, automatic software upgrades, and other functions also contribute to enhancing the technological aspect of the vehicle.
- Excitement: Excitement refers to an emotion or experience filled with excitement and stimulation. In the automotive field, high-performance engines, responsive suspension systems, sporty exterior designs, and challenging driving modes (such as sports mode) can enhance the excitement of driving. Additionally, elements like sound systems and simulated engine sounds can create a lively and exciting atmosphere inside the car.

3 Results

The three teams defined personas (i.e., target user groups) and corresponding scenarios through extensive investigation and analysis. They identified user pain points and needs through analysis and discussion, determining improvement measures to address these pain points. Subsequently, the research teams conducted three rounds of testing and improvement iterations on their respective design products. Firstly, they performed the initial UEQ user testing, improving based on benchmark results and UEQ scales [12]. Next, expert reviews were conducted, and dialectical analysis and optimization were performed based on expert suggestions. Building upon this, the final round of UEQ user testing was conducted, and refinements were made based on the results. The following sections introduce the user profiles, conceptual designs, and results of user testing for the three groups.

3.1 Fashion Designer

Young professionals often need to balance travel and work commitments. They require seamless device integration, instant idea recording, inspiration capture, and stimulation of creative thinking. These individuals typically appreciate novel and personalized interactions and assistance, and the combination of in-car voice DA with personalized artificial intelligence (AI) can provide these auxiliary functions.

Meet Jane, a fashion designer, who often struggles with a lack of design inspiration. Deciding to go on a field trip for inspiration, she finds herself having to check her schedule and destination on her phone while driving, then starting navigation. While driving to gather design inspiration, if she comes across elements or scenery worth referencing, she has to find a safe place to park, take out her camera, and capture the scenes. During the time spent on this, the elements (such as a group of birds or a cloud) may have disappeared, or her whimsical ideas may have been forgotten. Additionally, there may be some design materials that appeared during the drive but went unnoticed by her. After collecting enough materials, Jane feels overwhelmed by the multitude of photos and struggles with integrating them with her style or design requirements, requiring more creative thinking.

The team's design aims to help users capture and record real-time inspiration during the driving process, preventing the loss and missed opportunities of inspiration. Upon entering the car, the vehicle identifies the user's identity based on biological information, syncs the schedule, and automatically adjusts the seat to an ergonomically healthy position. Subsequently, the DA provides the owner with the ability to automatically capture specified creative elements while driving. During the journey, the DA can also recognize gesture captures, instantly recording scenes of interest to the owner. Upon reaching the destination, the DA provides three types of images: "AI Capture" displays scenes captured according to instructions; "Capture Materials" contains scenes captured by the owner using gestures during the drive. Dragging materials onto the windshield and windows allows for an immersive recreation of the scenes. "AI Generate" combines the captured materials of the day with the style of past works to automatically generate design sketches. Additionally, the touch display screen above the steering wheel can be used with the included stylus to modify the draft, creating a satisfactory piece. Similarly, details of the work can be displayed on the large screen through dragging.

UEQ user testing and expert reviews revealed good hedonic quality but slightly lacking in pragmatic quality, primarily in the following aspects: (1) The design is user-centered, fully considering the uniqueness and personalized needs of the designer group, and the custom features showcase the luxury experience brought by customization. (2) The functionality is innovative, with high attractiveness, and the immersive field trip and material capture functions grasp the passionate moments of a designer's inspiration. (3) Attention needs to be given to basic safety issues; improvements were made to address concerns about gesture capture during driving potentially disrupting driving safety, and pop-up prompts after photo capture potentially obstructing the driver's line of sight. (4) Building on the foundation of targeting specific groups, the design can be further expanded for broader applicability to serve more diverse groups, such as adding everyday functions like taking photos to find similar styles, and AI recommending scene-matching outfits for non-designer groups.

3.2 Beauty and Travel Blogger

Some young women enjoy solo travel, capturing vlogs, and aspire to always present their best selves in videos. They do not want to miss any scenic moments during the journey.

As single women, they have higher safety requirements for vehicles and expect a highly interactive and companionable in-car voice assistant.

Meet Xiaomei, a 23-year-old single beauty and travel blogger who frequently shoots travel videos. She needs a large amount of material but dividing attention between the camera and video content poses a risk to driving safety. Additionally, traditional video shooting methods on bumpy roads may affect video stability and quality. Furthermore, due to the filming needs, she needs to touch up her makeup frequently to ensure she looks perfect in the videos. However, makeup application in the car is affected by lighting issues. Importantly, as a single woman, Xiaomei often feels lonely on the road and is concerned about safety issues such as robbery and tire bursts.

Our aim is to design a personalized and companionable Porsche intelligent voice interaction assistant specifically for female drivers, providing truly considerate assistance in route planning, video shooting, social entertainment, and safe driving. Firstly, when the user sets off, the DA recommends different styles of routes for navigation and adjusts the in-car environment based on weather conditions. For instance, it may suggest wearing sunglasses if the ultraviolet light (UV) index is high. Before driving, it asks if she wants to activate the vlog mode anytime, opening nine camera angles for her to choose which ones to keep. During the journey, if the user sees a beautiful scenery and decides to get out for a photo, the vehicle automatically activates an alert mode. If it detects someone lingering nearby, it sends a real-time monitoring alert to the user's phone and provides the option to sound an alarm or attract attention with a loud noise. If the user feels tired during the journey, she can inform the DA, which will recommend the nearest service area for her to rest. Before resting, it asks if she needs a wake-up call, automatically lowering the interior brightness and playing white noise or music to create a sleep-inducing atmosphere. Upon waking up, the DA generates a sleep quality report. After waking up, based on the user's current makeup status, the DA asks if she needs a touch-up. If confirmed, it activates the makeup mode: the front windshield turns into a mirror, and the user can control the mirror's brightness through the center console. Next is the user's most concerned safety issue. In case of situations like kidnapping or robbery, the user can manually trigger an alarm by touching the back of the steering wheel. The vehicle will sound an alarm, send the location, and record the face of the intruder. If there's a tire burst or similar issues, the DA will display the rescue phone numbers for the current region and recommend solutions. Considering the user's feelings of loneliness, the vehicle also has social functions, such as sharing location with friends and voice chatting.

The results indicate that this design has a lower pragmatic quality but a higher hedonic quality. According to user feedback, the lower pragmatic quality may be due to the complexity of the functions provided by the voice assistant, without a clear focus on solving specific problems. The higher hedonic quality may stem from the voice assistant's ability to provide various interesting functions, such as schedule management, navigation planning, and video-assisted shooting. Users also provided specific improvement suggestions, such as adding the function to automatically recognize dangerous situations and take appropriate actions and setting the wake-up conditions for the voice assistant. Therefore, we propose the first version of improvement. Firstly, to improve pragmatic quality, we connected key functions and focus on their application in daily scenarios. Secondly, to prevent accidental touches, we changed the alarm button on the steering wheel to touch with the back of the hand. Thirdly, we set the wake-up conditions for the DA, and if there are no new requests within ten seconds, it automatically enters sleep mode. Building on the first improvement, combined with the positive feedback and suggestions from experts, we made a second improvement: Firstly, to ensure that the core driving functions are not affected, we changed the original anti-UV mode to directly display sunglasses. Secondly, we added more emotional design, reducing the user's feelings of loneliness, such as social functions in vehicle interaction. Thirdly, we improved existing functions, such as adding a fault handling function to the alarm button and changing the rest mode to go to the service station or rest area for rest and adding a timer function. Finally, we conducted a more in-depth and extensive user test. Combining users' firsthand experiences and suggestions, we once again improved the design. This time, the improvements were more subtle: Firstly, we numbered the people who wanted to share the car inside and outside, making it convenient for users to control through voice commands. Secondly, based on safety, privacy, and emotional considerations, we narrowed down the range of interactions in vehicle interaction functions to be limited to acquaintances.

3.3 Office Workers

The accelerated pace of life requires individuals to frequently switch roles between work and personal life. This shift involves not only a change in mindset but often requires adjustments in attire as well. As a successful "leading lady" in the workplace, a person might need to transition from a professional setting to a more relaxed one, such as a park, bar, or shopping center, on a Friday evening. In this context, the car, as a tool for location transition, plays a role in facilitating the transformation of both internal and external identities.

Meet Meimei, a 28-year-old independent woman of the Generation Z and the current president of a technology company. She is accomplished in her career and values personal life experiences and cost-effectiveness. She enjoys a comfortable and relaxed lifestyle and likes to drive to suburban markets and small shops in her leisure time. However, her busy schedule often leaves her with no time to change clothes after work. Consequently, she finds herself continuing to wear professional attire for casual entertainment, maintaining a tense demeanor. Despite going to places like parks or social gatherings, she struggles to fully relax, knowing that she would soon be immersed in work again. The precious downtime fails to provide sufficient rejuvenation, leaving her feeling helpless and distressed.

In response to the above scenario and needs, we propose a solution aimed at creating a "Cinderella carriage" for women to seamlessly transition between life and work. This design, based on Level 4 autonomous driving, aims to free up users' cognitive resources, facilitating a smooth transition and relaxation from internal feelings to external attire changes. In terms of mood transition, we've designed a "One-Click Disturbance-Free" mode and a "Leisure Mode." The One-Click Disturbance-Free mode connects with the user's mobile phone, helping to block work-related messages and providing a quiet rest environment. The "Leisure Mode" includes options for binge-watching, music playback, and chatting. Users can choose their preferred mode, and additional relaxation resources such as mindfulness meditation are available if desired. For attire changes, we've created a dressing mode that combines outfit recommendations, automatic ironing, and a private changing space. The voice assistant, "Xiao Bao," recommends suitable clothing based on the user's destination. Once the user selects the desired outfit, the rear seats fold forward to transform into an automatic ironing area, and the chosen clothing enters the automatic ironing area. During this process, the windows in the dressing mode fog up, allowing the user to see outside while maintaining privacy inside. After the clothes are ironed, the front driver's seat turns toward the rear, providing the user with a larger dressing space.

We conducted three rounds of testing and iterative improvements on our design product. In the first round of UEQ user testing, based on benchmark results and UEQ scales, we found that the pragmatic quality and hedonic quality levels were both relatively high, with pragmatic quality slightly lower. To address this, we enhanced the pragmatic system's functionality. We added automatic ironing to the existing "changing mode," making the feature more comprehensive. Additionally, we introduced the "One-Click Disturbance-Free Mode" and the "Leisure Mode." The former helps block work messages, creating a quiet rest environment, while the latter, linked between the car screen and the phone, allows screen mirroring for music or binge-watching, providing entertainment options for users. Next, we conducted an expert review, and experts provided two suggestions. First, they wanted more flexibility in the sequence of the three modes and a more convenient overall experience. Second, our "changing mode" requires a relatively large space, imposing certain requirements on the car model.

Addressing these suggestions, we carried out the second round of iterative improvements. In the interaction process, we allowed users to choose the sequence of the three modes, interact with the voice assistant as needed, and switch between the three main functions freely. For the Porsche car model, we selected the Macan, known as the "little Cayenne." This SUV-style model met our design's spatial requirements, ensuring the functionality could be implemented effectively. Its dynamic design and compact body style are more suitable for female drivers.

Building on this, we conducted the second round of UEQ user testing. The results showed high levels of clarity and attractiveness but lower scores in efficiency, reliability, novelty, and stimulation, with efficiency being the lowest. To address this, we incorporated Level 4 autonomous driving technology into the design prototype. Level 4 autonomous driving allows complete takeover of vehicle operations in specific areas, enabling users to engage in other tasks, such as changing clothes, during autonomous driving. This resolves the pain points of limited user time and numerous tasks, significantly improving efficiency. We also added dynamic facial recognition, allowing the driver to be recognized and unlocked upon sitting, streamlining the driving process and enhancing the owner's sense of security, reliability, and novelty. The three rounds of improvements deepened our understanding of user needs and refined our product design.

4 Discussion and Reflection

4.1 Innovative Classroom

The teacher advocates for a free and open atmosphere in the classroom, assigning a graduate student as a teaching assistant to guide each group. Students can boldly express their ideas in class and build good relationships with classmates and teachers. Adopting an educational approach that combines theory and practice, the first half of each class involves the teacher introducing theoretical knowledge, such as distinguishing terms related to UX, usability metrics, and user experience surveys. The second half focuses on enhancing students' practical skills, such as working in groups to define personas and engaging in DA-related design, conducting user experience tests, and continuously iterating and upgrading. With continuous learning of theory and increasing practical experience, each student personally experiences designing products for user pain points, constant iteration, and the product development process, gaining a deeper understanding of engineering psychology and user experience. This classroom model truly achieves "learning by doing," providing students with a sense of achievement and fulfillment.

4.2 Generation Z User Needs

The future belongs to the Generation Z, and understanding the characteristics and needs of this generation is crucial for product design. The three product designs provide innovative solutions that meet the practical needs of different segments of the Z generation. Fashion designers no longer need to worry about being unable to record their inspiration while driving; solo travel vloggers can confidently go out alone, capturing materials as they please without fear of loneliness; and workplace professionals can change outfits promptly after work, disconnecting from work. These three DA products designed for single women effectively meet the needs of female drivers, helping them smoothly complete work and relax, achieving a work-life balance. These creative works provide a fresh perspective for DA design.

4.3 Limitations

The three groups produced innovative results in class, but there are some common issues. Due to time constraints in the classroom, we did not conduct user research when considering user needs and pain points. Relying solely on our understanding and stereotypes of the user group, such as assuming "fashion designers must like more colorful personalized interiors," led to non-authoritative results. In the design processes, we considered conducting user research to identify product pain points and genuine user needs, designing more targeted solutions. During user and expert reviews, we invited members of the target audience to provide feedback and suggestions.

As it was our first encounter with engineering psychology and our first design for a company, our design ideas were somewhat fanciful and did not consider commercial scenarios. To increase the commercial value of the product, it needs a certain universality. The target audience range should be broadened, or functionality should be added to enhance the product's universality. For example, the "inspiration capture" feature designed for fashion designers could switch to an "outfit inspiration capture" feature or include "outfit recommendations and check-in spots matching the destination" for regular users.

4.4 Outlook for the Automotive Industry

The present landscape witnesses a widespread adoption of in-car voice DA, reflecting the escalating demand among consumers for diverse use cases and enhanced features. The pivotal role of elevating the existing in-car voice experience is evident, and there is an anticipation of continuous development and progress for in-car voice assistants within the rapidly evolving digital age. This project focuses primarily on addressing the needs of female users from the Generation Z. Building on this focus, certain expectations arise for the prospective evolution of in-car voice DA:

- Personalized UX: In the forthcoming era, in-car voice DA are poised to prioritize personalized user experiences. The intelligent assistant can adeptly grasp the driver's preferences and routines, delivering tailor-made services. Examples include curating music playlists in alignment with the driver's taste and furnishing intelligent calendar reminders synchronized with the driver's schedule.
- Enhanced Intelligence and Natural Interaction: Anticipated advancements indicate that future in-car voice DA can evolve to exhibit heightened intelligence and a more natural interaction paradigm. Integration with conversational AI, such as ChatGPT, is envisioned to empower these assistants to comprehend and interpret driver voice commands more effectively, fostering authentic and meaningful conversations. This enhancement aims to substantially elevate the overall interaction experience between the driver and the in-car assistant.
- Focus on Health and Safety: Future in-car voice DA is expected to place a more significant emphasis on addressing health and safety needs. Capabilities will extend to monitoring the driver's health indicators, including heart rate and blood pressure, offering timely advice and alerts. This holistic approach aims to contribute to enhancing the driver's safety and well-being by providing comprehensive safety protection features. For instance, in emergency situations for female drivers, the intelligent assistant may automatically send distress messages through emergency contacts or enable emergency calling functions.
- Integral Role in Autonomous Driving: With the continuous evolution of autonomous driving technology, in-car voice DA is foreseen to play a more integral role. Seamless integration with the vehicle's autonomous driving system will enable real-time navigation and provision of traffic information. Additionally, these DAs can automatically adjust driving strategies based on prevailing road conditions, aligning with the advancements in autonomous driving capabilities.
- Smart Home Connectivity: Looking ahead, in-car voice DA is anticipated to achieve seamless connectivity with smart home devices, facilitating a harmonious link between the home and the vehicle. Drivers can gain the ability to control home devices like lighting and temperature through the in-car assistant. This connectivity may even extend to activating home devices before arriving at the doorstep, ensuring a smoother transition of states and meeting the diverse needs of the driver.

The future trajectory of in-car voice DA in the automotive industry heralds a paradigm shift towards greater intelligence, personalization, and interconnectedness with the surrounding environment. Evolving into indispensable intelligent assistants and life companions for drivers, they are poised to offer a driving experience that is not only safer and more convenient but also remarkably comfortable.

References

1. Hernandez-de-Menendez, M., Escobar Díaz, C.A., Morales-Menendez, R.: Educational experiences with generation z. Int. J. Interact. Des. Manuf. **14**, 847–859 (2020)
2. Fan, A., Shin, H.W., Shi, J., Wu, L.: Young people share, but do so differently: an empirical comparison of peer-to-peer accommodation consumption between millennials and generation Z. Cornell Hospitality Q. **64**(3), 322–337 (2023)
3. Ozkan, M., Solmaz, B.: The changing face of the employees–generation Z and their perceptions of work (a study applied to university students). Procedia Econ. Finance **26**, 476–483 (2015)
4. Xin, X., et al.: X thinking in the experience economy era: 23 personas that identify generation Z interaction qualities. Creativity Innov. Entrepreneurship **74**, 86–94 (2023)
5. Liu, W., Lee, K.P., Gray, C.M., Toombs, A.L., Chen, K.H., Leifer, L.: Transdisciplinary teaching and learning in UX design: a program review and AR case studies. Appl. Sci. **11**(22), 10648 (2021)
6. Desmet, P.M., Xue, H., Xin, X., Liu, W.: Demystifying emotion for designers: a five-day course based on seven fundamental principles. Adv. Des. Res. **1**(1), 50–62 (2023)
7. Maedche, A., et al.: AI-based digital assistants: opportunities, threats, and research perspectives. Bus. Inf. Syst. Eng. **61**, 535–544 (2019)
8. Sachdev, S., Macwan, J., Patel, C., Doshi, N.: Voice-controlled autonomous vehicle using IoT. Procedia Comput. Sci. **160**, 712–717 (2019)
9. Chattaraman, V., Kwon, W.S., Gilbert, J.E., Ross, K.: Should AI-based, conversational digital assistants employ social-or task-oriented interaction style? A task-competency and reciprocity perspective for older adults. Comput. Hum. Behav. **90**, 315–330 (2019)
10. Visser, F.S., Stappers, P.J., Van der Lugt, R., Sanders, E.B.: Contextmapping: experiences from practice. CoDesign **1**(2), 119–149 (2005)
11. Liu, W., et al.: Designing interactive glazing through an engineering psychology approach: six augmented reality scenarios that envision future car human-machine interface. Virtual Reality Intell. Hardware **5**(2), 157–170 (2023)
12. Schrepp, M., Hinderks, A., Thomaschewski, J.: Design and evaluation of a short version of the user experience questionnaire (UEQ-S). Int. J. Interact. Multimedia Artif. Intell. **4**(6), 103–108 (2017)

Research on the Innovative Service System Design for Herbal Tea Driven by Circle-Breaking Trend

Yuxiao Xiao[✉] and Zhen Liu

School of Design, South China University of Technology, Guangzhou 510006, People's Republic of China
3273707036@qq.com

Abstract. Circle-Breaking means making something a widely known outside of the fixed circle. It has become a popular way of attracting more customers recently as it presents the product in a way that is outside the conventional perception.

Herbal tea is a type of traditional Chinese beverage based on the theories of traditional Chinese medicine. Herbal tea has medical and cultural significance as an important part of Chinese medicine culture, and has been selected as the first batch of national intangible cultural heritage in China. However, the herbal tea industry has been gradually declining, which has also affected the herbal tea culture, as its marketing methods are out of step with today's experiential economy. Additionally, there remains a gap in current research regarding the improvement of its marketing ways or the preservation of the herbal tea culture. Therefore, this paper uses the service design as the theoretical basis, employs the double drill model and co-design as research methods to develop an innovative service system for herbal tea. The service system is driven by the circle-breaking trend, aiming to improve the competitiveness of herbal tea and protect its culture. This paper develops a new design mode based on the service design and the circle-breaking trend in the heritage conservation research for the first time, which provides certain reference for cultural heritage conservation and the interdisciplinary research in design and marketing.

Keywords: Service Design · Circle-Breaking · Heritage Conservation · Herbal Tea · Double Drill Model · Co-design

1 Introduction

1.1 Circle-Breaking

Circle-Breaking refers to making something a widely known outside of fixed circle. It has become a popular way of attracting more customers as it presents the product in a way that is different from the conventional perception [1]. This can pique customers' curiosity and lead to increased interests in the product. The Temple coffee and the Moutai-flavored latte are both typical examples. In the case of Luckin Coffee's Moutai-flavored latte, for example, which recently gained notoriety for catching fire, the combination of coffee and Maotai creates a strong sense of contrast that effectively stimulates users' curiosity and attracts them to experience it. On its first day, a total of 5.42 million Moutai flavoured lattes were sold with sales exceeding 100 million RMB, setting a new record for Luckin Coffee's single product sales [2, 4]. Therefore, circle-breaking is currently a highly effective marketing strategy for attracting users.

The core of circle-breaking is to break the rules and catch people off guard. To successfully break the circle, we must first accurately define the product's circle model based on the user's perception [3]. The flow chat of the circle-breaking and the product's circle model are shown in Fig. 1. Then, we can choose a strategy to break the cycle based on the model. There are typically three types of circle-breaking: scene-breaking, crowd-breaking, and culture-breaking. Table 1 *gives a summary* of the three different circle-breaking types.

Table 1. Summary of the three different circle-breaking types.

Circle-breaking type	Definition	Examples
Scene-breaking	Explore new scenarios and cultivate new consumption habits by breaking away from fixed product scenarios	Temple coffee
Crowd-breaking	Break down the product's fixed user base so that previously unfamiliar user groups know and experience the product	Moutai-flavored latte, Moutai-flavored ice-cream
Culture-breaking	Incorporate specific cultural content into the product to attract users	CHAGEE

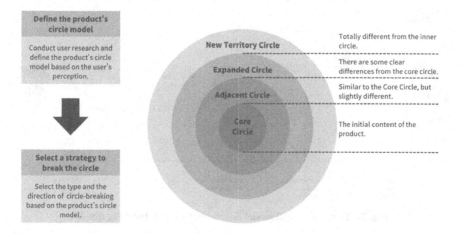

Fig. 1. The flow chat of the circle-breaking and the product's circle model.

1.2 Herbal Tea

Herbal tea is a kind of traditional Chinese drinks, which is based on traditional Chinese medicine theories and adapted to the climate of Lingnan. Herbal tea holds medical and cultural significance as a crucial component of both Chinese medicine culture and Lingnan culture [5]. In 2006, the State Council of China selected herbal tea as the first batch of national intangible cultural heritage.

However, the herbal tea industry has been in a state of gradual decline in recent years, and the herbal tea culture has also been impacted. Asia's ready-to-drink herbal tea market share declined by 27.1%. In addition, according to the Cato Consumer Index, herbal teas have declined from over 50% to 45% in terms of household penetration, a gradual shift towards weakness [6]. There are two main reasons for this. The first is that herbal tea is affected by the competition from other beverages. Secondly, its marketing ways do not align with the current experience economy, failing to meet consumers' demand for a satisfying service experience [6, 7].

2 Methods

Based on the current plight of herbal tea, this paper uses the service design as the theoretical basis, employs the double drill model and co-design as research methods to develop an innovative service system for herbal tea. At the same time, this paper innovatively applies the circle-breaking trend to the double drill model (see Fig. 2), with the aim of improving the attractiveness of the herbal tea service system and preserving the herbal tea culture.

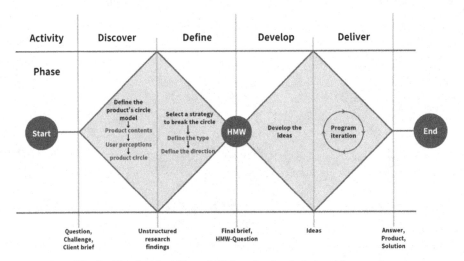

Fig. 2. The double drill model driven by the circle-breaking trend.

3 Conduct

3.1 Discover

Product Content Research. In order to accurately define the herbal tea's circle model, it is first necessary to have an accurate and comprehensive understanding of herbal tea. At this stage, two methods are mainly used: literature review and field research. By reviewing the literature on herbal tea and conducting field research at the Guangzhou Herbal Tea Museum, Shen Nong Herbology Museum and Wong Tai Sin Temple, it was found that herbal tea, as an intangible cultural heritage in Lingnan, is very rich in content: Firstly, the founder of herbal tea is Ge Hong, a famous philosopher of the Tao. He discovered herbal tea during his study of Taoism and medicine at Luofu Mount in Lingnan [12]. Therefore, herbal tea has a deep connection with Taoist culture. Secondly, herbal tea is based on traditional Chinese medicine (TCM) and made from Chinese herbs [14]. Herbal tea is an important part of Chinese TCM culture. In addition, herbal tea was developed by the people of Lingnan in the course of long-term disease prevention and health care according to the local climatic characteristics. Herbal tea is a representative of Lingnan culture [5, 13]. Use a relationship graph to summarise the content of the herbal tea (see Fig. 3). In this study, culture-breaking is selected as the circle-breaking strategy to design. On the one hand, herbal tea has a rich cultural content. On the other hand, culture-breaking is helpful to the culture conservation.

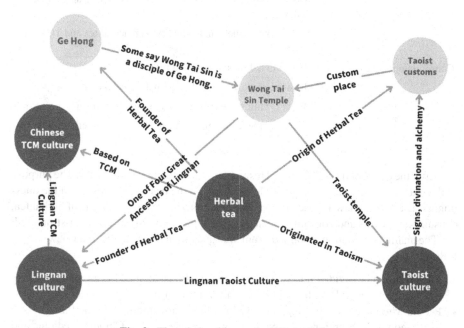

Fig. 3. The relationship graph of the herbal tea.

User Research. Two Main Methods are Used to Gain a Deeper Understanding of the User: Questionnaire and Interview. In the questionnaire, a total of 84 valid questionnaires are distributed. The purpose of the questionnaire is to understand the user's knowledge of herbal tea and daily consumption habits. The questionnaire consists of three main sections: the personal information survey, the perception survey and the consumption survey. The target of the questionnaire are people now living in the Lingnan. The content of the questionnaires is shown in Table 2.

Table 2. The questions in the questionnaire.

Section	Question
Personal information survey	What is your gender?
	What is your age group?
	Where are you from?
	How long have you lived in the Lingnan?
Perception survey	Do you know what herbal tea is?
	What do you think herbal tea is?
	Do you know the founder of herbal tea?
	Do you know the connection between herbal tea and Lingnan culture?
	Do you know the connection between herbal tea and Taoist culture?
	Do you know the connection between herbal tea and TCM culture?
Consumption survey	How often do you buy herbal tea?
	How much do you spend on herbal tea each month?
	What is your motivation for purchasing herbal tea?
	What are the factors that influence you to buy herbal tea?

After the questionnaire, 12 typical respondents are selected to interview. The purpose of the interview is to gain an insight into the users on the basis of the results of the questionnaire. The interview focused on: knowledge of herbal tea, perceptions of herbal tea, consumption habits and consumption needs. The type of interviews are semi-structured.

The main information obtained from the questionnaire and the interview are as follow:

- The users can be divided into two groups: those who have lived in Lingnan for a long time and those who have lived in Lingnan for a short time.
- People who have lived in Lingnan for a long time know more about herbal tea.
- Most people's perception of herbal tea remains at the level of Chinese medicine and Lingnan culture.
- People who have lived in Lingnan for a long time pay more attention to the effectiveness of herbal tea.

- People who have lived in Lingnan for a short time are more likely to be attracted to the culture of herbal tea.
- Cultural habits are an important part of people's motivation for herbal tea drinking.
- How to choose herbal tea is an important demand from users.
- The current way of purchasing herbal tea is not convenient.

Product's Circle Model. Based on the product content research and the user research, the circle model of the herbal tea shown in Fig. 4 is carried out.

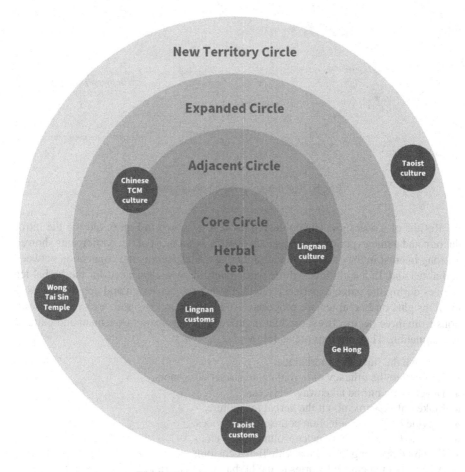

Fig. 4. The circle model of the herbal tea.

3.2 Define (Co-design)

Preparation for Co-design. In order to define the circle-breaking strategy, a co-design workshop is conducted. The co-design workshop is for herbal tea stakeholders. It provides a platform for them to express, aiming to ensure the accuracy of the design. The process of co-design needs to be carefully designed to be step-by-step (see Fig. 5).

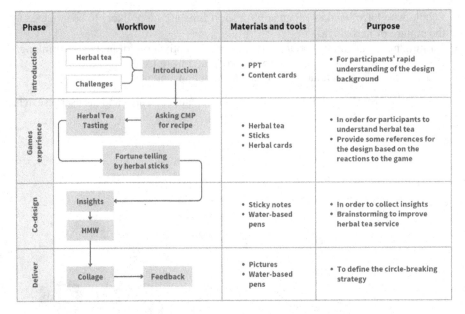

Fig. 5. The design of the co-design process.

Results of Co-design. The co-design process is shown in Fig. 6. During the introduction and game experience phases, it is observed that most of the participants showed a strong interest in the cultural content of herbal tea, especially the connection between herbal tea and Taoist culture. All the participants show a clear need for the herbal tea choices during the game experience phase. During the co-design and deliver phases, 5 main insights on herbal tea are proposed. And participants propose a total of 10 solutions from three perspectives: product improvement, service improvement and cultural dissemination. The solutions are as follow:

- Improve the flavour of herbal tea.
- Emphasize the efficacy of herbal tea to attract customers.
- Develop the online takeaway services.
- Make online game about the herbal tea culture.
- Provide herbal tea selection counselling services.
- Provide Chinese medicine consultation service.
- Combine drinking herbal tea with Taoist customs.
- Add herbal tea cultural stories to the herbal tea packaging.
- Provide DIY making herbal tea service.
- Reuse of herbs, for the environment.

3.3 Develop

Based on the above analysis, the herbal tea service system consists of an applet and a herbal tea experience hall. The applet and the herbal tea experience are closely linked in order to better serve the users.

Fig. 6. Co-design process (Left: game experience, right: co-design).

Fig. 7. Applet prototype.

Applet Prototype. In order to improve the service flow of herbal tea purchase, we design an applet for providing takeaway service and reservation service. Users can book services such as consultations and herbal tea purchases through the applet before visiting the herbal tea experience hall to save time waiting in line. In addition, there are cultural games and cultural stories in the applet so that users can easily understand the culture of herbal tea, which is conducive to cultural preservation. The prototype is shown in Fig. 7.

Herbal Tea Experience Hall Model. The herbal tea experience hall is the core place, which has the function of cultural heritage and the function of herbal tea service. Users can participate in various activities there, such as cultural experiences, medical consultations, tea selection, and tea drinking. The herbal tea experience hall is divided into nine areas: reception, sign requesting area, interpretation area, herbal medicine area, alchemy area, consultation area, drinking area, recycling area and wishing area. The model of herbal tea experience is shown in Fig. 8.

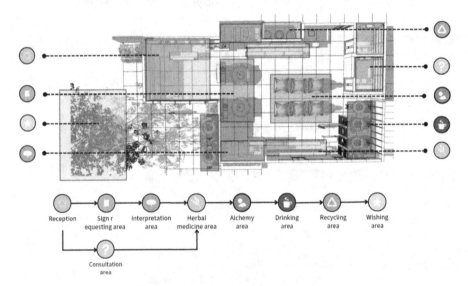

Fig. 8. The model of herbal tea experience.

3.4 Deliver (Usability Test)

Preparation for Usability Test. In order to evaluate and iterate the design, a usability test is conducted. A total of six typical users participate in this test. The test covers the entire process of the herbal tea service system. The content of the test is shown in Table 3. The testing tools are Figma and Unity 3d to test the applet prototype and experience hall model.

Results of Usability Test. The designer is responsible for communicating the task from the sidelines as well as observing and recording the tester's responses during the test. There are three types of responses from the testers: successful completion of the task

Table 3. The list of testing tasks.

NO.	Task
1	Use the applet to book an order for herbal tea
2	DIY herbal tea recipes using the applets
3	Where are you from?
4	Use the applet to book a consultation and then go to the experience hall to consult
5	Ask for a sign and get the result of it in the interpretation area
6	Make a wish in the wishing area with the sign

and no errors (Record with "√"), successful completion of the task with some confusion (Record with "O") and failure to complete the task (Record with "×"). The result of the test is shown in Table 4.

Table 4. The result of the tests.

Tester NO.	Task 1	Task 2	Task 3	Task 4	Task 5	Task 6
1	√	√	√	√	√	×
2	√	√	O	√	√	O
3	√	√	√	√	√	√
4	√	√	O	√	√	O
5	√	√	√	O	√	√
6	√	√	√	√	√	√

From the test result Task 1, Task 2 and Task 5 are completed well. The Task 6 with the most errors is due to a lack of instructions in the wishing area. The error in Task 3 is due to the unclear meaning of the text of the "Old Chinese Medicine Recipe" button in the applet. The error in Task 4 is due to tester's unfamiliarity with the process of asking for a sign.

Based on the above analysis, The improvement strategies are as follow:

- Change the text of the "Old Chinese Medicine Recipe" button in the applet to "Ask for a consult and recipe".
- Add some guidance to the applet and sign requesting area.
- Add some guidance to the wishing area.

4   Results

4.1   Persona

Our users are divided into two main categories: those who live in Lingnan for a long time and those who live in Lingnan for a short time. Their perceptions of herbal tea and their motivations for purchasing herbal tea are slightly different due to the differences in their living environments, but their needs for health and their interest in culture are the same. The personas are shown in Fig. 9.

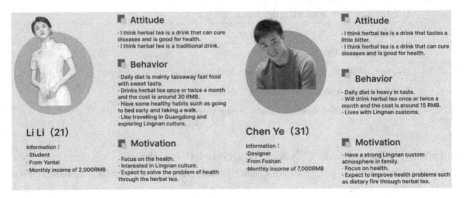

Fig. 9. Personas.

4.2 Service Blueprint

Based on the users' demand for health and their interest in culture, the herbal tea service system is designed to combine with Lingnan, Taoist and Chinese medicine cultures, driven by the culture-breaking. Through the design of cultural packaging and cultural games, users can learn about the cultural knowledge of herbal tea and feel the charm of herbal tea in the process of drinking herbal tea in an interesting way. We also improve the whole process of drinking herbal tea, such as booking, counselling and making herbal tea, to ensure that users choose the right herbal tea and drink it conveniently. The service design includes the applet and the herbal tea experience hall: the applet mainly undertakes the functions of service booking and online cultural popularisation, and the herbal tea experience hall as the activity place is mainly used to provide offline services and cultural popularisation. The final prototypes are shown in Fig. 10 and the blueprint is shown in Fig. 11.

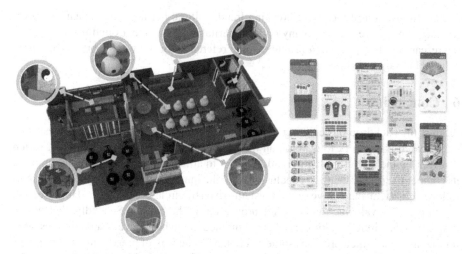

Fig. 10. Prototypes of the herbal tea experience hall and the applet.

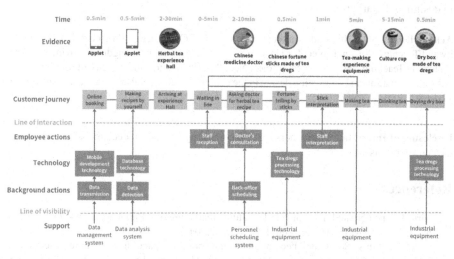

Fig. 11. Service blueprint.

5   Discussion

The preservation of cultural heritage has always been an important social issue. The preservation of cultural heritage is not only about the preservation of the past, but also about the transmission and dissemination of human wisdom, values and creativity. Taking herbal tea as the research object, this paper develops a new design mode based on the service design and the circle-breaking trend to improve the attractiveness of the service system. In this research, we unexpectedly discovered the great potential of the circle-breaking trend in cultural heritage preservation. With the rigour of design and the innovation of the circle-breaking trend, cultural heritage can appear in a user-friendly way. There are still many cultural heritages in decline around the world, and the research in this paper can provides some reference for the way of preserving these cultural heritages.

6   Conclusion

Against the backdrop of declining herbal tea culture, this paper uses service design as the research framework to develop an innovative service system for herbal tea, which is driven by the circle-breaking trend, in order to attract more consumers and improve its competitiveness. The main conclusions and the innovation points of this paper are as follows: Firstly, an innovative service system driven by circle-breaking trend is presented, which provides valuable guidance for protecting the herbal tea. Secondly, the service design and the circle-breaking trend are combined in the heritage conservation research for the first time which provides some reference for the way of preserving these cultural heritages. Thirdly, this paper proposes a new double drill design model driven by the circle-breaking trend, which provides certain reference for the interdisciplinary research in design and marketing.

Acknowledgments. This study was supported by "2022 Constructing Project of Teaching Quality and Teaching Reform Project for Undergraduate Universities in Guangdong Province" Higher Education Teaching Reform Project (project No. 386), 'Innovation and practice of teaching methods for information and interaction design in the context of new liberal arts' (project grant number x2sj-C9233001).

Disclosure of Interests. The authors have no competing interests to declare that are relevant to the content of this article.

References

1. Yiru, J.: The core and trend of "circle culture" marketing. Int. Public Relat. **04**, 7–12 (2022). https://doi.org/10.16645/j.cnki.cn11-5281/c.2022.04.001
2. Li, L.: Luckin's "Soy Latte" becomes a hit; how brands expand the boundaries of crossover co-branding. China Advertising **11**, 44–47 (2023). https://kns.cnki.net/kcms2/article/abstract?v=phUvsea1i7bPY2mPTggi2s6viG-4ME6EHnc9iZhJQ9ykvEsczAO6JlVf1O8nHnmCvElRlbK-1vxwSC7uOWPkAMO_BybhxhWt9RK1V78ikBG1N-vWcewUID4HYYFy84R9Arpw13xEgHg=&uniplatform=NZKPT&language=CHS
3. Peiyu, X.: What does crossover marketing rely on to attract consumers. People's Daily Overseas Edition, 12 October 2023. https://kns.cnki.net/kcms2/article/abstract?v=phUvsea1i7Y2jF5gQDXzrusKY9_5qT3e6dVI8S2j-WEMxgYBngRhjiwp6DMM5sPWqgSyTXa1TQF8jgsoakmsz-X3HtSUToQurPSnAaF-BYHP5YktbmLfsFS8o9Tkwb3qbcEJMRgz1yA=&uniplatform=NZKPT&language=CHS
4. Menghan, Y.: How far can the re-launch of the saucy chocolate co-branded model broaden the boundaries for Moutai? China Wine News, 30 January 2024. https://kns.cnki.net/kcms2/article/abstract?v=phUvsea1i7ZeL0TJgA1OJSVZK14id0Ag5tmgtvoiYpOX48kmwAyONXNz7ni_OTY3sviK4fsJx9aoSrIioV7nWdBwQ3ppxfoESkEu8vK74VR8Zc1qb4YlfI8kZqChDOll3g3BSfbZPAb0=&uniplatform=NZKPT&language=CHS

5. Junfa, L.: The past life of herbal tea. Guangdong Second Class **05**, 36–37 (2022). https://kns. cnki.net/kcms2/article/abstract?v=phUvsea1i7asFK-vrevTayDnbTr_iiU4Tqcig_7qohecn7p CZ1rqLg6Bell9xoPwE81QiRg9RBcco8Npzw3usfm1Ri7FImd8GbkybfikUcgQf_C8rkSb Spme2JadAR7uWN0aIyCgLqs=&uniplatform=NZKPT&language=CHS
6. Is the Herbal Tea Market "cold". Food Saf. J. **18**, 6 (2022). https://kns.cnki.net/kcms2/ article/abstract?v=phUvsea1i7aM1HD9SNJXxlrxHmX4dJxO49hAC-1wTXRrKRBd4rPC- pAFgWn8j_6SBVAff4mooljFORp3bYVUdrNMTTyDsrQk1nRCupo7A2fyqK5a_GBo6B3 MWSUtRMt9syQmRD4JDL4=&uniplatform=NZKPT&language=CHS
7. Zhiyin, L.: Herbal tea industry growth is weak and how to break out of the leading companies. First Financ. Daily (2022). https://doi.org/10.28207/n.cnki.ndycj.2022.000898
8. The double-diamond model. https://outwitly.com/blog/human-centered-design-series-1/
9. Morelli, N.: Developing new product service systems (PSS): methodologies and operational tools. J. Clean. Prod. **14**(17), 1495–1501 (2006)
10. Steen, M., Manschot, M., De Koning, N.: Benefits of co-design in service design projects. Int. J. Des. **5**(2) (2011)
11. Wu, Y., Chen, L.-Y., Ren, L.: Implementation of service design on innovation development of traditional handicraft: a case study of Yongchun lacquered basket. In: Rau, P.-L.P. (ed.) Cross-Cultural Design. LNCS, vol. 10281, pp. 232–240. Springer, Cham (2017). https://doi. org/10.1007/978-3-319-57931-3_19
12. Lingdi, L., Jipeng, D., Hong, G.: The contemporary value and inheritance of Lingnan regional cultural symbols. J. Huizhou Coll. **04**, 7–13 (2022). https://link.cnki.net/doi/10.16778/j.cnki. 1671-5934.2022.04.002
13. Jianmin, X., Hang, Y.: Analysing the culture of herbal tea and its transformation in Guang- dong. Editorial Board Res. Food Cult. **16** (2005). https://kns.cnki.net/kcms2/article/abstract? v=phUvsea1i7alpRxYZbLtnGYl72s86hwMn4ECDJ0K3CGDzle_bzWCOO-pBpBpDUW3 HVWS17tCePLnH4e_CPvftuN5h4iIScoBarNHb6KyNiQ0t58akHHb1zQQaYcrQV0KlG0 wxNXGTZw=&uniplatform=NZKPT&language=CHS
14. Hong, Z.: Lingnan medicine and Lingnan Culture. Chin. Med. Cult. **10**(05), 39–42 (2015). https://doi.org/10.16307/j.1673-6281.2015.05.009

Exploration of the Digital Twin for Prototyping the Product-Service System Design in a Bus Manufacturing Company

Zhang Yan🆔 and Tobias Larsson$^{(\boxtimes)}$ 🆔

Blekinge Institute of Technology, Karlskrona, Sweden
zhang.yan@bth.se, tobias.larsson@bt.se

Abstract. When bus manufacturing companies move forward in their servitization journey for providing service solutions for tourism industry, there is an increasing need to exploit the prototype way to support the realization of design solutions in the early stages of the Product Service System (PSS) design. Digital twin, a new emerging and fast growing technology which connects the physical and virtual world, has attracted much attention worldwide recently. This paper presents a new method for PSS design based on the digital twin approach. The development of product design is briefly introduced first. The framework of digital twin approach is then proposed and analysed. The main work in this research work is how to trade off the 'realism' of the design output of the virtual concept. A case is presented to illustrate the application of the proposed DT approach for product prototyping. Verification activities performed the case in a virtual simulation environment prototype the design concepts in the tourism industry.

Keywords: Digital Twin (DT) · Prototyping · Product Service System (PSS) · Service scenario · Tour bus

1 Introduction

The ongoing digital servitization transformation is pushing manufacturing companies to adopt innovative approaches to manage product development process with customers (Struwe and Slepniov, 2023). Manufacturing companies that were traditionally perceived as product-centered are today increasingly influenced by a service-oriented theory, which claims that manufacturing companies are driven to shift their business focus towards a strategy where customer-perceived value is in the spotlight and where products are bundled with services to offer Product-Service Systems (PSS) (Goedkoop et al., 1999). The industry companies need to move "downstream" knowledge from the entire lifecycle into the early phases of the PSS design process where critical decisions are made (Morelli 2006). At the same time, this raises the awareness of, and requirements for, a new emerging methods that support cross-disciplinary team collaboration in the process of designing and prototyping these PSS solutions. Digital twin (DT) consists of three parts: physical product, virtual product and the linkage between physical and virtual product

(Glaessgen and Stargel 2012). Building on such a gap, the paper aims to present an DT approach that allows the integration of the PSS design along with the service operational context for prototyping the concepts of the PSS (Furr and Dyer 2014). The intent is to enable the bus manufacturing industries to leverage the use of DT in their early design phase to make decisions on both, PSS design features and service operational strategy, ultimately enabling the prototyping of the potential impact of the transition toward digitalization of tour bus in terms of scenario performance, operational cost, and environmental impact. This paper's research question can be described as: How can product concepts be prototyped using digital twin in the early phase of product service system design?

The paper exemplifies the approach by scenario it in a tourism natural environment describing how the DT have enabled PSS concept design and prototype develop, and how prototype of service solutions is integrated into the digital twin of the operational scenario. The last section summarizes the main content, contribution, limitations, and future perspectives.

2 Research Approach

The research was conducted with guidance from the framework of Design Research Methodology (DRM) proposed by Blessing and Chakrabarti (2009) and is based on a single-Case Study Research (Yin 2014), which has also influenced the research approach in this work. First, the research motivation was clarified by reviewing the literature on PSS design and digital twin (DT), which provided a deeper understanding of the challenges and existing gaps in current research. The research question was defined in collaboration with a bus manufacturing company that designing tour bus for tourism industry applications. The initial dataset was collected through the case company and has been modified and complemented with realistic data and application environment in a nature tourism scenario. The digital twin model and systems simulations have been run using commercially available software. 3D gaming engine/Computer-based simulations. These data were used in the research to create preliminary demonstrators of digital twin, that were discussed with a cross-disciplinary group of experts having knowledge in engineering design, vehicle design, product planning and virtual prototyping). The verification of the impact of the Prescriptive Study results (the digital twin approach) corresponds to the 'Application Evaluation' phase of the DRM.

3 Scientific Background

3.1 Product Service System

A PSS is a marketable set of tangible products and intangible services that together can fulfil a customer's needs (Goedkoop et al., 1999). Product-Service Systems (Mont, 2002) is one of the industrial trends representing the shift in manufacturers' strategic focus from selling a physical product to providing performance and availability, as a way to satisfy more sophisticated needs and expectations (Baines et al. 2007).From the literatures, PSS has been categorized into three needs and expectations (Baines et al. 2007). From the literature, PSS has been categorized into three different groups by product ownership and type of service provided as follows (Tukker and Tischner 2006):

- Product-oriented PSS: Products are sold to the user, but additional services are added, such as maintenance or product-related consultancy.
- Use-oriented PSS: The business model is geared toward selling the product function through leasing or renting, and the product remains under the ownership of the PSS provider.
- Result-oriented PSS: The business model is geared toward selling a result and is closest to offering a pure service where no predetermined product is involved.

PSS are increasingly seen as business strategies created by companies that intend to strengthen their market position and create a competitive advantage through traditional transactional product sales. PSS emerged as a response to make both production and consumption sustainable, for example, by reducing waste by reuse, remanufacturing, and repair, similar to the contemporary recommendation of a circular economy to guide sustainable development. Despite the promises of PSS, manufacturers continue to struggle for optimized financial performance by integrating products and services. The existing research argues that this is largely due to the insufficient theoretical exploration in the manufacturing industry and the lack of a systems approach in PSS design (Rondini et al., 2017).

3.2 Prototyping for Design

The concept of prototyping is to gather information to help in the decision-making process of design creation and inter-disciplinary design, prototypes have a unique capability for enabling sensemaking between stakeholders with differing domain vocabularies by creating a "common language" (Exner 2016). Experiential prototyping techniques endeavor to accomplish three goals towards addressing the problem: understanding existing user experiences and context, exploring and evaluating design ideas, and communicating ideas to an audience (Buchenau et al., 2000). Furr and Dyer assert that rapid prototypes have a fundamental role in hypotheses validation (2014). They also discovered that in some cases it can be beneficial to fake the capability of a product if the experience is your key point of investigation (Furr and Dyer 2014). Prototypes enable sensemaking in design process via the following properties (Exner 2016):

- A prototype visualizes mental ideas
- A prototype supports the comprehension of complexity
- A prototype enables communication, thus removing cultural and linguistic barriers
- A prototype always contains a specific question and is limited due to given constraints
- A prototype tests functionalities and requirements.

3.3 Digital Twin for PSS Design

The concept of digital twin (DT) can date back to Grieves's description about Product Lifecycle Management (PLM) in 2003 (Grieves 2014). Rosen et al. believe that digital twin is the model which can interact between autonomous system behaviours and the environment in the physical world (Rosen et al. 2015). DTs are increasingly developed and used to integrate multidimensional simulation and support decision-making in complex situations (Tao et al., 2019). The applications of DT in the realm of products (Erkoyuncu et al., 2020), services (Stark et al., 2019), and product-service ecosystems (Tao et al., 2018). While a majority of the applications of DT are in the manufacturing/production-related (Jones et al., 2020). DT also seems to facilitate multi-disciplinary and heterogeneous simulations of complex systems, especially enabled by the building block correspondence of Model-based Systems Engineering (Schluse et al., 2017; Clement et al., 2017). Anchoring the inferences from these studies, one trend was clear that the DT embraced a high-fidelity representation of the physical space. Such an approach may not be suitable for early-stage design decision-making that is typically subjected to many uncertainties. Thus, the empirical study primarily focused on the collection of needs and expectations for the use of DTs in the early stages. More specifically, the focus was to utilize DT to enhance the design space exploration to the PSS level (comprising of the systems, the associated services, and the application environment), and finally to the scenario level (i.e. including the simulation of different operational context) (Bertoni et al., 2022).

Not much attention was paid to make use of digital twin in the first stage of product creation (i.e. the design stage). As pointed out and stated by Dassault, there is huge potential of digital twin in product design (Digital Twins 2015). In addition, if one could establish the product digital twin mode from the design phase, then more related design data, marketing data, user experience data, etc., can be integrated into the product digital mode, and this will result in better serve for the product prototype stage and operation stage (Bertoni and Ruvald 2021).

4   Result: The Proposed Digital Twin Approach for Prototyping

This study's main contribution is to develop the digital twin approach based on the data-driven method and to integrate it into the product development process for prototyping PSS design. To demonstrate the different types of data, application methods and software system collaboration support of digital twin in the product development of PSS design. To demonstrate the different types of data, application methods and software system collaboration support of digital twin in the product development process. Ultimately, both academia and industry can learn how to apply the digital twin approach for proto-typing of PSS design. The digital twin approach for prototyping the PSS was developed by the authors in previous research that built on a comprehensive literature review of relevant PSS design methodology and digital twin presented in Sect. 3. The digital app-roach is structured in a framework based on the product development process to ensure broad adoption in manufacturing companies (see in Fig. 1 below). The development and deployment of the DT in the framework consisted of the combination of different types of modules and virtual simulations at different levels of granularity that provide input and output to each other, respectively. Figure 1 shows the logical structure of the DT comprising of the PSS system and virtual prototype models connected hierarchically (scenario-, product-, feature-prototype). **The DT approach** requires selecting a PSS type for designing (Tukker and Tischner 2006). First, select the PSS category based on the high level of product development from three categories: **Product-oriented, Use-oriented, and Result-oriented.** Then value data needs to be collected for creating digital twin of product, and there are three categories of data should collect. For the collection of different types of data: scenario data, product data and feature data. The scenario data collect from different stakeholders, the product data from bus manufacturers, and the feature data from the supply chain. These three types of data mentioned above into the digital twin approach through the gaming engine, Unity 3D. The all three types of modules need to be developed as 3D modules and be bounded in virtual environment. Therefore, the data output of DT approach can generate three types of prototypes for decision making of PSS design, the result of prototype ensure data authenticity and usability from prototype simulation to data input during the product development process.

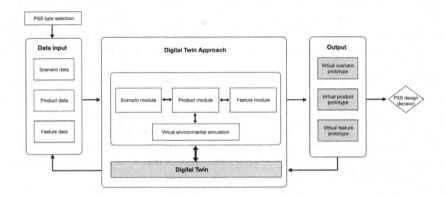

Fig. 1. Framework of digital twin approach for PSS design prototyping.

4.1   Application Case: Prototyping a Tour E-bus Concept for Tourism Industry

Smart E-bus have gradually become the direction of product development and competition in the automotive industry, and new product development methods are transforming towards by applying emerging tools and approaches of digitalization and intelligence. The global bus manufacturing company-King Long Group is also facing the challenge of the bus manufacturing industry needs to adapt to the tourism industry's demand for buses to provide diversified customer-oriented scenarios during nature tourism. It also requires tour buses to provide digital service capabilities for tourists during the journey. It is necessary to develop a virtual prototyping system for user usage scenarios based on King Long's product development platform using emerging technologies such as digital twin, simulation tool and AI, and provide data driven method in the early stage of the development of tour bus. Quantitative data analysis support is provided to ensure the competitiveness of new products and services in tourism service industry as smart products (smart cockpit + digital service), and at the same time applied the method and approach to the design and development of service solution for tourism service.

Creating Digital Twin via Data-Driven 3D Module. In this case, follow the framework of digital twin approach (see in Fig. 2 below). First, the digital twins are developed based on the King Long's tour bus product platform by research team. By using gaming engine, Unity 3D, the design team could develop 3D virtual models of bus products, including (exterior, interior and cockpit components, interface and passenger character models, etc.). When developing digital twins, it is necessary to comply with from the virtual environment level, such as (operation environment model, transportation systems and natural environment models) to meet the physical and activities requirements of scenario side cockpit components, interface and passenger character models, etc.). When developing digital twins, it is necessary to comply with from the virtual environment level, such as (operation environment model, transportation systems and natural environment models) to meet the physical and activities requirements of scenario simulation. For the product definition, such as develops product key systems of (product appearance, product cockpit, cockpit interior materials, product chassis and battery systems, etc.). For the feature definition, such as (component detail models, functional actions and interactive effects, components) can be grouped or separated for creating independently. The digital twin development is based on combining different types of data into the product 3D models. These data come from three categories: **scenario data, product data and feature data**. In the case, the scenario data is collected and analyzed by researchers through tourism industry data and interviews and collation of product positioning with internal stakeholders of local tourism company in. Product data and feature data comes from product data provided by King Long's R&D department. The three types of data have saved by researchers into Excel format as the input for creating digital twin. This step explores the method of combining the different types of data inputs by digital twins during the product development phase. It also allows product managers and design engineers within bus manufacturing company to see the visualization of the product concept as soon as possible to facilitate collaborative innovation works.

Verification of Design Concepts from Digital Twin. When evaluating the concept, product managers and design engineers first need to select a specific scenario from the scenario list from the approach (see in Fig. 3 below). Taking the bar scenario as an example in case, the description of the scenario, user needs and user tasks are all derived from market research data, allowing design engineers to have a common understanding and consensus on the scenario. Then the value dimension needs to be assigned a value, which is summarized into two categories: functional value and non-functional value. There are 6 value dimensions in total (Eco-friendly, Flexibility, Comfortability, Digitalized, Profitability and Total cost). Product managers and design engineers can adjust the value weight from 1 to 10 on the simulation interface, and the simulation system will set down the weights for each value dimensions. At the same time, the system uses EVOKE model proposed by Bertoni et al. (2018) to calculating the value evaluation score of the product. For example, the total score for the bar scenario concept = 7.7. The highest overall value score is Profitability = 8.96, followed by Eco-friendly = 8.37 and Flexibility = 8.12. This bar scenario consists of 10 feature items, and the system sorts the features list automatically. Product managers and design engineers can make decisions and analyze design options based on the result of value scores and chart analysis. At the same time, through digital twins, the virtual engine is directly rendering the 3D visualization solutions of the scenario model and product model. The design teams can interact with digital twin design concept from digital interface of the digital approach.

The scenarios and product design concepts completed can be brought into the virtual environment for concept verification through simulation tool. Product managers and

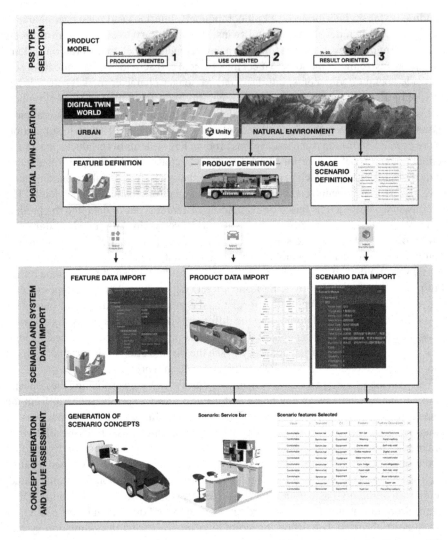

Fig. 2. The framework of the digital twin approach in early phase of tour bus development, King Long case.

design engineers will open the virtual environment in front of the big screen to verify the operational plan in a virtual natural environment in national park. During the simulation, the three visualized prototype modes (**Scenario, Product, Feature,** prototype) **of** the simulation vision can be adjusted to meet different visual needs and graphics performance for large-scale hybrid simulations. In the **Scenario prototype**, you can adjust the impact of factors such as (total service time, total customer number, energy consumption and CO2 saving, etc.). In the **Product prototype**, it shows that the (detailed interior materials of the vehicle cockpit, the passenger behaviours of objects and characters). Hence, the **Feature prototype** shows such as (air conditioning temperature adjustment,

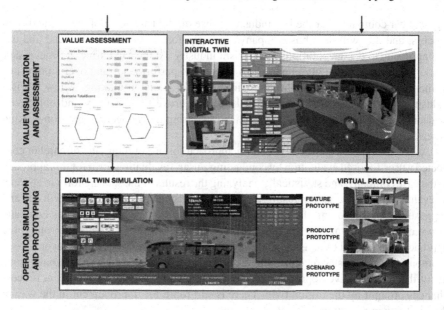

Fig. 3. The framework of the digital twin approach in in early phase of tour bus development for PSS simulation and prototyping, King Long case.

volume, screen con as (air conditioning temperature adjustment, volume, screen content and character movements, etc.). The virtual prototype makes product managers and design engineers interact with scenario performance, service process and customer usage effects in the customized tourism scenarios through digital twin of 3D prototyping. The virtual prototype makes product managers and design engineers interact with scenario performance, service process and customer usage effects in the customized tourism scenarios through digital twin of 3D prototype.

5 Discussion

The current recent research, and scientific literature have repetitively highlighted the potential of digital twin, data-driven decisions for providing a new way of approaching product development in the manufacturing industry. Nevertheless, when designing the product and service in the early design phase of PSS, there are many decisions are still made based on industry experience, intuition, and forward-thinking of engineers, managers, and decision-makers. The digital twin approach presented in this paper is a step toward a more extensive i, there are many decisions are still made based on industry experience, intuition, and forward-thinking of engineers, managers, and decision-makers. The digital twin approach presented in this paper is a step toward a more extensive integration of prototype into the early conceptual design of PSS. At same time, the value visualization of prototype can reduce the uncertainty concept selection in product development process. This paper demonstrates and discusses how the digital twin approach can participate in the early design and decision-making process of tour bus through a case of a global car company. For the bus industry to use digital twin technology in the design process, and this will help bus company's participators can easier understand and use this approach to design solutions for tourism industry. At the same time, it is necessary to use 3D visualized prototyping to show the service performance and operation results of the design concept in the virtual environment for decision-making. Allow tourism industrial stakeholders and decision-makers to improve the accuracy and objectivity of decision-making through value visualization during the subjective decision-making process.

As the verification for the digital twin approach for prototyping, the researcher conducted a user-focused evaluation by conducting a usage evaluation form for this approach in the case company, and statistically analyzing the results of the scoring form to conduct an evaluation. The evaluation results are evaluated through qualitative user feedback and suggestions on improving the approach. As a result, the design team in bus company also see that the digital twin approach is recognized as a convincing visual prototyping approach. The digital twin as the new way of prototyping the PSS design has only been promoted in the industry recently, and there is a lack of successful cases that have come about through effective approach and tools to prove the product development process changes brought by the digital twin. There is still room for improvement in the way of the digital twin prototyping the PSS concept.

6 Conclusion

This paper addresses the introduction of a digital twin approach for prototyping the PSS design in manufacturing industry. The paper introduces digital twin approach as the prototype tool to promote the product development process in a bus manufacturing company. A digital twin approach that supports prototyping in PSS design is proposed and developed. The approach has been described through the case of the development of tour bus in the early design phase for King Long to address digitalization and servitization transformation challenges. This paper has introduced and vitrificated the result of digital twin approach apply with the case company in the tourism scenario of a national park. Future research will try to apply the digital twin approach to prototype the concept for more service industries, which have relatively higher design requirements for completeness of service solutions, customer scenario, and total value creation for service companies.

Acknowledgment. The research has also received financial support from KKS, VINNOVA, BIGSimulo.

References

Baines, T.S., Lightfoot, H.W., Evans, S., et al.: State-of-the-art in product-service systems. Proc. Inst. Mech. Eng. Part B J. Eng. Manuf. **221**(10), 15431552 (2007). https://doi.org/10.1243/095 44054JEM858

Bertoni, A., Machchhar, R.J., Larsson, T., Frank, B.: Digital twins of operational scenarios in mining for design of customized product-service systems solutions. Procedia CIRP, 532–537 (2022). https://doi.org/10.1016/j.procir.2022.05.290

Bertoni, A., Ruvald, R.: Physical prototypes to foster value co-creation in product-service systems conceptual design: a case study in construction equipment. In: Camarinha-Matos, L.M., Boucher, X., Afsarmanesh, H. (eds.) Smart and Sustainable Collaborative Networks 4.0. IAICT, vol. 629, pp. 382–389. Springer, Cham (2021). https://doi.org/10.1007/978-3-030-85969-5_35

Bertoni, M., Bertoni, A., Isaksson, O.: Evoke a value-driven concept selection method for early system design. J. Syst. Sci. Syst. Eng. **27**(1), 46–77 (2018). https://doi.org/10.1007/s11518-016-5324-2

Blessing, L.T.M., Chakrabarti, A.: DRM, a Design Research Methodology. Springer, London (2009). https://doi.org/10.1007/978-84882-587-1

Buchenau, M., Suri, J.F.: Experience prototyping. In: Proceedings of the 3rd Conference on Designing Interactive Systems: Processes, Practices, Methods, and Techniques, pp. 424–433. ACM (2000)

Clement, S.J., McKee, D.W., Romano, R., Xu, J., Lopez, J.M., Battersby, D.: The internet of simulation: enabling agile model-based systems engineering for cyber-physical systems. In: 12th System of Systems Engineering Conference (SoSE), pp. 1–6. IEEE (2017)

Digital Twins Land a Role in Product Design (2015). Accessed 17 Aug 2007 http://www.digita leng.news/de/digital-twins-land-a-role-in-product-design/

Erkoyuncu, J.A., del Amo, I.F., Ariansyah, D., Bulka, D., Roy, R.: A design framework for adaptive digital twins. CIRP Ann. **69**(1), 145–148 (2020)

Exner, K., et al.: A transdisciplinary perspective on prototyping. In: 2015 IEEE International Conference on Engineering, Technology and Innovation/International Technology Management Conference, ICE/ITMC 2015 (2016). https://doi.org/10.1109/ICE.2015.7438659

Furr, N.R., Dyer, J.: The Innovator's Method: Bringing the Lean Startup Into Your Organization. Harvard Business Press (2014)

Glaessgen, E.H., Stargel, D.: The digital twin paradigm for future NASA and US air force vehicles. In: 53rd Structural Dynamics and Materials Conference Special Session: Digital Twin, pp. 1–14, Honolulu, HI, US (2012)

Goedkoop, M.J., van Halen, C.J.G., te Riele, H.R.M., Rommens, P.J.M.: Product Service Systems, Ecological and Economic Basics. Dutch Ministries of Environment and Economic Affairs (1999)

Grieves, M.: Digital twin: manufacturing excellence through virtual factory replication. In: White Paper (2014)

Jones, D., Snider, C., Nassehi, A., Yon, J., Hicks, B.: Characterising the digital twin: a systematic literature review. CIRP J. Manuf. Sci. Tech. **1**(29), 36–52 (2020)

Menold, J., Simpson, T.W., Jablokov, K.: The prototype for X framework: exploring the effects of a structured prototyping framework on functional prototypes. Res. Eng. Des., 187–201 (2018)

Morelli, N.: Developing new product service systems (PSS): methodologies and operational tools. J. Clean. Prod. **14**(17), 1495–1501 (2006)

Mont, O.K.: Clarifying the concept of product–service system. J. Clean. Prod. **10**(3), 237–245 (2002)

Rosen, R., Wichert, G.V., Lo, G., Bettenhausen, K.D.: About the importance of autonomy and digital twins for the future of manufacturing. IFAC-PapersOnLine **48**(3), 567–572 (2015)

Rondini, A., Tornese, F., Gnoni, M.G., Pezzotta, G.: Hybrid simulation modeling as a supporting tool for sustainable product service systems: a critical analysis. Int. J. Prod. Res., 1–14 (2017)

Schluse, M., Atorf, L., Rossmann, J.: Experimentable digital twins for model-based systems engineering and simulation-based development. In: 2017 Annual IEEE International Systems Conference (SysCon). IEEE 2017, pp. 1–8 (2017)

Stark, R., Fresemann, C., Lindow, K.: Development and operation of digital twins for technical systems and services. CIRP Ann. **68**(1), 129–32 (2019)

Tao, F., et al.: Digital twin-driven product design framework. Int. J. Prod. Res. **57**(12), 3935–53 (2019)

Tao, F., Cheng, J., Qi, Q., Zhang, M., Zhang, H., Sui, F.: Digital twin-driven product design, manufacturing and service with big data. Int. J. Adv. Manuf. Technol. **94**(9), 3563–3576 (2018)

Tukker, A., Tischner, U., Verkuijl, M.: New business for old Europe: product-service development, competitiveness and sustainability. Sheffield Greenleaf, 72–97 (2006). https://doi.org/10.1016/S0959-6526(01)00039-7

Yin, R.K.: Case Study Research: Design and Methods, 5th edn. SAGE, Los Angeles (2014)

Research on the Experience Design and Tourist Satisfaction of Rural Tourism in China: A Bibliometric Analysis

Zhiwei Zhou[1], Mengshan Chen[1], and Zhen Liu[2(✉)]

[1] School of Management, Guangzhou City University of Technology, Guangzhou 510800, China
[2] School of Design, South China University of Technology, Guangzhou 510006, China
liuzjames@scut.edu.cn

Abstract. Under the background of Rural Revitalization Strategy, rural tourism has become a "hot spot" in the tourism market. As a kind of experience economy, tourist experience has a significant impact on rural tourism satisfaction, so it has also become a key research topic of Chinese scholars in the field of rural tourism. In order to further sort out the research situation in the academic field of rural tourism experience design and user satisfaction in China, and provide reference for the follow-up academic research in this field, this paper uses the method of bibliometric analysis of scientific literature, selects the journal articles and master and doctoral theses of CNKI on "rural tourism, experience design and tourist satisfaction" from 2004 to 2023 as the research object, and uses CiteSpace visual literature analysis software for comprehensive analysis. The results show that: 1) the domestic research on the relationship between rural tourism experience design and satisfaction can be divided into two stages, and the research heat and the amount of literature show an overall upward trend; 2) the high-yield author group has not yet formed, and there is little cooperation between authors and research institutions; The majority of research institutions are in inland areas, and the main type of research institutions is universities; 3) the keyword analysis based on the knowledge map shows that the research hotspots mainly focus on the influencing factors of rural tourism satisfaction, product experience design such as rural home stay, and rural tourism development strategy.

Keywords: Rural tourism · Experience design · Tourist satisfaction · Bibliometric analysis

1 Introduction

With the advancement of urbanization, people's living pressure continues to increase, and their desire for the natural environment and rural local culture is also growing. Green and healthy leisure experience activities such as mountain home stay, characteristic picking, agricultural research and learning are constantly emerging [1], providing an ideal place for people to get close to nature, experience rural culture and release pressure. From the perspective of the development process, China's rural tourism has experienced three stages: the embryonic stage represented by farmhouse tourism from the 1990s to 2006; From 2006 to 2016, the development stage focused on leisure agriculture and tourism; After 2017, with the proposal of China's Rural Revitalization Strategy, the ministry of culture and tourism issued the guidance on promoting the sustainable development of rural tourism in 2018, which ushered in the upgrading and rapid development of China's rural tourism. According to the data of the Ministry of culture and tourism, from 2012 to 2019, the number of rural tourists nationwide jumped from nearly 800million to 3billion, with an average annual growth rate of more than 20%. Among them, the number of rural tourism visitors nationwide reached 3.09 billion in 2019, accounting for half of the number of domestic tourists [2]. From 2020 to 2022, affected by the new crown epidemic. The scale of rural tourism market fluctuates, but the overall growth trend is obvious.

Tourism provides experiential products. User experience and perception directly affect satisfaction evaluation, and then affect tourism desire and the sustainable development of rural tourism. Therefore, rural tourism experience design plays a vital role in improving tourist satisfaction and promoting the development of rural tourism. The issue of rural tourism experience and satisfaction has also become a hot topic in academic and industry research and attention. Therefore, the study of the development process of China's rural tourism experience design and user satisfaction, as well as the overall grasp of the current research situation in the academic field of China's rural tourism experience design and user satisfaction, can lay the foundation for the follow-up academic research in this field.

2 Methods

2.1 Data Source

The data in this paper comes from China National Knowledge Infrastructure (CNKI), with the themes = "rural tourism" and "experience design" and "tourist satisfaction", and the time span to 2023. And all the search results were selected for this study. The journals and master's and doctor's degree theses that have selected 423 articles are the object of literature analysis in this paper at last.

2.2 Research Methodology

This paper uses the bibliometric analysis method to analyze 423 literatures. The main tool is CiteSpace scientific literature analysis tool. CiteSpace software is a document visualization analysis tool. It can realize diversified, dynamic and time-sharing visual analysis of document samples, so as to help us find the historical research path and future development trend of academic research sites from a large number of sample documents [3]. Since its development, CiteSpace software has been widely used in a variety of disciplines. It is the most distinctive and influential knowledge mapping analysis tool among the literature analysis tools in recent years.

In this paper, CiteSpace software is used to analyze keywords co-occurrence, clustering, emergent words and to draw visual maps of keywords co-occurrence, frequency and centrality, clustering, timeline, emergence, etc. Through multidimensional comparative analysis of literature analysis samples, the knowledge map of China's rural tourism experience design and user satisfaction research is drawn, so as to grasp the research hotspots and trends of China's rural tourism experience design and user satisfaction from a macro perspective, it provides a reference for the further development of this field.

3   Results and Analysis

3.1   Analysis on the Time and Quantity of Literatures

The quantity and time of literatures published in the academic field is one of the criteria to judge the research hotspot in this field. This paper makes a statistical analysis of the number of published years of 423 literatures retrieved with the themes of "rural tourism", "experience design" and "tourist satisfaction", and the results are shown in Fig. 1.

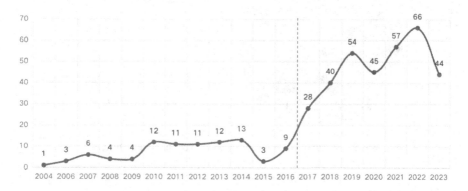

Fig. 1. The number of published articles in the CNKI from year 2004 to 2023.

From the time of publication, the research on experience design and tourist satisfaction of rural tourism in China can be divided into two stages. In the first stage (2004–2016), the literature on this research direction in this field began in 2004. The number of papers published in this stage was relatively low and the growth was relatively slow, with an average annual number of 7.42. In the second stage (from 2017 to now), with the "Rural Revitalization Strategy" proposed at the 19th National Congress of the Communist Party of China in 2017, rural tourism has become an important development direction of new rural areas, and academic research in this field has also shown a rapid growth trend. From 2017 to 2019, the average annual number was 40.67. In 2020, due to the impact of the new crown epidemic, the tourism industry was depressed, and the number of literatures in this field decreased to 45. From 2020 to 2022, there was another upward trend, with a maximum of 66 papers. Compared with 2022, the number of papers published in 2023 was in a downward state, and there were still 44 papers. From the perspective of the overall trend of the number of papers published, the research in this field will remain hot in the future.

3.2 Analysis on the Discipline Field of Literatures

By analyzing the distribution of the subject field of literature, we can find the distribution of the research topic of this paper in the subject field. From Fig. 2, we can see that tourism ranks first in the literature subject distribution of "rural tourism", "experience design" and "tourist satisfaction", accounting for 46.60%, agricultural economy ranks second, accounting for 36.32%, trade economy ranks third (4.41%), service economy ranks fourth (3.20%), followed by enterprise economy (2.40%), architecture and Engineering (1.60%), Tourism and agricultural economy account for a large proportion, a total of 82%.

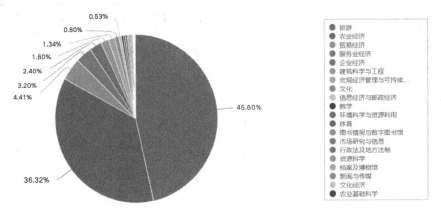

Fig. 2. Distribution of disciplines involved in the literature.

3.3 Analysis on the Author and Institution of Literatures

Analysis on the author of literatures. According to CiteSpace's visual analysis of the core authors of 423 papers selected, 133 N-nodes, 18 E-links, and a density network density of 0.0021 are obtained. It can be seen from Fig. 3 that the scale of the cooperation team is mainly 2–4 people. LiJinzhi and WangPing, ZhouHaiyan and YeJianming, Duan-Shengkui and ZhangLi, FengYanting and WuXinyu, DingYing and RenYisheng are two people's cooperation teams. ZhangYanli and MengChanglai, XuJia and HeYaping are four people's cooperation teams. WuJiang and Liu Yang, Mei Lin and Liu Jisheng are also four people's cooperation teams. Although there is cooperation between scholars, the degree of cooperation is not very close, which shows a decentralized state.

In addition, during the period from 2004 to 2023, the number of papers published by a single scholar on the themes of "rural tourism", "experience design" and "tourist satisfaction" was not high. Eight authors published two papers, and the rest were one. On the whole, the cooperation between most researchers in the research field of "rural tourism experience design and satisfaction" is sparse, and the degree of cooperation is not high. At present, the overall research field has not formed a large discipline research

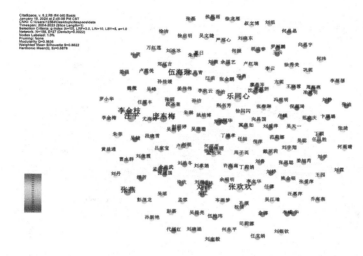

Fig. 3. Collaboration map of core authors.

team. And the researchers have not formed a coherent and continuous research, and the number of literatures published by a single researcher in this field is small.

Analysis on the institution of literatures. According to CiteSpace's visual analysis of research institutions in the literature selected in this paper, a co-occurrence map of research institutions with 125 N-nodes, 3 E-links and a density of 0.0009 is obtained, in which each node represents the corresponding institution, the node size represents the number of documents issued by the research institution, and each link represents the cooperative relationship between institutions. The thicker the link, the closer the cooperative relationship between institutions. It can be seen from Fig. 4 that there is less mutual cooperation among research institutions and they are in a decentralized state.

According to the number of papers published by the institutions, Central South University of forestry and technology ranked first with 10 papers; The second is Fujian agriculture and Forestry University, with 6 papers; The third is Hebei Agricultural University, with 5 papers; Guangxi Normal University, Henan Agricultural University and Zhejiang Ocean University have published four papers.

On the whole, the cooperation between most research institutions in the research field of "rural tourism experience design and satisfaction" is relatively small. The types of research institutions are mainly universities with the primary industry as the dominant discipline, and the geographical location of the institutions is mainly in the central and inland regions, and less in Southern China.

3.4 Keyword Map Analysis

Keywords are a highly summarized summary of the topic of an article, and their frequency, relevance, and prominence can reveal the research hotspots, internal connections, and research trends in the research field.

Keyword Co-occurrence Map Analysis. By using CiteSpace to conduct keyword co-occurrence analysis on the literature with the themes of "rural tourism", "experience

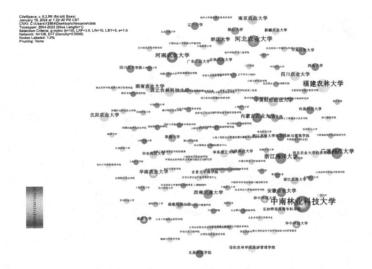

Fig. 4. Collaboration map of core institutions.

design" and "tourist satisfaction", we obtained the keyword co-occurrence map of N-node 295, link point 518 and network density 0.0119. Keywords are the core theme in the literature. If keywords appear more often, they are regarded as the research hotspot in this field. As shown in Fig. 5, the keywords that appear include rural tourism, satisfaction, experience, leisure agriculture, experience design, experience economy, rural revitalization, influencing factors, rural homestay, etc., and the links between keywords are rich and closely linked. At the same time, the nodes of these keywords in the figure are large, indicating that the research on rural tourism experience design and satisfaction is hot in these cross fields.

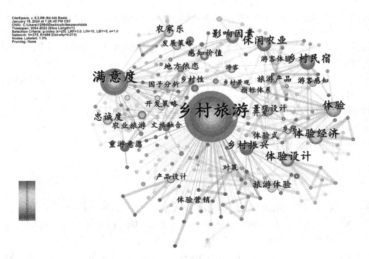

Fig. 5. Keyword co-occurrence map.

Further analyze the centrality of the core keywords through the list, as shown in Table 1. It is generally believed that keywords with higher frequency and higher centrality value are more important. In this research field, there are 4 high-frequency keywords whose centrality is higher than 0.1. Table 1 shows the top 10 keywords with the highest frequency and centrality. Frequency represents the number of occurrences in the literature analyzed in this paper, and centrality represents that keywords play a pivotal role between literature and literature. It can be seen from Table 2 that the keyword "rural tourism" has the highest frequency and centrality, followed by "satisfaction", "influencing factors", "rural home stay" and "experience". It can be seen that rural tourism, satisfaction, influencing factors, rural home stay and experience have larger nodes and higher frequencies, and these keywords can be regarded as the hot spots in the research fields of "rural tourism", "experience design" and "tourist satisfaction".

Table 1. High-frequency keywords, word frequency and centrality statistics.

Serial number	Keywords	Frequency	Centrality
1	Rural Tourism	178	1.02
2	Satisfaction	55	0.34
3	Influencing Factors	20	0.09
4	Rural Home Stay	20	0.15
5	Experience	16	0.1
6	Leisure Agriculture	15	0.09
7	Rural Revitalization	14	0.03
8	Experience Economy	12	0.09
9	Experience Design	11	0.07
10	Tourism Experience	11	0.02

Keyword Clustering Map Analysis. Keyword clustering analysis can explore the main research direction in this field. CiteSpace was used to cluster the selected literatures. The keyword clustering map has two values to evaluate whether the clustering is effective. One is the average contour value of silhouette clustering. S value > 0.5 means that the clustering structure is significant, and > 0.7 is convincing; One is the modular clustering module value. Q value > 0.3 means that clustering is meaningful. As shown in Fig. 6, the S value of this paper is 0.7331, and the Q value is 0.6089. Therefore, the keyword clustering map of this paper is convincing and meaningful. A total of six clustering blocks are screened out, which are 0 rural tourism, 1 satisfaction, 2 experience, 3 experience economy, 4 influencing factors, and 5 agricultural tourisms.

Further analysis of clustering contour value. This value is an evaluation method to measure the clustering effect. The closer the contour value is to 1, the better the clustering effect is. Through analysis, the clustering contour values of the above six clustering blocks are above 0.8, as shown in Table 2, indicating that the clustering effect is good.

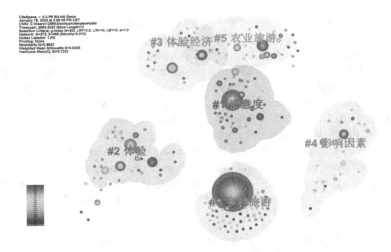

Fig. 6. Keyword clustering map.

Table 2. Keyword clustering table.

Serial number	Cluster tags	Cluster profile	Cluster size	Cluster keywords
1	Rural Tourism	0.993	57	IPA analysis, rural tourism, ssatisfaction, etc.
2	Experience Economy	0.944	23	experience economy, leisure agriculture, development strategies
3	Agricultural Tourism	0.926	16	orchards, rural landscapes, and rural revitalization, etc.
4	Experience	0.885	28	willingness, perceived value, local attachment, etc.
5	Influencing Factors	0.875	23	influencing factors, experiential marketing, factor analysis, etc.
6	Satisfaction	0.848	39	development strategy, loyalty, etc.

Keyword Emergent Map Analysis. Emergent words can reflect the sudden increase or obvious increase in the frequency of use of a keyword in a certain period. This paper analyzes the keyword emergence of the selected literature, and sets the minimum duration to 1 year, γ 0.5. As can be seen from Fig. 7, a total of 17 key emergent words were obtained.

From the perspective of the intensity of key words, the intensity of "Rural Revitalization" is the highest, which is 3.72, followed by "agritainment" which is 3.01, followed by "revisit intention", which is 2.73, and "satisfaction" which is 2.69. From the year of appearance of the overall key words, from 2010 to 2023, "rural revitalization, farmhouse entertainment, satisfaction, revisit willingness, tourist perception, rural homestay" are the main words of experience design and tourist satisfaction in rural tourism in this period. From the development of agritainment in 2010 to leisure agriculture and experience economy in 2012, as well as rural homestay and tourist perception in 2019, the development scale of rural tourism at this stage has changed from farmers' use of their own houses and fields for agritainment and rural tourism to leisure agriculture and rural homestay in 2012. It is no longer limited to "eating farmhouse meals and living in farmyard", but to a collection of sightseeing, leisure, entertainment A comprehensive rural tourism scenic spot integrating research and study. Satisfaction, Rural Revitalization and integration of culture and tourism will emerge in 2021. During this period, China has put forward more clear development goals and directions for rural revitalization, emphasizing the need to give full play to the advantages of rural resources, ecology and culture, and develop industries such as leisure tourism, catering and home stay, cultural experience, health preservation, and elderly care services that meet the needs of urban and rural residents.

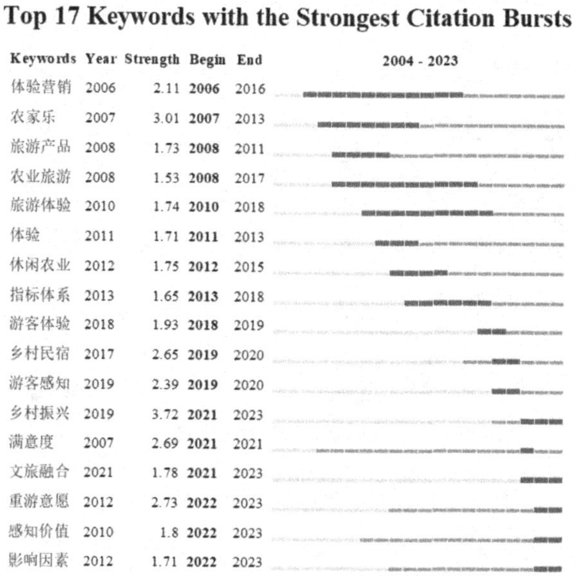

Top 17 Keywords with the Strongest Citation Bursts

Keywords	Year	Strength	Begin	End	2004 - 2023
体验营销	2006	2.11	2006	2016	
农家乐	2007	3.01	2007	2013	
旅游产品	2008	1.73	2008	2011	
农业旅游	2008	1.53	2008	2017	
旅游体验	2010	1.74	2010	2018	
体验	2011	1.71	2011	2013	
休闲农业	2012	1.75	2012	2015	
指标体系	2013	1.65	2013	2018	
游客体验	2018	1.93	2018	2019	
乡村民宿	2017	2.65	2019	2020	
游客感知	2019	2.39	2019	2020	
乡村振兴	2019	3.72	2021	2023	
满意度	2007	2.69	2021	2021	
文旅融合	2021	1.78	2021	2023	
重游意愿	2012	2.73	2022	2023	
感知价值	2010	1.8	2022	2023	
影响因素	2012	1.71	2022	2023	

Fig. 7. Keyword emergent map.

Keyword Clustering Timeline Map Analysis. The change of keywords over time can indicate the change and development trend of research topics. Through cluster analysis, CiteSpace can arrange the hotspots in the same year in chronological order and gather them in the same area. The clustering timeline map generated by CiteSpace is shown in Fig. 8. There are six clusters in total.

In the "rural tourism" cluster, the research content from the experience marketing, marketing strategy and cultural experience in 2012 to the development experience in 2020 and the transformation of digital footprint in 2023 can be seen that the research hotspots are closely related to the changes of social environment. In the "satisfaction" cluster, the nodes are relatively concentrated. Scholars focus more on the integration of satisfaction and perceived value, revisit intention, local attachment and culture and tourism, and less on the aspects related to experience. In the "experience" clustering, it mainly focuses on the content of experience, focusing on experience design, landscape design, rural revitalization, etc. In addition, it also pays attention to the experience of manor, homestay and participation. In the "experience economy" cluster, the research mainly focuses on leisure agriculture and development, focusing on leisure agriculture, development dilemma, development countermeasures, demand and other aspects. In the cluster of "influencing factors", the factor analysis in 2012 first appeared, and the empirical research focused on the model, index system and factor analysis. In the "agricultural tourism" cluster, the focus is mainly on different types of agricultural tourism, such as flower tourism, leisure farms, etc. After 2015, agricultural tourism will pay more attention to experience and product innovation. With the proposal of the Rural Revitalization Strategy in 2017, the concept of agricultural tourism has gradually been replaced by rural tourism.

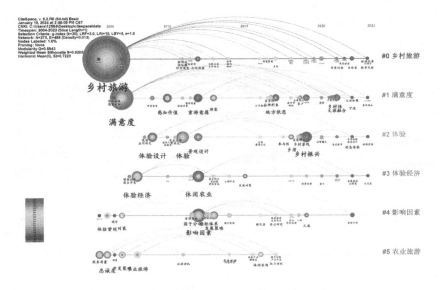

Fig. 8. Keyword clustering timeline map.

4 Discussion

4.1 Research Hotspots

This paper sorts out the academic research papers with the themes and keywords of "rural tourism", "experience design" and "tourist satisfaction". At the same time, combined with the analysis of keyword co-occurrence map, frequency and centrality of high-frequency keywords, clustering timeline map and keyword emergence map, it summarizes the hotspots of China's rural tourism experience design and tourist satisfaction research from 2004 to 2023 into three aspects.

Research on Influencing Factors of User Experience and Satisfaction. According to the keyword co-occurrence map analysis, the centrality of "rural tourism", "satisfaction" and "influencing factors" are 1.02, 0.34 and 0.09 respectively, indicating that the three are strongly related to other hot keywords. Combined with the literature analysis, it is found that the literature mainly focuses on the influencing factors of satisfaction. Around this theme, researchers combined different theories, through the construction of models and empirical research methods, to explore the influencing factors of rural tourism satisfaction in different regions.

Among the analysis methods, the number of literatures using IPA analysis method is the largest, reaching 80. IPA analysis, or immediate performance analysis, is an analysis method that directly obtains the importance and performance or importance and satisfaction of the research object by positioning the data through the quadrant diagram. The literature mainly processes the questionnaire data through descriptive statistical analysis, differentiation analysis and importance satisfaction analysis (IPA analysis), and draws IPA quadrant [4], so as to classify and sort the importance of factors affecting tourist satisfaction. In addition, 40 papers used structural equation modeling method.

In terms of research model and theory selection, 39 articles used satisfaction theory, 13 articles used SWOT model, 12 articles used experience theory, 8 articles used expectation difference theory, 5 articles used customer perceived service quality theory and perceived value theory, 5 articles used grounded theory, and 4 articles used ACSI satisfaction theory and KANO model.

In the research conclusion, the influencing factors of satisfaction can be summarized as "food, housing, transportation, travel, shopping and entertainment" [5] or the six structural dimensions of "facility value, sightseeing value, leisure value, cultural value, consumption value and fitness value" of tourism destination [6], or the seven standards of Tourism transportation, price perception, tourism resources, scenic spot facilities, tourism services, shopping experience and scenic spots [7]. Or it can be divided into four types of behavior, i.e. traffic, consumption, viewing and interaction [8].

Rural tourism with different characteristics has different factors affecting tourists' experience and satisfaction. For example, the influencing factors of rural sports featured tourism include "tourism element services, resources and environment services, scenic area facilities services, information publicity services, security services, personnel quality services" [9], while the impact of leisure agriculture focuses more on "Park reputation, tourism facilities and management, personnel services, perceived value, tourism and entertainment activities, tourism landscape and environment, and tourism transportation" [10], The influencing factors of homestay mainly include homestay environment, homestay service, homestay experience, homestay characteristics [11].

Research on Rural Tourism Product Design to Meet User Experience. According to the keyword co-occurrence map analysis, the centrality of "rural homestay", "experience" and "experience economy" are 0.15, 0.1 and 0.09 respectively, indicating that the three are strongly related to other hot keywords. Combined with literature analysis, it is found that there are 73 academic papers based on the keywords of product design to meet user experience, such as home stay, product experience, tourism products, experience design, etc. The content involves the research on farmhouse experience in scenic spots [12], leisure agricultural park [13] or orchard experience and design [14], ancient village tourism product experience design [15], home stay experience design [16], rural tourism landscape design from the perspective of cultural experience [17], and public space design [18]. In addition, there is also the perspective of studying service-oriented product design from the perspective of tourism process. Such as rural tourism public service process design [19], rural tourism map design based on experience perspective [20], personalized planning of rural tourism routes [21], tourism app interface design from experience perspective [22], rural tourism cultural and creative design [23], etc.

"Homestay" is an important research hotspot of rural tourism products. Combined with the analysis of keyword clustering timeline, the key word "rural homestay" was counted, and 40 research literatures on the subject were found. The main content involves the research on the development strategy of rural homestay based on the analysis of tourist satisfaction [24], the research on the spatial design or environmental art design of rural homestay based on the perspective of experience [25], the transformation of rural homestay [26], the research on the integration of cultural experience and natural experience of homestay [27].

Research on the Development Strategy of Rural Tourism Based on Policy. According to the analysis of the keyword emergent map, the emergent intensity of "leisure agriculture" and "Rural Revitalization" was high and lasted for a period of time. Based on the analysis of literature, it is found that there are 39 academic papers on the theme of development strategy research based on policy, such as agriculture, rural areas, leisure agriculture, rural revitalization, development strategy, path, planning, etc. The main contents include: first, the construction strategy of high-quality rural tourism product system under the background of "high-quality development" policy [28], the high-quality development path of rural tourism with sports characteristics [9], etc.; Second, under the background of "Rural Revitalization" policy, research on the development strategy of characteristic mountain village tourism [29], the development countermeasures of rural tourism in minority areas [30], the development path of leisure and sightseeing agriculture [31], the development dilemma and Countermeasures of leisure agriculture [32], etc.; Third, the rural night tour experience and digital art design under the background of "digital countryside" policy [33], and the digital development of rural tourism [34]; Fourth, the development of agritainment Tourism under the "three rural" policy [35], the coordinated development of rural areas and tourist attractions [36], and the rural tourism development strategy based on the perceived value of tourists [37].

From the specific content of the literature, in addition to the policies mentioned above, there are also research on development strategies around other policies such as "supply side reform", or research on Rural Tourism Satisfaction Based on the policy background. China is a large agricultural country. In order to adapt to the development of the times, the policies on agriculture, rural areas and farmers are also changing. As an important branch of the three rural areas, rural tourism has become an important research topic and research hotspot in recent years.

4.2 Research Trends

Based on bibliometric analysis, feature analysis and content analysis, the academic research in the field of rural tourism experience design and user satisfaction in China in the past 20 years since 2004 has obvious policy orientation and market frontier. The research in this field has experienced obvious advanced development, the research attention has increased rapidly in the past six years, and the number of papers has increased rapidly. As China's social and economic development has entered a new stage of high-quality development, the development of rural tourism experience design is facing new historical opportunities and new market challenges. Combined with the concentration analysis of China's rural tourism experience design and user satisfaction in recent years, the future research on China's rural tourism experience design and user satisfaction may focus on the following areas.

Research on comprehensive application of user oriented rural tourism experience and satisfaction influencing factors. According to the above analysis, rural tourism experience and satisfaction are affected by many factors, including tourism resources, service quality, infrastructure, tourism environment, etc. These dimensions change with the changes of policies, markets, technologies and user groups. Future research will continue to focus on the impact of tourists' perceptions and expectations on rural tourism satisfaction, and pay attention to the comprehensive analysis of the changes and updates of these dimensions, as well as the joint impact of multiple factors on satisfaction and the interaction between them. In addition, previous scholars have focused on empirical research, through a large number of field surveys and data analysis, to explore the actual situation and influencing factors of rural tourism satisfaction, but there is a lack of applied research. Therefore, it will be a long-term trend for China's rural tourism experience design and user satisfaction research to explore the changes of influencing factors of rural tourism satisfaction, transfer the results into applied research, and translate them into specific practical measures to promote the sustainable development of rural tourism.

Research on diversification and personalization of market oriented rural tourism experience design. With the diversification of consumer demand and the continuous upgrading of consumption, rural tourism experience design is developing towards diversification and personalization. In the rural tourism planning, the tourism destination excavates the local cultural characteristics and natural resources, such as farming, picking, handicrafts, folk activities, cultural and creative IP, theme home stay and other characteristic experience design is gradually becoming the mainstream of the market, so as to provide tourists with unique and attractive tourism experience and improve tourist satisfaction. In addition, as young people gradually participate in rural tourism, in order to further meet the needs and interests of young people, rural tourism began to design more novel and interesting themes, such as music festivals, animation exhibitions, E-sports events, etc., which can attract young people's attention and increase their participation and stickiness. Therefore, how to keep up with the pace of market development, integrate diversified and personalized elements, and realize the transformation of rural tourism from tradition to innovation and youth will be the key research trend in this field.

Research on the digitalization and industrialization of rural tourism under the policy background. With the high-quality development of rural industry, the continuous deepening of policies such as "prospering agriculture through digital commerce" and "Internet+" agricultural products, and digital countryside, the research hotspots of China's rural tourism experience design and user satisfaction are also closely following policy changes. With the continuous development of Internet technology, the digitization of rural tourism has become a new development trend. Through the Internet platform, it is more convenient to publicize and promote rural tourism resources, and improve the popularity and reputation of rural tourism. At the same time, digital technology can also provide tourists with more convenient tourism services, such as analyzing tourists' preferences and needs through big data and providing customized tourism routes and activities; Improve the experience of tourists through intelligent technology, so as to improve the satisfaction of tourists. In addition, the experience economy of rural tourism is gradually industrialized, and the sustainable development of rural tourism is realized through product innovation, service improvement, industrial integration, structural optimization and other measures. It can be seen that policies play an important guiding role in the development of rural tourism. It is a new trend in the research of rural tourism experience design and user satisfaction in China to study the digitalization and industrialization of rural tourism development in combination with the frontier dynamics of policies.

5 Conclusion

This paper uses CiteSpace software to make a bibliometric analysis on the experience design and tourist satisfaction of rural tourism in China from 2004 to 2023, and makes a visual knowledge mapping study on the literature, and draws the following main conclusions.

In terms of the number and time of papers published, the overall time distribution of literature shows an upward trend, which can be roughly divided into two stages: the period of gentle growth (2004–2016), with an average annual number of literature searches of 7.42; During the rapid development period (2017–2023), the average annual number of literature searches in this stage was 40.67, and has maintained a high degree of research interest. With the continuous deepening of the Rural Revitalization Strategy, it can be judged that the research in this field will continue to grow in the future.

From the perspective of disciplinary fields and publications, the interdisciplinary nature of the research on rural tourism experience design and user satisfaction in China is weak, and the main disciplinary fields are concentrated in tourism and agricultural economy, accounting for more than 82%.

From the analysis of the cooperation of the authors, the cooperation among scholars is relatively decentralized as a whole, and the group of authors presents the characteristics of "individual concentration, overall dispersion". The research field of rural tourism experience design and user satisfaction in China is extensive and there are many representative scholars (teams). The inland area is the main area of the core high-yield scholar group of rural tourism experience design and user satisfaction in China.

From the analysis of the cooperation of the issuing agencies, the cooperation between the issuing agencies is not close enough, and there is a lot of cooperation space. Colleges and universities are the main types of institutions for rural tourism experience design and user satisfaction research in China, and the distribution agencies are concentrated in areas with rich tourism resources, and the cross regional cooperation among distribution agencies is still affected by geographical location.

From the perspective of research hotspots and trends, through the analysis of keyword commonality map and cluster map, the research hotspots of China's rural tourism experience design and user satisfaction mainly focus on the empirical research of satisfaction influencing factors, the research of rural tourism experience product design and the research of development strategies and paths. With the changes of policies, markets, technologies and users, the future research trends in this field may focus on the influencing factors of satisfaction and their comprehensive application, the diversification and personalization of experience design, and the digitization and industrialization of experience economy in rural tourism.

Acknowledgments. The research is funded by Key Research Base of Humanities and Social Sciences in Universities of Guangdong Province: Research Base for Digital Transformation of Manufacturing Enterprises (2023WZJD012) & Principles of Marketing Course Ideological and Political Demonstration Course (57-S23120001).

References

1. Zhu, X., Liu, H.: Research on the development of digital enabled rural tourism. Smart Agricult. Guide **21**, 80–83 (2023)
2. Zhang, J.: Improving the quality and upgrading of rural tourism to help the overall revitalization of the countryside – the fifth series of reports on the high quality development of tourism since the 18th CPC National Congress. China Tourism News, 27 September 2022
3. Chen, C., Hou, J., et al.: CiteSpace II: identification and visualization of new trends and trends in scientific literature. J. Inf. Sci. **28**(3), 401–421 (2009)
4. Qiu, L.: Research on the development strategy of rural tourism in Zouping city based on tourist satisfaction. Shandong Normal University (2023)
5. Ailing, C.: Analysis of rural tourism development in Anshi village, Yibin City based on tourist satisfaction. Guilin University of technology (2023)
6. Fan, X.X.: Research on influencing factors of tourist satisfaction in Zhangguying village from the perspective of nostalgic tourism. CSU of Forestry and Technology (2022)
7. Han, Y.: Research on tourism development strategy of Qiaojiayuan based on tourist satisfaction analysis. Northwest Normal University (2023)
8. Zhou, L., Zhang, X., Yin, Q.: Satisfaction survey of rural tourism spatial experience–a case study of Zhenbei village in Harbin. Small Town Constr. **40**(08), 101–110(2022)

 9. Lijie, X.: Research on the high quality development path of rural sports tourism. Guangzhou Institute of Physical Education (2023)
10. Qi, Z.: Research on Influencing Factors of tourist satisfaction of leisure agriculture in Conghua District. Hainan University, Guangzhou (2023)
11. Liu, J.: Investigation and Analysis on the satisfaction of rural home stay tourists in Jizhou District. Hebei University of Technology, Tianjin (2023)
12. Xu, X.: Research on tourist satisfaction of scenic area dependent "farmhouse entertainment". Zhejiang University (2007)
13. Wang, X.: Research on tourist satisfaction in leisure agricultural park. Nanjing Agricultural University (2009)
14. Xu, H.: Applied research on experience design of sightseeing orchard. Central South University of Forestry and Technology (2009)
15. Meng, M., Yu, Y., Zhang, J.: Research on experiential design of tourism products in Ancient Villages – a case study of Zhuge village, Lanxi City, Zhejiang Province. Bus. Res. (01), 195–198 (2008)
16. Chen, J., Le, T.: Research on experience design of rural tourism oriented accommodation. Archit. Cult. (03), 73–74(2018)
17. Zhu, S.: Research on rural tourism landscape design from the perspective of cultural experience. Qilu University of Technology (2021)
18. Yang, X.: Research on public space design strategy of new rural complex in Chengdu based on tourist satisfaction. Southwest Jiaotong University (2021)
19. Guo, J.: Research on improving tourist satisfaction with rural tourism public services in Xiaoguai Township. Shihezi University, Karamay City (2023)
20. Zhang, D.: Research on rural tourism map design based on experience perspective – Taking Zhejiang Tianmu Mountain tourism map as an example. Western Tourism 02, 85–87 (2023)
21. Lixiao, F.: Personalized planning method of rural tourism route based on landscape gene. J. Hebei North University (Nat. Sci. Edn.)37(07), 47–51 (2021)
22. Zhu, J.: Research on the interface design of the ancient village tourism app with the sinking immersion experience from the perspective of beautiful countryside – Taking Yongtai village as an example. New Meiyu (08), 134–136 (2022)
23. Qin, S., Dong, H., Guo, J.: Design value and interactive experience of rural tourism cultural innovation from the perspective of IP creativity. Soc. Sci. (03), 50–55 (2022)
24. Wang, M.: Research on the development strategy of rural B&B based on the analysis of tourist satisfaction. Zhejiang Ocean University (2019)
25. Hu, Y.: Research on the environmental art design of rural home stay based on experiential tourism. Huazhong University of Science and Technology (2017)
26. Le, T.: Research on the application of experience design in rural accommodation under the background of rural tourism. Zhejiang University of Technology (2018)
27. Wang, J., Lou, Y.: Research on the experiential design of rural home stay. Design 32(11), 57–59 (2019)
28. Li, Z.: Research on the construction strategy of high quality rural tourism product system in Jiangsu Province – taking the implementation of the Rural Revitalization promotion law as the background. Ind. Innov. Res. 22, 87–89 (2023)
29. Zhan, G.: Research on tourism development strategy of Taishan village, Longhu town under the background of Rural Revitalization. Guangxi University for Nationalities (2023)
30. Zhang, J.: Research on Countermeasures for rural tourism development in ethnic minority areas. Henan Agricultural University (2019)
31. Luyi, Z.: Research on the development path of leisure and sightseeing agriculture in Qingjiang Town. Jiangxi Agricultural University, Yueqing City (2022)
32. Yong, F.: Research on the dilemma and Countermeasures of leisure agriculture development in Xipeng Town. Southwest University, Jiulongpo District (2022)

33. Zhang, H.: Rural night tour experience and exploration of digital art design. Donghua University (2022)
34. Ren, Y., Zha, Z., Cheng, Y., et al.: Research on satisfaction of digital development of rural tourism in Wuyuan County from the perspective of tourists. Sci. Aechnol. Ind. **21**(10), 161–168 (2021)
35. Luo, P.: Research on the development of agritainment tourism in Changsha. Hunan Agricultural University (2012)
36. Li, H., Li, S.: Analysis on the coordinated development of beautiful villages and scenic spots. Henan Agricult. **13**, 60–61 (2016)
37. Chen, S.: Research on rural tourism development based on tourists' perceived value. Southwestern University of Finance and Economics (2010)

Author Index

Printed in the United States
by Baker & Taylor Publisher Services